Software requirements

Software requirements

Styles and techniques

Soren Lauesen

 Addison-Wesley

An imprint of Pearson Education

London/Boston/Indianapolis/New York/Mexico City/Toronto/Sydney/Tokyo/Singapore
Hong Kong/Cape Town/New Delhi/Madrid/Paris/Amsterdam/Munich/Milan/Stockholm

PEARSON EDUCATION LIMITED

Edinburgh Gate
Harlow CM20 2JE
Tel: +44 (0)1279 623623
Fax: +44 (0)1279 431059
Website: www.pearsoned.co.uk

First published in Great Britain in 2002

ISBN: 0 201 74570 4

British Library Cataloguing in Publication Data
A CIP catalogue record for this book can be obtained from the British Library.
Library of Congress Catalogue in Publication Data
Applied for.

10 9 8 7 6 5 4 3 2
08 07 06 05 04

Typeset by Pantek Arts Ltd, Maidstone, Kent.
Printed and bound in Great Britain by Biddles Ltd, King's Lynn, Norfolk

The Publishers' policy is to use paper manufactured from sustainable forests.

Contents

Preface

Have you ever used a new piece of software that didn't meet your expectations? If so, it might be because nobody stated the expectations in a tangible manner. Software requirements are about writing the right expectations in the right way.

These days, many people get involved in writing requirements. It is not only a job for specialists; users, customers, suppliers, and programmers also get involved. In small companies we sometimes even see employees without special training being asked to write requirements for a new software product. Furthermore, the roles of expert user, analyst, designer, and programmer seem to blend more and more. This book is important and relevant for many people involved in software requirements:

The analyst, working as a requirements engineer or a consultant, can find tricks here and there, and he can look at requirements written by other specialists.

The customer can find ways to ensure that the new product will meet his business goals, and suggestions for handling contracts and tenders.

Software suppliers can find ideas for helping the customer and for writing competitive proposals.

Users can prepare themselves for working with specialists or the developers. They can also find ways to describe their work tasks, and examples of what to write and what not to write in their requirements.

Programmers and other **developers** can learn how to express requirements without specifying technical details, and how to reduce risks when developing a system.

IT students can learn about theory and practice in requirements engineering, and get a foundation for case studies and projects.

You don't have to read the whole book. How can we cover so many topics for so many audiences? The answer is simple: you don't have to read all of the book. If you read most of Chapter 1, you should then be able to read sections of the book in almost any order, according to your needs.

Background

When I began to work in the software industry in 1962, software requirements were relatively unimportant since at the time hardware was very expensive, and software was comparatively cheap. Renting a computer for an hour cost the same as paying someone to work for 30 hours and computers were 5000 times slower than they are today.

Software development was carried out either on a time and materials basis, or as a small part of the really important job – making better hardware. The customer paid until he had a program that printed results he could use with some effort. Nobody thought of usability. Everything to do with computers was a specialist's job.

Today things have completely changed. Hardware is cheap, and software development is expensive and very hard to keep within budget – particularly if the customer wants a result matching his expectations. For this reason software requirements are growing in importance as a means for the customer to know in advance what solution he will get and at what cost.

Unfortunately, software requirements are still a fuzzy area. Little guidance is available for the practitioner, although several textbooks exist. One particularly critical issue is the lack of real-life examples of requirements specifications.

This textbook is based on real-life examples, and it discusses the many ways of specifying software requirements in practice. We emphasize practical issues such as:

- what analysts write in real-life specifications; what works and what doesn't work
- the balance between giving the customer what he needs and over-specifying the requirements
- the balance between completeness and understandability
- the balance between describing what goes on in the application domain and what goes on in the computer
- reducing the risk to both customer and supplier
- writing requirements so that they can be verified and validated
- writing low-cost requirements specifications.

During my time in industry, I have worked as a programmer, a project manager, and later as a department manager and quality manager. However, I always loved programming and had a key role in the critical parts of the programs. We programmed many things, from business applications, scientific applications, and process control, to compilers, operating systems, and distributed databases.

When I worked as a developer from the mid-1970s, our team had to write software requirements, but we always felt uncertain about what we wrote. Was it requirements or design specifications? We realized that requirements were important, but felt stupid not knowing what to do about it. Furthermore, nobody else in our multinational company could show us a good example of software requirements, although there were corporate rules and guidelines for what to write.

In the mid-1980s I became a full professor in software engineering at Copenhagen Business School. That let me see development from two other sides: the user side and the customer side. I didn't have the constant pressure of turning out code and products, so I had time to look at the industry from another perspective.

For a long period I studied human–computer interaction and came up with systematic ways of developing good user interfaces – the missing links between studying the users and producing a good prototype. To my disappointment, industry didn't care at that time (the Web has now changed that attitude).

In the early 1990s, I decided that it was time to change subject. I asked around in industry to find out what was the most difficult part of development. Everyone I asked said "requirements and all that stuff at the beginning of the project." That was how I became interested in requirements.

I went to my research advisor, Jon Turner of New York University, and said, "Jon, I want to do research in requirements." He looked at me for some seconds and said, "Don't." "Why?" I asked. He replied that it was impossible to do anything significant in that area, and what researchers actually did had little to do with what industry needed. Alan M. Davis (1992) has observed the same thing.

This was a real challenge to me. To begin with, I had great problems in getting to see other people's requirements. I talked to developers from many companies and asked them: "Do you write software requirements?" Usually they said yes. I then asked, "Could I see the one you are using or writing right now?" There was a pause – then various replies, such as, "No, it's confidential, and it would be too much trouble to get permission for you to read it." Or, "Well, it isn't quite finished yet; maybe you could see it later." Or even this amazing variant, "Well, we're working on it, but right now we are too busy testing the system. When we have finished testing, we will write the requirements, and then you may see them."

Every now and then I got permission to see some real-life software requirements. Usually they were inspired by the IEEE 830 guidelines, since they contained all the introductory sessions such as Scope and Audience. However, when it came to the specific requirements, they were bewildering, and IEEE 830 suggested no guidance. Part of what I saw was program design; there were also some dataflow diagrams, and the rest made little sense to me. Where were the requirements?

Six months later, I saw some software requirements that were so good that I could learn from them. Jens-Peder Vium was the first to show me a good requirements specification, and it is included in this book as the Danish Shipyard case (see

Chapter 11). Although vastly better than anything else I had seen at that time, it too had deficiencies, and together we worked on improving the various techniques involved. Soon my studies gained momentum, and I got to see many other good requirements, some of which are included in this book. A year later, so many people wanted me to look at their requirements that I had to say no to many of them.

My conclusion from these initial studies was that people were ashamed of the requirements they had written, but they didn't know how to make them better. Furthermore, everybody had some good parts in their specification, and some serious weaknesses. If all the good things could be combined, we would be close to a general solution. However, there were some important problems that none of the practitioners seemed able to solve:

- How do you avoid writing anything about the product, yet be able to verify its requirements?

- How do you ensure that the requirements correctly reflect the customer's business goals?

- How do you specify quality factors such as usability or maintainability in a verifiable manner?

Research, experiments, and luck helped me develop answers to these questions. These answers are included throughout the book, for instance in sections 3.8, 6.6, 6.11, and 8.7.

Using the book for courses

The book is a considerably extended version of an earlier book, which we used successfully at professional courses for analysts and developers, as well as for computer science students. Depending on the audience, we selected different parts of the book for discussion. We have even used the book with Information Systems (IS) students with no understanding of programming. In this case we combined it with a short course in data modeling, data flow, and basic understanding of development activities.

The figures in the book are available in PowerPoint format, and the checklists as Word documents. Solutions to some of the exercises are available for teachers. E-mail the author at slauesen@itu.dk. Most of the figures are rich in detail, and as a result, you can easily spend 5–30 minutes discussing a single figure. In a typical course, only about one-third of the figures are discussed.

The book suggests two kinds of course activities, *discussions* and *exercises*. Discussions are themes for course room discussions, and may also be used for homework. Exercises are for homework or for teamwork during course hours.

Exercises and training projects

You can run the exercises in many ways. At professional courses, we assign exercises to teams of three to five participants. Each team has to outline the answer in one to two overheads. That should be possible in about an hour, depending on the participant's background and level of knowledge.

For university students, the exercises are given as homework, but here too we tend to restrict answers to a few overheads. One or two teams present their solution to the other students. About 15 minutes are allowed for a presentation, including discussion. The students are asked to control the presentation themselves. They should usually imagine that they are developers or consultants, while the other students are "customers". It is important to listen to the "customer", explain the solution again if the customer hasn't understood it, and identify weaknesses in one's own solution. A successful presentation identifies many weaknesses. This attitude is extremely important in practice, but difficult to achieve because we all tend to defend our own solutions.

However, exercises alone are not sufficient for training in requirements engineering. While programming exercises may give you programming training, this is not so with requirements. The art of discovering real demands and stating real requirements cannot be practiced through written exercises.

It is necessary to practice using real companies. For university courses, we always combine the course with the students doing project work in a real company. The first part of the project is that the students have to find a company or organization on their own. This also trains them to find the way to the right people; a very important skill in requirements engineering.

Acknowledgements

This book has only one author, yet I mostly write "we" in the text. This is because most of the experiences I discuss and report here have originated in talks and collaboration with someone else. Thus a large and varied selection of my colleagues have contributed to the book and justify my use of "we".

I would particularly like to thank the following:

Jens-Peder Vium, of Innovation & Quality Management, for permission to use the Danish Shipyard case (Chapter 11), and for many inspiring discussions and joint presentations. He has been a consultant for many years, and is an important source of knowledge about many different kinds of projects.

Susan Willumsen, at that time a masters student, for her collaboration and sharp observations during the Danish Shipyard study.

Houman Younessi, of Swinburne University, now Rensselaer at Hartford, for many theoretical and practical discussions that were the starting point of this book, and for some of the ideas behind the style concept and the maintainability requirements.

Otto Vinter, of Bruel & Kjaer, for permission to use part of the Noise Source Location requirements (Chapter 14), some of the case studies, and for many inspiring discussions, particularly about error sources and prevention methods.

Karin Lomborg (now Karin Berg) of Deloitte & Touche, for permission to use part of the Midland Hospital case (Chapter 12).

Jan C. Clausen, of Katalyse, for helping me to see the basic difference between tasks and use cases, and for many inspiring discussions about requirements and usability.

Klaus Jul Jeppesen, of Asea Brown Boveri, now the IT University, for information about large projects in control and manufacturing, customer negotiations, etc.

Marianne Mathiassen, masters student, and Lotte Riberholt Andersen, Jeanette Andersen, and Annemarie Raahauge, of West Zealand county, for collaboration when developing the technique first known as 'use cases with solutions', later renamed to Tasks & Support.

Lene Funder Andersen, Lene Frydenberg, Jens Wolf Frandsen, and Marc Olivier Collignon, diploma students, for being the first to try Tasks & Support in real life. They successfully managed to use the technique for writing requirements and run the tender process for a large telecommunications company. They also helped the company select the right proposal from among twenty suppliers.

Dorte Olesen, Lars Henrik Søfren, and Jette M. Rosbæk, of West Zealand county, for their impressive work when trying out Tasks & Support in a new hospital project.

Erik Simmons, Intel Corporation, for teaching me Planguage and for reviewing the book as carefully as if it had been a requirements document. (Like a typical developer, I couldn't repair all the defects. ☺)

Soren Lauesen
June 2001

slauesen@itu.dk

1

Introduction and basic concepts

A requirements specification is a document that describes what a system should do. It is often part of a contract between a customer and a supplier, but it is used in other situations as well, for instance in in-house development where "customer" and "supplier" are departments within the same company.

Specifying requirements is recognized as one of the most difficult, yet important areas of systems development. Little guidance is available for the practitioner, although several textbooks exist. One particularly critical issue is the lack of real-life examples of requirements specifications.

The structure of the book

We have based this book on real-life examples and in it we discuss the many ways of specifying requirements. It contains a requirements specification for a total business administration system in a shipyard (Chapter 11), a short, but adequate specification for a membership administration system (Chapter 15), excerpts from two hospital systems (Chapters 12 to 13), and excerpts from a 3D sound measuring system (Chapter 14).

After the introductory chapter, the book has five long chapters on various ways to state requirements, illustrated by examples. Most readers don't understand why this comes so early. They find it more logical to start with elicitation techniques, i.e. techniques for gathering requirements, such as interviews, prototypes, and brainstorms. Elicitation is needed before any requirements can be defined, so why not start that way?

The reason is a simple observation: if the analyst doesn't know how requirements can be stated in real life, he cannot elicit them. He may ask the customer a lot of questions but not the crucial ones; or he may use a technique such as prototyping in situations where it is a waste of time.

Specification styles. A requirement can be specified in many styles. We may specify it in plain text, as a diagram, as a table, etc. We may specify what the software system must do, or specify the type of user activity it must support. These possibilities may be combined in many ways, giving rise to many styles.

Techniques. With an understanding of the styles involved, we introduce the various techniques for elicitation, checking, and validation. The many styles and techniques available are options for practical use, not something you have to do in every project.

Many practitioners ask why all these styles and techniques are necessary. Why can't we just present the best ones, those which always lead to a good result? I wish we could – give all of you the silver bullet that kills any monster. But my experience in the IT industry has taught me that every project is different. What is crucial in one project may be a waste of time in another. The best advice is to become a good analyst:

> *The good analyst knows many techniques, but also knows when to use them and when not.*

> *He combines and modifies techniques according to specific needs.*

The aim of this book is to help you on that path; to teach you many techniques, and advise you on when to use them and when not. To get you started, however, section 1.7 and Chapter 15 show examples of good combinations of techniques and requirements styles.

References

The book has a practical aim and is light on references and bibliography. Usually we don't try to tell you about the origins of the topics or compare what different experts have said. The general approach is to give a few references that will allow a practitioner to read more when needed. Many topics are also covered by other comprehensive books on requirements, and for these topics we don't give specific references. Use the annotated references in Chapter 17 to find other requirements books.

Sometimes we present more recent or controversial issues. In these cases we give references to different views of the issue.

1.1　The role of requirements

Highlights

Tacit demands are necessary – we cannot specify everything.
Elicitation and analysis: finding and structuring requirements.
Validation: the customer's check that requirements match demands.
Verification: checking that the product fulfills the requirements.

A requirements specification plays several roles during a project. Typically the customer and supplier (or their representatives) write it in close collaboration; later programmers and other developers use it. If things go wrong, the requirements specification may end up in court as evidence of what was agreed.

The development process

The requirements specification is produced early in system development. Figure 1.1 shows the traditional waterfall model for systems development. In this idealistic model, development starts with an *analysis* phase that produces the requirements specification. Often the specification is part of a contract between customer and supplier.

Later the specification serves as input to the design phase, which in turn produces input to programming, and so on, ending with the operation and maintenance of the system. At the end of development, both the supplier and customer test that the requirements are fulfilled. This is known as *verification* of the requirements.

The waterfall model represents an ideal. Real projects don't work like that: developers don't always complete one phase before starting on the next. Often they realize that something went wrong in an earlier phase, so part of it has to be redone. Sometimes it is an advantage to do some design work during analysis in order to produce a better requirements specification. Sometimes developers also carry out iterative analysis, design, and even programming, thus intentionally repeating several phases.

All this means that the phase idea of the waterfall model is wrong. The activities are not carried out sequentially and it is unrealistic to insist that they should be. On the other hand, developers do analyze, design, and program. The activities exist, but they are carried out iteratively and simultaneously. See Boehm (1989) and Pressman (2000) for alternative ways of organizing systems development.

One consequence of this is that requirements will change during development as developers and customers find missing, wrong, and unrealistic requirements. This is called *requirements management*. Requirements management is also important during maintenance, since many changes are caused by changing requirements.

Analysis and elicitation

Where do the requirements come from? In principle, they come from users and other *stakeholders* of the system. Part of the requirements work is to elicit the requirements from the stakeholders.

The assumption is that stakeholders have some *demands* and the role of the analyst is to *elicit* these demands, *analyze* them for consistency, feasibility, and completeness, and *formulate* them as requirements. The people eliciting and formulating requirements are called *requirements engineers* by some people, *analysts* by others. This book will use both terms.

In practice, the analysts can be developers, expert users (preferably a team of both), independent consultants, marketing people, and so on.

Stakeholders include users with various roles, the customer (who pays for the product), the customer's IT department, and sometimes external parties with whom the customer co-operates. If the system is a product offered to a broader market, stakeholders may include the distributors and sometimes software houses adding special features to the product.

Elicitation is a very difficult process for many reasons:

- Stakeholders may have difficulty in expressing their needs, or they may ask for a solution that does not meet their real needs.

- Stakeholders can have conflicting demands.

- Users find it difficult to imagine new ways of doing things or to imagine the consequences of things they ask for. When they, for instance, see the system that has been built for them, they often realize that it does not fulfill their expectations, although it fulfills the written requirements.

- Sometimes there are no users because the product is completely new, and nobody has used IT for this purpose before.

- Demands often change over time. When users, for instance, see a smart system somewhere, they may realize that they need something similar themselves. External factors may change too, such as new operating system releases or new laws.

Even when users can express their needs, requirements engineers find it difficult to write them down in a precise way without designing the solution at the same time. The result is that the real demands and the written requirements do not match.

For this reason, it is important for stakeholders to check that requirements meet their real demands. This type of check is called *validation*.

Fig 1.1   The role of requirements

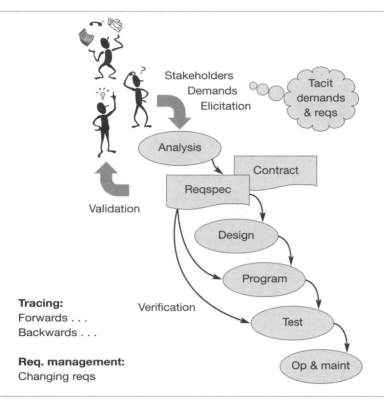

Tacit requirements. When a demand is not reflected in the requirements specification, we say it is a *tacit requirement*. We also talk about tacit demands, i.e. demands that the user is not aware of or cannot express.

In practice, most requirements are tacit. It is also widely recognized that if you try to write down all requirements, you end up with a huge specification that nobody can validate or use in development. The secret is to specify only what the developers cannot guess – plus a bit more – just to make sure. In order to do that, the analyst has to know what kind of developers are likely to use the requirements (see section 1.6).

A summary of the roles

No wonder it is difficult to write a requirements specification. It has to be used for many purposes:

Validation. The customer must be able to validate the requirements to see that they correctly reflect his needs. This means that he must be able to read the specification, understand it, and say, "Yes, this is what I need. This system will solve my problems."

In practice it is a good idea to validate intermediate work products, for instance designs of screen pictures, to see that everything still matches the customer's expectations.

Verification. Verification is carried out to check that the product satisfies the requirements. As a minimum, this is done in an *acceptance test* where the parties go through the requirements one by one and check that the product satisfies them.

It is also a good idea to verify that intermediate work products satisfy requirements. Developers as well as customers need to convince themselves that all requirements are being considered during development.

Tracing. Requirements tracing is needed to compare requirements against other information. There are four types of tracing:

Forward

1 Tracing from requirements to program to see that all requirements are dealt with. This is roughly the same as verification.

2 Tracing from demands to requirements to see that all demands are reflected in the requirements. This is part of validation, but often neglected with the result that important business goals may be lost.

Backward

3 Tracing from requirements to demands to see that all requirements have a purpose. This is another part of validation.

4 Tracing from program to requirements to see that all parts of the program are required. This is neither validation nor verification, but a useful check to avoid feature creep, that is, to prevent developers from wasting time producing things that the customer did not ask for.

Requirements management. In spite of attempts to get it right the first time, requirements change during development. It must be easy to update the specification, add new requirements, and assess the consequences of change.

Chapter 7 explains more about the role of requirements. See also Wiegers (1999).

Court cases. If things go wrong, the requirements specification and the contract may end up in court as evidence of what was originally agreed. Many developers believe that if they satisfy the written requirements, they will win the court case. However, in most countries courts don't work that way. If the customer had *reasonable* expectations that were not written in the specification, the court will rule that the supplier must fulfill this expectation. In other words, courts acknowledge reasonable tacit requirements.

The tricky point is of course what "reasonable" means. Assume for instance that the customer's system breaks down whenever the user forgets to fill in the discount field on the order screen. This is an error that the supplier has to repair; it is not a requirements issue, because any developer can see that this is a program error.

As a second example, assume that the customer's system has adequate response times, but over time the database becomes fragmented and response times become intolerably long. The product, however, has no feature for restructuring the database. The court would rule that such a feature is a reasonable expectation and that the supplier should have known about it, whereas the customer couldn't be expected to know about such things.

Finally, assume that the customer received a business application that could produce invoices, but had no feature that would do the opposite, that is, produce credit notes. This is more of a gray area. It is likely the court would say that such a feature is standard in business applications and the supplier should have known about it.

1.2 Project types

Highlights

There are many types of project: in-house development, buying commercial
software, tenders and contracts, etc.
Requirements have different roles in different types of projects.
Sometimes the project type is unknown.

Requirements play somewhat different roles in different types of projects. Here are
some typical projects (also see Figure 1.2):

In-house development. The system is developed inside a company for the company's
own use. The customer and the supplier are departments of the same company.

This situation often occurs in larger companies, for instance in banks, insurance
companies, and large manufacturing companies. Traditionally, these projects are
carried out without specified requirements, and many projects end in disaster. To
avoid this, many companies now try to use written requirements.

Product development. The product is a commercial product to be marketed by a
company. The development project is carried out inside the company. The "customer"
is the marketing department and the "supplier" the development department.

The parties often use requirements on many levels, for instance market-oriented
requirements stating the demands in the market, and design-level requirements
that specify exact details of the user interface. A frequent problem in these
situations is that developers never see the real customers (those buying the
product). Developers have to rely on the translation of requirements by marketing.
We have seen many cases where this has caused tremendous problems in
development as well as in market acceptance of the product.

Time-and-material based development. A software house develops the system on
a time-and-materials base, i.e. the customer pays the costs, for instance month by
month. Requirements are informal (unwritten) and develop over time.

In the old days this was the usual way to develop systems, and it still thrives in
some areas, for instance some Internet software houses. Over time, the parties tend
to realize that such projects can easily get out of control. The costs skyrocket, and
the parties fight over what has to be delivered and who is to blame.

Introducing written requirements is an improvement, since it becomes clear what is
to be delivered. The supplier may still develop the system on a time-and-materials
basis, so the costs are only partly controlled. In this version, we could just as well
call the project a contract-based development with a variable price.

Fig 1.2 Project types

Project types	Customer	Supplier
In-house Product development Time and materials	User dept. Marketing Company	IT dept. Software dept. Software house
COTS	Company	(Vendor)
Tender Contract development Sub-contracting	Company Company Supplier	Supplier Software house Software house
Unknown		Inhouse? COTS?

COTS purchase. COTS is an acronym for Commercial Off The Shelf and denotes a commercial package that you can buy – more or less off the shelf. Examples are Microsoft Office, development tools, Lotus Notes, large business applications (e.g. SAP, BAAN, or Navision), commercial bank or hospital systems, and so on.

Some of these products are fully off the shelf (e.g. Microsoft Office and some development tools). Others can be configured in so many ways that the customer needs a consultant to do it (e.g. SAP). Many COTS systems can be extended according to the special needs of the customer (e.g. bank or hospital systems), and some COTS systems are only frameworks where all the customer logic has to be built in (e.g. Lotus Notes).

The large business applications (SAP, BAAN, and so on) are often called ERP systems, Enterprise Resource Planning systems.

When we use the term *COTS purchase* in this book, we mean the purchase of a fully off-the-shelf product. Whatever extensions and configurations are required, the customer takes care of them himself. What role do requirements have in this case? Here, you don't set up a formal contract with requirements no more than when you buy a fridge, but it is still a good idea to figure out what your needs are so that you – in a structured way – can choose between the alternatives. Some forms of requirements are suited to that, as we will see throughout the book.

When we want a COTS product including some tailor-made configuration or extension, we use the term *COTS-based acquisition*. Requirements and contracts are very important here, so that you get the additional things that you need. The product you get consists of the COTS-part itself plus the tailor-made things. The situation can be handled as a tender project or a contract development. For a discussion of various types of COTS projects, see Carney and Long (2000). For a discussion of changed development processes to cater for COTS, see Brownsword *et al.* (2000) and Maiden and Ncube (1998).

Tender. The customer company starts a tender process and sends out a request for proposal (RFP). Several suppliers are invited to submit proposals. The tender documentation contains an elaborate requirements specification. The customer writes the specification or asks a consultant to do it. Later the customer selects the best proposal.

This approach is used more and more often today, particularly by government organizations, since they have an obligation to treat all suppliers equally and avoid any hint of nepotism or corruption.

Writing requirements for these situations is a real challenge. You have to write for a broad audience that you don't know, and you end up signing a contract for delivery, based primarily on the supplier's reply to the requirements. In many countries the customer is not allowed to bargain over features and prices after having sent out the request for proposal.

The tender approach is used for tailor-made systems as well as COTS-based systems. For the COTS parts of the system, you cannot specify product details such as screen pictures, since the screen pictures are largely determined by the product, which you of course have to choose later. This makes COTS tenders even more difficult from a requirements viewpoint. See sections 7.3 to 7.5 for more about tender projects.

Contract development. A supplier company develops or delivers a system to the customer company. The requirements specification and the contract specify what is to be delivered. The two parties will often work together for some time to write the requirements and the contract.

The system may be tailor-made or a COTS-based system with extensions.

This approach has been used for a long time in public as well as in private organizations. It is often a good idea to make two-step contracts where the first contract deals with making the detailed requirements, while the next one deals with developing the system. Prices can be fixed or variable, or a combination. See more on this in section 1.7.4.

Sub-contracting. A sub-contractor develops or delivers part of a system to a main contractor, who delivers the total system to a customer. Sub-contracting can be requirements-based or time-and-materials based without written requirements.

Sub-contracting differs from other situations in that both parties usually speak the "IT-language" and agree on technical interfaces between their products. Often the main contractor has several sub-contractors who develop different parts of the total product. Sections 5.4 and 5.5 discuss these situations.

Situation unknown. In many cases the customer doesn't know what he should do. Should he buy a COTS system or have the system developed in-house? Should he try to play the role of a main contractor and integrate several products, or should he contract with someone else to do it? See Sikkel *et al.* (2000) for a discussion of such situations.

High-level requirements can help to resolve these issues. They may help compare the alternatives from a cost/benefit and risk perspective, and they may help in looking for potential suppliers in-house or outside. The membership system in Chapter 15 handles such a situation.

1.3 Contents of the specification

Highlights

Data and functional requirements.
Quality requirements: system speed, ease of use, etc.
Floating transition to contract issues.
Parts to help the reader: business goals, diagrams, etc.

What should the requirements specification contain? Theoretically it is simple: it should specify the input to the system and the output for each input. In principle, that is what the user will see in the final system, so nothing else needs to be specified. (Theory says that the specification should also state how fast the system shall produce this output, and other performance matters.)

This is the traditional idea in computer science, and scientists have developed many ways of specifying input and output in exact detail. In order to write the specification, the analyst must elicit the requirements by studying users and business goals. The assumption, however, is that the end result is a specification of input and output.

Unfortunately, real-life systems are usually too complex to specify in this way, so it is necessary to specify them on a higher level. Furthermore, it is not a simple matter to derive precise specifications that ensure good user support and meet the business goals.

Let us look at the situation in more detail. Figure 1.3 shows the system as a black-box with *interfaces* to the surroundings. First of all, the system has user interfaces to various user groups. It also has interfaces to the supporting hardware and software platforms, for instance commercial products such as Pentium PCs, Windows NT, Oracle databases, and SAS (for data analysis).

The system may also have interfaces to external technical systems, for instance special sensors and devices, public data-bases, document-handling systems, natural language processors, and so on. The diagram is actually a *context diagram* – a very useful part of requirements explained in section 3.2.

Data requirements

An important part of the requirements is *data requirements*: What data should the system input and output, and what data should the system store internally?

Database. Most systems have to keep track of information about their surroundings, for instance customers, or valves and temperatures in a chemical

Fig 1.3   Contents of ReqSpec

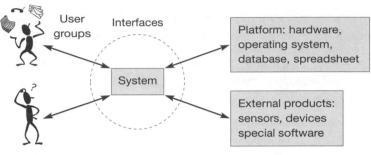

Data requirements:
System state: Database, comm. states
Input/output formats

Functional requirements, each interface:
Record, compute, transform, transmit
Theory: F(input, state) -> (output, state)
Function list, pseudocode, activity diagram
Screen prototype, support tasks xx to yy

Quality reqs:	**Managerial reqs:**
Performance	Delivery time
Usability	Legal
Maintainability	Development process
. . .	. . .

Other deliverables:	**Helping the reader:**
Documentation	Business goals
Install, convert,	Definitions
train . . .	Diagrams . . .

plant. The system has to store the corresponding data in some kind of database or other internal objects. It is important to specify this data, and in Chapter 2 we explain various ways to do this. Database data is independent of the interfaces and is most conveniently described in a separate section.

Some analysts claim that these data details are internal computer matters and should not be specified in requirements. However, there is almost a one-to-one relationship between information found in the surrounding domain, and the data stored in the system. As a result, specifying the data has very little to do with designing the system.

Input/output formats. Input and output data appear on the various interfaces. The data requirements should in principle specify the detailed data formats for each interface, but in practice many details are specified indirectly through the database description. This saves a lot of writing because database data may appear through many parts of the interfaces.

Communication state. Each interface will have some data that is only indirectly visible in the surroundings. This data keeps track of the communication state on that interface, what has been processed already, what is allowed next, etc. As an example, for a user interface the system keeps track of the current state of the user dialog, who is logged on, what the user has entered already, which user windows are open, etc.

The communication state is closely associated with the functionality provided by the system and is often described as part of the functional requirements.

System state. Developers often talk about the *system state*. This means all the data stored in the system; that is, database contents plus communication states. When talking about a specific part of the system, system state may also mean a subset of database and communication states.

Functional requirements

Functional requirements specify the functions of the system, how it records, computes, transforms, and transmits data. Each interface has its own functions. Typically, the user interface is the most important interface, since most of the data are recorded and shown through it.

Styles. Functional requirements can be specified in many ways. In this book we will call them *styles*. Here are some examples of styles:

1 A list of the functions to be provided.

2 A textual description of what each function does (mini-spec or pseudo-code).

3 An activity diagram showing what each function does.

4 The detailed user interface shown as a prototype of the screens.

5 A description of the user's work tasks and a requirement saying that these tasks must be supported.

Chapters 3 and 4 explain these styles and many others in detail. Some of the styles focus on identifying the necessary functions (e.g. 1, 4, and 5 above). Others focus on specifying details of the functions (e.g. 2 and 3 above). In practice most functions are trivial, so a detailed description is rarely needed (see section 4.1).

Theory and practice. According to tradition in computer science, a system function F is defined as follows:

F(input, system state) $\rightarrow$ (output, new system state)

This means that for any given input and any given system state, function F will deliver some output and set the system state to something new.

In practice this means: when you give the system a command, the response depends not only on the command, but also on the contents of the database and other variables. The response may be some visible output, and some invisible change in database contents and other variables.

In theory, the functional requirements should specify this transformation, but in practice the specification is very indirect because most functions are trivial. The main problem is often defining which functions are needed rather than what they do in detail.

Data versus functions. Usually requirements engineers include data requirements as part of functional requirements. This is logical since functional requirements draw on data to describe the function. From a practical view, however, it is often convenient to separate them.

Quality requirements

Quality requirements specify how well the system performs its intended functions. Quality requirements are also called *non-functional requirements*. Figure 1.3 shows three quality factors (i.e. categories of quality requirements):

Performance. How efficiently should the system work with the hardware: how fast should it respond, how many computer resources should it use, how accurate should the results be, how much data should it be able to store?

Usability. How efficiently should the system work with the users: how easy should it be to learn, how efficient should it be in daily use, etc.

Maintenance. How easy should it be to repair defects, add new functionality, etc.

There are many more quality factors, each of which can be specified in several ways or styles, as we will see later.

Other deliverables

Usually the supplier delivers more than hardware and software. Documentation, for instance, will usually be required.

The requirements can also specify services, for instance who does what in order to install the system, convert data, train users, operate the system, and so on.

Managerial requirements

Managerial requirements are in a gray area between requirements and contractual issues. It is not sufficient to specify the deliverables: you also need to know when they will be delivered, the price and when to pay it, how to check that everything is working (verification), what happens if things go wrong (legal responsibilities, penalties), etc. Sometimes you have to specify who owns the software and other intellectual properties.

Managerial requirements may also include a specification of the development process to be used.

It is largely a matter of company tradition which of these subjects are included in the requirements and which in the contract. The important thing is to remember to include them somewhere.

Helping the reader

Some specifications are just a long list of numbered requirements. Others go into great detail to explain the background of the requirements, the customer's general business, etc.

We recommend that you take some time to explain the background (rationale) for each requirement; to state in which work processes the requirement is important, which problem is it supposed to solve, and so on. Customers and suppliers understand the requirement itself much better when they know its purpose. Understanding its purpose may also help the parties find a better alternative requirement.

Other things may also help the reader, for instance explanation of terms used in the customer's world (*definitions* or *glossary*), or examples and diagrams.

Business goals. One very important thing is often missing: the business goals or success criteria of the system. Why does the customer want to spend money on the new system? This information is not, strictly speaking, requirements because it is not the supplier's responsibility to reach the customer's business goals. However, explicit business goals allow the customer as well as the supplier to convince themselves that the requirements actually enable the customer to reach his goals. It is even better if the analyst documents how each business goal is reflected in the requirements. Sections 8.7 and 10.7 show examples of this.

Organizing the parts

There are many ways of combining requirements and auxiliary information into a specification. The best-known standard in the area is IEEE Recommended Practice for Software Requirements Specification (IEEE 830). It suggests a standard structure of the introductory parts and several alternative ways of structuring the detailed requirements: according to the interfaces, according to user classes, according to application domain objects, etc. It states explicitly that what we have termed "managerial requirements" above should not be part of the requirements, but should form part of some other document.

If you want to see a very short specification template, have a look at the membership system in Chapter 15. You may also use the contents checklist in section 9.2.1 as a template. Robertson and Robertson (1999) have their own, very comprehensive template for specifications.

For a sample of full requirements specifications, have a look at Chapters 11, 12, and 15. Furthermore, Dorfman and Thayer (1990), Kovitz (1999), and Martin *et al.* (1999) show large parts of specifications.

We will discuss some different ways of organizing the specification in section 1.7.

1.4 Problems observed in practice

Highlights

Relatively few problems in data and functional requirements.
Serious problems ensuring efficient task support and meeting business goals.
Quality requirements: important, but what should be written?
Parts to help the reader: important, but often ignored.

The requirements specification contains many things. What is most important, and where do problems arise in practice?

Data and functional requirements. In all the specs I have seen, data and functional requirements are by far the largest part of the requirements.

Although there are many incomplete, wrong, ambiguous, and badly phrased requirements, they cause few problems in the final product as long as the developer can see that something is vague or missing. Apparently developers make good guesses in these cases, or they ask stakeholders for clarification. At the same time, analysts complain that they spend too much time writing these requirements and have doubts over whether they do it right.

Expectations not met. Usually we see serious problems of another kind in the final product. Even though the requirements are implemented as intended, the final product doesn't support the user tasks adequately. Furthermore, the product doesn't enable the customer to obtain his desired business goals. In other words, even if the customer gets what the requirements say he should get, he gets a system that doesn't fully satisfy his real needs. We show examples of this in sections 8.7 and 10.7.

These problems are to a large extent caused by insufficient functionality. The necessary functions are missing, or they are not provided in a useful form. In these cases the developers can't see that something is wrong because they don't know enough about the user tasks and business goals. One solution is to state goals explicitly, and carefully trace them to requirements. Section 1.6 discusses a case where goals were explicitly stated, but not traced adequately to requirements.

Helping the reader. In many specs there is very little information to help the reader, and what is there is of an introductory nature. The Midland Hospital system in Chapter 12 is a typical example. In other specs, however, there is good background information for each of the requirements. The Noise Source Location product in Chapter 14 is a good example.

Background information is crucial to help the supplier understand the customer's real needs, and many software disasters could have been avoided in that way.

Quality requirements. Many analysts agree that quality requirements are very important, and that many problems in the final product are quality defects. Yet quality requirements occupy little space in requirements, particularly the "soft" ones such as usability and maintainability. Why?

One reason is that analysts don't know how to specify quality requirements, although they know that they are important. Chapter 6 discusses ways to specify quality requirements.

1.5   Domain level and product level

Highlights

Product: the system to be delivered.
Domain: the product and its immediate users and other surroundings.
Clients: people served by the domain.
System: the product, the domain, or software plus hardware?

In many cases it is pointless to describe the detailed input and output from the system. An example is a tender process where the suppliers are expected to propose solutions based on their own commercial application. Describing the detailed user interface in detail is pointless, since it differs from one potential supplier to another. Specifying the functions on a more abstract level helps only slightly. How, then, should requirements be specified?

The solution is to describe the activities that go on in the system surroundings and then require that the new system supports these activities. We will introduce two terms here: the *product* is the new system to be developed; the *domain* includes the activities going on around the product when it is used. Figure 1.5A illustrates this principle.

Product. The product to be delivered is the box in the middle. Typically it consists of software, and possibly some hardware.

(Inner) domain. The inner domain is the product plus the surrounding work area, in the figure consisting of the immediate users and their activities, as well as any special systems that the product must communicate with.

The example illustrates a mixed business and technical system: a computerized elevator management system. It keeps track of repair staff, schedules their visits to elevator sites, keeps track of customer calls and billing, etc. It also communicates with special systems (*control computers*) that supervise a number of elevators and report problems and alarm calls. The domain includes these special systems, and it includes staff working directly with the product.

To simplify matters we will usually just say *domain* rather than *inner* domain. We include the product as part of the domain because we need a term for what man and computer do together – irrespective of how the work happens to be divided between them.

Clients – outer domain. Outside the domain we have customers and repair staff who communicate with domain staff. We call these second-level users the *clients* and what goes on in that area is the *outer domain*.

Fig 1.5A Domain and product level

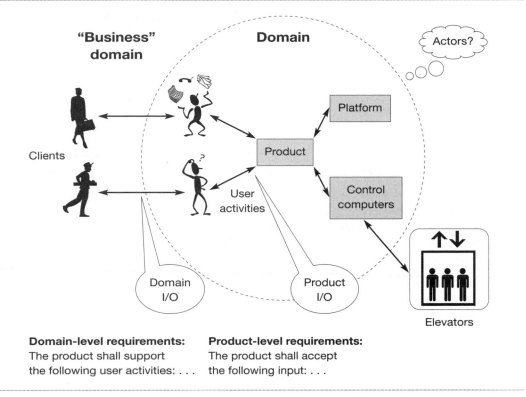

Domain-level requirements:
The product shall support
the following user activities: . . .

Product-level requirements:
The product shall accept
the following input: . . .

In the outer domain we also find the elevators themselves, since they communicate with the special systems and not directly with the product to be delivered. In principle the elevators are clients too, although this sounds strange. Some people use the term *business domain* to denote the outer domain – even when talking about a non-profit organization.

The term *product-i/o* means input and output between the new product and the domain. The term *domain i/o* means input and output between the domain and the next level of surroundings.

The product-domain distinction allows us to talk about two kinds of requirements:

Product-level requirements: these specify what should come in and out of the product.

Domain-level requirements: these describe the activities that go on outside the product – in the domain. The requirements are to *support* those activities.

We will see more levels of requirements in the next section. Many analysts are skeptical about domain-level requirements. Are they good requirements? Can we validate and verify them? Yes we can – quite well, in fact. Sections 3.6 and 3.8 show how.

Quality requirements can be at a product level as well as at a domain level. One example is performance. You can specify the response time for the computer system (product level), or the performance time for a user task consisting of manual time as well as computer response time (domain level).

Terminology

Domain. The term *domain* is normally used in a more vague sense to denote the application area. Here we use it to denote the product and its immediate surroundings.

System. What does "the system" mean? This term is used all the time, but it has many meanings depending on the context. In requirements contexts it often means the product to be delivered. However, if the product is software only, analysts tend to use 'system' for a combination of hardware and software. They also talk about system requirements versus software requirements.

From an abstract viewpoint, the domain is also a system, but it is wider than the product to be developed since it also contains the activities around the product. In our example, this large system consists of people as well as computers. The wide system also has users – the clients.

Actor. If we do not want to specify whether we are talking about human users, clients, or external products, we use the term actor. An *actor* is a human or some external system that communicates with the system under discussion.

User requirements. Sometimes requirements engineers use the term user *requirements*. It is tempting to believe that they mean domain-level requirements, and sometimes they do, for instance Wiegers (1999). Mostly, however, they mean product-level requirements expressed in a way that the user easily understands, while *system requirements* or *software requirements* are very technical and oriented towards the developer.

Defining product limits

Let us as an example assume that the customer changes his mind. He doesn't want the product as we outlined it above. He wants to buy a total package consisting of the central computer plus all the control computers.

So, what is the product now? Figure 1.5B shows that the product box grows to include the control computers. The elevators also change from being "clients" to being actors inside the domain. In this new situation the requirements deal with what the central computer and the control computers do together. It is not even certain that several computers are needed; maybe one computer is enough.

Fig 1.5B Redefined limits

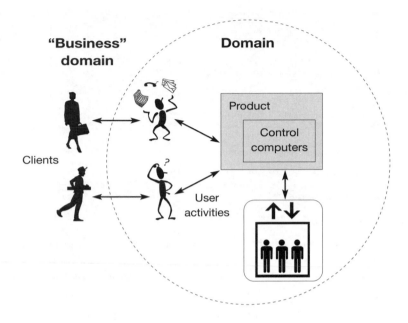

Defining the limits of the product is very difficult in some projects, to the extent that it blocks more important discussions about business goals or task support. Sections 5.3 and 5.4 show how to deal with this problem.

1.6 The goal–design scale

Highlights

Goal-level requirement: why the customer wants to spend money on the product.
Domain-level requirement: support user tasks xx to yy.
Product-level requirement: a function to be provided by the product.
Design-level requirement: details of the product interface.

Tradition says that a requirement must specify

what the system should do

without specifying how.

The reason is that if you specify "how", you have entered the design phase and may have excluded possibilities that are better than those you thought of initially. In practice it is difficult to distinguish "what" from "how". The right choice depends on the individual situation.

We will illustrate the issue with an example from the Danish Shipyard (Chapter 11). The shipyard specializes in ship repairs. The values of orders range from $10,000 to $5 million, and as many as 300 workers may be involved in one order. Competition is extremely fierce and repair orders are usually negotiated and signed while the ship is at sea.

The management of the shipyard decided, for several reasons, to replace their old business application with a more modern one. One of their business goals was to achieve a better way of calculating costs.

When preparing a quote, the sales staff precalculate the costs, but often the actual costs exceed the precalculation, causing the shipyard to lose money. Or the pre-calculated cost is unnecessarily high, causing the shipyard to lose the order. What is the solution to this? Maybe the new IT system could collect data from earlier orders and use it to support new cost calculations. Experience data could for instance include the average time it takes to weld a ton of iron, the average time it takes to paint 100 square meters of ship, etc.

Figure 1.6A shows four possibilities for the requirements in this case, which we will discuss one by one.

Goal-level requirement

R1 The product shall ensure that precalculations match actual costs within a standard deviation of 5%.

Fig 1.6A The goal-design scale

R1. Our precalculations shall be accurate to within 5%	Goal-level requirement
R2. Product shall support cost recording and quotation with experience data	Domain-level requirement
R3. Product shall have recording and retrieval functions for experience data	Product-level requirement
R4. System shall have screen pictures as shown in app. xx	Design-level requirement

Which requirement should be chosen if the supplier is:
- A vendor of business applications?
- A software house concentrating on programming?
- PriceWaterhouseCoopers?

This requirement states the business goal, which is good because that is what the shipyard really want. Note that we call it a goal-level requirement because it is a business goal that can be verified, although only after some period of operation. Unfortunately, if you ask a software house to accept this requirement, they will refuse. They cannot take the responsibility for R1, because it requires much more than a new IT product: it is also necessary to train and motivate the shipyard staff, build up an experience database, etc., and even then it may be impossible to reach the goal. The customer has to take responsibility for that.

Domain-level requirement

R2 The product shall support the cost registration task including recording of experience data. It shall also support the quotation task with experience data.

This is a typical domain-level requirement. It outlines the tasks involved and requires support for these tasks. The analyst has carefully identified the right tasks. For instance, he hasn't specified a new user task to record experience data, because his knowledge of the shipyard and its day-to-day work tells him that then the recording would never be done. It must be done as part of something that is done already – recording the costs. Sections 3.6 and 3.8 explain more about domain-level requirements.

Could we give this requirement to a software house? That depends. If it is a software house that knows about shipyards or similar types of businesses, it may work. It doesn't matter whether the software house offers a COTS-based system with the necessary extensions, or whether they develop a system from scratch. However, if we choose a software house that is good at programming, but doesn't know about business applications, it would be highly risky, because they may come up with completely inadequate solutions.

Can we verify the requirement? Yes, even before the delivery time. We can try to carry out the tasks and see whether the system supports it. Deciding whether the support is adequate is a matter of assessing the quality. We discuss this in section 7.3.

What about validation? Can the customer reach his business goals? We can see that there is a requirement intended to support the goal, but we cannot be sure that it is sufficient. Here the customer runs a risk, but that is the kind of risk he should handle and be responsible for: he cannot transfer it to the software house.

Product-level requirement

R3 The product shall have a function for recording experience data and associated keywords. It shall have a function for retrieving the data based on keywords.

This is a typical product-level requirement, where we specify what comes in and goes out of the product. Essentially we just identify the function or feature without giving all the details. Section 3.4 tells more about this kind of requirement.

Could we give the requirement to a software house? Yes. If it is a software house that knows about shipyards there is no problem. Using COTS or developing from scratch are both acceptable. If we choose a software house that doesn't know about business applications, we would have to add some more detail about experience data, keywords, etc., then they should be able to provide the features we have asked for. Can we verify the requirement? Yes, before the delivery time. All that needs to be done is for us to check that the necessary screens are there and that they work.

What about validation? Here the customer runs the same risk as for R2. However, we run an additional risk. We cannot be sure that the solution adequately supports the tasks. Maybe the supplier has designed the solution in such a way that the user has to leave the cost registration screen, enter various codes once more, and then enter the experience data. A likely result would be that experience data isn't recorded.

Design-level requirement

R4 The product shall provide the screen pictures shown in app. xx. The menu points shall work as specified in yy.

This is a typical design-level requirement, where we specify one of the product interfaces in detail. Although a design-level requirement specifies the interface exactly, it doesn't show how to implement it inside the product.

R4 refers to the shipyard's own solution in app. xx. If they asked a business system supplier for R4, they might not get the best system. A supplier may have better solutions for experience data, but they are likely to use different screen pictures than those in app. xx. Insisting on the customer's own screen pictures might also be much more costly than using an off-the-shelf solution.

However, if the product was a rare type of system, the shipyard might have to use a software house without domain knowledge and have them develop the solution from scratch. In that case, R4 might be a very good requirement, assuming that the shipyard has designed the solution carefully. The shipyard would thus have full responsibility for ease of use, efficient task support, and its own business goals.

Choosing the right level

The conclusion of the analysis is: *choosing the right level on the goal-design scale is a matter of who you ask to do the job.*

You should not give the supplier more responsibility than he can handle. He may refuse to accept the added responsibility, or he may accept it but deliver an inadequate solution. Neither should you give him too few choices. It may make the solution too expensive, and if you haven't validated the requirements carefully, you may get an inferior solution.

In practice, the shipyard case is best handled through R2, the domain-level requirement. The main reason is that R2 ensures adequate task support and allows us to choose between many COTS suppliers. However, R1 is still important, although not as a requirement, but as a measurable goal stated in the introductory part of the spec. R4 may also be a good idea, not as a requirement, but as an example of what the customer has in mind. Of course, the customer shouldn't spend too much work on R4 since it is only an example.

R3 is rarely a good idea. The customer runs an unnecessary risk of inefficient task support and missed goals. Unfortunately, most requirements specs work on that level, and it is often a source of problems.

In the discussion above, we discarded R1, the goal-level requirement, because a software house couldn't take responsibility for it. Could we find a supplier that could accept this requirement? Maybe, but we would have to use a completely different type of supplier, for instance a management consultant such as PriceWaterhouseCoopers, Ernst & Young, etc. In their contract with the consultant, R1 would be the requirement, and R2 would be an example of a possible (partial) solution.

It is, however, likely that not even the consultant would accept R1 at a fixed price. Instead he might work on a time-and-material basis, tell the customer about other solutions and advise him whether experience has shown that 5% deviation was achievable in a shipyard, how to train staff, etc. In essence, the customer would get an organizational solution, possibly including some IT.

Quite often it is a good idea to use different requirement levels for different interfaces, or change from one level to another during the project. In section 1.7 and Chapter 5 we show ways of combining the levels.

What happened in the Danish Shipyard?

You may wonder what actually happened in the Danish Shipyard case discussed above. The full requirements specification is in Chapter 11. There are eight business goals, clearly stated in section 4 of the spec, which is an introductory section intended to help the reader. The real requirements are in section 5, which uses product-level requirements similar to R3 above. (Each sub-section has also an introduction that explains a bit about the tasks involved.)

When the system had been in operation for about a year, we assessed it and noticed that sales staff didn't use the experience data. Why? The financial manager, who had been closely involved in the development, said it was because sales staff were reluctant to use computers and they should be replaced by younger staff. A closer study revealed, however, that the system had no features to enable it to record experience data, and the feature for retrieving experience data was difficult to find and use from the quotation windows.

Further study revealed that the requirements didn't mention recording of experience data – it had accidentally been replaced by a reference to *retrieval* of experience data. The spec mentioned retrieval of experience data but didn't make it clear that this should be done during quotation. So, although all the requirements were verified at delivery time, nobody noticed that a highly important goal was lost.

How could this have been avoided? One possibility would be to trace the eight business goals to requirements and check them several times during development to ensure that the project remains on-track. A good quality manager would have ensured this. Another possibility would be to use domain-level requirements rather than product-level ones.

Asking "why"

In practice it is not always easy to choose the right level on the goal-design scale, and analysts often make mistakes. They should try to slide up and down the scale by asking "why" each requirement is necessary and "how" it can be achieved. Then they can select the requirement appropriate for the project.

Figure 1.6B shows some "why" questions for a device that measures neural signals in human patients. The customer developed medical equipment and had sub-contracted the software and part of the hardware development. One requirement said that the product should have a special mini-keyboard with start/stop button, repeat button, and a few other buttons.

Fig 1.6B Ask "why"

> **Neural diagnostics**
>
> System shall have mini-keyboard with start/stop button, ...
> Why?
>
> So that it is possible to operate it with the "left hand"
> Why?
>
> Because both hands must be at the patient
> Why?
>
> To control electrodes and bandages, and to calm and reassure the patient.

The supplier could deliver that, but just to make sure he understood the requirements, he asked "why" the mini-keyboard was necessary. The answer was that it should be possible to operate the device with "the left hand." Still a bit puzzled, the supplier asked "why" once more.

The customer explained that, "both the surgeon's hands have to be at the patient, so the surgeon couldn't use an ordinary keyboard."

"Why?" insisted the supplier.

"Because the surgeon has to fix electrodes to the patient's body, and sometimes keep bandages in place, and at the same time calm the patient because the electrical signals can be painful," was the answer.

Now the supplier understood the goal, but also understood that the requirements were too design-oriented. Since the supplier also supplied part of the hardware, more freedom was possible. The most important point was that both the surgeon's hands had to be at the patient.

The parties could now see various other ways to satisfy the real need, for example with a mini-keyboard attached to the surgeon's wrist, with foot pedals, or with voice recognition and a headset microphone.

They ended up with the requirement outlined in Figure 1.6C. Note that it includes both a domain description and some examples in order to help the reader and to record the ideas generated at an early stage.

Fig 1.6C Recommendation: why and how

Measuring neural response can be painful for the patient. Electrodes must be kept in place . . . so both hands should be at the patient during a measurement.	Domain – why
R1: It shall be possible to perform the commands *start*, *stop* . . . with both hands at the patient.	Requirement
Might be done with mini-keyboard (wrist keys), foot pedal, voice recognition, etc.	Example – how

Recommendations

In general it is an advantage to include "business" goals, domain-descriptions and – using more caution – examples.

Business goals and goal-level requirements are not requirements to the supplier, but:

1 they improve the supplier's understanding of the domain, and

2 they allow you to check that the goals are fully reflected in the requirements and that they are considered during development.

Domain-descriptions are sometimes requirements, sometimes not. If you use product-level requirements, make sure that you add some domain description to explain the *purpose* and the context of the requirements. Domain descriptions:

1 improve the supplier's understanding of the domain,

2 help the supplier to guess tacit requirements or ask for further information,

3 take additional space unless you use domain-level requirements.

Examples of design are not requirements, but:

1 they improve the supplier's understanding of what the customer had in mind,

2 they record early ideas,

3 they should be used with caution to avoid requirements issues turning into design issues.

1.7 Typical project models

Highlights

Product-level requirements: elicited from users. A lot of work.
Domain-level requirements: describe user tasks. Much faster.
Two-step approach: domain-level first, design-level later with careful checks.
Contracts and price structure: can reduce risks.

In the preceding sections we have mentioned many possibilities: requirements on various levels from goal-level to design-level; different requirements styles from plain text to diagrams, and from data requirements to quality requirements; many techniques and methods from elicitation and analysis, to validation and verification.

The rest of the book gives details of all these possibilities, but how do you combine them in practice? There is no fixed, standard way to do it, because projects are so different. What is excellent in one project may be a waste of time in another. In spite of this, we will explain a couple of models below. You may use them as a basis for your project and adjust them according to actual project characteristics. Figures 1.7A and 1.7B give an overview of the possibilities.

1.7.1 The traditional approach: product-level requirements

In this classical model you interview the stakeholders, study existing documents, conduct workshops and brainstorms. Finally you analyze and write the requirements specification. In the basic version of the model you don't need to specify business goals, because the decision to get a new system has already been made. In the extended version, you also conduct interviews and brainstorming sessions to identify business goals.

The specification will contain the following central parts:

- Introductory parts (including business goals in the extended version).

- The limits of the system: what is to be delivered; what are the interfaces (for instance shown as a context diagram; see section 3.2).

- Data requirements, for instance as a data model with a data dictionary (see sections 2.2 and 2.3).

- Product-level functional requirements, for instance as function lists, feature requirements, and textual process descriptions (see sections 3.3, 3.4, and 4.3).

- Quality requirements for critical quality factors (see section 6.2).

Fig 1.7A Typical project models

Traditional: Product-level requirements

Ask users, study documents, extract features.
- Introduction, [business goals]
- System limits, e.g. context diagram
- Data requirements, e.g. data model, data description
- **Product-level functional requirements, e.g. features**
- Critical quality requirements

Fast approach: Domain-level

Describe user tasks, study documents . . .
- Introduction, [business goals, **BPR tasks**] . . .
- System limits, e.g. context diagram
- Data requirements, e.g. verbal data description
- **Domain-level requirements, e.g. Tasks & Support**
- [Trace analysis: **goals to tasks**]
- Critical quality requirements

Two-step approach: Domain-level + design-level

- All the fast-approach stuff
+
- **Design-level requirements**, e.g. prototypes, protocols

The IEEE standard 830 gives additional guidance on how to organize each part, particularly the introductory matters and the functional requirements. The Volere Template (Robertson and Robertson 1999) has a much longer list of things to consider in the specification.

After the first draft of the specification, it is necessary to review it, have the customer validate it, check it for consistency, and so on. Chapter 9 describes ways of doing this.

The work may take a long time, and often the analyst has to do most of it himself. Usually there is insufficient time to do it right and get information from all the stakeholders. Furthermore, analysts tend to focus on the trivial parts, leaving the difficult parts till later when – alas – time runs out.

In some cases, the work is primarily done by users and co-ordinated by the customer's IT department, for instance as follows: the IT team asks all user departments involved to submit their requirements to the new system. The departments have no requirements expertise, but they try to come up with something. The IT team then collects and edits the submissions and sends them to the suppliers.

Fig 1.7B Recommended project models

Project type	Project model		
	Trad.	**Domain**	**Two-step**
In-house	?	OK	OK
Product development	?		OK
Time and materials	?	OK	OK
COTS business	?	OK	
COTS tools	OK		
Tender COTS	?	OK	
Tender tailor	?	OK*	OK*
Contract COTS	?	OK	
Contract tailor	?	OK*	OK*
Sub-contract	OK		OK
Maintenance	OK		

? Used, but dubious * Variable price

In the West Zealand Hospital case, explained in section 3.8, the IT teams worked in this co-ordinating way. They didn't fully understand what the users submitted, but assumed that the supplier would understand it. The supplier actually understood some of it because he had domain expertise from many other hospitals, but unfortunately he didn't understand many parts. "We will find out more during the implementation process," he reasoned and signed the contract. No wonder that the system later failed to meet several business goals.

Apart from the long time spent in analysis, the traditional approach has some inherent weaknesses. In general, it is difficult to ensure that product-level requirements provide adequate task support and that they satisfy the business goals. Furthermore, even if customers can read the requirements, they will not know whether they are adequate. If you invite stakeholders to submit requirements, they also tend to come up with long wish lists that are difficult to prioritize afterwards.

Product-level requirements are well suited to three kinds of projects, as shown in Figure 1.7B:

1 COTS purchases where the customer wants a development tool or a technical component. The requirements are a list of desired features, and the different products are compared against the list.

2 Sub-contracting where customer and supplier agree on a technical sub-product and its features.

3 Maintenance projects where an existing, deployed system gets new features.

In all of these cases, the customer knows the user tasks and the supplier doesn't need to know about them. Furthermore, the best type of solution has been decided. What remains to be found is the exact list of features needed.

1.7.2 The fast approach: domain-level requirements

In this model you primarily focus on describing the user tasks in co-operation with expert users. You also collect information on the data to be stored in the computer. In the basic version of the model you don't need to specify business goals, because the decision to get a new system has already been made. In the extended version, you also conduct interviews and brainstorming sessions to identify business goals. Part of describing the business goals may be to describe high-level tasks or BPR (Business Process Re-engineering) tasks.

The specification will have almost the same central parts as the traditional approach, with important deviations shown in bold:

- Introductory parts (including business goals and **BPR tasks** in the extended version; see section 3.11).

- The limits of the system: what is to be delivered; what are the interfaces (for instance shown as a context diagram; see section 3.2).

- Data requirements, for instance as a data dictionary (see section 2.4). Sometimes a data model is useful too.

- **Description of user tasks** plus a requirement saying that these tasks have to be supported (see sections 3.6 and 3.8).

- A **trace analysis** showing how each business goal is reflected in the tasks (extended version only). See section 8.7 for an example.

- Quality requirements for critical quality factors (see section 6.2).

Before sending the specification for review, you conduct a CRUD check (Create-Read-Update-Delete check, section 9.2.3) to see that all required data are handled in some task. Usually they are not, so then you need to describe the missing tasks.

Next you send the specification out for review and conduct review meetings. Stakeholders are primarily invited to correct the task descriptions. They may also suggest solutions, but these are examples and not requirements.

Chapter 15 shows an example of this approach in a small, low-cost project expected to take only a few weeks.

In section 3.8 we explain how this approach worked in a hospital case, and we contrast it with the traditional approach above. The analysts reported that the domain-level approach reduced analysis hours and calendar time by a factor of 5 to 10. Selecting the right product was speeded up in a similar way.

The weakness of the approach is that some functional requirements are hard to specify through user tasks. It is of course acceptable to specify them in other ways as a supplement.

The approach is suitable for most types of projects, with a few exceptions:

1 It is not suitable for COTS acquisition of development tools or technical components. In these cases the customer wants certain features, and the domain aspects have already been resolved.

2 It is not suitable for sub-contracting of technical parts for the same reasons.

3 It is only suitable for product development as the first step of a two-step approach. In product development we strongly recommend that you design the user interface and test it carefully as the second step of requirements.

1.7.3   The two-step approach: domain-level requirements plus design-level requirements

The first step of this model is the domain-level approach above. It produces the first level of requirements exactly as above with business goals, data requirements, task descriptions, etc. Reviews and checks are also carried out.

The second step is a design task that produces *design-level requirements* for the complex interfaces.

For the user interface, developers design a prototype of the screens. The basis is the task descriptions and the data description. Section 2.5 outlines a systematic way to do it. The design is usability tested to see that the user interface is sufficiently easy to learn and effectively supports the tasks (see section 6.6). The result is a new requirement on design level:

■ The product shall have a user interface with screens, menus, etc. as shown in app. xx.

Review and validation of this requirement has been done by means of the usability test.

For complex technical interfaces, developers design and specify communication formats, protocols, etc. (see section 5.5). It is also a good idea to make a functional prototype that tests whether the communication really works.

In principle the design-level requirements replace the domain-level requirements from step 1. Verification at the end of development is now a test to see that design-level requirements are fulfilled, e.g. that all parts of the user interface prototype now work as specified. However, don't throw away the requirements from step 1 just yet. Let us see why.

Requirements management. During design, developers detect many errors and omissions in the domain-level requirements. For instance, they may detect missing user tasks or new task variants. Should they update the domain-level requirements when they are no longer needed for verification? Yes, they should! There are several reasons for this. First, the team needs the domain-level requirements to validate the design-level requirements. Second, the domain-level requirements are excellent for requirements management. They serve as justification for the design-level requirements and show what the consequences would be of a change.

Finally, in practice it is also useful to verify the domain-level requirements at the end of development, including testing that the user interface is still easy to use. The reason for this is that deviations may sneak in during development and make the user interface less useful. A typical example of this is a creative Web designer, who adds fancy colors to the final Web page, unintentionally making it hard to read on the screen.

The two-step model is suited to many types of projects:

1 In-house development, time-and-material based development, and sub-contracted projects.

2 Product development. We have seen repeated success with the two-step model in product development where programming, etc. became much more predictable, client satisfaction sky-rocketed, and sales prices could be doubled (Lauesen and Vinter 2001).

3 Tailor-made systems, either in tender projects or contract development.

4 The add-on parts of COTS-based products, either in tender projects or contract development.

In 3 and 4 above, a contract is involved and it is important to find a fair way to specify the costs. See the discussion below.

The two-step model is not suited to the standard parts of COTS-based systems. They already have their own interfaces, so defining new ones is meaningless.

1.7.4 Contracts and price structure

When you use the two-step approach in tenders or contract development, deciding on a final price can be tricky because the size of the project is only partly known at the beginning of step 2, the design step. Do you write one contract for the design work and another for the development work? Or could you write one contract for the whole thing? Figure 1.7C shows an overview of the various possibilities.

Fig 1.7C Contracts and prices

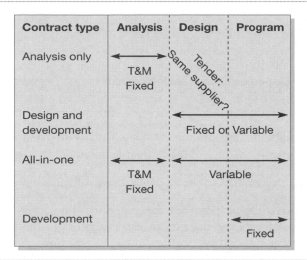

Initial analysis contract. You may draw up a contract for the initial analysis that ends with domain-level requirements (step 1). Most consultants prefer to do this on a time-and-material basis.

Some consultants offer a fixed-price contract for the initial analysis. This may sound risky, since the amount of work involved is unknown. However, from an initial investigation of the customer's situation, consultants can often tell roughly how much time will be needed – and how much the customer is willing to pay.

The result should be the necessary requirements and other material for a tender process or a contract negotiation. The price in the contract may either be fixed or variable, as explained below.

Some consultants are also suppliers of tailor-made solutions or COTS-based solutions. In this case a consultant may not be allowed to submit proposals in the tender process. However, if the requirements are truly domain-oriented, all potential suppliers have equal opportunities and the consultant who wrote the requirements can also qualify as a supplier.

In contrast, if the requirements are more design-oriented, the consultant will most likely favor a particular supplier, typically himself, and he is disqualified since he has a de facto monopoly. There are two ways out of this: (1) Avoid the design-oriented requirements in the tender and use only domain-oriented requirements. (2) Avoid the tender situation and go for an all-in-one contract that includes analysis and development (see below).

Design and development contract, fixed price. When responding to a domain-level specification with a fixed price, suppliers will essentially have to do some design work and calculate prices based on that. There are several drawbacks here: this is a lot of work, and if the supplier loses the contract, he has wasted a lot of money. Furthermore, a good design job requires close user interaction, usability tests, and so on, which cannot be done prior to signing the contract. So the real design work has to be done later and the initial cost estimate may be very inaccurate, particularly if much new development work has to be done.

Many suppliers quote a fixed price, and some even succeed in delivering an adequate system without losing money. Others do a bad job and lose money initially, but formally they fulfill the written requirements. Later they recover the loss through expensive additions to the system. They have a monopoly when it comes to system additions, so they can charge a high price for these.

Design and development contract, variable price. Instead of a fixed price, the customer can ask for a fixed price for the basic system (the built-in COTS parts) plus a unit price per "addition". Additions can be measured as the number of new screens graduated according to screen complexity (sections 3.16 and 5.1 gives examples). Additions can also be measured by means of Function Points or Object Points, which are standardized ways of measuring the essential size of an IT-system (see Thayer 1997 and Furey and Kitchenham 1997).

This type of contract often specifies the development approach to be used, for instance how users should be involved, how to review and test designs, etc. The supplier should include these costs in the fixed price he quotes. The advantage to the supplier of this is that writing a proposal will be much less work, and at the same time he reduces his risk because more work later means more money.

The advantage to the customer is that he doesn't end up paying a high price for additions when the supplier has got a monopoly. He can compare suppliers' prices, but to do this he must have some idea of what the supplier provides as a standard solution and what has to be added. The Midland Hospital requirements in Chapter 12 show a way of doing this based on product features. The Task & Support style shown in section 3.8 and in the West Zealand Hospital case (Chapter 13) show how to do this with domain-oriented requirements.

In practice we see amazingly few contracts made with variable prices. For one reason or another, the parties prefer a fixed price in spite of the associated risks. Sometimes the parties add a clause saying that either party, up to a certain point in development, can withdraw from the contract against paying compensation to the other party. This is a good way out if the supplier turns out to be less competent, or the customer more demanding, than expected.

All-in-one contract. An all-in-one contract includes analysis and development. This form is widely used in cases where the customer has little IT expertise, doesn't want an expensive consultant, and feels confident that a supplier can provide what he needs. The supplier will carry out the analysis, design the solution and develop the product. It is unwise to do this on a time-and-material basis, but which price should be agreed on initially, and what are the requirements? The real requirements develop over time, so the only requirement the parties should agree on initially is the development process to be used. For instance, they could state in the contract that a two-step approach is to be used with details described further (see section 3.16).

The contract might be a combination of an initial analysis contract and a design-and-development contract with variable price. The price structure could be composed accordingly: fixed price or time-and-materials basis for the initial analysis; fixed price plus a unit price per "addition" for the rest of development.

Contract outlines and price structures of this type also allow the customer to compare several suppliers.

Development contract, fixed price. If the customer has used design-level requirements, it is fairly simple to draw up a contract for the rest of development. The risk to the developer is small, since it is clear what has to be developed. The customer has taken the risk that his design is adequate.

We see this type of contract in industry, for example, to develop the software for a mobile phone where the customer has designed the exact user interface of the phone. It is also common in aviation and the aerospace industry. Since the system may change over time, it is also a good idea to contract on a unit price per "addition" to prevent the supplier from exploiting his monopoly later. In most of these cases, the customer is a main contractor.

2

Data requirement styles

In some systems the content of the database is the most important part, while the functions are relatively trivial because they mostly deal with maintaining the data and presenting it in various ways. Many business applications are of this kind.

In other systems (such as technical systems or some Web applications) there is not a real database, because the system stores its data in other ways, for instance as objects in main memory or as simple files.

In any case, it is important to specify the data to be stored in the system, no matter whether data is stored as a database or in some other way. It may also be important to specify the data that enter and leave the system.

Some analysts claim that details of the stored data are internal computer matters and should not be specified in requirements. What we should specify is only the information of importance in the domain. However, there is almost a one-to-one correspondence between information in the domain, and the data stored in the system. As a result, specifying the data is not really a design issue.

In this chapter we will look at four styles for specifying data. They are all suited to describe data stored in the system, be it a technical system or a business system. Most of the styles are also useful for describing data entering and leaving the system.

2.1   The hotel system example

In what follows, we will often use a hotel system as an example. We have chosen this example because most people have some idea what the application is about, yet we can also show requirements that may surprise the typical software developer. Once he has seen such non-trivial requirements, he can see that they are necessary, but he may not have thought of them on his own. In most of the examples, we ignore some of these non-trivial requirements. For instance we usually ignore that rooms are not booked by room number, but by room type; hotels usually overbook, i.e. book more rooms than they have, expecting that some customers will not turn up.

Other non-trivial requirements are discussed over the chapters. In this way, the hotel example illustrates a basic point in all requirements engineering: You cannot sit in your office and produce requirements based on intuition and logic. You have to discover the non-trivial requirements from users and other stakeholders.

Our initial definition of the hotel system is shown in Figure 2.1. It is relatively simple: we want to support the hotel reception, in particular the tasks of booking rooms, checking in, checking out, changing rooms for a customer who has already checked in, and recording services such as breakfasts on a guest's bill. To do this, the system should record data about guests, rooms, and services.

Fig 2.1 The hotel system

Task list

Book guest
Check in
Check out
Change room
Breakfast list and
other services

Data about:

Guest
Rooms
Services

2.2   Data model

What is it?

Block diagram describing data inside and outside the product.
Excellent for experts – difficult for users.
For COTS-based systems: focus on non-standard data.

A data model specifies the data to be stored in the system and the relationships between the data. Figure 2.2A is a data model for a simple hotel system. There are many variants of data models. The one in the example is an *Entity/Relationship model*, also called an *E/R model* or a Bachman diagram. In object-oriented development, analysts use a variant called a *class diagram* (see section 4.7).

Each box corresponds to a collection of records of the same type. The *Guest* box, for instance, contains records about all guests that the hotel system must keep track of. The connectors between the boxes show *one-to-many relationships*. For instance, the connector between the Guest box and the Stay box shows that one guest may have one or more stays. We have shown the connectors as "crow's feet", but there are many other ways to show them.

Requirements

The requirement says that 'the system shall store the following data'. This does not mean that the data is to be stored in one particular way. The E/R model is a logical model, and the data may be stored in several ways: as a relational database, as objects using C++ or Java, etc. All these versions can satisfy the requirement.

Looking at the real-life specifications in Chapters 11 to 15, you might notice that only the shipyard specification (Chapter 11) contains a data model, and it is not explicitly stated as a requirement. However, the specifications in Chapters 13 to 15 used data models as intermediate work products to guide the analysts.

The hotel data model

We will explain the example in some detail. The model shows that the hotel system has to keep track of guests (one record per guest), and a number of stays at the hotel (one record per stay). The connector between Guest and Stay shows that one guest may be connected to several stays. Reading the same connector the other way, it shows that each stay is connected to exactly one guest. In simple terms, this means that each guest may stay a number of times at the hotel.

Fig 2.2A Data model

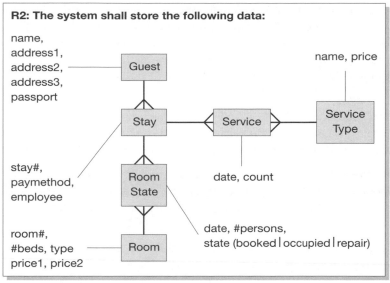

R2: The system shall store the following data:

name,
address1,
address2,
address3,
passport

stay#,
paymethod,
employee

room#,
#beds, type
price1, price2

name, price

date, count

date, #persons,
state (booked | occupied | repair)

Guest — Stay — Service — Service Type — Room State — Room

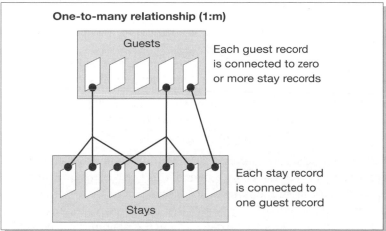

One-to-many relationship (1:m)

Guests

Each guest record
is connected to zero
or more stay records

Each stay record
is connected to
one guest record

Stays

The diagram at the bottom of Figure 2.2A shows how you can imagine the one-to-many (1:m) relationship. The Guest box contains a record or index card for each guest. The Stay box contains record or index card for each stay. The crow's foot connects each guest with his stays. Furthermore, each stay is connected to only one guest.

Guest. The model also shows the data we must keep track of for each guest: his name, address, and passport number (for foreigners only). These pieces of data are called *fields* or *attributes*. In practice, there will be many more guest attributes, such as a telephone number, e-mail address, or contact person.

A typical commercial (COTS) system for business applications might have 150 fields for each customer in the database. An amazing number – how can that be? If you look at the fields one by one, you will realize that each field could be useful in some applications. However, no company will ever use all the fields in their application. During installation, the IT staff will select those fields useful for this particular company.

Stay. According to the model, we have to keep track of the following information for each stay: the stay number (also called a booking number), the pay method (whether the customer pays by cash, credit card, or has a company account), and an employee name (only when the 'guest' is a company and one of its employees stays at the hotel).

ServiceType. The system also needs a list of various types of services, e.g. breakfast or telephone. The *ServiceType* box has a record for each type of service, stating its name and price. In simple terms, it is a price list, and each record corresponds to a line on the list.

Service. For each stay, the guest may receive several of these services, and the *Service* box keeps track of them. Each service record is connected through the crow's feet to exactly one stay and one type of service. The service record fields show which day the service was received and how many items were received. The connectors point to the appropriate stay and service type. As an example, a record might have connectors specifying that stay 714 received some continental breakfast. The fields of the service record show that two continental breakfasts were served on 23/11/2001. Each service record will appear as a separate line on the customer's invoice for that stay.

Room. The *Room* box corresponds to the list of rooms. For each room there is a record with room number (corresponding to the sign on the door), the number of beds in the room, the type of room (whether it has bath, toilet, etc.), and prices.

RoomState. We need some information about the room for each day, e.g. whether it is free, booked, occupied, being repaired, etc. The records in *RoomState* keep track of this. In principle each room has a RoomState record for each date, showing the actual or planned state that date. Notice that a stay relates to one or more RoomStates corresponding to the dates where the customer has booked a room or actually stays in it.

Did you notice how many non-trivial details we mentioned above? They all related to some field or some connector in the model. A data model is an excellent way of getting an overview of lots of detail. If you know something about the domain, you can usually guess the meaning of most boxes and many of the fields. However, you can rarely guess the meaning of it all. For instance, you might not guess why and when we record a passport number. In practice a data description (for instance a data dictionary) is important for understanding the details. Section 2.3 explains more on this.

Normalization

Database analysts talk about normalizing the data model. This means to break each record into smaller records in order to give each record a fixed size and to prevent the same data being stored in several places. Normalization is an almost mechanical process that we will not discuss here, but we will give two examples from the hotel system:

1 **Fixed size.** We don't combine a Room record with all its RoomState records. At first sight combining them seems a good idea because the Room record now would contain a "calendar" for the occupation of this particular room. However, if we want the system to cover varying lengths of the calendar, we would have violated the principle of a fixed record size.

2 **Data in one place only.** We don't combine a stay record with its associated guest record. If we did so, a guest with several recorded stays would have his name and address stored in each of his stay records and it would be difficult to handle the situation where he changes his address or phone number.

It is often convenient to model the domain information without normalizing the data. However, when developers plan a corresponding relational database system, they will always normalize according to rule one, because a relational database cannot handle variable length records. Usually, they will also normalize according to rule two. If data are to be stored as objects, normalization is not quite as important, because objects may have a more complex internal structure.

Implementation

An E/R model is a model on a logical level, and there are many ways of storing the data in the product. Figure 2.2B shows two of them.

Database. In business applications, the data will typically be stored in a *relational database* as tables of records, with one table for each box of the data model. A 1:m connector is implemented as a reference from the m-side record to the 1-side record. These references introduce the need for *keys* in the database.

Every table that must be referenced from another table needs a unique identification of the records. This identification is called the *primary key*. It is implemented as one or more fields. For example, in the hotel system, the stay table has a good key field: the stay number. It is unique and it also makes sense to the users, who talk about booking numbers or stay numbers. But often a table has no natural key fields. The guest table is an example. We cannot be sure that the address or the name is unique, and they are difficult to spell in a consistent manner. So in practice we would have to introduce an artificial, primary key for the guest, for instance a guestId (an identification number) that the system might assign automatically. The users need not know about it.

Once we have the primary keys, we can store references corresponding to the connectors. As an example, we would store a guest identification number in each stay record. This additional field is called a *foreign key* because it points to a foreign table. The foreign key allows the database system to find the guest record connected to the stay record. The database system can also find all stay records connected to a particular guest, but that involves searching through all stay records looking for the particular guest identification. Fortunately, database systems have advanced techniques for optimizing such searches.

Linked objects or nested data structures. In technical systems, the data can be stored in many ways, for instance as arrays and records nested in several levels. With the object-oriented (OO) approach, each record would be stored as an object. In many technical systems, data is stored entirely in main memory. A 1:m connector will usually be pointers (memory addresses) from the m-side object to the 1-side object. Additional pointers link the 1-side object to a chain of associated objects in the m-side box. The lower part of Figure 2.2B shows this principle.

When pointers are used, there is no need for artificial primary keys or foreign keys. Furthermore, the system works 1,000 to 100,000 times faster because everything takes place in the system's memory. Unfortunately, memory space is severely limited, and data in memory cannot survive a power failure or other such disasters. Non-trivial approaches are needed to extend the apparent memory size and ensure data persistency.

For technical systems as well as database systems, there may be small differences between the logical data model and what is implemented. In the hotel system, we could for instance omit RoomState records that show that the room is free. If there is no RoomState record for a specific date, the room is free. This might save space if we want to book far into the future. However, such details are not relevant when the data model is used as a requirement.

Terminology

Data modeling occurs in many flavors, and the terminology varies from one school to another.

In the database world, the boxes are called *entity classes*, *relations*, or *tables*. In the object-oriented world they are simply called *classes*. (Classes not only store data, they also have functionality; see section 4.7.)

The records in the boxes may be called *entities*, *instances*, *records*, or *objects*.

The attributes may be called *fields*, *attributes*, and sometimes *table columns*.

Fig 2.2B Implementation of data models

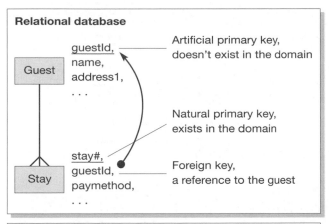

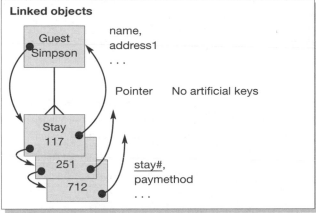

The connectors are called *relationships* in the database world and *associations* in the object world. In some data-modeling schools they are called *relations*, whereas relations in other schools mean the boxes. This double meaning of "relation" can be very confusing.

The term *association* chosen by UML (see section 3.21) is a good choice since it avoids the confusion about relations versus relationships.

Cardinality

A connector has a *cardinality*, i.e. whether it connects one A record to many B records, or one B record to many A records. Often it is useful to be more specific about the cardinality of a relationship. Does a guest always have at least one stay, or are zero stays allowed? Does a RoomState always relate to one stay or can it be stay-less? Figure 2.2C shows how this can be expressed by means of crow's feet.

Fig 2.2C Cardinality

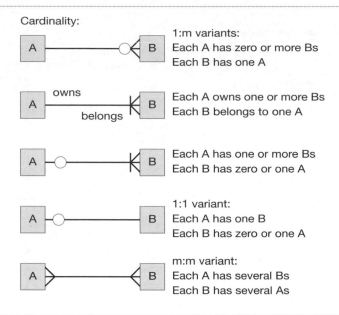

Cardinality:

1:m variants:
Each A has zero or more Bs
Each B has one A

owns
belongs
Each A owns one or more Bs
Each B belongs to one A

Each A has one or more Bs
Each B has zero or one A

1:1 variant:
Each A has one B
Each B has zero or one A

m:m variant:
Each A has several Bs
Each B has several As

The first three relationships in Figure 2.2C are variations of the one-to-many relationship. In the second of these, we have shown names for the relationship. If we read from A to B, the relationship is called "owns" (*A owns B*). If we read the other way, it is called "belongs to" (*B belongs to A*). Sometimes one name suffices.

The fourth relationship is a one-to-one variant. Each A has one B, and each B has zero or one A.

The last relationship is a many-to-many variant. Many-to-many crow's feet are often convenient in modeling and requirements, but they cannot be implemented directly. We have to transform the many-to-many relationship into a connection class and two crow's feet, as explained below, under Transformation rules.

Sub-classing and specialization

Sometimes an entity can occur in several variants. In the hotel system, for instance, we have two kinds of guests: an ordinary person and a company. A company will have some attributes that a person doesn't have, for instance several contact persons and phone numbers.

We can model this as shown on Figure 2.2D. The open-headed arrows show that *Person* is a sub-class of *Guest*, sometimes called a specialization. Similarly, *Company* is a sub-class.

Fig 2.2D Sub-classing and specialization

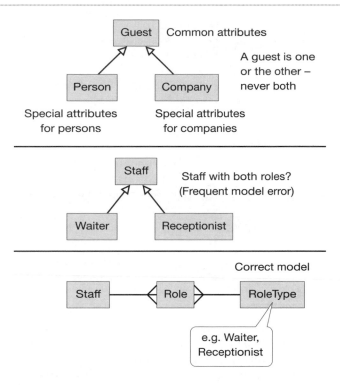

What does that mean? First of all, a guest must be either a person or a company. The guest cannot be both at the same time. Second, a company has the common attributes found in *Guest* plus the special attributes found in *Company*. If you think of this in terms of records, a guest has only one record, but the person record is not the same length as the company record. In most systems, an entity cannot change sub-class once it has been created.

Sub-classing is very important in object-oriented development, and the programming languages support the concept well. In more database-oriented systems, sub-classing is rarely used, partially because relational databases don't support the concept directly.

As an example, in order to handle the person/company situation in a database, developers are likely to define a long record with fields for person as well as company. A tag field would say whether it *is* a company or a person. Depending on the tag, some fields have to be empty (null). If this leads to a lot of wasted space, developers might split the guest table into two or three and connect these with relationships.

Fig 2.2E Other notations

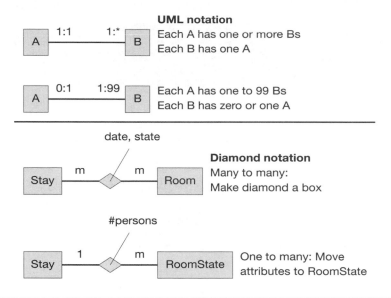

UML notation
Each A has one or more Bs
Each B has one A

1:1   1:*
A — B

0:1   1:99
A — B
Each A has one to 99 Bs
Each B has zero or one A

date, state

Diamond notation
Many to many:
Make diamond a box

Stay — m ◇ m — Room

#persons

One to many: Move
attributes to RoomState

Stay — 1 ◇ m — RoomState

We often see analysts with an object-oriented background favor the sub-class concept so much that they use it wrongly. The middle part of Figure 2.2D shows an example of this. It is tempting to specify that staff persons have sub-classes: waiters and receptionists. The two classes might have some different attributes. What is wrong with this? If you go to any small hotel, you will see the same person working sometimes as a waiter, sometimes as a receptionist. This cannot be modeled as sub-classes. The person cannot belong to both sub-classes at the same time, and most systems don't allow dynamic changes of sub-class.

Instead, you have to model the possible types of roles as a separate class, and then connect a staff member to one or more of these role types. The model could be like the third one in Figure 2.2D. If necessary, you can divide the role types into sub-classes. This is possible since role types don't change sub-class dynamically.

Notations

We can show relationships in many other ways than crow's feet, and the notation varies from one school to another. Figure 2.2E shows the same one-to-many relationship in different notations. They mean the same as the crow's feet that were used above, although they look different.

The notation at the top is used in UML (see more on this in section 4.7). It allows more precision than the crow's feet notation. You could for instance specify that a stay may have a maximum of 99 room states.

The diamond notation can be confusing because the diamond can have attributes. Thus it serves partly as a crow's foot and partly as a box. It can always be transformed into a new box and two crow's feet, but in many cases the new box is superfluous. The rules for this are:

■ Without attributes the diamond corresponds exactly to a crow's foot.

■ If it has attributes and is a 1:m relationship, the attributes could as well be added to the m-side box. The diamond then becomes a single crow's foot.

■ If it has attributes and is a m:m relationship, it corresponds to a connection box and two crow's feet like RoomState on Figure 2.2F.

■ If it is a ternary relationship, i.e. with three lines jutting out, it corresponds to a box and three crow's feet.

Transformation rules. To a large extent the preferred notations are mostly a matter of habit and practice. Personally, I read a lot of data models in all the notations, but I much prefer the crow's feet because you can see their meaning at a glance. Figure 2.2F illustrates this. If you read towards the toes, a crow's foot means, "fan-out". Read the other way, it means an arrow pointing at one object. You can visually trace a path in the diagram and, if it is a sequence of fan-outs, the result is a "large fan-out". Read the other way, it is a "long pointer".

If there are fan-outs in both directions along the path, the end-points are connected in a many-to-many way (unless additional consistency rules say differently).

The bottom diagram in Figure 2.2F shows that you can also go the other way. If you have a many-to-many relationship in your model, you can resolve it by means of a connection box inserted between the two existing boxes. The hotel system offers an example. If you look only at the boxes Stay and Room, you will realize that they have a many-to-many relationship: one room may be used by many stays, and one stay may comprise several rooms. If we invent the RoomState box and insert it between Stay and Room, the result is two simple crow's feet.

Usually an m:m relationship becomes two 1:m relationships when you insert a connection box – just as in this case – but sometimes it turns into several relationships.

The visual ability to track a sequence of connectors is particularly important in larger models, where you often have to mentally combine several relationships. Even the simple hotel system can provide an example:

According to the model in Figure 2.2A, how many guests are related to one service object? And how many guests are related to one service type object? With the UML notation and some practice, you have to focus hard to answer those questions (try it on the UML model in section 4.7). With the crow's feet and the same amount of training, you can answer at a glance. (By the way, the answers are: Only one guest is related to a service object, while several guests are related to a service type object. This is also what is expected from an understanding of the domain, so the model passed the "test'")

Advantages of data models

A data model is a very precise description of data. Furthermore, it is amazingly insensitive to the level we work on. If we make an E/R model of the information occurring in the domain, the model will be similar to an E/R model of the data inside the final product. In other words, the domain-level description and the product-level description are the same. This means that an early analysis of the information in the domain will create a model that can survive to implementation with only minor modifications. This is an important point. As we will see in Chapter 3, the same does not apply to the functions in the system.

Verification. Many developers are very experienced with E/R models, finding flaws in them, and using them to implement the product. It is also simple to verify that the data handled by the product matches the requirements.

Disadvantages of data models

Unfortunately data modeling takes time to learn. A good developer will need a week or two to be able to use it, but some IT people never learn it. The notation itself is not difficult to learn, but applying it is difficult because the real world is not divided into obvious boxes or objects (in spite of what the object community says). There are some obvious objects, such as guests and rooms, but a connection object such as *RoomState* is strange. If you don't normalize the model, you may hide connection objects to some extent. An object-oriented implementation can sometimes implement the unnormalized model directly.

In practice, it can be difficult to decide how much detail to include in the model. If too much is attempted, modeling will take forever. The expert knows when to stop. The model can never become a perfect model of the world.

Sometimes the modeling exercise can be immense, yet a waste of time. This happens for instance if we want to purchase a commercial business application. You will have to work for a long time to come up with all the classes and attributes that such a system contains as a standard. A typical company will only need a fraction of them. However, some companies do have special needs that are not covered by the commercial systems. In that case it will be very useful to model the data in this area. As usual in requirements, the problem is to recognize that a situation is special.

Fig 2.2F Transformation rules

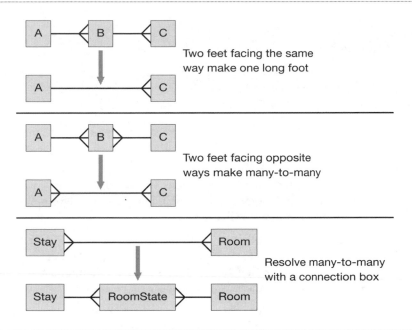

Two feet facing the same
way make one long foot

Two feet facing opposite
ways make many-to-many

Resolve many-to-many
with a connection box

Validation. Customers without basic training in E/R modeling find the diagrams difficult to understand. Even with some training, there is a long way to go from understanding the diagrams to really understanding their consequences for daily user tasks. Is it possible, for instance, for a customer to have two rooms at the same time? Or change room during a stay? This creates a serious communication gap, and the analyst must perform many checking activities to ensure that the model is correct. One way to overcome the communication gap is to use the *virtual window model* (section 2.5). Another is to write a data dictionary (section 2.3).

2.3   Data dictionary

What is this?

A textual description of data inside and outside the product.
Excellent for expert as well as user.
For COTS-based systems: focus on the non-standard data.

In many projects, you don't have to make a data model, but you can in plain text describe the data to be recorded in the system. It is the developer's job to transform these descriptions into a data model and possibly a database. This is the approach used in the Midland Hospital in Chapter 12.

Even if you have a data model, it is usually insufficient for describing details, special cases, and the relation to domain concepts. A verbal data description is needed. The shipyard system in Chapter 11 has both a data model and a verbal data description (under "definitions and terms").

A *data dictionary* is a verbal data description structured systematically. You may arrange it alphabetically according to field names, but this can be confusing unless you also have a data model to explain how fields belong together. If you have a data model – or an outline of one – structure the data dictionary according to the classes of the model.

The analysts behind the Membership system in Chapter 15 used an outline data model, which is not part of the requirements specification. Next they wrote the data dictionary that *is* part of the specification. There were some problematic parts of the data model that could be modeled in different ways. Instead of jumping into an implementation-oriented model, the analysts chose to write the data dictionary on a slightly more abstract level.

Figure 2.3 shows part of a carefully written data dictionary from the hotel system. Each entity (object or record) has its own description, including a description of each of its attributes. We explain what the entity means and mention other names used in practice for the entity. We have also given a few examples of the entity, particularly unusual ones.

For each attribute, we explain what it means and specify its type (text, number, etc. and the length of the field).

Often we see trivial descriptions, e.g.

guestName: Text, 120 chars. The name of the guest.

This is hardly worth writing. A good description tells the reader something non-trivial.

Fig 2.3   Data dictionary

> **Class: Guest** [Notes a, b ... refer to guidelines]
> The guest is the person or company who has to pay the bill. A guest has one or more
> stay records. A company may have none [b, c]. "Customer" is a synonym for guest, but
> in the database we only use "guest" [a]. The persons staying in the rooms are also called
> guests, but are not guests in database terms [a].
>
> **Examples**
> 1. A guest who stays one night.
> 2. A company with employees staying now and then, each of them with his own stay
>   record where his name is recorded [d].
> 3. A guest with several rooms within the same stay.
>
> **Attributes**
> name: Text, 50 chars [h]
>   The name stated by the guest [f]. For companies the official name since the
>   bill is sent there [g]. Longer names exist, but better truncate at registration
>   time than at print out time [g, j].
> passport: Text, 12 chars [h]
>   Recorded for guests who are obviously foreigners [f, i]. Used for police
>   reports in case the guest doesn't pay [g].
> . . .

Figure 2.3 may give some ideas. Notice that there is information about where the guest name comes from and what it is used for, which is not trivial. In order to write it, we need domain knowledge, and that is an essential part of requirements work.

We have also made a brave decision: we won't use more than 50 characters for the name. This is not so much to save space, but to help users. Some people have long names, but if the receptionist enters the entire name, it is not easily visible on the screen, and when printed out, the system has to cut it, sometimes into something funny or incomprehensible. It is better to have the receptionist truncate it in a meaningful way in the first place.

Below are some questions that may help the analyst to write better data descriptions. To illustrate the principle, we have added references such as [a] to the figure to show how the questions have been addressed.

Warning: You don't have to answer all the questions for every entity and attribute. However, if you don't know the answer, there is a good reason to ask expert users.

Check questions for each entity

a) Which entity name is used in the product? How does it relate to other names used by people in the domain?

b) How does the entity relate to other entities?

c) Are there cases where it doesn't have the usual relation to other entities?

d) Are there special things to consider when creating or deleting the entity?

e) Give a typical example of the entity. Give also unusual examples of the entity.

Check questions for each attribute

f) Where in the domain do the values come from?

g) What are the values used for in the domain?

h) Which values are possible for this attribute?

i) Can the attribute have special values, e.g. blanks, and when?

j) Give typical and special examples.

Data dictionaries as requirements

How can we use data dictionaries as requirements? There are at least three possibilities:

1 Use the data dictionary as an explanation of the data model, which is already a requirement. Example: the shipyard system in Chapter 11.

2 Use the data dictionary as a requirement, for instance:

R1 The product shall store data according to the data dictionary in xx.

In this case there is no need for the data model in diagram form, although it may give the reader an overview. Example: the membership system in Chapter 15.

3 Split the data description into separate feature requirements, for instance:

R2 The product shall record guests and remember the guests from stay to stay (regular customers).

R3 The product shall record companies as customers. When an employee from the company stays at the hotel, the company shall be the "guest" and be sent the invoice, but the name of the employee shall be recorded for the stay.

The last possibility, splitting the data description into several requirements, is popular in practice, but it tends to become long-winded (the Midland Hospital example in Chapter 12 is an example). It may, however, help the supplier to indicate which data he supports and which data he might handle in some other way.

Advantages of data dictionaries

A data dictionary can specify all the necessary details and the special cases. Some analysts say that a data dictionary lacks precision, which is true if the analyst has not followed the guidelines about what to write. In general, however, data dictionaries work best in combination with data models.

Validation. Customers and expert users can validate the description immediately. If the description gives non-trivial information, the customer may be encouraged to explain about special situations that the system also has to support.

Disadvantages of data dictionaries

The biggest disadvantage with data dictionaries is that they may take a long time to write, and since the person writing it can dig into detail and special cases, it can be hard to decide when it is good enough. A long description is also harder to validate, and validation may end up being cursory.

Good advice to you, as the analyst: Time and deadline will usually determine when it is "good enough". So start with the difficult parts of the data description, those that you don't know how to explain. If you have time, also take some less difficult parts. Omit the trivial parts.

And what do you think most analysts do? The opposite. They take the easy parts first and feel they have produced something today. They leave the hard parts until later, and the approaching deadline means that they never resolve the issues. Later, what will the developer do? Deliver his best guess. That works fine for the trivial data – even without verbal description – but not for non-trivial data, because the developer can't make any better guesses than the analyst.

2.4   Data expressions

What is this?

Compact formulas that describe data sequences.
Useful for composite data and message protocols.
Excellent for experts, acceptable for many users.

A data dictionary can give a lot of detail, but tends to be long. Furthermore, it is not suitable for showing how different pieces of data combine into structures. In contrast, a data expression is short and can show the structure of data. Data expressions are also called Regular Expressions or Backus-Naur Form (BNF). Just to warn you, some authors, e.g. Shneiderman (1998), call data expressions a *data dictionary*.

Figure 2.4A shows examples of data expressions. There are several notations, but the ones we have used in this figure are commonly used.

Details of the examples

The first example specifies the data that the user has to enter in order to request booking of a room:

booking request = guest data + period + room type

The formula shows that the user has to enter guest data, a specification of the desired period, and a specification of the room type. The plus sign is a concatenation operator showing that these pieces of data have to follow each other in that sequence.

The second formula shows that the guest data is composed of several parts:

guest data = guest name + address + pay method + [passport number]

Here we have enclosed the passport number in brackets, which show that the passport number may be omitted. (In the hotel, passport numbers are only required for foreigners.) We have shown the format of a passport number as follows:

passport number = letter + {digit}*8

The formula says that a passport number consists of a letter followed by exactly eight digits. The braces show that the inner part is repeated a certain number of times, as specified by the star. Other variants of repetition could be:

Fig 2.4A Data expressions

Notation with plus as concatenator
booking request = guest data + period + room type
guest data = guest name + address + paymethod
                    + [passport number]
passport number = letter + {digit}*8
room state = {<u>free</u> | <u>booked</u> | <u>occupied</u> | <u>repair</u>}
account data = transfer + {account record}* + done

Notation with implicit concatenation
guestData = guestName, address, paymethod
                    [, passportNumber]
ifStatement = if condition <u>Then</u> statement
                    [<u>Else</u>: statement <u>End If</u>]

{digit}*   Any number of digits

{digit}*(0:8)   Between 0 and 8 digits.

{digit}*(4:*)   At least 4 digits.

The next example shows that there are four possible room states:

room state = {<u>free</u> | <u>booked</u> | <u>occupied</u> | <u>repair</u>}

The brackets enclose the four possibilities that are separated by vertical lines. We have underscored the possibilities to show that they are literal values, i.e. that the actual value of the room state could be the text *free, booked,* etc.

Message sequence. An interesting possibility is that each data part is a separate message. In that way we can describe the possible message sequences on a technical interface. Figure 2.4A shows how the hotel system could send data to the account system. First it sends a *transfer* message, then a number of account records, and finally a *done* message.

The principles

We can summarize the basic principles of data expressions in this way:

+   Shows the sequence of data. What comes after what.

[ ]   Shows that something is optional.

{ }*   Shows that something is repeated a number of times.

{ | | }   Shows a choice between several possibilities.

B = C   Shows that the composite data structure B is composed as shown by C.

<u>free</u>   Shows a literal value.

Concatenator. The plus sign is a concatenation operator; it does not indicate that there is a separator between data parts. For instance, the characters of the passport number are not separated by anything – in spite of the plus sign.

The notation we have used is on a logical level, where we don't care how the different parts of the data are separated. They could be separated by spaces as in natural text, on separate lines on the screen, in separate fields, or separated by commas in a text file.

Implicit concatenation. In other notations, the plus is not used as above. We just write the data parts in the sequence they must occur. Spaces are assumed to separate parts where needed. If we want a comma to separate the data parts, we show a comma in the formula. The lower part of Figure 2.4A shows the formula for guest data as an example, but this time we have specified that the parts have to be separated by commas. Note that we now have to write each data name without embedded spaces. Otherwise it is ambiguous whether something is a single piece of data or two pieces separated by a space.

The notation with implicit concatenation is often used to describe programming languages. Figure 2.4A shows how we could describe the rules for an if statement in Visual Basic. Note that the keywords are underlined to show that they have to be written exactly as stated. Note also that the Else-part is optional since it is enclosed in square brackets.

Data model. Figure 2.4B shows how we could write part of a data model as data expressions:

Guest = name + address + {Stay}*

Stay = paymethod + [employee] + {room + date}*

We have written that Guest consists of name, address, and a list of stays. Further, a Stay consists of paymethod, an optional employee name, and a list of room numbers and associated dates. The latter list corresponds to some of the room states in the data model.

This example might suggest that it is easy to write a data model as data expressions, but we soon run into problems. For instance, why don't we extend the description of Stay to show that a stay also refers to a guest, as suggested on the figure? The problem is that a data expression is a formula for generating texts. When we include Guest in Stay, the text that describes a stay will have to include the text that describes a Guest. A first step in generating the text for a stay could produce this if the stay is for an ordinary guest who has only one room for one night:

Stay = <u>cash</u> + <u>room23</u> + <u>8/6-2001</u> + Guest

Now we have to replace Guest with name, address, etc. which could produce the following if the system has recorded two stays for the guest:

Stay = <u>cash</u> + <u>room23</u> + <u>8/6-2001</u> + <u>J. Simpson</u> + <u>Ringroad 23</u> + Stay1 + Stay2

Fig 2.4B Data model vs. data expressions

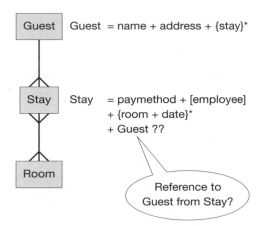

Next we have to replace Stay1 with the first stay of the guest and Stay2 with the second stay of the guest. And for each of these we have once more to include the Guest. As you can see, the text will never end.

Actually, we have constructed a recursive data structure that never ends. Recursive data structures are very useful in other cases, for instance to describe a programming language where one statement consists of other statements. In these cases the data structure ends, because these other statements become smaller and smaller, and the last statements are simple statements without sub-statements.

Data models don't end this way, so what should we do? One way out is to describe each class as a simple list of fields. Furthermore, we should describe each relationship as a separate text that gives the names of the two classes and the cardinality. This corresponds closely to the data descriptions you meet in many relational database systems.

Advantages of data expressions

A data expression is a very compact, yet precise, description of a sequence of data. It describes the formal rules for what must follow what.

Data expressions are traditionally used to describe the data that flows in a dataflow diagram, to describe languages (natural languages as well as programming languages), and sometimes to describe communication protocols and data formats in technical interfaces.

Validation. Customers without IT background find simple data expressions easier to understand than E/R models. Checking that they match existing or planned data is more difficult, however.

Verification. Developers can easily understand data expressions, and there are systematic ways of transforming a data expression to a program that handles the data. Data expressions are also an excellent source of test data for verification.

Disadvantages of data expressions

If you try to describe entire data models by means of data expressions, you lose the visual overview of the data, and the expressions become so complex that they are much harder to understand than data models. However, you can use data expressions to describe parts of the model, and then the two techniques supplement each other well.

Data expressions may be used to outline the data flowing across the user interface, but only on a high level where the data does not reflect the actual user dialog. They cannot provide the semantic richness of a good data dictionary, but the two techniques may supplement each other.

2.5   Virtual Windows

What is this?

Simplified screen pictures with graphics and realistic data, but no buttons and menus.
Excellent for experts as well as users.
Excellent for planning new user interfaces.
But don't overdo it and start designing the user interface.

A virtual window is an idealized screen picture. Graphically it looks like a screen picture, but it has no functions or menus. It also assumes that screens can be larger than normal if necessary. The idea is to visualize the system's data in a way that the user readily can relate to.

Virtual windows serve three purposes:

1   They allow customer and developer to validate the data model.

2   They can be used to plan data screens that effectively support user tasks.

3   They allow the customer to validate the screen design at a very early stage.

The first purpose is important in all cases. The other two are only interesting when a new system is to be developed, rather than bought.

The hotel example

Figure 2.5 shows four virtual windows that together cover all data from the hotel data model. They are also sufficient to support all daily activities in the reception, except for the fact that we need some search mechanisms to find guests and free rooms.

The *guest window* shows the data involved in a stay: guest data, rooms charged, service notes, rooms booked. (The rooms booked are shown below the dotted line.) If we later add proper buttons and menus, the screen supports booking, check-in, and check-out in addition to change of room, cancellation of a booking, etc.

The *rooms window* shows data for each room: prices, type, and when they are occupied or booked. With the addition of some search criteria, it supports finding free rooms and checking room state in general.

The *breakfast window* shows which rooms have received which kind of breakfast on a specific day. The screen supports the task that a waiter brings the list of breakfast servings from the restaurant, and the receptionist has to enter it. In the restaurant, guests are identified by their room number, so the list contains the servings by room number. The list contains only data that is shown in other screens too (the guest windows), and in principle, the breakfast data could be entered through the

Fig 2.5   Virtual windows

R1: The product shall store data corresponding to the following virtual windows:
R2: The final screens shall look like the virtual windows??

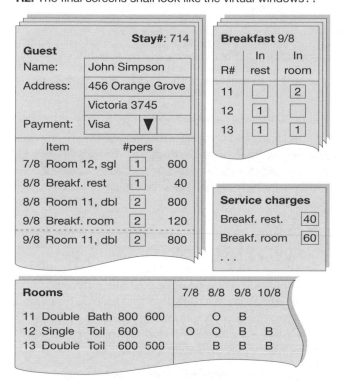

guest windows. This would be an inefficient way to support the task, however, even if we helped the user to browse the guests in room sequence.

The *service charge window* shows the charges for each type of service. It doesn't support any daily tasks, but is essential for updating the service charges. (Room prices can in theory be updated through the rooms window.)

Virtual windows as requirements

How can we use the virtual windows in requirements? On Figure 2.5, requirement R1 uses the virtual windows as data requirements:

R1 The product shall store data corresponding to the following virtual windows . . .

This is acceptable as a data requirement. The format of the windows does not have to be used in the actual screens.

An extreme version of this requirement style is to attach a print of all existing screens and forms, call them virtual windows, and require that the new system shall provide all data from these windows (although not necessarily in that form). To the customer this is a labor-saving way of writing data requirements. Unfortunately it may be very time-consuming for the supplier.

We might also use the virtual windows as requirements for new screens:

R2 The final screens shall look like the following virtual windows . . .

This is of course only meaningful if new screens must be designed. For existing parts of COTS systems, it is meaningless.

Even if new screens are to be developed, such a requirement might be premature – it may limit later interface design and consequently the usability of the final system. However, let us assume that you have designed the virtual screens carefully, taking all data and all tasks into consideration. Let us also assume that you have tested the understandability of the screens. Then R2 would be a good design-level requirement.

Validation and checking

The major advantage of virtual windows is that users and customers easily understand them and readily go into detail and discuss special cases to be supported. It is important, however, that the screens have a realistic graphical look, for instance with frames indicating where the user might type something, as shown in Figure 2.5. The screens must also show realistic data, preferably including unusual situations. Our experience is that otherwise critical problems are not revealed.

If you look closely at the guest screen, you will notice that Mr Simpson didn't follow the simple, expected pattern of room booking. First he stayed in a single room and had breakfast in the restaurant, then he moved to a double room and had two breakfasts in the room, and he plans to stay one extra night.

Receptionists grasp this situation immediately and come up with more complex examples to be supported. The result in this case was that the whole guest concept was restated. The result was documented in the E/R data model and the data dictionary.

Together these four screens contain all the data in the data model. When we add suitable functions (menus, buttons, etc.) to the screens, they can support, create, read, update, and delete all data. It is straightforward to check this. The screens also efficiently support all user tasks, except that there is no window suitable for searching guests, and no search criteria for finding rooms. We can check efficient task support by walking through the task descriptions (see section 3.6) or by explicitly writing down how tasks use the virtual windows (see section 3.13).

Designing the windows

If parts of the system need a new user interface, we know from practice that virtual windows are an excellent intermediate design step. We will briefly outline a systematic design approach based on task descriptions, an E/R model, and virtual windows (Lauesen and Harning 2001).

Starting with a common or critical task, we compose screens that include the necessary data for the task. Next we consider new tasks one by one, and expand the previous screens or add new ones to include the necessary data for these tasks. During the process, we try to keep the number of different screens at a minimum. We don't care about buttons or other interface functions at this stage.

Finally, we review the E/R data model to check that all data can be handled through the virtual windows. The checking activity usually reveals flaws in the E/R model as well as in the virtual windows.

The result is a low number of different windows, what helps the user better understand and master the system. The number of filled windows per task is also low, which improves user efficiency.

We make a simple usability test of the virtual windows, an *understandability test*. We simply test whether typical users can understand the virtual windows and figure out which screens to use for various tasks. This test is possible much earlier than traditional usability tests of prototypes. The understandability test ensures that the virtual windows can serve as a sound basis for the development of real screens with high usability. In practice, we find many serious usability problems at this early stage. Fortunately, it is cheap to redesign the virtual windows. Usually we make a few iterations of virtual window design and understandability testing in order to reach a satisfactory result.

Designing the rest of the user interface is now mainly a matter of adding buttons and functions to the virtual windows. Sometimes, however, we have to cut or combine virtual windows, add dialog boxes and search screens, etc.

Advantages of virtual windows

Validation. Virtual windows are first of all an excellent way to make the customer understand the system data, detect special cases, etc. They are also excellent for checking that data model and data descriptions are adequate. It is also a good idea to include them as examples of screen pictures, since they help the supplier to understand what it is all about. If a new user interface is to be developed, virtual windows are a good intermediate design step.

Verification. Developers can easily verify that the system contains data as specified. They can design the real screens based on the virtual windows.

Disadvantages of virtual windows

If you are not familiar with the virtual window technique, it can easily take up a lot more time than reasonable for requirements. Inexperienced developers tend to design real screens with buttons, menus, etc. that are not relevant for virtual windows. They also tend to spend a lot of time with their favorite design tool making screens look "pretty". Furthermore, they are tempted to make virtual screens for all those parts of the system that need not change because an adequate version exists already.

3

Functional requirement styles

Data requirements specify the data to be stored in the system. In contrast, functional requirements specify what data is to be used for, how it is recorded, computed, transformed, updated, transmitted, etc. The user interface is in most systems an important part of the functions because many data are recorded, updated and shown through it.

In this chapter we will discuss some of the many *styles* for stating functional requirements. These styles differ in several ways, in, for instance:

■ their notation (diagrams, plain text, structured text),

■ their ease of validation (customer's check),

■ their ease of verification (developer's check),

■ whether they specify something about the surroundings or the product functions,

■ whether they simply identify the functions or give details of what they do.

Most of the styles in the chapter primarily identify the necessary functions. The last styles from section 3.15 and on use indirect ways of specifying the functions, for instance through standards or required development processes.

In this chapter we don't describe styles that can specify details of what the functions do. We have devoted Chapter 4 to this.

Real requirements specifications use a combination of styles. Most importantly, the different kinds of interfaces need different styles. For instance, the user interface needs a style that the expert user can validate, while the technical interfaces need more precise styles aimed at IT professionals.

In most systems the user interface is the most difficult to deal with, and in this chapter we primarily look at the styles from a user interface viewpoint. Chapter 5 discusses special interfaces, for instance printed reports or technical interfaces. In those sections we show how to combine the various styles to deal with the special interface.

The proper combination of styles also depends on the type of project (in-house, tender, COTS, etc.) and the way the project is carried out (up-front requirements, or detailed analysis leading to design-level requirements; see section 1.7).

3.1 Human/computer – who does what?

Highlights

Domain model: humans and computers united.
Physical model: what each of them do.
Product requirements divide the work.

A pervading issue is how the work is divided between human and computer. The division is not given in advance, but is decided more or less through the requirements.

Figure 3.1 illustrates the problem through a part of the hotel system: how to find a free room for the guest. At the top of the figure we see what human and computer must do together. Based on data about free rooms and the guest's wishes, human and computer must find a free room for the guest. We call this the *domain model* of the functionality.

We could have used various UML notations to illustrate the principle, but have chosen a simple *dataflow diagram*. A bubble means a function that uses some data fed to it through the arrows and computes a result leaving it through other arrows. Data is stored in 'files' shown as double lines, suggesting a pile of paper sheets.

In the lower part of the figure we see a possible division of labor between human and computer. The receptionist (the user) receives the guest's wishes and tells the computer about the dates in question and the kind of rooms needed. The computer scans the list of rooms and shows a list of those available. The receptionist chooses one of them. The computer saves the choice for later use when the guest has been recorded, etc. This is the *physical model* of functionality. In this model we have split the work between human and computer.

However, we may divide the work in other ways. We could for instance let the computer choose the first room on the list without asking the user. Or we could let the guest choose a room on the Web, seeing a floor map of the hotel. It is still the same domain task, but the division of labor is very different.

No matter how carefully we study the present user tasks, there is no automatic way of identifying the 'correct' functions in the product. Some creativity is necessary, particularly if we want a new system that is markedly better than the present one.

With data requirements it is easier. If we study the information used in the present tasks, we can almost automatically specify the data to be stored in the new system.

What should we specify as functional requirements to the product? The functions the product should have, for example, the screens we want? If we do this, then we

Fig 3.1   Human/computer – who does what?

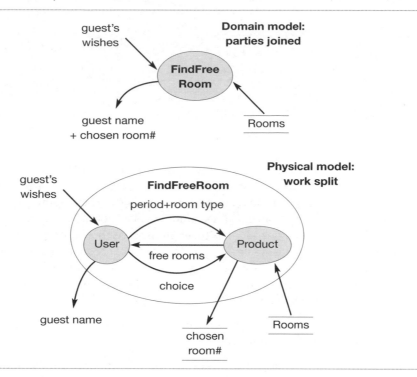

have chosen the division of labor, and we have decided much of the future human work and the business processes. That is a huge responsibility to the requirements engineer. We should either do it very carefully at *requirements time*, or we should avoid specifying product functions until *design* time.

Furthermore, if we want to base the future system wholly or partly on existing commercial products, they already have their built-in functions and we shouldn't specify our own.

The rest of the chapter looks at ways of dealing with these fundamental issues.

3.2   Context diagrams

What is this?

A diagram of the product and its surroundings.
It shows the scope of the product.
It is important but often overlooked.

The context diagram (Figure 3.2) shows the product as a black box surrounded by user groups and external systems with which it communicates. Arrows show how data flow between the product and its surroundings. In the figure, you see that the hotel system communicates with receptionists about booking, checking out, recording service charges, etc. The hotel guest receives a booking confirmation and invoices printed by the system. There is an external accounting system that receives account records corresponding to the printed invoices. There is also a telephone system (a local exchange) that controls the hotel room phones and sends billing information to the hotel system.

The notation is a kind of dataflow diagram. It should be supplemented with a plain text explanation of each interface.

The arrows show transfer of data. For instance, the diagram on the figure shows that the receptionist exchanges booking data with the product. However, sometimes analysts let the arrows show events rather than data. The arrow then shows who takes the initiative. For instance, there is an arrow from the hotel system to the accounting system, indicating that the hotel system takes the initiative to transfer data to the accounting system. Data may actually flow both ways during the transfer, because the accounting system sends various confirmation data back to the hotel system. A plain text explanation could help to clarify these matters.

Requirements. The context diagram gives an excellent overview of the required product interfaces. It reflects an early decision about the scope of the product: what is included in the new product and what is outside (domain). The example shows clearly that the accounting system and the telephone system are not included in the hotel system in this project.

You can use the context diagram as a requirement, for instance in this way:

R1 The product shall have the interfaces shown on the context diagram.

You might help the reader by outlining also the domain, as shown at the bottom of Figure 3.2. This is not a requirement specification, however.

Fig 3.2 A context diagram

R1: The product shall have the following interfaces:

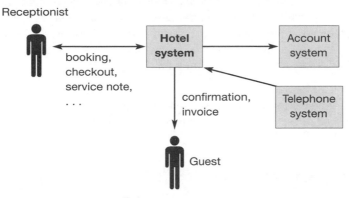

R2 ??: The reception domain communicates with the surroundings in this way:

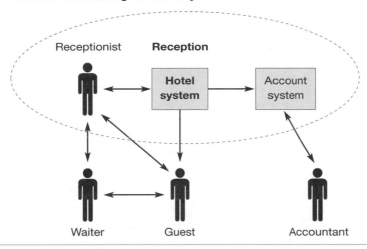

Sometimes analysts show data flowing between the surrounding users and products. As an example, we have shown that the guest communicates with the waiter, and the receptionist. This has nothing to do with the product requirements, but may help the reader understand the context.

Practice. It is extremely useful to outline a context diagram early in the project and keep it updated during analysis. Making the diagram can reveal amazing differences in the understanding of what the product really comprises. For instance, what do we mean by a reception system? Does it include the telephone system?

Should we require both systems as one package? Does it communicate directly with the waiter or only with the receptionist?

Surprisingly, we rarely see context diagrams in larger requirement specifications. None of the specifications in Chapters 11 to 14 have any. Many external systems were mentioned in these requirements, but it was difficult to see to what extent the product communicated with them – or whether these systems were part of the required package. A context diagram would have been very useful.

The membership system in Chapter 15 has a verbal version of a context diagram and requirement R1 says that the system shall support these interfaces. (Actually, the analysts had sketched a diagram but included only the text version in order to save time.)

Advantages of context diagrams

Verification. The context diagram gives developers an over-view of the interfaces and serves as a high-level checklist over what to develop. It is easy to verify that all interfaces are dealt with during and after development.

Validation. Most customers can readily understand the context diagram, spot missing interfaces and discuss what is to be delivered and what is outside the product.

3.3 Event list and function list

What is this?

Events to be handled by the product (or a list of product functions).
Events to be handled by human + computer (or a list of user tasks).
Product events are design-level issues.

An *event* is something that requests a system to perform some function. Usually an event arrives with some data telling the system what to do.

An event list shows the types of events that can arrive at the system. Since an event causes the system to perform a function, we can make a similar list of the functions that the system can perform.

The terminology and the details vary depending on whether we talk about events arriving at the domain or at the product. Figure 3.3 shows two lists of events for the hotel system: domain events and product events.

Domain events

Domain events arrive to the domain from the surroundings. Sometimes domain events are called *business events* or *triggers*.

In the hotel case, the domain has to respond to events such as a guest phoning to book a room, a guest arriving to check in, a service note arriving from the waiter who has served breakfast to room 14, etc.

All these events have data attached to them, for example the name and address of the guest for a booking event, or the room number and type of breakfast for a service note event.

Each domain event will cause the receptionist to perform an activity, often called a *task* or a *use case*. Thus we can also look at the list of events as a list of tasks.

The more complex tasks on the list need more explanation than simply the task name. This can be done by means of task descriptions, use cases, dataflow diagrams, activity diagrams, etc. As part of the task, the receptionist will ask the hotel system to perform various functions, i.e. he will send events to the hotel system.

Domain-level requirements. The requirements are that the product shall *support* the various domain events or tasks. It is left to the developer to design the necessary product events and product functions.

Fig 3.3   Event list and function list

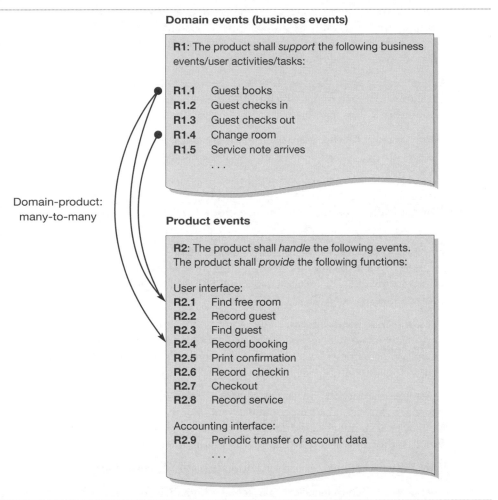

Domain events (business events)

R1: The product shall *support* the following business events/user activities/tasks:

R1.1	Guest books
R1.2	Guest checks in
R1.3	Guest checks out
R1.4	Change room
R1.5	Service note arrives
	. . .

Domain-product: many-to-many

Product events

R2: The product shall *handle* the following events. The product shall *provide* the following functions:

User interface:
R2.1	Find free room
R2.2	Record guest
R2.3	Find guest
R2.4	Record booking
R2.5	Print confirmation
R2.6	Record checkin
R2.7	Checkout
R2.8	Record service

Accounting interface:
R2.9	Periodic transfer of account data
	. . .

Product events

Product events arrive at the product from the domain. In the hotel case, the product has to respond to events such as the receptionist asking the system to find a free room, asking the system to record a guest, asking the system to record a service note, etc. The hotel system would also have to respond to a clock signal every night asking it to transfer accounting data to the accounting system.

It is a good idea to organize the event list according to the product interfaces, as outlined on Figure 3.3. The events are often called *messages* to indicate that they also carry data.

Each product event will cause the system to perform an activity, usually called a *function*. Thus we can also look at the list of events as a list of functions. The more complex functions on the list need more explanation than simply the function name. This can be done by means of dataflow diagrams, informal algorithms (mini-specs or pseudo-code), activity diagrams, mathematical specifications, etc.

When dealing with the user interface, we have to break down each user task into smaller steps, each requesting a product function. As illustrated on Figure 3.3, the booking task uses the *Find free room* function, the *Record booking* function, etc.

Some product functions are used by many tasks. Finding a free room, for instance, is used during booking, check in, and if a customer wants to change room.

It is easy to construct another hotel user interface that is based on a different set of product functions. For instance, we could let *Record booking* allocate a room automatically, thus avoiding the need for a *Find free room* function.

There are two conclusions from this discussion: (1) The relation between domain events and product events is many-to-many, and the product events cannot be defined in a simple manner from the domain events. (2) Deciding on a precise list of product events is a design issue, and it should only be done for certain types of projects (see section 1.7).

Product-level requirements. The requirements are that the product shall *handle* the various events or *provide* the various functions. Here the subtle difference between events and functions becomes important. If we list the events as requirements, the product has to handle exactly these events.

If we list the functions instead, analysts interpret it in the way that the product shall somehow provide that functionality. We do not insist that functions named that way shall appear in menus, etc. but only that the user is somehow able to invoke that functionality. In this way we can avoid premature design – at least to some extent.

The shipyard requirement specification (Chapter 11) uses function lists extensively.

User-interface versus technical interface. For human–computer interfaces, the list of functions is reasonable as a product-level requirement, while a detailed list of product events is a design-level requirement. For technical interfaces to other products, the detailed list of product events may be highly important. For example, the telephone system sends events to the hotel system. It is important to list these events in detail. The reason is that in this case, the product events are determined by an existing system, whereas for the user interface, they have to be determined during system design.

Advantages of event and function lists

Event and function lists are primarily checklists for what to develop. The lists should be supplemented with more detailed descriptions of the non-trivial items on the list. Often these detailed descriptions form the major part of the functional requirements.

Verification. Developers can easily check that each event/function on the list is supported or implemented.

Validation. Customers can to some extent validate the domain-level lists of events and tasks. However, they may find it difficult to check whether all events are included. One of the problems is that there are many variants of each event or activity. For instance, is arrival after having booked and without having booked two different events? Section 3.6 explains how to deal with event variants, and section 3.10 explains how to identify the important events.

Analysts can make a consistency check to see that the lists are logically complete. They compare the lists against the data model: Is there an event/function that can Create, Read, Update, and Delete each entity in the data model? If not, some event or function is probably missing. The check can be made on the domain level as well as the product level. Section 9.2.3 explains this.

Disadvantages of event and function lists

The event list for the user interface is a design issue. Make it only if you need design-level requirements. If you want a commercial product, the list will be useless since the product has defined its own events already.

The lists may give you a false sense of security because they appear to contain the full truth. However, they are only close to the truth if you have elicited the requirements carefully, for instance identified all the user tasks in the inner domain as well as the outer domain. See section 3.10 for techniques for doing this.

Customers cannot usually validate the list of *product* events and functions. Unfortunately, they are often asked to do so. Customers can better validate the list of domain events and tasks.

3.4　Feature requirements

What is this?

Text form: the product shall record/show/compute . . .

Many people believe that this is the only acceptable type of requirement.

Can lead to a false sense of security for user and analyst.

It is difficult to ensure that users are adequately supported and business goals covered.

A feature is one or more related product functions and related data. The most common way to write requirements is to specify features in plain text, and many customers and analysts cannot imagine other ways to specify functionality. Figure 3.4 shows some examples that could occur in the hotel system.

R1: room repair

R1 suggests several things at once, more or less explicitly. A room state called *repair* is needed and it must also be possible to set that state. It is tacitly assumed that it must be possible to reset the state to normal. It is also tacitly assumed that the room cannot be occupied or booked when it is in that state. Translation of the requirement into these more precise program specifications is left to the supplier. In practice a requirement like R1 is sufficient if developers have some domain experience.

The requirement specifies something about data as well as functions, and in general there is a gradual transition between the two kinds of features.

R2: staffing

R2 is an important requirement dealing with a real need, finding out how many staff members to allocate in the near future. It is clearly a product function, since the product has to make a calculation. However, the designer is given no clues about the work situation where this function is needed. Will this be needed frequently? In a hurry? In combination with other functions? Since the specification doesn't give any clues, it is difficult for the developer to design a good user dialog where the function is used.

With some domain understanding, we can guess that the function is intended to support the bi-weekly roster planning. The manager has to figure out which staff he should call in on duty during the next two weeks. To do that, he needs an estimate of the number of rooms that will be occupied. This estimate can be made from statistics about previous room occupation combined with seasonal variations.

Another puzzling thing with R2 is that details of the function are intentionally left to the supplier. This makes sense in a tender situation, because suppliers have different solutions. Furthermore, suppliers specializing in hotel systems know more

Fig 3.4   Feature requirements

R1: The product shall be able to record that a room is occupied for repair in a specified period.

R2: The product shall be able to show and print a suggestion for staffing during the next two weeks based on historical room occupation. The supplier shall specify the calculation details.

R3: The product shall be able to run in a mode where rooms are not booked by room number, but only by room type. Actual room allocation is not done until check-in.

R4: The product shall be able to print out a sheet with room allocation for each room booked under one stay.

> In order to handle group tours with several guests, it is convenient to prepare for arrival by printing out a sheet per guest for the guest to fill in.

about such forecasts than the average hotel owner does. At the same time the customer has avoided specifying something that no supplier could provide as a COTS-part. A professional supplier will not only outline the computation in his proposal, but also give evidence of the reliability of the forecasts. The customer can use this information to choose the right supplier.

R3: booking mode

R3 says that the product shall be able to book rooms by room type and delay the choice of the actual room to check-in time. R3 looks innocent but may be a disaster to a supplier that hasn't read the requirements carefully. The rest of the requirements assume that booking is by room number, but R3 changes a lot of things. The data model is not valid anymore, and it is difficult to come up with one that satisfies R3 too. Many parts of the program will not work because they carry room numbers around, rather than room type. Furthermore, new user dialogs are needed.

This is an example of how important it is for the supplier to scrutinize every requirement, imagining how it could be handled. Ignoring something like R3 might lead to a disaster to the supplier.

A warning: R3 is only an example. Real hotel systems always support booking by room type, otherwise there could be a situation where the hotel has a free room every day, but not the same room. As a result, the last guest has to move from room to room during his stay. We have ignored this problem in other parts of the book. A supplier with little domain knowledge might not know about the problem.

R4: print rooms

R4 is confusing and ambiguous. Does the customer want the system to print a list of room numbers on a single sheet, or to print a sheet for each room? The customer himself cannot see any ambiguity. To him the requirement is obvious.

In tender situations we often see such ambiguities. Amazingly, the supplier often responds with a proposal, fully aware that he doesn't understand all the requirements. "We want the order," he thinks, "so we will resolve the problems later." This usually ends well, but if the requirement was a dangerous one like R3, it could be very expensive – to both parties.

As an analyst, you might spot the ambiguity and try to reword the statement. After a few minutes you will have come up with a formulation that you consider unambiguous. Be warned: like the customer, you may not realize if your result is ambiguous too.

Instead, ask the customer why he wants that requirement. He might explain about the situation where he has to check in a whole group of guests. Each guest has to sign a form before getting his room key, and he wants to print all these forms in advance so that everybody can be checked in within a few minutes.

Then write down the problem, for instance as outlined in Figure 3.4, and put it just in front of the requirement; now the developer will understand the problem. This is often the best way to resolve ambiguities. The requirements for the Noise Source Location system (see Chapter 14) use this approach extensively.

Features often originate in preliminary work products made in other notations. The examples on Figure 3.4 show features that could originate in state-transition analysis or event lists (R1), critical situations in tasks (R4), or problems that different kinds of users have talked about (R2 and R3). Other work products could also be sources, for instance data models, dataflow diagrams, activity diagrams, or process descriptions.

Advantages of feature requirements

Features are usually straightforward to implement if the supplier understands them. In many cases he can directly translate them to functions in the program; he does not have to worry about whether they allow the customer to achieve his business goals.

Feature requirements are appropriate if the customer knows the user tasks very well and the supplier doesn't have to know about them, for instance when buying a technical component and in some maintenance projects (see section 1.7.1).

Validation. Customers love features. They use the customer's language.

Verification. It is straightforward to check that all the features are implemented in the final product. This will be time-consuming, of course, if there are many features.

Disadvantages of feature requirements

It is a problem that features are easy to formulate, because customers may dream up so many features that the whole system becomes unrealistic. In a tender situation, the result may be that no serious suppliers write a proposal. One remedy for this is to insist on a task where the feature is needed, and describe that task, for instance as in R4 above. Experience shows that many features are abandoned in this way because the customer realizes that no such task exists and there is thus no need for the feature.

If the customer expects to select a COTS-based system, for instance during a tender process, he may be tempted to write down the features of one particular system that he knows. This will favor the supplier of this particular system although other suppliers might have better solutions to his real problems.

Validation. Although the customer readily understands the features, he has great difficulties in checking that the features allow him to reach his business goals.

3.5   Screens and prototypes

What is this?

Screen pictures and what the "buttons" do.
Excellent as design-level requirements if carefully tested.
Not suited for COTS-based systems.

Under certain circumstances it is an excellent idea to design the final screen pictures and specify that they are requirements. Doing this goes much further in the design direction than specifying features. The two-step approach in section 1.7.3 shows one way to utilize this in the project.

Screens as requirements

If we specify the screen pictures, much of the user interface is defined. Figure 3.5A shows the requirement:

R1   The product shall use the screen pictures shown in app. xx

Figure 3.5B outlines what that appendix might contain, in this case finished screens made with the tool to be used for the final product. Simpler screen outlines might work just as well; even hand-drawn screens will work.

Unfortunately, the user interface is not defined sufficiently through the screen pictures. A prototype of the interface should also specify what the functions do. Some of the functions are non-trivial and have to be defined more precisely. Also, error messages may be important. R2 specifies it in this way:

R2   The menu points and buttons shall work according to the process description in app. yy. Error messages shall have texts as shown in app. ee.

Figure 3.5B outlines the contents of that appendix. The buttons, etc. are grouped according to the screens, and the non-trivial ones have pseudo-code that explains what they should do. Note that Check-in is far from trivial. Its function depends on the many situations in which it can be used.

If we want to choose a COTS-based system, R2 is completely senseless, of course, because the screens exist already in the system. Even if parts of the system have to be developed as extensions to the COTS system, it is unwise to specify the screens, because an economic solution requires that you adjust the design to what the system can do easily, and you haven't chosen the system yet – only set up the requirements.

In case you have more freedom to design the screens or if the entire system has to be developed from scratch, it may be a good idea to specify the screens. Just remember that now the customer and the analyst have taken full responsibility for

Fig 3.5A Screens and prototypes

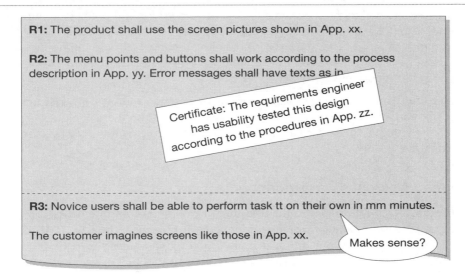

R1: The product shall use the screen pictures shown in App. xx.

R2: The menu points and buttons shall work according to the process description in App. yy. Error messages shall have texts as in

Certificate: The requirements engineer has usability tested this design according to the procedures in App. zz.

R3: Novice users shall be able to perform task tt on their own in mm minutes.

The customer imagines screens like those in App. xx.

Makes sense?

the ease of use and the ability to support the tasks. This implies that R1 and R2 may conflict with a usability requirement such as R3:

R3   Novice users shall be able to perform task *tt* on their own in *mm* minutes. (May conflict with the defined screens.)

The defined screens may not allow users to learn the system so quickly. On the other hand, R3 asks for more than R1 and R2 can specify, for instance that product response times are adequate.

If R1 and R2 must ensure usability, it is not sufficient to design the screens by means of logic and sound judgment. Experience shows that although it helps to use expert advice, user interface standards, and participatory design, it is not sufficient to ensure a good user interface (see section 6.7).

A good user interface requires:

- careful analysis of the tasks to be supported (see section 3.10)

- early prototypes, preferably as mockups

- usability tests to see that the prototype actually allows typical users to perform all the tasks without assistance (see section 6.6.2)

- several revisions of the prototype and new tests.

Figure 3.5A shows that the design has been carefully tested in this case, so the design should be adequate as a requirement.

Screens as examples

If you don't make all the design efforts at this stage, it is still possible to outline screens and use them as examples, for instance as shown on Figure 3.5A as an explanation of R3. Now, the screens are not requirements, but examples that help the supplier understand what the customer has in mind. The requirement is the task performance time specified in R3.

Warning: You should state clearly that the screens are examples, otherwise the customer may believe they are requirements and insist on them being implemented. If the screens are fancy and hard to implement, it may become an expensive lesson.

Advantages of screens as requirements

It is quite possible to design the user interface as part of requirements, for instance as part of the two-step requirements approach (section 1.7.3). It is not as expensive and time-consuming as it may sound. Experience shows that the benefit is a much smoother programming phase and a higher user acceptance of the product (see section 6.6).

Validation. The customer can ensure that the screens are able to support the tasks and provide high usability. However, it is not enough to review the screens. Task analysis and usability tests have to be made.

Verification. It is straightforward to verify that the final user interface is as specified. Experience shows, however, that it is a good idea to repeat the usability test with the final product. Some problems may have crept in during development, for instance that the creative screen designer introduced flashing fields or fancy colors that make the screens less useful than in the prototype, or that the system response time is inadequate.

Disadvantages of screens as requirements

Don't use this requirements style when the product under consideration is a commercial product – with or without modifications.

If the tasks are not well defined or the scope of the entire product is dubious, it is much too early to design screens and use them as requirements. It is a big job, and the effort may turn out to be wasted when the project scope is settled. However, prototypes may be very useful to help illustrate the various possibilities.

If screen design is not suitable for one reason or another, we recommend that task descriptions be used as requirements (see sections 3.6 and 3.8).

Fig 3.5B Screens and prototypes

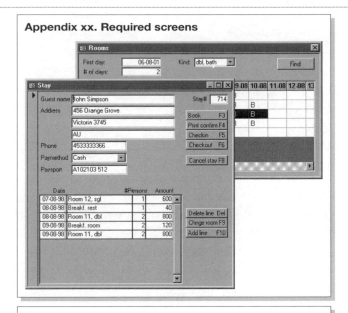

Appendix xx. Required screens

Appendix yy. Required functions

Stay window
Book:

. . .

Checkin:

If stay is booked, record the booked rooms as occupied.

If stay is not recorded,

Check selected rooms free and guest information complete.

Record guest and stay. Record selected rooms as occupied.

If stay is checked in, . . .

3.6   Task descriptions

What is it?

Structured text describing user tasks.
Easy to understand for user as well as developer.
Easy to specify variants and complexity.
Simple to verify.
Domain-level requirements – also suited to COTS.

The new product must support various user tasks. Figure 3.6A shows a structured way to describe them. The description consists of several parts, one for each work area, and one for each task in the work area.

In Figure 3.6A, we have not only described the tasks; we also use them as requirements:

R1   The product shall support tasks 1.1 to 1.5.

This is a domain-level requirement. We have described the activities in the domain, and the requirement is to support these activities. The description says what human and computer should achieve together, and it doesn't mention any product features.

Many developers find this kind of requirement surprising. Can the requirements be verified, they may ask. Yes, we can easily check that the final product can support these activities. However, the support may be good or bad, efficient or cumbersome, so we are left with a quality comparison. We might specify the desired quality, but it is not sure we can get it. In practice, the customer will more likely compare several solutions and find the preferred one. More about that in sections 3.8 and 7.3.

If you are familiar with *use cases*, you will probably notice that task descriptions look very much like use case descriptions. What is the difference? The difference is whether we describe what humans do or what the computer does:

■ A **task** is what user and product do together to achieve some goal. (The product is usually a computer system.)

■ A **use case** is mostly the product's part of the task (see more below).

■ A **human task** is the user's part of the task.

When the customer gets a new product, he changes the balance between what the user does and what the product does. Often, some kind of computer system was used before, and with the new product the computer system takes care of more of the task. In some cases the human part of the task disappears all together, and we have a total automation of the task.

Fig 3.6A Task descriptions

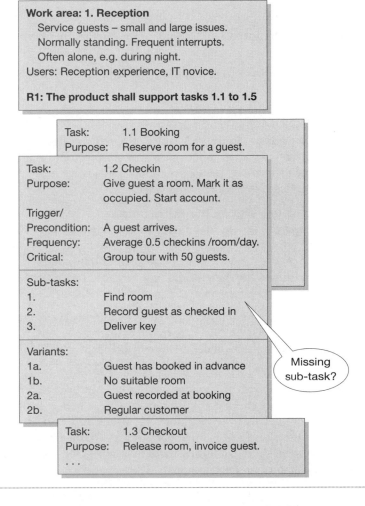

The term task is traditional in ergonomics and human–computer interaction, and it has focus on the human part of the total task. The term *use case* is traditional in UML and object-oriented analysis, and it focuses on the computer part of the total task as explained in section 3.12. A few authors say that use cases really are tasks, e.g. Stevens and Pooley (2000) and Wiegers (1999). Some developers use the term 'user story' to mean the same. To avoid these conflicting definitions, we use the term *task* for the combined action of human and computer.

In Figure 3.6A we describe tasks by means of a template inspired by Cockburn's *Use Cases with Goals* (Cockburn 1997, 2000).

Requirements. Task descriptions can serve several purposes in requirements:

- They can specify requirements without specifying anything about the product features.

- They can explain the purpose of traditional product requirements (explained in section 3.7).

- They can balance user demands against feasible solutions (explained in section 3.8).

Work area, background information

Let us look at the details of Figure 3.6A. The example describes the work area *reception*. In the hotel system we are using as an example, there is only this work area, but a more realistic hotel system would also have work areas such as staff scheduling, purchasing, and room maintenance.

The work area description explains the overall purpose of the work, the work environment, the user profile, etc. You might wonder whether this information is requirements. As it appears in the example, it is not. It is background information that helps the developer understand the domain. No matter how complete we try to make the specification, most real-life design decisions are based on developer intuition and creativity. The background information sharpens the developer's intuition.

In the example, the background information tells us that the system should support several concurrent tasks because there are frequent interrupts; a mouse might not be ideal when standing at a reception desk; allowing computer games or Web access during night shifts might be an advantage to keep the receptionist awake, etc.

The work area description is the common background information for all the tasks in that work area. Most authors don't use separate work area descriptions, but give some description of the user (the actor) for each task. This duplicates information because the same users perform many tasks. As a result, the background descriptions tend to be short. Collecting them in a work area description encourages a more thorough description.

Individual task descriptions

Below the work area description, we find descriptions of the individual tasks. Each task has a specific goal or purpose. The user carries out the task and either achieves the goal or cancels the whole activity.

In the example, we recognize the booking, check-in, and check-out tasks. Let us look at check-in in detail.

Purpose. The purpose of check-in is to give the guest a room, mark it as occupied, and start the accounting for the stay. This translates well into state changes in the database. If the user cancels the task, there should be no traces in the database.

Trigger/Precondition. The template has space for a trigger or a precondition. A trigger says when the task starts, e.g. the event that initiates it. On Figure 3.6B the trigger is the arrival of a guest – he reports at the reception desk. In some cases there may be several triggers, for instance for the task *look at your new e-mails*, as shown on Figure 3.6B. This task has at least three triggers, and the last one is a weak trigger that occurs because "the user is curious".

A precondition is something that must be fulfilled before the user can carry out the task. In the check-in case we have specified a trigger, but not a precondition. There is rarely a need for both. We explain more about preconditions below.

Frequency and critical. The fields for frequency and critical are very important in practice. The requirement on Figure 3.6A is to support 0.5 check-ins per room per day, and support critical activities with 50 guests arriving. What can that be used for in development?

Imagine 50 guests arriving by bus and being checked in individually. Imagine that each guest reports at the reception desk, the receptionist finds the guest, prints out a sheet for the guest to sign, and then completes the check-in of that guest. This could easily take over a minute per guest. The last guest will be extremely annoyed at having to wait one hour! Maybe we should provide some way of printing out a sheet for each guest in advance with his room number on it?

What about 0.5 check-ins per room per day? How many rooms are there? Well, a large hotel has 500 rooms, meaning that there are approximately 250 check-ins per day, with most guests probably arriving in peak hours. We definitely need a multi-user system – so that the system can deal with concurrent check-ins and ensure that no two customers end up being assigned to the same room. We can derive several design constraints from these two lines.

Sub-tasks. Next comes a list of sub-tasks. The receptionist must find a suitable room for the guest, record guest data, and record that the guest is checked in and the room occupied. Finally he must give the guest the room key.

These sub-tasks are on the *domain level*. They specify what the user and the computer must do together. Who does what depends on the design of the product. It is likely that the computer will help in finding free rooms, but the receptionist will make the final choice. What about the sub-task *Deliver key*? Should that be computer-supported too? Maybe. Some hotel systems provide electronic keys, unique for each guest, but that is expensive. Obviously the solution has to be decided later in the project, depending on the costs and benefits involved.

One of the advantages of task descriptions is that the customer readily understands them. If we try to validate the check-in task with an experienced receptionist, he will immediately notice that something important is missing: "In our hotel, we don't check guests in until we know they can pay. Usually we check their credit card, and sometimes we ask for a cash deposit. Where is that in your task description?"

"Oops" said the analyst and added this line between sub-task 1 and 2:

2. Check credit card or get deposit

Variants. Finally, there is a list of variants for the sub-tasks.

Sub-task 1 (find room) has two variants: (1a) The guest may have booked in advance, so a room is already assigned to him. (1b) There is no suitable room (suggests some communication between receptionist and guest about what is available, prices, etc.).

Sub-task 2 (record guest) also has variants: (2a) The guest may have booked in advance and is thus recorded already. (2b) He is a regular customer with a record in the database.

Variants are a blessing for customers as well as for developers. You don't have to describe rules or specify logic for the many special cases; simply list the variants to be dealt with. Experienced developers say that as long as there are below 20 variants, this is manageable. Above that, consider redefining the task or splitting it into several tasks.

Task sequence. Although the sub-tasks are enumerated for reference purposes, no sequence is prescribed. In practice users often vary the sequence. It is a good idea to show a typical sequence, but it doesn't mean that it is the only one. In a small hotel you may, for instance, see a regular guest arriving, and since the receptionist knows him and knows that his favorite room is available, he hands him the key and later records that he has checked in. The system should allow any sequence as long as it makes sense.

Sometimes one or more sub-tasks are optional. Usually that is clear from the context, or you may specify it in the sub-task. You may also specify it as a variant of that sub-task, but that is cumbersome. As an example, let us look at the case where a guest phones to change his booking. Here we have a clear event, but it is not clear what kind of change we end up with. Maybe the guest just wants to inform us of his new address; maybe he wants to book an additional room; maybe he wants to bargain since he has found a cheaper alternative; maybe he ends up canceling the booking.

Some analysts attempt to define separate tasks for each of these possibilities, but that is cumbersome and doesn't reflect the true user situation. Figure 3.6B shows how to solve the problem by using optional sub-tasks.

Fig 3.6B Triggers, options, preconditions

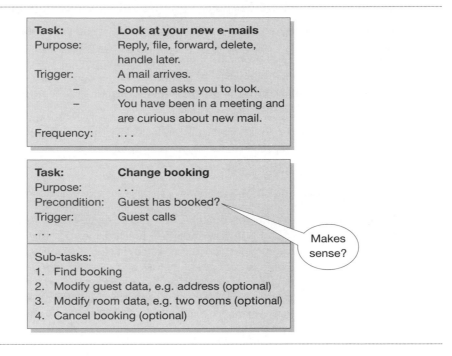

Preconditions and sub-tasks

Some developers find preconditions very important. Our experience is that they may be important for use cases in order to help the programmer, but not for tasks. (There are exceptions, as discussed below.)

As an example, Figure 3.6B shows the task *change booking*. It is logical to assume that the guest actually has a booking, and the example shows it as a precondition. This makes sense if the example specified what the computer should do. The programmer would then know that some other part of the program had checked that the guest has a booking, so his program part doesn't have to check once again. Use cases focus on what the computer should do, so here we have an example of the usefulness of a precondition in a use case.

But is it really a precondition for the task? Are we sure that the guest actually has a booking? And if not, which task specifies what to do if he believed he had a booking, but actually had no booking?

The answer is simple. Sub-task 1 says what is necessary: the receptionist will find the booking and thus see whether the guest has booked. Or rather, the receptionist will find out whether the system has recorded a booking for that guest. (Maybe the guest booked on a day when the system was down, so that the booking is on a slip of paper somewhere.)

Consequently, we shouldn't specify any precondition in this case. We might specify a variant of sub-task 1, *No booking recorded*, but that is too obvious to specify.

As another example, some analysts insist that we specify a precondition for check-in, saying that the receptionist has to be logged on to the system. This makes more sense since the receptionist should get nowhere without logging on. On the other hand, this is so obvious that there is no need to mention it. Or we could claim that logon is not an essential part of the task, and that it is more relevant as a security requirement.

As a final example, assume that we had split the check-in task into two: (1) checking in a previously booked guest, (2) checking in an unbooked guest. It might then make sense to specify a precondition, for instance:

Check-in a booked guest

Precondition: Guest has booked in advance

Even this use of precondition is dubious. It somehow suggests that the receptionist knows for sure whether it is this case or not. In practice, the guest may believe that he is checked in, and only during the task is it revealed whether the 'precondition' is true. If it is not, the receptionist has to back out of the task and select another path through the system. This can be annoying, particularly if the receptionist has to enter guest data once more. For this reason, the solution in Figure 3.6A treats the difference between booked and non-booked guests as variants. Notice that the trigger event is the same in both cases.

Preconditions may be more relevant for sub-tasks in order to show restrictions on the sequence. For instance we could have described check-in in this way:

Task: Check-in

Sub-tasks:

1   Find room

2   Record guest data

3   Record check-in (precondition: free rooms selected and guest data recorded)

4   Deliver key

The precondition on *record check-in* reflects that guest data as well as one or more free rooms are needed to check in a guest. This is obvious to the user, but may be a useful hint to the developer.

In some cases a sub-task is so big that it deserves a separate task description. Essentially, task A will call task B. In this case it may be useful to have a precondition on task B stating what should have been checked before task B is started.

Extends, includes, etc.

Many analysts take great care to specify various relationships between use cases. This is very useful if we think of what the computer should do, since it helps to structure the program. The same principles are sometimes useful on the task level too. One task may, for instance:

- **include** another one as a sub-task (e.g. task A calling task B as above)

- **extend** another one, because it uses some additional variants

- be the **equivalent** to another one – only the names differ.

It can be useful to specify some of these things to avoid writing things twice and to help designers use common solutions wherever possible. However, users find them confusing, particularly if the analyst is dogmatic about the terms, which often happens. (Many developers find the terms confusing too and spend hours discussing what is what.)

Our best advice is to be pragmatic. Work on a task-oriented level that keeps the number of task descriptions at a manageable level. Use *variants* rather than a plethora of extends and includes. We have modeled large application areas by means of twelve task descriptions, each with an average of four variants. We have also seen systems of similar complexity modeled with 200 use cases on such a low level that they failed to reflect true, closed tasks.

Useful for technical systems?

Task descriptions are primarily intended as domain-level requirements for the user interface. What about the technical interfaces, for instance the interface between the hotel system and the accounting system? There are two ways to deal with the issue:

Part of a larger task. A technical interface will ultimately serve some purpose to humans, and in principle we could simply describe this user task. In the accounting case, the accountant's task is to balance the bank account, send invoices, etc. This task is an indirect requirement to the technical interface, exactly as it is an indirect requirement to the user interface. Section 5.3 explains this approach in detail.

Technical transaction. A task is a closed and meaningful piece of work for a human user. What is the equivalent concept when two technical systems (actors) communicate? It is a *transaction*. A transaction is an interchange of messages that achieves something meaningful. Maybe a task description is a good way to describe such a transaction, but I have not seen this done in practice. The advantage should be that we don't try to divide the work between the two technical systems too early. This seems promising when a main contractor tries to find suitable sub-contractors. However, if one of the systems already exists, we might better use design-level requirements. Sections 4.9 and 5.5 show ways to specify the interfaces between technical systems on the design level.

Advantages of task descriptions

Validation. Customers find it easy to validate the task descriptions because they speak the customer's language. Customers can also identify special cases to be dealt with, and the requirements engineer can deal with them immediately, simply by adding them as further sub-tasks or variants.

Trace to development. Developers can easily understand the task descriptions, but find it somewhat difficult to design the corresponding product functionality. However, once a screen design is available, it is fairly straightforward to check that it supports the task. The check can for instance be done as a walk-through of task descriptions and associated screens. An expert user should participate in this.

Verification. Checking the final system against the task descriptions is straightforward. The task description and the variants generate good system test cases. Verification is possible before the system is put into operation.

Domain-level. Task descriptions are on the domain-level and involve no product design. Task descriptions improve the intuitive understanding of the domain, omitting the need for a lot of detailed requirements.

Suitable for COTS. Task descriptions are excellent for COTS-based systems since they are supplier-independent. Different COTS products have different user dialogs, although they all support the same tasks. It is often the *quality* of their task support rather than their features that makes one COTS system better than another.

Complexity. Task descriptions can specify complexity and many variants in little space.

Disadvantages of task descriptions

No data specified. Nothing is shown about the data required for the tasks. In principle, this information is needed for developers to produce appropriate screen pictures and to check that the necessary data is available in the database. Often intuition suffices but, if not, we suggest *tasks with data* (section 3.13) to overcome the problem.

Non-task activities. Some activities may not be real work tasks, but they may still require product functionality. Examples are ad hoc reports and surfing the Web without precise goals. Section 3.10 give hints to deal with them.

Design is harder. Some developers find it difficult to translate the task descriptions into good product functions. The naive solution would be to develop special screens for each task, but this can result in too many screens, which is expensive and may also confuse the user because the data can look different in the various tasks. So, how do you get the same functionality with fewer screens? The Virtual Windows technique (section 2.5) is one answer.

3.7 Features from task descriptions

What is it?

Product features explained by means of task descriptions.
Improves understanding and validation of the features.
You can rarely guess user tasks from the features.

Some developers strongly resist task descriptions as requirements. They insist that requirements must be specified as traditional product-oriented features, for instance:

R1 The product shall be able to find free rooms of various types in a specified period.

From task description to feature

One way to combine the two worlds is to take the task descriptions, derive product features from them, and leave some pieces of the task description as justification for the features.

Figure 3.7 shows an example derived from the check-in task. Some of the requirements correspond closely to sub-tasks (R1.3, R1.4, and R1.6); the rest correspond to the general background information of the task. The text introduction to the requirements gives the supplier a much better understanding of the requirements and also serves as a justification of them.

With this approach, the task descriptions from section 3.6 could be a preliminary work product, but are no longer requirements.

Differences between task descriptions and feature requirements

What is the real difference between tasks as requirements and traditional feature requirements?

First, we have made some design choices that are reflected in the feature requirements. This is most obvious in R1.1 (no mouse), R1.6 (electronic keys), and R1.7 (preprinted registration forms). We could think of other solutions that might work just as well or even better.

Second, we are verifying something very different at delivery time. With tasks as requirements we verify that the tasks and their variants can be supported. With feature requirements we verify that certain features are present, regardless of whether they are sufficient to support the tasks. The responsibility for task support is thus with the analyst who drew up the specification.

Fig 3.7   Features from task descriptions

Work area: 1. Reception

The product is normally operated standing, and there are many interruptions.
R1.1   Product shall allow mouse-free operation.
R1.2   Product shall support switching between incomplete tasks.

The product must support check-in, i.e. the guest must get a room and a key, and accounting must start.
R1.3   Product shall find free rooms of various types.
R1.4   Product shall record check-in and rooms occupied by that stay.
R1.5   Product shall collect pay information for the stay.
R1.6   Product shall provide electronic keys.

It may take too long time to check in a bus of pre-booked guests if they are checked in one by one.
R1.7   Product shall print registration forms in advance for group stays.

It should now be obvious why some suppliers resist task descriptions as requirements. It is much easier for the supplier to satisfy feature requirements, particularly if he has stated them himself, than it is to ensure a good support of the user tasks.

We have seen many bad results from feature-oriented requirements, for instance systems that have the required functionality, but where the user has to go through a lot of screens to perform simple tasks.

From feature to task description?

We can derive product features from tasks, but can we go the other way? Can we derive task descriptions from features? The answer seems to be no. What we can sometimes do is make a guess about the user tasks, but it *is* pure guesswork. For instance, the information about critical situations and variants is difficult to guess. Writing down task descriptions is not something you can do in isolation in your office. You have to interview and study users.

Experience with several large tender projects based on feature requirements shows that suppliers usually fail to understand the real work situation of the user. Can't they derive the task understanding from the feature descriptions? It seems impossible unless they already know the domain through other channels.

A couple of times, I have asked the customer's analyst – who wrote the requirements – whether he could describe some of the user tasks. He said that he could only guess at them. He had never seen the tasks being carried out and hadn't asked about them. This is not that surprising: if the analyst follows the traditional approach he ends up with a long list of desired features, but no information on the tasks to be supported.

3.8 Tasks & Support

What is it?

Structured text describing tasks, domain problems, and possible support for them.
Identifies critical issues.
Discusses product features in a structured way.
Easy to understand for user as well as developer.
Easy specification of variants and complexity.
Simple to verify.
Domain-level requirements – also suited to COTS.

Plain task descriptions as discussed in section 3.6 are *domain-level models* of the activities, in the sense that we only explain what human and computer do together. We don't even distinguish between how we did the task in the old days and how we want to do it in future. We don't require a specific solution, but leave that to the supplier or developer, as long as the solution supports the user tasks.

However, the customer often wants some influence on the solution or he may have suggestions for solutions. Understandably, he is tempted to specify product features. On the other hand, the supplier may not be able to provide those features at a reasonable price – or he may have better solutions than those envisaged by the customer.

Tasks & Support resolve this dilemma. Figure 3.8A shows how we could use this style to specify the check-in task. Here are the differences from plain task descriptions:

- Each sub-task is described in two columns.

- **Domain-level.** The left column explains the domain-level activity, i.e. what human and computer should do together.

- **Problems.** The left column also explains any issues or problems in the old way of doing things.

- **Solution.** The right column describes a possible solution that could support the sub-task. Supplier and customer may later co-operate to specify another solution.

- **Example vs. agreed.** The heading of the right column changes during the process, for instance from *Example solution* to *Proposed solution* to *Agreed solution*.

The Task & Support idea was developed by this author and Marianne Mathiassen in close co-operation with a large customer (a hospital) and three COTS suppliers (Lauesen and Mathiassen 1999). Section 10.7 has more information on the case study. The technique has since been used successfully in several large projects, both by vendors, customers, and product developers.

Fig 3.8A Tasks & Support

Task:	1.2 Checkin
Purpose:	Give guest a room, Mark it . . .
Frequency:	. . .

Sub-tasks:	**Example solutions:**
1. Find room. **Problem:** Guest wants neighboring rooms; price bargain.	System shows free rooms on floor maps. System shows bargain prices, time-and day-dependent.
2. Record guest as checked in.	(Standard data entry)
3. Deliver key. **Problem:** Guest forgets to return the key; guest wants two keys.	System prints electronic keys. New key for each customer.
Variants:	
1a. Guest has booked in advance **Problem:** Guest identification fuzzy.	System uses closest match algorithm.

Past: Problems

Domain level

Future: Computer part

Requirements

What are the requirements with this approach? There are two options:

R1 The product shall support tasks 1.1 to 1.5 and remedy the specified problems.

R2 The product shall provide the features in the right-hand column of tasks 1.1 to 1.5.

The first possibility corresponds to plain task descriptions, although with emphasis on issues and problems. The solutions are just examples. This is usually the best choice since the supplier has to ensure adequate task support.

The second possibility corresponds to *Features from task descriptions*. It is a good choice at a later stage when the parties have agreed on the way the tasks must be supported. It is useful to preserve R1 as a requirement to ensure task support also in matters not covered by R2.

Domain-level activity. Let us look closer at the example in Figure 3.8A. The left-hand column describes the domain-level activity – human and computer together. The description of this activity is very short; simply the name of the sub-task. In real specifications, more may be needed (see the hospital example in Chapter 13).

We suggest that imperative language should be used here, e.g. *Find room*, to hide whether a human or a computer carry out the sub-task.

Problem. The problem part is the only part of the description that mentions something about what happens in the old system. You only specify problems if there are any. As an example, sub-task 2, *Record guest*, doesn't have any significant problems, so a description of the domain activity suffices.

Note that the problem part gives us an opportunity to specify things we cannot specify in the other requirement styles. As we show in section 10.7, the problem part also serves as an important link between requirements and business goals.

Solution. In the right-hand column we outline how the new system could support the activities and how it could solve problems. This part shows something about the future and what the product should do. In practice this is an area for discussion between customer and supplier, who should try to arrive at an agreement based on the benefit to the customer and the cost of providing the solution.

Figure 3.8A shows *example solutions* as indicated by the right-hand column heading. In a later version, the supplier may change this column to reflect new ideas or proposals, and the heading should change to "Proposal". Finally, the column is changed to what the two parties eventually agree to provide, and the heading should change accordingly to "Agreement".

To emphasize the computer aspect, we suggest that statements with an explicit subject should be used, e.g. *System shows free rooms* or *Product shows free rooms*. Traditional wording such as *The system shall show free rooms* may be used if you like, but only if the parties decide that the right-hand column is the requirement, thus giving up the explicit requirement to support the user tasks and solve the user problems.

Figure 3.8A shows various non-trivial solutions to the problems. For instance, some hotels may be willing to negotiate a discount if the customer arrives in the afternoon and the hotel has many vacancies. The system could guide the receptionist in these matters. Perhaps one supplier has realized that the weather has an influence on such negotiating, since customers would be more reluctant to go to other local hotels in rainy weather, so he offers a feature for entering weather conditions, thus exceeding the customer's expectations. The supplier specifies this proposal in the solution column.

In some cases the solution is trivial. Sub-task 2, for instance, calls for ordinary data entry only; nothing needs to be specified. Many sub-tasks in real systems are trivial data entry tasks. In these cases there is not much difference between the domain activity, the user activity, and the computer activity. The feature requirements are trivial.

West Zealand Hospital

We developed the Task & Support technique in close co-operation with a local government that operated a couple of hospitals. After a few weeks of studying what they had experienced in other acquisitions, we came up with the Task & Support idea. Next we wanted to test the idea on a realistic scale in the same organization.

We took an existing system recently contracted with a supplier but not yet delivered, and developed Tasks & Support for the most difficult application area: roster planning. This was also the most business-critical area because many savings were expected from improved roster planning. Modeling this area required eight task descriptions, as explained in section 10.7.

Figure 3.8B shows an abbreviated version of the most critical and complex task: make roster. The task is actually carried out over a period of several days where the user tries to allocate staff and get feedback from others about the allocation. Some of the sub-tasks are carried out several times during the total planning task.

Note sub-task 3, Allocate staff for unstaffed duties. It is the most critical part because most of the economic advantage must be obtained there. Although the monetary benefits are not shown there, you can clearly see that this is a very important sub-task.

Another interesting thing is variant 3b, No staff available. The user (planner) works for a single hospital department and doesn't have information on staff in other departments. Because qualified staff are becoming scarcer, the users dreamt of getting on-line information about available staff in other departments. They reasoned that the system ought to know the roster for other departments too, so it should be able to list staff whom they might call on for additional help.

When we later checked the approach with three suppliers, one of them laughed at this "primitive requirement". His company provided computer services for all the local hospitals, and they could easily provide access to available staff there too. The requirements format enabled him to tell the customer that he could exceed his dreams.

What is covered by the technique?

To what extent can Tasks & Support replace traditional functional requirements? We checked that in the hospital where we developed the technique. When we had developed the Task & Support requirements in co-operation with super-users, we compared the 38 original, feature-based requirements with those expressed through the task descriptions. Figure 3.8C shows a summary of the results.

Sixteen original requirements were covered by the task descriptions.

Seven original requirements were not covered by the task descriptions, but we estimated that they would have been if we had made a data model and cross-checked it against the tasks (see section 9.2.3). For instance, we had overlooked that the system had budgets for each department, and some tasks dealing with budgeting were needed to provide the budget data.

Fig 3.8B Hospital roster planning

Task	1.2 Make the roster	
Goal	Staff all duties. Ensure regulations . . . Ensure low cost	
Frequency	Once every two weeks. In some departments . . .	
Critical	Vacation periods . . .	
Sub-tasks:		**Example of solution:**
1	**Initialize new roster period**	System generates roster for new period based on . . .
2	**Record staff leave** Two kinds of leave: ... **Present problems:** Leave requests kept on manual notes, often months into the future.	System can record leave one year into the future. System warns if leave is against regulations. It must be easy to record a long period of leave (several months).
3	**Allocate staff for unstaffed duties.** Ensure level of competence, regulations, leave days, and low cost. **Present problems:** Difficult to ensure this manually. Costs are higher than necessary and errors occur.	System shows unstaffed duties and suggestions for staffing. User selects the actual staff. System warns if duties are unstaffed, leave or regulations violated, or cost unnecessary. Warnings must be immediate to support the "jigsaw puzzle". System supports extensive undo and several temporary versions.
4	**Send roster for review**	A print of the roster is sufficient.
5	**Modify roster**	Steps above suffice
6	**Authorize roster**	. . .
Variants:		**Example of solution:**
3a	**Staff not yet recorded in the staff file**	User enters preliminary data for new staff.
3b	**No staff available** **Present problem:** No information about staff in other departments	System suggests staff from other departments based on their authorized rosters.

Fig 3.8C Match with old feature spec

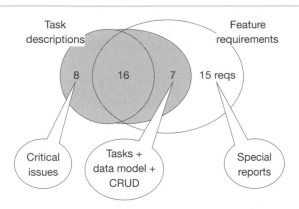

Fifteen original requirements were not covered, and we had difficulty seeing how this could have been done. They all specified some special report to be produced, and the old system had these features. However, nobody we talked to could explain what these reports were used for, so it was impossible for us to identify any tasks needing these requirements. We believe that some of them were actually used somewhere, while others were just relics of the old system. Section 5.1 explains ways to deal with such reports.

Eight requirements were new. The task descriptions clearly showed a need for these eight things, but they were not mentioned in the old requirements. All were critical for some reason. Half happened to be provided by the supplier anyway, but the rest were not. This led to great consternation in the IT department as these deficiencies were realized, particularly because some of the business goals could thus not be met. Section 10.7 gives more details about the case.

The conclusion is that Tasks & Support can reveal critical requirements that can otherwise be easily overlooked. However, supplementary techniques have to be used too in order to cover all functional requirements.

Cost of the technique

The Task & Support technique doesn't require a lot of time, training, or tool support, but it needs close guidance by an expert. We will illustrate the typical pattern with what happened in another project.

The hospital decided to use Tasks & Support in a new COTS acquisition, possibly with tailor-made extensions. The application was about patient administration across all departments. The value of the contract was expected to be approximately $4 million plus around $2 million per year for operating the system. Here is a brief account of the work.

- A consultant trained two expert users and one IT specialist for two days. They had been involved in traditional feature-oriented requirements before, but had never seen task or use case techniques.

- As part of the two days of training, they outlined a single high-level task that covered most of the system as seen from the patient's point of view. This outline used nine ordinary task descriptions to be specified later.

- The two expert users worked part time on some of these task descriptions for seven days and sent the result for review by the consultant. The result almost made the consultant cry: the task descriptions had all been misunderstood! The expert users had kept the task headings, but had written the usual feature-oriented requirements to the *left* in the task template. The user and his problems had not been taken into consideration anywhere. (I have illustrated a wrong solution in Figure 3.8D with a task description from roster planning, although the actual example dealt with patient administration.)

- The consultant met with them half a day and explained that the idea was to shift the features to the right column and then fill the vacant space to the left with user-oriented task descriptions. They then worked together with the consultant to use this principle in one of the tasks.

- Next, they completed the entire spec in ten more days, including reviews in the departments. Then they sent it for a blitz review by the consultant. This time he was truly impressed. They had not only made excellent task descriptions, but they had also found a creative way to use the same template for non-task issues, such as maintenance, daily operation, and usability.

- The consultant had only minor comments, and the spec was sent out for tender. Total man days: around 25. Total consultancy days: 3.

Variant: Expert developers
- Seasoned developers who know about use cases, tend to master the Task & Support idea faster. They get it nearly right the first time.

The hospital team later reported that similar projects used to take six months with feature-based requirements, rather than the three weeks with the new approach. Furthermore, the new approach ensured that they got what they needed.

Comparison of the suppliers' proposals also went much more smoothly than usual. The team spent 20 man days comparing the two best proposals in detail. Essentially they made a kind of acceptance test of the existing versions of the products, working through all the task descriptions and variants to see and describe how well the systems and the promised extensions would support them. Their comparison convinced stakeholders without further discussion. The traditional approach used to take ten times as long because many stakeholders had to review and comment on the proposals.

Fig 3.8D Mistaken first-time use

Task	1.2 Make roster	
Critical	Vacation periods . . .	
Sub-tasks:		**Example of solution:**
1	**Initialize . . .**	
2	**Record staff leave** System shall record staff leave one year ahead. System shall print a list of warnings.	See example list in xx.
3	**Allocate staff for unstaffed duties.** System shall compute a roster proposal. System shall allow users to modify the proposal easily. System shall compute financial consequences of roster.	*Feature style in disguise* For instance in a local PC.
4	**. . .**	

Fig 3.8E Early experiences

Traditional	**Tasks & Support**
Write requirements Everybody asked. All dream up requirements. Combined into one spec. Few understand it.	**Write requirements** Expert users describe tasks. Everybody can correct tasks and add *wishes*.
Time: 25 weeks	Time: 3 weeks (first time)
Assess proposals Everybody has a say	**Assess proposals** Carry out the tasks – give scores.
Political choice	Selected stakeholders asked. No doubt.
Time: 10 man months	Time: 1 man month

Old approach. Why did requirements specification now go so fast? Figure 3.8E shows a summary. Previously, the IT department had asked each user department (wards, labs, personnel department, etc.) to write down their requirements, and the IT department then edited the whole thing and sent it for comments and approval in the departments. This caused a lot of debate on whether the spec was complete and whether this or that was needed.

Amazingly, although the IT department had edited the spec, they often didn't understand the requirements, but assumed that the user departments knew what they had asked for and that the supplier would also know. Our later talks with the suppliers revealed that they too weren't sure what the hospital asked for, but assumed it could be resolved during the project.

New approach. With the Task & Support approach, a small group of expert users, assisted by the IT department, wrote a set of task descriptions (12 in this case), sometimes with suggested solutions. The expert user's deep task understanding was a key factor in the approach. Then they sent it off for comments and approval as usual. The departments now commented primarily on the completeness of the task descriptions, which are facts, rather than on the required features, which tend to be a matter of opinion. When a department suggested some solutions, they were simply included as possible solutions in the right-hand column, i.e. as an example rather than a requirement.

It should be mentioned that in this example, the hospital had a fairly good idea what kind of system they wanted and what kind of business goals to go for. There was also a reasonable commitment by all departments involved. This had been the case both when the old feature-based method had been used, and when Tasks & Support had been used.

In other organizations, goals and commitment may be serious issues. Resolving them may take a long time, making it difficult to see the full effect of the Task & Support approach.

Advantages of Tasks & Support

Validation, verification, etc. Tasks & Support have the same advantages as plain task descriptions. The customer can easily validate them; developers can better understand the requirements and check that their design is adequate; the parties can easily verify the requirements at the end of development.

Tenders. We have much experience with the technique from tenders, where the customer announces a request for proposal and several suppliers reply. Whether we are dealing with COTS-based products or custom-made products, suppliers as well as customers report these further advantages:

■ It is much easier than usual to understand what the customer really needs and what kind of solution he has in mind.

- It is possible to trace between requirements and business goals. The suppliers really want to help the customer and therefore care about his business goals too.

- The supplier can specify the advantages of his solution by relating it to the user tasks.

- The supplier can also show where his solution exceeds the customer's expectations.

- The supplier can demonstrate to the customer how his tasks will be supported, and how his critical issues will be handled.

- All suppliers get equal opportunities since no solution is prescribed.

- It is possible to adjust ambitions in the solution according to needs and costs.

Disadvantages of Tasks & Support

No data specified, non-task activities. Just as for plain task descriptions, nothing is shown about data required for sub-tasks. Also, some activities are hard to describe as tasks.

More work for the supplier? Some vendors are concerned that the approach takes longer than traditional approaches. Previously, they could just cut and paste from other proposals. With Tasks & Support they have to understand the user's tasks, they complain. This is true, but a clever customer will insist on task descriptions for just that reason.

More work for the customer? Some vendors suggest that it is more laborious for the customer as well. In our experience, this is not true. The specification work is actually reduced drastically compared to traditional specifications. Of course, compared to the approach where the customer doesn't specify anything but leaves it to the supplier to set up a specification, it is more laborious.

Unusual reply format. We have found that many suppliers hesitate to modify the right-hand column to show their solution. They prefer to specify their solution in attachments. This, however, makes it more difficult for the customer to evaluate the proposals. Skilled suppliers modify the text in revision mode, thus clearly showing what they have changed. They sometimes attach product descriptions, for instance screen pictures, and then refer to them from the task description. Section 7.5 and 7.4 show examples of the supplier's reply to Tasks & Support and the customer's evaluation of the reply.

We suggest that customers draw up a more elaborate guideline for how to modify the descriptions, preferably with a good example, in order to help less skilled suppliers. When supplier and customer jointly develop Tasks & Support, there is no such problem with modifying the description.

3.9   Scenarios

What is it?

A case story illustrating one or more user tasks, or a specific case to be tested.
Improves developer intuition.
Not requirements.

The term *scenario* has many meanings (Campbell 1992; Constantine and Lockwood 2001; Weidenhaupt *et al.* 1998). For requirements purposes, it either means a small story with a vivid illustration of the work area, or a specific case of a task.

Vivid scenarios

Figure 3.9 shows an example of a vivid scenario. Note how we can derive several things from this scenario: the critical task variant with the bus full of tourists; the problem with adjoining rooms; the need for night entertainment for reception staff.

Scenarios are attractive, but not suitable as requirements. They don't pretend to cover all tasks, and they are difficult to verify and trace during development.

Case scenarios

UML defines scenarios in another way:

> *A scenario is an instantiation of a use case.*

This means that a task description (use case) is the general pattern for doing certain things, while a scenario is how it is done in one particular case. We will call this kind of scenario *case scenarios*. Case scenarios are not quite the same as vivid scenarios. Vivid scenarios may comprise several case scenarios and they give a more stimulating description of the situation. Here are some simple examples:

- *Checking in a guest is a task* (the general case – any guest).

- *Checking in John Simpson who has booking number 2533 is a case scenario.*

- The *evening duty* (Figure 3.9) is a vivid scenario.

- *Checking in Sheik Ibrahim and his three wives and six children* is a case scenario that happens to be vivid at the same time.

Case scenarios are useful as test cases when testing usability or testing the final product. In contrast, the vivid scenario in Figure 3.9 is not suitable as a test case.

Fig 3.9 A vivid scenario

Scenario: Evening duty

Doug Lawson had studied all afternoon and was tired when he arrived at 6 pm to start his shift on reception. His first task was to prepare for the arrival of a busload of tourists expected at 7 pm. He printed out all the check-in sheets and put them on the desk with the appropriate room key on each sheet.

In the middle of that, a family arrived asking for rooms. They tried to bargain, and Doug always felt uneasy about that. Should he give them a discount? Fortunately Jane came out from the back office and told them with her persuading smile that she could offer them 10% discount on the children's room. They accepted, and Doug was left to assign them their rooms. They wanted an adjoining room for the kids, and as usual he couldn't remember which rooms were adjoining.

Around 10 pm, everything was quiet, and he tried to do some of his homework, but immediately became sleepy. Too bad – he wasn't allowed to sleep at work until 1 am. Fortunately the office computer allowed him to surf the net. That kept him awake and even helped him with some of his homework.

3.10 Good tasks

Highlights

Closed task = meaningful user goal.
Check that you have identified all tasks.
Bundle small, related tasks.
Don't program the user dialog.

What makes a good task?

The task concept sounds simple. In practice, however, analysts often define tasks poorly, choosing tasks that are too vague or too small. Here are some rules for selecting good user tasks:

1 **Closure rule.** Each user task must be "closed", i.e. finish with a meaningful goal that makes the user feel he has achieved something.

2 **Session rule.** Small closed tasks performed in the same work session should be grouped together under a single task description.

3 **Don't program.** Don't go into detail with how the task is performed, the exact sequence of steps involved, how to deal with special cases, etc.

The concept of "closure" originates from task analysis in human–computer interaction. A closed task has a goal that is meaningful to the user. Completing the task gives the user a pleasant feeling – he feels he has achieved something; maybe he deserves a cup of coffee. Psychologists say that most of us love closed tasks so much that we prefer to do the small things that we can complete now, rather than the large things that may take days.

While a task has to be closed, the sub-tasks in the description are usually so small that they are not closed, and consequently they are not real tasks.

Some tasks are closed when looked upon individually, but they belong together and are carried out in a single session, so they should be described as a single task. The reason is that we want efficient support for the group of tasks rather then the individual, small tasks.

Some developers specify too many details of the task, e.g. what to do if the booking number is not correct, which conditions trigger alternative paths among the sub-tasks, etc. These are programming details. At best they describe what is going on inside the computer, but that is premature design; also, the customer can rarely validate such details.

Fig 3.10 Good tasks

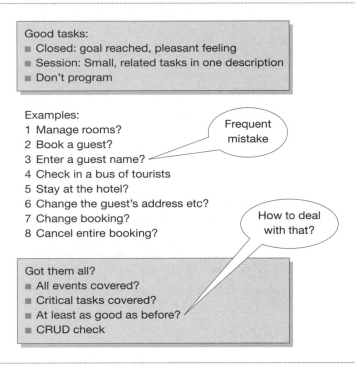

The task description should explain what the user does or wants to do, and users are not programmed in the same way as computers. You should use variants to handle the complexity, not programming.

Examples

Let us try to apply the rules to the examples in Figure 3.10. Which of the examples are good user tasks?

Manage rooms is an important activity, but it is not closed. You cannot say that now you have finished managing the rooms. It is an ongoing activity and thus not a good task.

Book a guest is a good task. It is closed and, when the receptionist has done it, something meaningful has been done. It may also be the time for a break – unless other guests need attention.

Enter guest name is not a good task. There is no closure. Receptionists would not feel that they have achieved something after entering the guest name. Entering the guest name is part of a larger, more meaningful activity, e.g. booking the guest. Surprisingly many tasks (use cases) seen in practice are defined on such a detailed, but meaningless level. This also means that the number of use cases is much too high.

Check in a bus of tourists is a good task. Although checking in one of them may be considered a closed task, the receptionist would feel that there is no time for a break until all are dealt with. The small tasks form a single session to be supported efficiently.

A stay at the hotel seems at first sight to be a strange task. It is not a task for the receptionist, but if we look at the guest as a type of user, staying at the hotel is a meaningful activity. Handling such activities is the whole purpose of the hotel. In section 3.11 we shall look at this from the guest's point of view and see how it gives rise to business process re-engineering.

Change the guest's name and address can be a closed task, for instance if a booked guest phones and says that he has moved house and want the confirmation to be sent to the new address. *Change the booking and cancel the booking* can also be separate closed tasks. However, the three tasks are often done in the same session and should be grouped into a single task description with optional sub-tasks like this:

> **Task:** Change booking
>
> **Sub-tasks:**
>
> 1 Find booking
>
> 2 Modify guest information (optional)
>
> 3 Cancel booking (optional)

Completeness

How can we ensure that we identify all tasks? First of all, you need to interact with users to learn about the tasks. Section 8.2 explains about using interviews, observations, etc. to identify user tasks. Many developers try to guess the tasks by means of logic and common sense, sitting in their offices, but they fail to really understand what is going on.

However, even interviews and observations may not reveal all the tasks. How can we ensure that all tasks have been covered? It is impossible to guarantee such completeness, but here are some guidelines for getting close.

All domain events covered? An event is something that requests a service of our system. If our "system" is the reception, a domain event requests a service from the reception. Examples are that the guest calls to make a booking, that a guest arrives, etc. Each domain event gives rise to a user task. In this way we identify tasks for booking, check-in, etc. You should make a list of the domain events and ensure that each has a corresponding task.

Critical tasks covered? Critical tasks are those that are time-consuming, frequent, difficult, or performed under stress. It is important to identify these because they need careful support. When observing users, you may see the time-consuming and frequent tasks, but rarely the difficult or stressful tasks; you have to ask about them. In the hotel reception scenario above, you might only identify the busload of tourists as a critical task if you asked about stressful and difficult situations.

At least as good as before? There is a difficult problem in this area: introducing a new system may turn a non-critical task into a critical one. As an example, one manufacturing company replaced their old IT system with a new COTS-based one. The old system had a very sophisticated screen picture that gave an excellent overview of pending repair jobs in the factory. However, the users were unaware that they used a sophisticated screen. The new system only showed traditional lists of data records that didn't give the same overview, and it would be very expensive to create new sophisticated screens. The old task using the repair list had not been stressful using the old system, but it was using the new one. Although the analysts had catered for all critical tasks, they had not realized that the new system would create a new critical task.

This is one of the reasons the customer often wants a requirement like this:

R2 The product shall perform at least as well as our present product.

Suppliers strongly resist such requirements since it may be an immense task for them to study the old system in the detail necessary to meet this requirement. Verifying the requirement would be hard for the same reason. In this case, a skilled analyst might have spotted the sophisticated screen when studying the users, and identified it as something crucial.

Another technique that can help is to give the supplier a screen dump of all screens in the system, thus allowing him to spot unusual screens. Goal-domain tracing may sometimes identify unnoticed, but critical, tasks. Section 8.7 explains the technique and shows how it detected such a task in the shipyard.

CRUD check. CRUD stands for Create-Read-Update-Delete. In order to make a CRUD check of the user tasks, you need a description of the data to be stored in the system. (Any of the descriptions mentioned in Chapter 2 will do.) You now look at each piece of data and ask yourself how that piece is created, read, updated, and deleted, and whether some task description deals with it.

If no task description deals with it, you will probably have to add such a task. Usually you identify some surprising new tasks in this way. In other cases there may be good reasons for not adding the task, for instance because the data is maintained in another system.

Some of the missing user tasks are often small tasks, such as updating the customer's address or deleting the customer. They may be grouped together according to the session principle into larger maintenance tasks. Section 9.2.3 explains more about CRUD checks.

Hard-to-catch activities Some activities may not be real work tasks or they may be hard to identify, but they may still require product functionality. Examples are ad hoc reports, games, surfing the Web without precise goals, supervisory functions (e.g. checking that everything in the plant is running smoothly).

An example from the hotel system is the need for an estimate of staff numbers needed in the next period (see section 3.4). Once this is suggested, the need is obvious, but would you have identified that need? There is no clear task or external event dealing with it, and there is probably no data in the database suggesting such a need.

We have no special remedy for identifying these activities. All we can suggest is that you have to study the domain better to ensure that all such activities are recognized; it is important to study all user groups. See Beyer and Holtzblatt (1998) for good techniques in that area. Identifying the business goals and tracing them to user activities and requirements may also help (see section 8.7).

New tasks may sometimes be created when the new product is introduced. Jan C. Clausen (personal communication) has for instance pointed out that when automatic workflow is introduced, a new task is created; the task of manually sorting out all the electronic documents that don't find a receiver in the automated way.

3.11   High-level tasks

What is it?

Total business cases as seen by the clients.
Independent of existing user tasks.
Idea generating – business process re-engineering (BPR).
Rarely used as requirements.

Most systems have both users and clients. The users of the hotel system, for instance, are the receptionists. The clients are the guests. The users and the hotel system work together to serve the clients.

For fully automated systems such as automatic teller systems or shopping sites on the Web, there is nobody to help the client. As a result, the client is also the user.

If we look at the hotel from the guest's point of view, staying at the hotel is a kind of task. It is not a task in the immediate surroundings of the product since the guest may not interact directly with the computer, but it is an interesting task anyway, because the ultimate success of the system depends on how well it serves the clients.

Figure 3.11 shows the sub-tasks of a hotel stay as seen by the guest. Now we see the previous tasks, Book, Check-in, etc. as sub-tasks of this higher level task.

We also see two new tasks: select a hotel and reimburse expenses. Are they of interest when defining the product requirements? They may very well be. For instance, a business guest needs an invoice to claim reimbursement, but some of his expenses will not be reimbursable and it simplifies matters to the guest if they do not appear on the main invoice. (In fact, some expenses might be outright embarrassing to have on the main invoice!)

Our preoccupation with the receptionist has so far prevented us from seeing the client's needs, so a high-level task description will help us to see the key business needs here. We can use the high-level task as an analysis tool to reveal additional requirements. In this case we identified a need for separating reimbursable expenses from other expenses. We could add it as a feature requirement or we could state it as a problem in the Task & Support description for check-out.

Business process re-engineering (BPR)

Business process re-engineering uses radical restructuring of a company to better serve the clients and reduce costs. The present user tasks are not taken for granted. Some of them may disappear, others are redefined, and new ones may come up. High-level task descriptions can help in that process. For instance, we might ask whether we could support the hotel-stay task any better.

Fig 3.11 High-level tasks

Task:	1. A stay at the hotel
Actor:	The guest
Purpose:	. . .

Sub-tasks:	Example solution:
1. Select a hotel. **Problem:** We aren't visible enough	?
2. Booking. **Problem:** Language and time zones. Guest wants two adjoining rooms	Book room on Web. Choose rooms on Web at a fee.
3. Check in. **Problem:** Guests want two keys	Electronic keys.
4. Receive service.	
5. Check out. **Problem:** Long queue in the morning	Use electronic key for self-checkout.
6. Reimburse expenses. **Problem:** Private services on the bill	Split into two invoices, e.g. through TV.

In the example shown in Figure 3.11, we first used Tasks & Support to identify the client's sub-tasks and problems. In a later brainstorming session, we came up with possible solutions to some of the problems.

The general trend in the solutions is to allow the client to do more for himself. We could help him to book through the Internet, and why not allow him to select a room too? We could also allow him to order services electronically during his stay. He could check out electronically by inserting his electronic room key into a slot at the reception desk, thus bypassing the morning queue of other guests checking out.

Could we use high-level task descriptions as a requirement? In principle, yes, but often these things are so business-critical that the customer wants to analyze the business impacts more closely, and end up with ordinary task descriptions.

Actor, product and system

Let us finish this discussion by recapping some theory. In section 1.5 we introduced the terms "product" and "domain". *Product* is the system we want to achieve, typically a software system or hardware plus software. *Domain* includes the immediate actors using the product, i.e. human users plus other products that interact with our new product. *Business domain* is the domain outside the inner domain around the product. Just as the users work in the inner domain, the clients "work" in the business domain. When we restructure the domains, we carry out business process re-engineering.

An *actor* is something that interacts with a system. What is the "system"? That depends on the context. If we look at this from a receptionist's point of view, the 'system' is the product (the hotel system). The receptionist is the actor who interacts with the product. The task descriptions correspond to this view.

If we look at it from a client (a guest)'s point of view, the "system" is the entire reception including the product used by the receptionist. The client is the actor who interacts with the reception. The high-level tasks reflect that view.

3.12 Use cases

Highlights

Widely used styles.
Some styles are good for designing user dialogs.
Most ignore the user's part of the tasks.
Not suitable as requirements for COTS-based projects.

A use case is primarily the product's part of a task, including its interaction with the user. Use cases were introduced by Ivar Jacobson *et al.* (1994) as a literal translation from Swedish, and the term is now used extensively in connection with object-oriented software development (Booch *et al.* 1999; Stevens and Pooley 2000). However, the term use case has been used in so many ways that it is hard to know what people are really talking about when they use it (Cockburn 1997; Constantine and Lockwood 2001). In this section we will illustrate some of the many kinds of use cases.

Although widely used for analysis and design, most kinds of use cases are on a too detailed level to be used as domain-level requirements, because they specify parts of the user interface design. However, some kinds of use cases are suited as product-level requirements and for designing the detailed user dialog.

3.12.1 Use case diagrams

We will first look at the UML version of use cases. UML (Unified Modeling Language) is a standard notation introduced by one of the object-oriented schools (Booch *et al.* 1999). UML definitions of use cases have changed over time. Here is my attempt to define the UML idea, based on definitions by Rumbaugh *et al.* (1999):

A use case is a sequence of related messages exchanged among the system and outside actors, together with actions performed by the system.

Here is the original definition by Rumbaugh *et al. (1999): A use case is a coherent unit of functionality provided by a classifier (a system, subsystem, or class) as manifested by sequences of messages exchanged among the system and one or more outside users (represented as actors), together with actions performed by the system.*

And here is the one by Booch *et al. (1999): A use case is a description of a set of sequences of actions, including variants, that a system performs to yield an observable result to an actor.*

Fig 3.12A Use cases vs. tasks

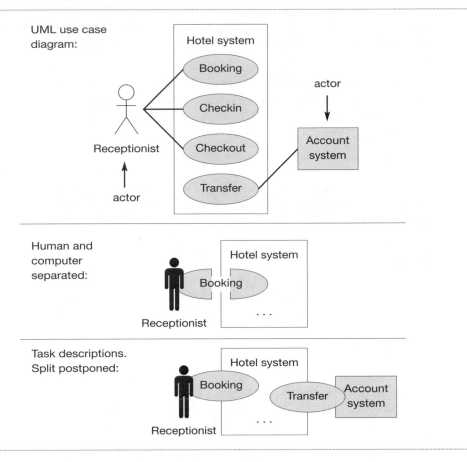

Note that the definitions only talk about the actions performed by the system (in our terminology the product), not the actions performed by the user.

UML comprises several types of diagrams, the use case diagram being one of them. The first diagram on Figure 3.12A shows four UML use cases. The box represents the product and the diagram shows that the receptionist can carry out (be the actor) of the use cases *booking*, *check-in*, and *check-out*. These use cases are handled by the product, i.e. the computerized hotel system, as illustrated by the bubbles inside the box. In product terms, each use case bubble might involve several product functions, for instance listing free rooms and recording guest information.

Note that the accounting system is an actor too. It transfers accounting data from the product, and the bubble shows the hotel system part of the transfer.

The diagram in the example simply lists the use cases. It adds a graphical hint of the actor who initiates the use case inside the product. In more elaborate use case diagrams, use cases may be connected to each other by means of lines that show extend, include, and other relations between the use cases (see section 3.6).

The graphical representation suggests that the use case is something done by the product, not something done by user and product together. The figure reflects the current thinking that use cases are computer-oriented. It also matches the UML definition above with the bubble representing the actions performed by the system, and the line representing the messages exchanged.

However, there are other types of use cases than the one defined in UML. In the second diagram in Figure 3.12A, we have illustrated a kind of use case where we can see user actions as well as computer actions. The diagram shows that the entire booking task consists of two parts, one carried out by the user and one carried out by the product.

The last diagram in Figure 3.12A illustrates the task concept. The bubble represents the entire task. It floats over the product boundary, illustrating that the task is carried out by human and computer together, but the division of labor is not yet determined. The transfer task also has a hotel system part and an accounting system part, with a division not yet determined.

3.12.2 Human and computer separated

We will now look at a text-oriented version of use cases where we split the work between human and computer. Figure 3.12B shows how that works for the check-in procedure. To keep it short, we only look at an example where the guest has booked in advance. The example and the formats were inspired by Constantine and Lockwood (2001).

In the top box of this figure, there are two columns. The left-hand one specifies what the human does, the right-hand one what the computer does. Time runs down the page, so we see clearly how the dialog progresses. Notice that we have specified how the guest identifies himself: through a booking number. We have also specified that the computer chooses the rooms (allocate free room(s)), presumably based on the guest's booking information. Finally, we can see why the computer displays the room number: the receptionist needs it in order to select the right room key.

Now, what is wrong with this? As a preliminary stage in designing the user dialog, such use cases are fine. But from a requirements viewpoint, we have arbitrarily divided the task between human and computer. For instance, the receptionist has no say in which room is allocated to the guest. The computer decides based solely on room type (single, double, etc.). This dialog will be inadequate if the guest wants two adjoining rooms, for instance.

Fig 3.12B Human and/or computer

Human and computer separated

Use case: Check in a booked guest

User action	System action
Enter booking number	
	Show guest and booking details
Edit details (optional)	
	Store modifications
Push checkin	
	Allocate free room(s)
	Display room number(s)
Give guest key(s)	

Computer-centric use case

Use case:	Check in a booked guest
Trigger:	Receptionist selects check in

Read booking number
Display guest and booking details
Read and store modifications
Wait for checkin command
Select free room(s)
Mark them as occupied
Add them to guest details
Display room number(s)

End use case

Furthermore, the dialog goes into too much detail, yet fails to deal with important variants on that level. What if the receptionist types a wrong booking number or the guest cannot remember his booking number?

Compared to the task descriptions, we have prematurely decided on too much. Maybe the chosen dialog has low usability (the comments above suggest that). It is better to either complete the design and carefully test it with real users, or to leave the use case at the task description level, where we haven't split the work between human and computer.

3.12.3 Essential use cases

We may remove some of the restrictions from the dialog above and make it more technology-independent. The first part could for instance look like this:

User:	Computer:
Identify booking	
	Show guest details and booking details
Verify details . . .	

Here we have opened up various ways of identifying the guest and his booking, e.g. by booking number, name, or electronically. The use case is now in the form introduced by Constantine and Lockwood (1999, 2001) as "essential use cases". They have used the model widely and successfully for dialog design.

Constantine and Lockwood use the term "essential use case" for closed use cases that are implementation-independent (technology free), yet describe user intentions as well as computer responsibility. The only problem with this is that it may be hard to separate user from computer without deciding on some kind of technology.

In contrast, the task descriptions are truly technology free since they don't split the work between user and computer.

3.12.4 Computer-centric use cases

Many developers reduce the use cases so that the user isn't visible anymore. The second box in Figure 3.12B shows an example. Apart from the trigger, the use case only mentions what the computer does. It is now almost a program that the computer could follow. The example comes very close to UML's definition of a use case. The messages sent between the actors are clearly visible in statements such as *read booking number* and *display guest and booking details*.

And what is wrong with that? Well, there is the same problem with premature design, yet a lack of detail, but new problems have been introduced:

■ The user finds such use cases meaningless. He doesn't care about what the computer does, but he does care about what he does, and that is not visible anymore. For instance, it is unclear why the computer ends up showing the room number. If the analyst had forgotten this piece, the user would probably not have noticed it, and the final system would have been very hard to use.

■ The use cases may misguide the programmer, so that he implements a dialog strictly following the use case sequence, although this was not the intention of the analyst. A more modern dialog lets the user have control and choose his own path through the task. However, such a dialog is event-driven and far from the "program" in the use case.

Fig 3.12C Detailed product activities

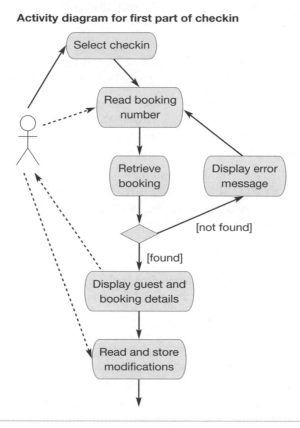

Activity diagram for first part of checkin

3.12.5 Detailed product activities

Faced with the problem of missing detail, e.g. what to do if the booking number is wrong, many analysts switch to even more program-oriented descriptions, for instance in the form of UML activity diagrams. Figure 3.12C shows an activity diagram for the first half of the check-in procedure. We have seen developers spend weeks designing the dialog as detailed as this figure.

Each rounded box contains an activity carried out by the computer, and the arrow leading away from a rounded box shows what the computer should do next. A diamond shows a choice between two paths. The activity diagram shows a little about the user. The dotted lines indicate that he interchanges data with the computer.

Activity diagrams are useful for other purposes (section 4.6), but from a requirements viewpoint, they should not be used to specify dialog details. They also take up a lot of space for the trivial things they usually express. So although they are supposed to help developers, many developers find them a waste of time and prefer to go straight to outlining the real program.

Advantages of use cases

Since use cases are widely used, the analyst should know about them and their limitations. In some cases the customer may insist on them being used.

The UML use case diagrams may be used as top-level checklists for what to specify further and what to develop. This may support validation as well as verification. Experts agree, however, that the diagrams should be supplemented with text-based versions.

Essential use cases have proven useful for designing the user interface (Constantine and Lockwood 2001). They share many advantages with task descriptions, although they are more design-oriented and thus less suitable for requirements, particularly for COTS-based acquisition.

Disadvantages of use cases

All the use case styles have the same disadvantages as task descriptions. They say little about the data used in the tasks, and they cope poorly with non-task activities.

When applied to the user interface, the computer-oriented use cases reflect a design of the user dialog. They are too detailed to be used as domain-level requirements, thus they are not suited to COTS-based acquisition. They are supposed to help the programmers implement the user interface. This seems true for strictly computer-controlled dialogs, such as the ATM often used as a textbook example. For more modern, user-controlled interfaces, the computer-oriented use cases are very different from the program to be produced.

None of the use case styles support the problem-oriented or cost/benefit-oriented view covered by Tasks & Support (section 3.8).

3.13 Tasks with data

What is it?

Structured text describing user tasks and data needed for each sub-task.
Useful for screen design and tracing to development.
Difficult to validate.

A common problem with all the use cases styles above and the task descriptions is that they don't say much about the data needed to carry out the various sub-tasks. In this section we will look at a task style that solves the data problem. The author developed this technique as part of a more systematic way of designing complex user interfaces.

The need for visible data

Figure 3.13 shows a task with data. It is based on a task description, in this example the check-in task. The left-hand column lists the sub-tasks, while the second column shows the data needed to support each sub-task. Sometimes we add a third column to show how the planned windows match the needs.

In practice we move the variants of each sub-task up to the sub-task itself, as shown on the figure. This gives a better overview of the data needs for the entire sub-task, what later helps the detailed design of the user interface.

Let us look more closely at the first sub-task, *Find room*. The second column says that the receptionist should be able to see free rooms of a certain kind, including the price and other attributes of the rooms. It is a tacit assumption that he should also be able to select any of these free rooms for the guest.

We might be more explicit about "free rooms", for instance stating that they must be free for the period in question. For space reasons we have not shown this on the figure.

Now look at variant 1a, *no suitable room*. In this case the receptionist should be able to see all free rooms of any kind, and the product should also show available discounts, for instance if a single customer stays in a double room.

Finally, variant 1b explains about the situation where the guest has booked in advance. Then the receptionist needs to see the booking information for the guest (stay details).

Instead of explicitly listing the required data, it is possible to refer to existing screens or printouts that contain the necessary data. This can vastly simplify documentation.

Fig 3.13 Tasks with data

Task:	1.2 Checkin	
Purpose:	Give guest a room. Mark it as occupied. Start account.	
Trigger:	Guest arrives	
Frequency:	Average 0.5 checkins/room/day	
Critical:	Group tour with 50 guests	
Sub-tasks:	**Visible data**	**Virtual windows**
1. Find room	Free rooms of kind x, price	Rooms. Crit: kind, dates
1a. No suitable room	All free rooms, price, discount	Rooms. Crit: dates
1b. Guest booked in advance	Guest and stay details	Stay. Crit: name . . .
2. Record guest as checked in	Guest detail, chosen rooms	Stay, Rooms
2a. Guest recorded at booking	Guest and stay details	Stay
2b. Regular customer	Guest detail, chosen rooms	Rooms, Stay. Crit: name . . .
3. Deliver key	Room numbers	Stay

Related windows/screens

Tasks with data are a good link to the design of the actual screens. A first step might be to develop virtual windows (section 2.5) that cover the data needs in few windows, reusing windows from task to task when possible.

Once the designers have virtual windows or final screens, they can check their design against the tasks with data. Figure 3.13 shows this check in the right-hand column. The column indicates the related virtual windows that satisfy the data need. For screens with a search criteria, we have also specified the criteria to be used to obtain the needed data.

Requirements? Are the visible data in the task description requirements? They may be. Although the visible data reflect a division of work between human and computer, they also reflect a deep understanding of the domain. The receptionist has to see this information in some form to serve the guest. He cannot leave it to the computer to select the rooms, for instance if a guest wants two adjoining rooms.

He also needs to handle price negotiation in the situation where the hotel could offer another type of room at a discount. So the requirement might look like this:

R1 The product shall show the data needed for each sub-task, as specified in the task descriptions.

Design? Are these requirements premature design? In some ways, yes. We have assumed a certain division of labor between human and computer. In the example we have assumed that the computer shows the room options and the receptionist chooses among them. Are there other ways to implement the aim of this division of work, without actually dividing the specified way? Well, we might define further criteria for the rooms and let the computer use them in its search. We could for instance require the receptionist to specify whether the guest wishes a smoking/non-smoking room, two adjoining rooms, rooms with a view, rooms on the ground floor, etc.

This solution will not work for several reasons: The list of criteria tends to become endless and all this information would have to be added to the database, instead of relying on the tacit knowledge of the receptionist. So the specified data actually reflect a careful choice of what the computer might be good at and what the receptionist might be good at. It is not completely technology-free, but it is good enough as a requirement.

Tasks with data: pros and cons

Validation. Users can validate the data needs, but not reliably because the approach is abstract. From a validation viewpoint, it is far better to design virtual windows and validate them with the users by walking through the tasks.

Trace to development. Tasks with data are excellent for deriving virtual windows or the final screens. They are also good for checking a proposed design.

Verification. Checking the final product against the tasks with data is straightforward. Verification can be carried out during development.

If you plan for a COTS-based system, it is easier to verify the task support directly, instead of specifying the data needs and then verifying them.

It is more work. It is difficult to keep track of the many right-hand columns in the task descriptions, although tool support might help. You might end up with task descriptions having four columns:

- The domain-oriented sub-tasks and the problems

- Solutions

- Data needs

- Related windows.

3.14 Dataflow diagrams

What is it?

A bubble diagram showing functions, and data flowing between the functions.
Compact specification of the needed data.
Good as an intermediate work product.
Useful as requirements for workflow applications.

A dataflow diagram shows activities and the data they use and produce. Figure 3.14A shows the activities triggered by three events in the hotel domain: a guest books a room, a guest checks in with a booking, a guest checks in without a booking. We explain the details in the next section.

Each bubble is an activity, which roughly is the same as a process, an action, a function, or a task, depending on the level of abstraction. The bubble transforms incoming data to outgoing data. The data flowing in and out is shown by the arrows, and further specified in the data description below the diagram. Data stores are shown as two parallel lines, symbolizing a pile of documents. In a computerized system, a data store will typically be part of the database.

With dataflow diagrams, you can describe tasks in a technology-independent way – what human and computer do together (the domain model). Or you can describe what the computer should do (the physical model). You may also describe how several tasks relate to each other, for instance how documents flow from one office to another in a large organization. Figure 3.14A shows a domain model. It describes how human and computer together perform three different reception tasks: the booking task and two variants of the check-in procedure.

The strength of dataflow diagrams is that they can specify the exact data needs for each activity in a very compact manner. Some of the data flows are associated with an event, but the diagram cannot show this explicitly.

Customers find dataflow diagrams much more understandable than E/R data models. Still, they may have problems in seeing whether the diagrams correctly reflect the work processes and the desired functionality.

3.14.1 Dataflow – domain model

According to Figure 3.14A, the booking activity receives data in the form of a booking request. The booking activity sends guest data to the Guest data store, i.e. it records the guest in the database. It also sends a room number and the period of stay to the Rooms data store, i.e. it records that a room has been booked for that period. Finally, it sends data as a confirmation letter to the guest.

Fig 3.14A Dataflow – domain model

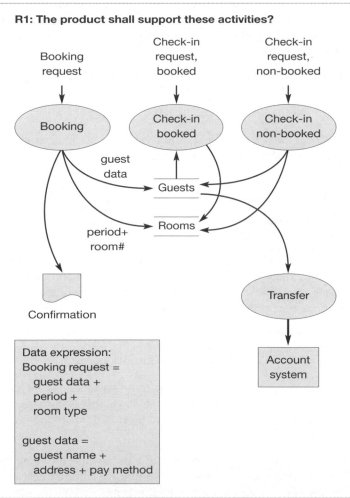

R1: The product shall support these activities?

Booking request

Check-in request, booked

Check-in request, non-booked

Booking

Check-in booked

Check-in non-booked

guest data

Guests

Rooms

period+ room#

Confirmation

Transfer

Account system

Data expression:
Booking request =
    guest data +
    period +
    room type

guest data =
    guest name +
    address + pay method

It is of course important that only a free room is booked, so the Booking activity has to find a free room. In order to do that, it has to read the Rooms data. Strictly, this should have been shown as an arrow from the Rooms store to the Booking bubble, but such trivial data retrievals are usually omitted from the diagrams, because this level of detail would result in a messy criss-cross of arrows.

The two check-in activities are described in the same way. The figure also shows an activity called *Transfer*, which transfers guest data to the accounting system. Here is an example of a data flow between two technical components. We cannot see the triggering event, but might specify it as a void data flow representing the midnight clock signal.

Usually, the detailed contents of each flow are described in a data expression, as outlined on the figure. It shows that a booking request consists of guest data followed by the period wanted and the type of room wanted. Guest data consists of guest name followed by address and pay method (plus phone number, etc.). Section 2.4 explains the notation in detail.

When a bubble describes a complex activity, we should specify it further. There are two ways to do that:

- Break the bubble into lower-level bubbles. Figure 3.14B shows examples of that.

- Write a piece of text that explains what the bubble does. The section on process description (4.3) shows examples of this.

3.14.2 Domain model, second level

Figure 3.14B shows how we can decompose the top-level activities from the previous figure into simpler activities.

Now the booking activity consists of four smaller activities. First somebody finds a free room. This activity uses data from the booking event and data about rooms. The activity selects a suitable free room and passes the room number and the booking request on to the next activity, Record Guest, which updates the Guest data store.

The data flow on to RecordBooking, which updates the Room data store to reflect that a room has been booked by this guest. Finally, data may flow on to Send Confirmation, which sends a confirmation letter to the guest.

The diagram describes the two other tasks in the same way. Note that some activities occur in more than one task. For instance, this is the case with FindFreeRoom and RecordGuest, which are used in the booking task and in non-booked check-in.

The nature of dataflow diagrams do not allow us to reuse the same FindFreeRoom bubble. It would tangle up the data flows so that we couldn't keep track of the tasks anymore. This is why we show the same bubble twice. (In the programming world, you would call a common sub-routine, FindFreeRoom.)

Still a domain model?

We might break down the bubbles to even simpler bubbles. For instance, RecordGuest could be split into recording the guest's name, address, etc. How far should we go?

When we break down the activity into very small activities, we either describe the existing activity in detail, or we start designing the new activity in the domain. Describing the existing activity in detail is not much use as a requirement, since the old activities are likely to change. Describing the new ones, however, requires that we know more about the new division of labor between human and computer.

Fig 3.14B Domain model, second level

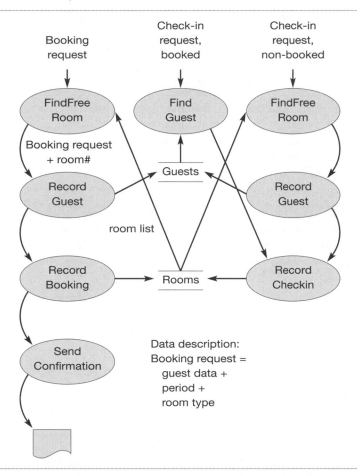

Data description:
Booking request =
  guest data +
  period +
  room type

The version shown on Figure 3.14B is almost too detailed. As an example, the diagram shows that booking always starts with finding a room, then recording the guest, and so on. This may be the way it is done at present or explained by receptionists, but it need not be the best way. Studies show that sometimes receptionists record the guest first (they may know that there are lots of rooms available in the period concerned), and sometimes they don't record the guest at all because he is a regular customer.

The problem is that dataflow diagrams tend to be overly concerned with the sequence of actions. You can modify the diagram to cater for the alternate sequences, but they become more complex. It is usually better to tacitly assume that sequences are not as strict as the diagrams suggest.

3.14.3 Dividing the work

It is possible to use dataflow diagrams to describe what the product should do. In principle, we split each domain-level bubble into two: one to be performed by the user and one to be performed by the product. If we carefully model what the product should do, amazingly we get rid of the concern for sequences. Figure 3.14C shows an example of how the split could be made for the booking task.

The activity *FindFreeRoom* is split into two. The receptionist receives the booking request. Then he sends the period to be booked and the room type to the computer, which in turn sends him a list of free rooms. The user could do this by entering the period and the room type on the screen and pushing a *FindRoom* button. The computer replies with a list of free rooms. The diagram doesn't specify these details, and it shouldn't since they are design matters.

Next the user selects a room from the list and tells the computer his choice. The computer saves the room number in the temporary data store *Current*. All these actions are part of the FindFreeRoom bubble. We could break the user bubble or the product bubble into smaller bubbles to reflect further details, but the risk is to over-specify the activity.

The next step in booking is to record the guest. This bubble is also split into two. The user, booking request still at hand, sends the guest data to the computer for later storing in the database. The computer temporarily stores the guest data in *Current* to keep track of the entire booking transaction.

Finally the user can ask the computer to record the booking. The computer uses the information in *Current* and updates Rooms to reflect the booking. Note that no arrow transfers data from RecordGuest to RecordBooking. In the domain-level diagram, the arrows between FindFreeRoom, RecordGuest, etc. carried guest data as well as room number. In the physical model, *Current* carries the information.

Since no arrow carries data from RecordGuest to RecordBooking, the receptionist could in principle perform RecordBooking at any time. However, as suggested by the diagram, RecordBooking will check to see that some booking data is stored in *Current*, so there is an implicit restriction on the sequence of steps. The restriction corresponds exactly to what we expressed by means of preconditions on sub-tasks in section 3.6. Furthermore, the receptionist should also be allowed to perform record guest before finding free rooms, although the dataflow diagram doesn't show it. We handle that in Figure 3.14D.

Although the principle of splitting the bubbles is simple, there are many ways to do it. Basically, it is a matter of designing the human–computer dialog. From a requirements point of view, this is premature design unless we want to end up with design-level requirements.

We should mention that dataflow diagrams never show bubbles nested inside each other. We have only done this here to illustrate the division of work.

Fig 3.14C Dividing the work

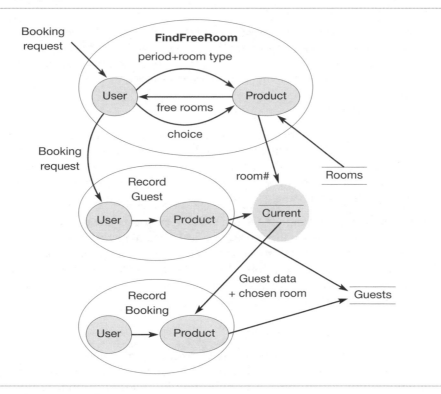

3.14.4 Dataflow – product level

If we collect all the product bubbles of the previous diagram, we get a dataflow diagram on product level. The result is what experts call a *physical model*. It describes the functions to be provided by the product. Figure 3.14D shows the result. The diagram is a top-level model of what the computer does. This means that for each product-level event, there will be only one bubble. So roughly speaking, we have a bubble for each button or menu point on the user interface. The diagram shows that the receptionist can use these buttons in any sequence, although the product will reject some sequences, for instance recording the booking before the guest and room have been specified.

Note that although FindFreeRoom occurred twice in the domain model because it was used in two tasks, it occurs only once in the physical model because there is only one FindRoom button.

The receptionist invokes the function FindFreeRoom when he has entered the period and room type. This detail is shown in the data expression at the bottom of the figure. FindFreeRoom uses room data to find free rooms and allows the receptionist to select one of them. FindFreeRoom then records the selected room in the temporary data store, *current*.

Current keeps track of the current state of the dialog with the receptionist. It remembers the free rooms selected, the guest selected, and a period for the stay. In this way, activities such as *RecordBooking* or *PrintConfirmation*, can perform their job without the receptionist having to provide the same data over and over.

Relation to domain level

In this example, the product-level model allows the user much more flexibility than the domain model. According to the product model, the receptionist may find rooms and record the guest in any sequence, whereas the domain model prescribes a strict sequence. So the product model does not follow the domain model strictly. However, this is an advantage here.

In the domain-level diagram, we can to some extent see the user activity as a sequence of smaller activities. In the product-level diagram, this information disappears completely. The functions can be used in many combinations to support check-in, booking, etc. Unfortunately this also means that a developer working on the basis of product-level diagrams loses an understanding of the user tasks. The result may be an inconvenient human–computer dialog.

Product-level data flow in practice

The dataflow diagram is a vague way of describing the intended functionality. Many developers report that a dataflow diagram is helpful if it closely models the program to be implemented. Each bubble could for instance model a specific procedure or sub-routine in the code.

In the example, each bubble is activated by a button or menu on the user interface. The bubble corresponds closely to the central event procedure in the final program, so it is a reasonable specification of the program.

If modeling is done in a more abstract way without concern for implementation, developers find it very difficult to use the diagram as a guide during implementation.

Advantages of dataflow diagrams

Since dataflow diagrams are widely used, the analyst should know about them and their limitations. In some cases the customer may insist on them being used.

The strength of dataflow diagrams is that they can specify the exact data needs for each activity in a very compact way.

Dataflow diagrams are useful for the following:

1 Outlining user tasks in a graphical way. This is primarily a help to the graphically oriented reader. You might state as a requirement that these tasks must be supported. However, such a requirement cannot give the richness of task descriptions.

Fig 3.14D Dataflow – product level

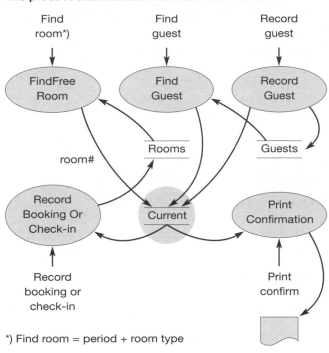

The product shall handle the events as follows:

*) Find room = period + room type

2 Specifying communication between technical components, e.g. between the hotel system and the accounting system. The data aspect is particularly important here.

3 Designing the new human activities in the domain. In this case the requirement to the product is to support these new activities. A special example of this is workflow modeling, where the analyst models the old and new routing of documents between departments.

4 Outlining the internal structure of the program.

Validation. Customers without an IT background can fairly easily understand dataflow diagrams, particularly those describing domain aspects.

Disadvantages of dataflow diagrams

Dataflow diagrams are not suited to describing user tasks with many variations. They don't support the problem-oriented or cost/benefit-oriented view covered by Tasks & Support (section 3.8). They are rarely useful for describing the functions of the product, unless the diagram closely models the actual program to be produced.

3.15 Standards as requirements

What is it?

Text requirement: the product shall follow standard xx.
Transfers the problem to the supplier.
Sometimes leads to a false sense of security.
An important type of requirement.

Standards are used for many purposes in requirements. In general they specify some functional requirements by referring to a standard. Some analysts (as well as IEEE 830) call such requirements *constraints*. In some cases they are mandatory and deserve the name 'constraint', in other cases they are not different from other functional requirements, except that the analyst has chosen to refer to the standard rather than attempting to specify the requirements in his own language. Figure 3.15 shows five examples of standards as requirements or constraints.

R1: Interface to another system

Interfaces between technical systems are often governed by standards. The hotel system must interface to the computerized account system, and it is likely that the account package has such an interface. The example assumes that it is a simple file transfer and that the format is described in the documentation of the package (the product name is fictitious).

This requirement is adequate if we look at the hotel owner's requirements to the hotel system. We might even have already gone into too much detail since the hotel owner doesn't really care whether the communication is through file transfers or not. His only concerns are that the proper account numbers are used, that all the account transactions get there within a reasonable time, and that they get there only once.

If we look at the hotel system *developer*, he wants to describe more about the interaction with WonderAccount. How is the standard to be utilized in the product? When is the data transfer to take place? Which records (of the specified format) are to be transferred? How must the system recover if the transfer is unsuccessful? However, these are design considerations and not part of the user requirements. Sections 5.3 to 5.5 discuss external interfaces in more detail.

R2: User interface style guide

There are guidelines for lots of areas. The example refers to a guideline for user interfaces, but something is added: a specific application is to serve as a model of how to use the guideline.

The analyst in this case was an experienced interface developer, who knew that the referenced guideline was often insufficient and had led to much time being wasted

Fig 3.15 Standards as requirements

R1: Data transfer to the account package shall be done through a file with the format described in WonderAccount Interface Guide xx.yy. The account numbers shall be . . .

R2: The user interface shall follow MS Windows Style Guide, xx.yy. The MS Word user interface should be used as a model where appropriate.

R3: Shall run under MS Windows release xx.yy. Supplier shall port product to new releases within _____ months.

R4: Shall follow good accounting practice. The supplier shall obtain the necessary certification.

R5: The supplier shall update the payroll computations in accordance with new union agreements within one month of release of the agreement.

---

by developers. He knew that referring to the interface of a specific product could resolve ambiguities in many cases.

The use of style guides such as these during development helps users to switch between different applications. They are not, however, a guarantee for high usability of the product. Many products follow the style guide, yet are very hard to use. See more in section 6.7.

It is possible, but laborious, to verify that the standard has been followed. There are usually many rules in the guide, and matching them against all the screens is time-consuming and prone to errors.

R3: Platform specification

The typical way of specifying the platform on which the system will run is to specify the platform products and release numbers. One concern is to what extent the supplier is obliged to update the product for future platform releases. R3 says that he should port the product to new releases within a certain number of months. This might also be dealt with as part of maintainability requirements (see sections 5.2 and 6.11).

R4: Domain standards

The product may have to follow standards defined in the domain. The example is from an accounting system. Auditors have descriptions of *Good Accounting Practice*. This covers many things, for instance that the system must keep an audit trail of all account entries, must allow an auditor to inspect all transactions, make statistics, etc. The standard usually also covers topics that do not directly relate to the product, e.g. management responsibilities.

The requirement implicitly says that it is the supplier's responsibility to find out what these standards are, and it explicitly says that he has to obtain certification for the product. (The concept of Good Accounting Practice and the issue of certification vary from country to country.)

R5: Pay agreements

Sometimes standards are subject to frequent change. It doesn't help the customer that the delivered product follows a standard at the time of delivery, if the standard has changed within a year. R5 is an example of this: the supplier has to support all union agreements now and in the future. It is a matter of taste whether we classify the requirement as a functional requirement, a maintenance requirement, or a requirement for daily operation.

The example is from the Midland Hospital in Chapter 12. It was a key requirement for the customer, and since Denmark is a small country with its own unions, only two suppliers were able to fulfill the requirement. The free market in the European Union was an illusion in this case.

The pros and cons of standards

In many cases standards are important requirements that cannot be omitted. In other cases they are an easy way out, because the alternative is for the analyst to study the standard himself and transform it into suitable product features.

Validation. Customers often rely on standards to ensure some unspecified goal. This may lead to a false sense of security. It is important to specify the goal of the standard in each project to be able to check that the standard achieves the goal.

Sometimes it is necessary to specify how the standard is to be applied, e.g. for the interface to the account system (R1 above).

Verification. Some standards can be reasonably well verified before the system is put into operation. This is the case with R1, R2, and half of R3. In other cases, a long period of operation is needed, such as with the second half of R3, and R5. In these cases the customer runs a significant risk since the supplier may not fulfill his promises. One way to reduce the risk is to look at the supplier's track record: How fast has he released new versions previously? How is his financial status – it is likely that he can continue doing so?

R4 (good accounting practice) may be verified by the customer's auditor or another third party before deployment. If certification is already available from a third party, they have done most of the verification for the customer.

3.16 Development process requirements

What is it?

A requirement to follow procedure xx to find the real requirements.
The best way if real requirements are uncertain.
Management control and price formulas can limit the risks.

In some situations, only vague requirements are available, and better ones cannot be made in time. Instead of these vague requirements, you can specify a suitable development process that will lead to the real requirements. Some analysts insist that such project specifications are not part of requirements, but part of the contract. IEEE 830, for instance, insists on that. What matters is that you write the process requirements somewhere. See also section 1.7.4 on contracts. Figure 3.16 shows several examples of development process requirements.

R1: Use iterative development

R1 specifies an iterative development process based on prototypes. The details of the process are important and should be specified. Some iterative processes don't deliver what is needed because the user/developer team loses sight of the real system objectives (see section 8.2.11). In other cases the design team produces and tests a prototype of the user interface, but when the programmers take over, they believe that it is only a guideline and develop the user interface as they see fit. Often the solutions they come up with cannot support the tasks as efficiently as the prototype.

To keep development on the right track, it is important to define the real requirements during the specified process. These requirements could for instance be *task descriptions* (domain-level requirements) or *usability-tested screen pictures* (design-level requirements). It is important to check that system objectives are met with these requirements. It is also important to record the requirements; otherwise there is nothing to verify at delivery time. See also the project models in section 1.7.

R2: Price per screen

The main problem with process-oriented requirements is that the supplier cannot give a fixed price in advance, because he does not know what has to be delivered until the required process has been carried out. There are various ways out of this dilemma, for instance, agreeing on a price formula based on the number of screens, as outlined in R2. Section 1.7.4 explains more about this.

In spite of careful requirements engineering, many things can wreck development, for instance misunderstandings, tacit requirements, and changing demands. R3 to R5 try to prevent this from happening.

Fig 3.16 Development process as requirement

R1: System development shall use iterative development based on prototypes as described in App. xx.

Generates new requirements?

R2: Supplier shall deliver additional screens with a complexity like that of screen S3 at a price of $____ per screen.

R3: All developers shall spend at least two days working with the users on their daily tasks.

R4: A special review shall be conducted at the end of each development activity to verify that all requirements and system goals are duly considered. The customer's representative shall participate in the review.

R5: Customer and supplier shall meet at least two hours bi-weekly to review requests for change and decide what to do, based on cost/benefit estimates of the changes.

R3: Spend time with users

R3 ensures that developers get domain knowledge, allowing them to avoid misunderstandings, understand the real demands, and make better design decisions.

R4: Review development activities

R4 specifies a special kind of review intended to ensure that all requirements are handled in all development activities. The customer is obliged to participate, which gives him a chance to correct misunderstandings and verify that requirements still reflect real needs. Can the supplier bind the customer by means of such a requirement? Yes, to a large extent. If the customer violates his part of the requirements, he will have a very difficult case if the supplier violates some other requirements. Both parties have to do as contracted – otherwise the contract may be terminated.

R5: Structured requirements management

R5 specifies how to handle changing requirements. The essential points are that requirement changes are recorded, evaluated against real demands, and prioritized based on cost and benefit. Section 7.8 explains more on this.

Pros and cons of development process requirements

Validation. Usually the customer has little understanding of how a process relates to the quality of the product. There is a tendency to rely on process standards, although little is known about their effect on product quality. As a result, most customers have little chance to validate that the process is adequate. However, the customer can validate the final requirements, and the purpose of the process is to support this.

Verification. Quite often developers commit to a specific process, yet go ahead and do something different. Verifying that the process is carried out is thus important. The customer should take some responsibility for this, for instance by participating in reviews or inspecting documents.

What can we verify in the final product? The process has been carried out some time ago, so if we are to verify something, we should formulate some of the results as requirements.

4

Functional details

The previous chapter with functional requirements didn't go into detail about what the functions did. We assumed that it is somehow obvious how a booking is recorded, how we find free rooms, and so on. The focus was on identifying these functions, and sometimes also on specifying the input and output of the functions. Essentially, this is what we do by means of event/function lists, task descriptions, use cases, or dataflow diagrams.

Usually this level of specification is sufficient, because a programmer with little domain knowledge can guess what output the function should produce for any given input. It is not only obvious what should come out of the function, but it is also straightforward to program (implement) the function. If the programmer makes mistakes but tests the system carefully, he can see himself that something is wrong.

There are several situations, however, where we need more precision. This chapter explains ways to do it. The first styles are best suited for discussions with expert users, while the later styles mainly are for IT professionals.

In many cases the styles are not suited for stating the requirements, but they can be very useful as intermediate work products. In some of the case studies in Chapter 11 onwards, analysts used technical diagrams for the initial analysis in order to find the real requirements and check that they were complete and consistent.

UML notation. We illustrate many of the styles with the notation used in UML. UML stands for *Unified Modeling Language* and is a standard notation introduced by one of the object-oriented schools (Booch *et al.* 1999). The UML school has selected several kinds of traditional diagrams, modified and standardized the notations, and given some of them new names.

4.1 Complex and simple functions

Highlights

Ignore trivial functions.
Describe semi-complex domain functions in requirements.
Describe semi-complex product functions as part of design.
Specify complex functions by performance or standards.

When do you need to describe a function in detail? You might believe that it is when a function is complex, but that is not the correct answer. In general it only makes sense to describe the semi-complex functions. It is waste of time to describe the simple functions, and the really complex functions must be handled in indirect ways.

Figure 4.1 summarizes these situations. Essentially there are two problem dimensions, one dealing with the obviousness of the domain and one dealing with the complexity of the program or algorithm.

Whether some part of the domain is obvious to the developer or not is not a clear-cut distinction. The analyst has to know the kind of developers involved, and if in doubt, he should assume that the domain part is non-obvious. Do we need the distinction?– Couldn't we just assume that it is all non-obvious? In principle yes, but in practice we have to distinguish in order to save time and in order to avoid hiding all the important things in trivialities. Remember: We have to live with tacit requirements.

Domain obvious, simple program

If the domain is obvious, it is clear to the programmer what the function should do. If the corresponding program part is simple, programming the function is straightforward. Fortunately, most functions are of this kind. Examples are FindFreeRoom, RecordBooking, PrintInvoice. No details of the function are needed. It is sufficient to find a good title for the function, provide some understanding of the context in which it will be used, and sometimes specify the input and output formats.

Domain obvious, interaction complexity

If the domain is obvious, it is also obvious to the programmer what the function should do. However, the interaction between several functions may make the program somewhat complex. An example is the Check-in function, as it must work differently depending on the situation, i.e. depending on other functions that have been used before Check-in.

Fig 4.1 Complex and simple functions

	Domain obvious	**Domain non-obvious**
Simple program	FindFreeRoom PrintInvoice	Discount calculation Business rules

Interaction complexity	Checkin
	  if booked
	  if non-booked
	  if add room
		Tax calculation
		Payroll

Hard to program	Fastest truck route Voice recognition?	Optimize roster Voice recognition?

Possible requirement styles:
A. (Leave to intuition)
B. Natural language or tables
C. Process description (algorithm)
D. Performance specification
E. Refer to laws and agreements

Suitable choices?

Since the domain aspect is simple, this is not really a requirement issue, but a design and programming issue. However, if we design the user interface as part of the requirements, we have to deal with interaction complexity in the user interface functions. The rest of this chapter shows many ways of specifying this complexity, ranging from state diagrams and textual process descriptions to activity diagrams and sequence diagrams.

Domain obvious, hard to program

In some cases the domain is obvious, yet the function is hard to program. Here are two examples:

Fastest truck route. Given a database of road sections and travel times per section. Find the fastest truck route between point X in city A and point Y in city B.

Everybody can understand what this function should produce as output. It is somewhat difficult to program the function for a small road network, but a good programmer should be able to handle it. However, if we talk about large national networks with a million roads, it is very hard to obtain a reasonable response time. Only a few specialists in the world are able to handle this.

If we specify requirements for a system that includes such functions, we should not attempt to specify the algorithm. Instead we should specify the performance of the system, e.g. the response time and the size of the network. These requirements are quality requirements, however, and not functional requirements.

If we know an expert in the area or know a paper that describes a solution, we might help the supplier with a reference to these sources. This is helping the reader, of course, and not a requirement.

> **Voice recognition.** Given the digital recording of a spoken sentence, print the sentence. Or a simpler variant of the above: recognize the statement as a request to push some button, and then push that button.

Everybody knows what the result of such a function should be. At present, however, nobody can fully implement the function. Some software suppliers have programs that can do this, but with limitations: only for a particular language, a particular group of speakers, when spoken carefully, and with little background noise. Even under these conditions, the program has a limited hit-rate.

If we want to develop a system that includes such features, we shouldn't attempt to specify the algorithm. We should instead specify the precision of the system, for instance the expected hit-rate for a certain group of speakers with a certain level of background noise. Again these requirements are quality requirements rather than functional requirements.

Domain non-obvious, simple program

When the programmer has inadequate knowledge of the domain, he cannot program the function on his own. However, once he understands the domain, the function is fairly simple to program. Here are some examples:

> **Discount calculation.** Business customers usually get discounts depending on the kind of product they buy, the order size, and the total yearly size of their purchases.

> **Business rules.** Companies usually have many more or less explicit rules, for instance about when a deposit is needed, when the supervisor's signature is needed, etc.

Sometimes there are written rules that cover these functions. It might then be sufficient to refer to those rules, but as an analyst you should check that the rules are also adequate from a developer's perspective. A good way is to work through a couple of examples with an expert user in order to see that the written rules are unambiguous. Usually, you will have to write some additional comments or write down some examples to guide the developer. These examples also make good test cases later.

In other cases, the rules are shared oral knowledge. Sometimes you don't have to care about the rules if the user interface allows the user to exercise his usual judgment. At other times you have to write them down and check them with expert users. One solution is to make a table of the possibilities and the outcomes (section 4.2 has an example), or you may write a textual process description (section 4.3), or you may draw activity diagrams (section 4.6), state diagrams, etc.

Domain non-obvious, interaction complexity

In some cases a typical programmer may have inadequate knowledge of the domain, and it would take him a long time to get information about all the rules that apply. Although each rule is simple, it is not straightforward to make the program because the many rules interfere with each other. Here are some examples:

Tax calculation. Given a person's or a company's income, expenses, etc. compute the tax to be paid.

Payroll calculation. Given the necessary information about work hours, age, job type, etc. calculate the pay.

These functions are not computationally complex, but it is very difficult to find out exactly what they should do because there are so many rules to handle. You have to study tax laws or union regulations and extract the necessary algorithms. As an example, in some countries union regulations for wages are extremely complex, and not even the workers themselves are sure what their salary should be.

Should the analyst extract this information and specify the algorithm? Usually not; unless he is a specialist in that area he cannot do it properly.

Suppliers that develop tax programs or payroll programs usually have an entire department for the purpose. These people have law and domain expertise, and they spend most of their time translating laws and agreements into programs. A requirements specialist requiring tax calculation as a part of a larger system should not attempt to compete with these specialists, but should use them as suppliers or sub-contractors.

Usually the solution is to write a requirement referring to laws or standards (see section 3.15).

Domain non-obvious, hard to program

In some cases a typical programmer has inadequate knowledge of the domain and, even if he knew the domain, the algorithmic complexity would be high. These situations are frequent and are important for both business and society in general. Here is an example:

Roster optimization. Calculate rosters for hospital staff so that adequate capacity and qualifications are ensured at all times and total wage expenses are minimized.

Sounds easy? It is not. First of all, you need a lot of domain knowledge about hospitals. You also need knowledge of all the union regulations that influence the wage. Given all this knowledge, the problem has also a very high computational complexity. In principle, you could let the computer generate all possible rosters, check whether it fulfills the rules, calculate the wage expense for that roster, and then simply select the best roster. Unfortunately, there will typically be more than a trillion possible rosters, so finding the best among them in this simple way might take a fast computer more than a thousand years.

There are many ways to deal with the computational complexity. Tricky optimization algorithms can sometimes cut the run time by a factor of millions. Being satisfied with sub-optimal solutions may also help a lot. Making an interactive system where computer and user co-operate to produce a good roster can be significantly better than the present manual system. But all of this needs a concerted effort between several domain experts and algorithm specialists. So what should be written in the specification? You may simply write a requirement like this:

R1: The system shall calculate rosters for hospital staff so that adequate capacity and qualifications are ensured at all times and total wage expenses are kept low. The solution might work as a close interaction between user and system. The supplier should specify how much better the rosters are than typical manual rosters.

This requirement assumes that the supplier has the necessary domain and algorithm expertise. If there are several potential suppliers, select the best one based on the quality of their solution. It is possible to verify that the quality is as promised. In case of COTS-based solutions, it can even be done before signing the contract.

Voice recognition. In Figure 4.1, we have put the voice recognition problem in both the obvious and the non-obvious domain categories. Its position depends on how much domain expertise the developer needs. There are simple approaches for identifying single words, where the word is compared against a large collection of spoken words to find the best match. These solutions do not require domain knowledge, only the algorithmic complexity must be mastered. On the other hand, if we want sentences to be recognized, a lot of linguistic and phonetic knowledge is needed, so a combination of domain expertise and algorithmic expertise is needed.

From a requirements viewpoint, it is simply a matter of specifying the required accuracy level for the voice recognition. The problem comes when the customer approaches potential suppliers. Will he need a specialist in algorithms, or a specialist in linguistics, or both?

4.2 Tables and decision tables

What is it?

Tables listing all the possibilities.
Easy to validate.
Easy to verify for user as well as developer.
Suited for business rules.

Sometimes a non-trivial procedure or set of rules exists in the domain in some form. As an example, many companies have rules for discounts, when a deposit is needed, when the supervisor's signature is needed, etc.

Informal table

You can describe such rules in a kind of programming language, but often a table is better. Figure 4.2A shows an example from the hotel system showing the various discount rules. These rules vary from hotel to hotel, so the figure is just an example.

This particular hotel is placed in a popular vacation area. Some tourists try to get discounts on the advertised room rates. Management give discounts when a customer wants a single room, but only double rooms are available. They also give discounts to families who want more than one room. Finally, they know that when it is early in the day and the weather is fine, people may shop around asking for cheaper rooms. For this reason management allows discounts if they think the hotel will have vacancies that night. But if people come late, and if the weather is bad, they are unlikely to shop around, so there is less need to give them a discounted rate.

The table shown in Figure 4.2A tries to set all these rules out. It also sets out whether two discounts can apply at the same time. In the example, discounts 1 and 2 cannot at the same time. This means that if a single parent arrives with two children, and want one single and one double room, but the hotel has only double rooms, they have to choose between discount 1 and 2. However, discounts 1 and 3 can apply at the same time, thus the guest would save 25% twice in the example (he would then pay 75% of 75%, i.e. 56.25%).

Discount rules can be very complex – and very critical to the business. The example here is very simple. Note that R1 says that the product shall suggest these discounts, not that it shall include them automatically. Here we are given some intuition about the task behind these requirements. Note also that the rules are shown with example discount rates. R2 explains that the rates are changeable. Showing the rules with examples is often a good way to make them easier to understand.

Fig 4.2A Business rules (informal table)

> **R1. The product shall suggest the following discount rates if a customer asks for a discount:**
>
> | 1. Double room used as single | 25% |
> |---|---|
> | 2. Family with more than one room, discount for additional rooms | 10% |
> | 3. Discount at immediate checkin:
3a. Before 6pm and hotel less than 50% booked, fair weather
3b. Before 6 pm and hotel less than 50% booked, bad weather | 25%

0% |
>
> Case 1 and 2 cannot apply in the same stay
>
> **R2: Managers shall be able to change the rates**

Decision table

There is a standard approach, called *decision tables*, that allows a more precise description of rules. Figure 4.2B shows the same example in the form of a decision table.

The top of the decision table has a line for each of the basic conditions that enter into the decision. In the example there are six basic conditions: the issue of a double room used as a single, additional family rooms, immediate check-in (without previous booking), the time of the day, the percentage of the hotel's rooms that are booked, and the weather conditions. Some of these conditions the system knows in advance, for instance 4 and 5 (and perhaps 6, with an outside sensor provided by the supplier?). Others must be entered by the receptionist.

Now, look at the grid to the right of these conditions. Y (Yes) shows that a basic condition has to be true; N (No) that a condition has to be false; and an empty cell that the condition does not matter. As an example, the first column applies when condition 1 is true and 2 is false. The rest of the conditions do not matter. This is the situation where a double room is used as a single, and it is not part of a family stay.

Look at the last column. It shows the situation of a guest wanting an immediate check-in, early in the day, when the hotel is far from full, and the weather is fair. There is a high risk that the guest will leave again looking for better options. Give him a discount.

The bottom of the decision table has a line for each action that might come out of the decision. In the example, the actions are two types of room discount (a and b), two types of early-in-the-day discount (c and d), and an error action because a combination is invalid (e). The grid to the right shows when one of these actions is to be carried out. Action (a), the first room discount (25%), is used when the double room is used as a single, no matter whether it is early or late in the day, fair or poor weather, etc.

The error action is taken if we have a double room used as a single as well as a family stay. This may happen if the receptionist has somehow specified this. In this case the receptionist must choose one of the two conditions.

What happens if an action is pointed out twice through two different combinations of conditions? As an example, action (a) might have two check marks in its line. The rule is that the action is carried out once only.

Let us illustrate the rule with a discussion of action (c), the first early discount. This gives 25% discount for the last column, where it is an immediate check-in, early in the day, the hotel is not full, and the weather is fair. Why use that rule? We already have action (a) with a 25% discount. Why not just choose this discount instead? If we did that, action (a) would be taken in the event of the double-as-single situation or in the event of the fair-weather situation. When both situations occur at the same time, the action is taken only once (it is an "or" condition). This means that the customer would receive only one discount, contrary to the rule in Figure 4.2A. It would also mean that the hotel management could not control the two types of discount separately.

The condition table is a strong tool for specifying such rules. It helps us to consider the different situations in detail, and it doesn't have the ambiguity of the more informal table shown in Figure 4.2A.

If we actually showed the table on the user interface, and allowed the user to set check marks, change the discount percentages, etc. we might let the manager specify the rules himself. Note that requirement R2 has been changed to include that possibility. If we had used the informal table shown in Figure 4.2A as a specification of rules, a computer program with linguistic abilities would be needed to allow the manager to change the rules.

See Davis (1994) or Pressman (2000) for more about decision tables.

Fig 4.2B Business rules (decision table)

R1: The product shall suggest the following discount rates if a customer asks for a discount:

1. Double room if used as a single	Y	N	Y		
2. Family, additional rooms	N	Y	Y		
3. Immediate check-in				Y	Y
4. Before 6pm				Y	Y
5. Less than 50% booked				Y	Y
6. Fair weather				N	Y
a. Room discount 25%	v				?
b. Room discount 10%		v			
c. Early discount 25%					v
d. Early discount 0%				v	
e. Error		v			

R2: Managers shall be able to change the rates and the rules

Pros and cons of decision tables

Decision tables and more informal tables are excellent for describing business rules. The customer has a good opportunity to validate and verify them, and the developer can easily transform them into programs and verify that the program works according to the requirements. It is even possible to allow the user to modify the rules without him having to know about programming.

Although the customer can validate the rules, this may be difficult. The analyst should help the customer to go through the table and look at examples, much as we have done in the explanations above.

Only mildly complex rules can be handled by decision tables. Rules expressed as programs with loops or recursion are not suitable for such tables.

4.3 Textual process descriptions

What is it?

Outline of the program (the algorithm) in text form.
Sometimes called *mini-specs* or *pseudo-code*.
The only way to provide fine detail.
Useful for design-level requirements, e.g. buttons in prototypes.
Sometimes useful for business rules.

A textual process description shows the details of what a function should do. The text can have many forms, from very sketchy, to mathematical specifications, or outlines of the actual code. The terms *mini-spec* and *pseudo-code* are used when the text is an informal program.

The function can be the action invoked by a product-level event, a method (operation) in a UML object, a line of text in a use case, a low-level bubble in a dataflow diagram, a box in an activity diagram, etc.

Process descriptions are only needed for some functions. Most functions are so simple that intuition suffices. Others are so complex that only the high-level result can be specified, while experts are needed to develop the algorithm. Section 4.1 discusses those issues.

Process descriptions may be used for some domain-level functions (business rules), but the most important use is in design-level requirements. For example, the design-level requirements for the user interface should be a prototype where screens are shown, almost in their final form. In addition we have to define the functions, i.e. buttons, menu points, etc. These functions are product functions that don't exist in the domain but are defined during product design. Most are trivial, but some are complex because they depend on the dialog state or interact with other functions. We need some kind of detailed specification that the developer can read.

What should be specified?

When a developer-oriented process description is appropriate, we recommend that you describe these aspects:

a) input to the function

b) the expected entry state (where appropriate)

c) changes made to the system state (e.g. changes in the database)

d) output from the function

Fig 4.3   A process description in pseudo-code

The product shall provide the following functions:

1.1 FindFreeRoom (type, period)
List rooms of the requested type that are free in
the period requested.
Allow the user to select some of them as
CurrentRooms in the requested period.

1.2 CreateNewStay (partial guest data, guest record)
Create a temporary CurrentStay.
If guest record exists then
fill CurrentStay with recorded guest data
else
fill CurrentStay with partial guest data.
Note: The product should look for similar records too.

1.3 Checkin (CurrentStay, CurrentRooms)
If CurrentStay is booked,
record rooms in stay as occupied.
If CurrentStay is not recorded,
check CurrentRooms free.
If guest not recorded,
check guest data complete, record guest.
record CurrentRooms as occupied, record stay.
If . . .

Figure 4.3 gives three examples from the hotel system, corresponding to three product-level functions. Although the examples are informal, they follow the recommendation.

a) The input is shown as parameters, e.g. (*type, period*). Usually the current state (database contents or dialog state) is used as an implicit input too, e.g. *rooms free* or *CurrentStay*.

b) The expected entry state is specified as a check of the state, e.g. *if CurrentStay is booked*. Some analysts prefer to replace the check with a precondition.

c) Changes to the system state are explained as verbs, e.g. *Create* a temporary xx or *record* CurrentRooms as yy.

d) The output from the function is given by other verbs, e.g. *List rooms*. In these examples most output is implicit in the form of state changes. In many other cases, output is returned through parameters.

Most parts of the process descriptions fall in one of the categories above, but there is a strange statement in RecordGuest:

The system should look for similar records too.

This is intended as a note to *If guest record exists*. The statement is informal, but mentions a real concern. Guest names and addresses are not spelled the same way each time. There are many ways to deal with this problem. Depending on the project type, this can be specified in more or less detail, for instance by referring to a standard way to do it. In other cases the supplier is invited to suggest possible solutions.

Requirements. The requirement is not that the product shall follow the process descriptions in detail, but only that it shall produce the same result as the specification.

The pros and cons of textual process descriptions

In some cases process descriptions are needed, because we cannot leave it to the developer to guess what to do. Textual process descriptions are the ultimate way to describe the details. Other approaches, such as activity diagrams and state diagrams, can give an overview, but cannot provide all the details.

Verification. A well-written process description can be used directly as basis for implementation, although it may be reshuffled completely in the code. (For example, in a graphical user interface, FindFreeRoom will be implemented as several pieces of code spread over many control objects.)

Verifying the requirements in the final product is done through testing. The process description implicitly mentions many cases to be tested in the final product. As an example, *Check-in* is to be tested with a booked stay, a new stay, and a checked-in stay.

Validation. Product function descriptions are mainly intended for developers. Some customers can understand the descriptions, but few customers are willing to try, since the amount of detail involved can be overwhelming. The customer should validate the product functions indirectly, for instance through tests of the prototype in which the functions are embedded. In sub-contractor projects, where supplier and customer are both technical experts, the parties are more likely to scrutinize the process descriptions.

4.4 State diagrams

A state diagram describes how a certain entity changes state as a result of various events. As an example, we will show how a room in the hotel changes state, from free to booked, from booked to occupied, from free to under repair, etc. The situation is slightly complicated because we not only talk about the state of the room today, but also about the planned state of the room at some time in the future. For this reason, each room has a RoomState record for every date in the calendar.

We will look at how the room state for a specific date changes as a result of events that happen today. For instance, the receptionist might change a room state for next week to *repair* because the carpenter has promised to come that day and repair the cabinets.

Figure 4.4 shows how a RoomState record for a specific date might change state. The four possible room states are shown as four rounded boxes. The black dot to the left of the figure represents the state before the RoomState record is created. The bull's eye at the bottom of the figure represents the deletion of the record. The diagram shows the life cycle of the RoomState record.

Let us first look at the events we have seen earlier. The RoomState is initially *free*. A booking event will change it to *booked*. A check-in event will change it to *occupied* whether it is free or booked already. A check-out event is only allowed in the *occupied* state and changes the room state to *free*. These events are shown as black arrows.

(We should add that a book event can apply to a room state record for some future date, because the idea of booking is to do it in advance. In contrast, a check-in event can only apply to a room today, because we cannot check in a guest before he arrives. We have not shown these details on the diagram.)

If these were the only events handled by the system, we can see from the figure that something is missing. The room cannot enter the *repair* state since no black arrow leads to that state, so we need a function or event to do that. Let us call it *repair* and put it on the event/function list. We also need an event to revoke the repair state. We have added it as a *done* event. We may also wonder whether a booked room could become free again. In real life it could, for instance when a customer cancels a booking, so a *cancel* event is needed too. Similarly, it is unclear

Fig 4.4   State diagrams

Rooms have a RoomState for each day in the planning period. The status shows whether the room is free, occupied, etc. that day.

R12: RoomState shall change as shown in Fig. 12.

Fig. 12. RoomState

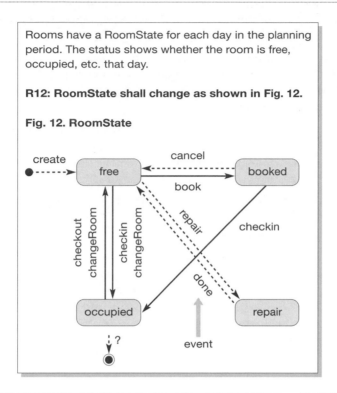

how a RoomState is created. Is it when the room is created? Which event does that? And for which period in the calendar? We have thus also added this event. We have also shown that somehow the entity has to be deleted at some time. The issues of when to create and delete the RoomStates is a good topic for discussion with the customer. It has to do with the planning period (months or years) and the retention period (how long data should be kept for statistical use). We have shown the new, non-obvious events as dotted arrows on the figure.

Requirements. In the example, the state diagram has primarily helped us to reveal missing events. We can also use the state diagram as a requirement, for instance as shown on the figure. The requirement specifies several things: the possible states of the entity, the function of various events, and the admissible sequence of events.

What do we model?

We can model the life cycle of any entity or group of entities with a state diagram, for instance entities in the data model, dialog states, data communication states, etc.

However, most entities have trivial life cycles consisting of two states (the entity exists or it does not exist) and events such as *create, update, delete*. Specifying these is rarely necessary. The recommendation is to specify state diagrams only for entities with a complex behavior and several states.

Another issue is whether we should specify the domain or the product. For data model entities there is little difference since data models tend to model the domain and the product at the same time. The only difference is whether we look at the domain events or the product events.

State diagrams are used extensively in Web-related systems to describe how the user can navigate from one Web page to another. The diagram models the state of the user's screen. Arrows show how links can move the user from one page to another. Web developers call these diagrams *site maps* and would be puzzled if you called them state diagrams.

Notation

State diagrams use a fairly standard notation. There are extensions of the notation that deal with parallel states of two entities, sub-states, etc. See for instance the UML notation in Booch *et al.* (1999) or Davis (1994). In the world of data communication, 'dialog' states are very important and very complex. Special notations are used in that domain, for instance SDL (Specification and Description Language), as described by Ellsberger *et al.* (1997).

The pros and cons of state diagrams

Verification. State diagrams are an excellent basis for development and testing. Most developers are familiar with them.

Validation. Huge state diagrams, for instance for Web sites, can easily extend over several pages and still retain their readability. Some customers can understand and comment on state diagrams, particularly if the analyst walks through the situations with them. Other customers cannot distinguish state diagrams from dataflow diagrams or activity diagrams.

4.5 State-transition matrices

What is it?

Table showing how something reacts in all possible cases.
Better than state diagrams for finding missing or obscure functions.
Use it only for complex life cycles.

What do they do?

State-transition matrices are another way to show state transitions. Figure 4.5 shows the matrix for the RoomState, i.e. the record that describes the state of a particular room for a particular date. The matrix lists events down one axis and states along the other axis. Each cell in the matrix describes what happens when that event occurs in that state. In the cell we show the new state and sometimes output from the system and other actions or conditions. In Figure 4.5 these additional items are written as footnotes.

Let us look at some details. The first column shows state 1, *free*. When the *Book* event happens in that state, the room state should change to state 2, *booked*. Similarly, when *Repair* happens in the free state, the room state should change to repair.

All state-event combinations. The advantage of the state-transition matrix is that we are forced to look at every combination of state and event. Furthermore, we have the opportunity to write notes on what should happen apart from a state change. In my time as a developer, state-transition matrices have always helped us resolve the real hard problems in the product, particularly for critical programs such as operating systems, compilers, or process control.

If we continue down the first column in Figure 4.5, we have to consider check-in when the room state is *free*. Assume that the guest wants to stay for several nights. The room state for the check-in date becomes *occupied*, but what do we do to the room states for the remaining days of the stay? Do we make them occupied too, although the guest might change his mind and leave earlier than planned, or do we make them booked?

As note (a) below the table explains, we have discussed that with an expert user and decided to record the first room state as *occupied* and the later room states as *booked*. The matrix cell shows this in the way that the new state may be either three or two. The decision influences other actions, for instance the check-in action when the room is booked in advance. We have shown that as note (b).

Let us continue down the first column. What about *Check-out*, *Cancel*, and *Done*? They should have no effect in the free state. What if the user tries to push these buttons? Maybe the system should beep, or those buttons should be gray. We have shown this as a dash.

Fig 4.5 State-transition matrix

	1. free	2. booked	3.occupied	4. repair
Book	2	–	–	–
Checkin	3/2(a)	3 (b)	–	–
ChangeRoom	3/2	? (c)	1	–
Checkout	–	?	1	–
Cancel	–	1	? (d)	–
Repair	4	–	–	–
Done	–	–	–	1

(a) RoomState for the check-in date becomes occupied.
   For later days it becomes booked.

(b) RoomState for the check-in date becomes occupied.
   For later days it remains booked.

(c) Can we change room for a booked stay before the
   guest arrives?

(d) Can we cancel a check-in without the guest paying?
   Yes, it happens when . . .

The middle column is more interesting, the booked state. There is no problem with the *Book* and *Check-in* events, but what if *ChangeRoom* happens to a booked room? Assume for instance that a guest has booked by phone and later calls to change the booking from, say a single room to a double. We ought to be able to handle that, but it has been forgotten on the state diagram in Figure 3.16.

In the column for *occupied* we encounter another problem. Could we use *Cancel* in this state? In other words, could the guest check in and then decide to leave without checking out and paying the bill? This happens in real life. A guest arrives and checks in, gets the room key and goes to the room. Five minutes later he returns with his luggage and says that this room is not what he expected. He wants to leave. The receptionist has to cancel the check-in. We also forgot this possibility on the state diagram.

Advantages of state-transition matrices

The state-transition matrix is a strong tool for checking that all situations and features have been covered. We usually find obscure situations that have to be dealt with. We can discuss these situations with the expert user, but we can rarely let him validate the matrix on his own. It is too abstract.

We can use the state-transition matrix as a requirement in the same way as a state diagram. It is easy and very efficient to make a program that closely follows the matrix. Essentially, the matrix is stored as a table in the program and each event makes a lookup in the table to see what to do.

Disadvantages of state-transition matrices

For some systems the state-transition matrix becomes too large and sparsely populated, for example where most of the cells contain *not possible*. This would be the case with a large Website system, where each page corresponds to a state and each possible click corresponds to an event. All cells will contain *not possible* except for clicks belonging to the page in question. In these cases, a state diagram is much simpler and more readable than a state-transition matrix.

4.6   Activity diagrams

> **What is it?**
>
> A diagram showing the flow of control and the flow of data (objects).
> Handles concurrency and synchronization.
> Good for analysis.
> Useful as requirements for workflow applications.

Activity diagrams are another kind of UML diagram. Originally, they were just traditional flow charts that showed the flow of control – what was done in which order. Today they have been expanded to show object flows (similar to data flows) and concurrent flows of control as well.

Note that the traditional flow charts and dataflow diagrams are two completely different things. A flow chart shows what the system does step by step with conditions and loops, while a dataflow diagram shows the data coming in and out of each function or activity. The activity diagram combines both in one diagram.

Example. Figure 4.6A shows an activity diagram that models the activities of three actors: a hotel guest, the hotel, and a bank clearing-house. Each of these three actors has what is called a *swim lane* running down the diagram.

Let us first have a brief look at the guest lane. The guest starts to book a room by sending some booking data to the hotel system, including a credit card number. Next he waits for a reply in the form of a reject or a confirmation with a booking number. Then he travels, checks in, etc. As part of checking in, he presents his booking number.

The hotel waits for a booking event (or some other event) and first checks to see that there is a free room. If so, they send a credit-check message to the bank and wait for a reply. If the customer's credit is acceptable, they record the booking and send a confirmation to the guest. The booking data lies waiting for the guest to arrive and present his booking number (we have not shown check-in details).

Finally, the bank waits for a credit check event (or some other event) and sends a reply. If credit was acceptable, the bank posts a deposit transaction, which means that the amount is not yet drawn on the guest's account, but it is reserved for a certain period and transferred to the hotel when the guest checks out. (Banks can do such things, although few customers are aware of this.)

At this stage, you may wonder whether "hotel" is a human receptionist or a computer. In fact, it might be either. The figure covers both possibilities, although we have a fully automated Web-booking system in mind. Checking in, however, will still be handled by a human receptionist, we believe.

Fig 4.6A Activity diagram, workflow

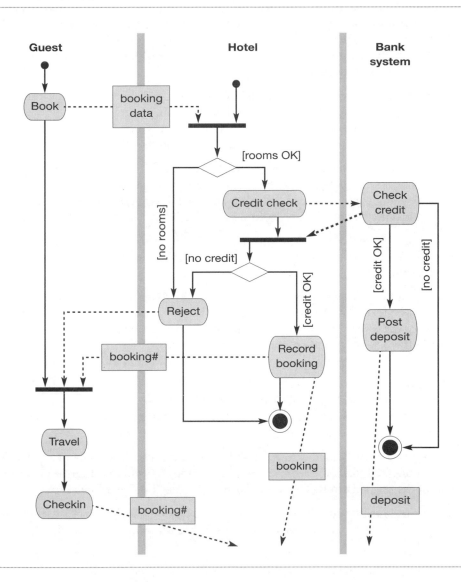

The flow-chart part. Let us look more closely at the notation on the diagram. The barrel-shaped boxes show activities. The actor carries out these activities. UML terminology distinguishes between actions, which are atomic functions that take place instantaneously, and activities that take longer. For simplicity, we have not distinguished between activities and actions.

The black arrows show the sequence of activities. When the actor has completed an activity, the black arrow shows what to do next. But what about the two black arrows coming out of the bank's *Check credit* box? Which one should be taken? Note that they are labeled with text in brackets. That label is called a *guard* and it says under which conditions each branch should be taken. The rule, however, is that only one arrow may be followed.

Does the diagram resemble a state diagram? Yes – and it *is* a state diagram. The state is the current point of control for that actor. The diagram shows how the actor goes from the state of performing one activity to the state of performing the next. This idea is very similar to the idea of a site map on the Web.

In the figure there are three state diagrams, one for each swim lane. Each of the actors carries out his own activities according to the state diagram. Thus the guest lane does not show several entities, but only one: the guest. Each rounded box shows a state the guest can be in, and he can be in only state at a time.

Once you know that the diagram is a special kind of state diagram, you can also recognize the start and stop markers showing where an execution thread starts and terminates.

Note that the boxes are slightly different. Activity diagrams use barrel-shaped boxes. The text in the box shows the action carried out before the state is left, for instance *Check credit* or *Reject*. State diagrams use boxes with rounded corners. The text in the box is the name of the state, for instance *free* or *occupied*. In this case the name corresponds to a value of the RoomState attribute in the data model.

The activity diagram also contains diamonds, which also have arrows leading away from them representing a choice of execution path. They work exactly like a rounded box, but their action is simply to ask a question, so for that reason nothing is written inside the diamond.

Object flow. The dashed arrows don't represent a state transition, but an object communicated to another activity. Sometimes the object in question is shown on top of the dashed arrow. The dashed arrows are used much as data flows.

In Figure 4.6A, the guest's Book action sends booking data to the hotel. The hotel may send a reject object to the guest, but this has not been shown explicitly.

Note that the black arrows cannot carry data. They are *not* messages sent to another box, but a transition from being in one box to being in another box.

Concurrent threads. The thick horizontal lines on Figure 4.6A are synchronization bars. Execution stops on the line until the other arrows have delivered their result to the line. As an example, the guest sends his booking data and waits on the synchronization line until he receives a reject message or a booking confirmation. Strictly speaking, the diagram shows that he must wait for both to occur, but we will ignore that detail. Waiting on the bar until others have arrived is called a *join* operation.

As another example, the "hotel" is started at some time and now waits at the synchronization bar for booking data to arrive. Next, the hotel checks room availability. When the hotel has served the booking request it terminates, according to the diagram. We have to imagine that new hotel activities pop up all the time and start at the top of the lane. A different model would be to let the hotel activity continue at the top of the lane rather than terminating.

Several arrows can start from a synchronization bar. Each starts its own thread of execution so that several threads can execute concurrently. This is called a fork operation. There is no example of this in Figure 4.6A, since each actor is only executing a single thread of activities.

Crossing the lane. You might notice that no black arrows cross the border to another lane. Is that a coincidence? No; crossing the border would mean that the actor continued his execution in another lane, which would be wrong here. The actor may send a message (an object) to another lane, but may not start working there.

Some analysts would model the interaction between guest and hotel as in Figure 4.6B. Here the guest forks into two execution threads right after Book. One thread continues in the hotel lane where all the checks are made. That thread ends up joining the main guest thread again. This model has black arrows crossing the lanes. You might interpret this as the guest "borrowing" the hotel and getting them to do something for him.

Note that the booking data cannot be carried by the black arrow crossing the lane. For this reason we still need a dotted line carrying the booking data.

Advantages of activity diagrams

Activity diagrams have a lot in common with the much older dataflow diagrams and flow charts, but they are more expressive. Activity diagrams are widely used, and analysts should know about them and their limitations. In some cases the customer may insist on them being used.

Activity diagrams are useful for

1 Designing new human activities in the domain. In this case the requirement to the product is to support these new activities. A special example of this is workflow modeling, where documents are routed between departments in a large organization or between organizations. The synchronization bars allow simple modeling of the situation where several documents have to meet each other before the case can proceed.

2 Specifying communication between technical components, e.g. between the hotel system and other products. The thread and synchronization aspects are also important here.

3 Outlining the internal structure of large programs.

Validation. Customers with no IT background can often read activity diagrams, particularly those describing domain aspects. Seeing whether they correctly reflect the requirements is much more difficult, however. Their expressive power is also a drawback since users find it difficult to distinguish dotted arrows from black arrows, appreciate fork and join operations, etc.

Disadvantages of activity diagrams

Activity diagrams are poor at describing the actual data communicated between actors, although they have a notation for sending objects around. It would be an advantage to combine activity diagrams with data expressions (see section 2.4).

Activity diagrams take a lot of space, as shown in Figure 4.6, where a few trivialities take a lot of space. In order to give the overview intended, the details, such as all the obvious checking actions, should be omitted.

Activity diagrams are often used to describe details of product functions, as illustrated in section 3.12.5. In this role they work as a reinvention of the old flow charts, which were abandoned long ago when structured programming became popular. Flow charts were known to lead to messy programs based on goto statements, which structured programming and the associated way of thinking avoided.

Fig 4.6B Fork and join operations

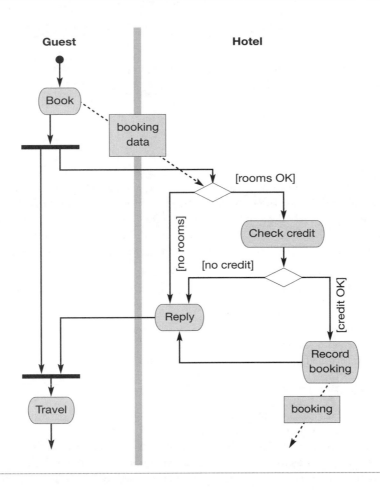

4.7 Class diagrams

What is it?

A data model where entities have data and can perform something.
For users, even harder to understand than data models.
Widely used – even when unsuccessful.
Useful as requirements for some technical systems.
Not suitable as requirements for business applications.

In this section we will look at the *static class diagram*, which is basically an extension of the E/R model (the entity/relationship data model; see section 2.2). The extension is that each class not only stores data, it also contains functions that work on that data. Class diagrams are widely used, and the analyst should know about them although they are more suitable for program design than for requirements.

Figure 4.7A shows an example of a static class diagram in UML notation. A box corresponds to a class of objects or records in a very similar way to the E/R diagram from Figure 2.2. Both pictures model the hotel system.

There are many variations of class diagrams, particularly concerning how the relationships are shown. UML shows relationships as simple lines with numbers indicating *cardinality*, i.e. whether the relationship is one-to-many, many-to-many, etc. For example, Figure 4.7A shows that a stay may have one or more *room states* (1..*) and a *room state* may belong to zero or one stays (0..1).

In this way, UML allows more precision than the crow's feet of the E/R diagram. You could even specify that a stay may have a maximum of 99 room states. Unfortunately, at the same time the UML notation has lost the visual overview provided by the crow's feet. The problem is that you cannot at a glance see how a chain of relationships combines into a single relationship. Section 2.2 explains this in detail.

Note that in UML, a relationship is called an *association*. This terminology avoids the traditional data model confusion about relations versus relationships (see section 2.2).

Operations. Inside each box, Figure 4.7A shows three things:

1 The name of the class.

2 The attributes of the objects.

3 The *operations* of the class (the functions, sometimes called *methods*).

An operation is a kind of procedure or sub-routine. It can create and delete objects of the class, it can update and read attributes, and it can compute results based on the attributes. It can also call operations in other classes.

Fig 4.7A UML class diagram

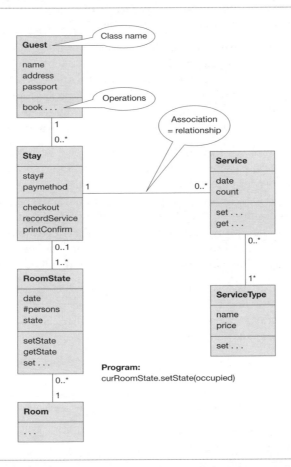

Since the operation is a sub-routine, it is called with parameters. As an example, the room state class has an operation *setState* that is called with two parameters: (1) a reference to a room state object; and (2), the new state to be set. As an example, assume that curRoomState is a reference to a RoomState object. The call to set that RoomState to *occupied* might look like this in a traditional programming language:

setState(curRoomState, occupied)

An object-oriented language recognizes that the operations are analogous to attributes, so the call is written in the same way as when we address an attribute of a record. In this case the call would be:

curRoomState.setState(occupied)

Operations to get and set attributes, and to create and delete objects, are usually taken for granted, and not mentioned explicitly in these diagrams. However, there are more interesting operations in the example.

The *check-out* operation works primarily on a stay record, so it is modeled as an operation in the *stay* class. Supposedly it will create a bill by combining related data in the guest class, the service class, and so on. To do this, it needs data from all the other classes in the diagram. It will retrieve this data by calling appropriate operations in the other classes. It will do other things too, for instance, cancel remaining room bookings if a guest leaves earlier than planned, record how the bill was paid, etc.

Messages. *Calling* an operation is not the proper term in the object-oriented world. In OO terms it is called sending a *message*. The message is sent to the proper object in the class and carries parameters as data in the message. Usually the caller will immediately wait for a reply message with return parameters, and in this case we have a traditional sub-routine call. However, the caller need not wait for the reply – or there need not be a reply, and then we have an asynchronous message. The message concept is thus broader than the call concept. In practice, however, most messages correspond to calls. Section 4.9 explains more about messages.

Encapsulation. The basic idea behind class diagrams is to combine data and functions into one concept. Data are *encapsulated* because they are only available through the functions (operations) of the object. Other classes don't have to know how data is represented; the operation will do any conversion needed.

In some sense class diagrams try to combine data models and dataflow diagrams. This is an ambitious goal, which unfortunately causes many frustrations in large development projects, particularly in business applications. The object concept seems so simple and convincing, so why does it lead to frustration?

Domain versus product. It was known from theory and practice that data models are independent of whether we model information about the application area (the domain) or data in the database (the product). The principle works excellently for small as well as large systems. Researchers jumped to the conclusion that the same applied to functions, and they came up with tiny examples where it seemed to work. But in general it does not! The functions working on the objects are generally completely different in the domain (what people do) and in the product (what the computer does). The functions are not even given in advance, but depend on the chosen division of labor between human and computer. Section 3.1 explains this in detail.

Requirements. The elusiveness of transferring functions from domain to product makes it difficult to use the object approach for requirements. If you try to make domain-level object models (human and computer together), you have defined several operations that cannot be used later in design. If you instead try to model the objects inside the product, you have made design-level requirements.

This is the basic, theoretical explanation. There are many other problems with modeling the domain by objects, one being that users have difficulties seeing that a hotel stay or an invoice can perform operations, such as object modeling suggests. Object modeling also suggests that users are objects with operations, which users find strange.

Another problem is that class models are not suitable for describing how objects co-operate to support the user tasks. For this purpose, the object community introduced use cases, collaboration diagrams, and sequence diagrams.

Object-suited domains. However, there are systems where the object approach works well for analysis and requirements:

■ IT tools that provide a service to users or developers, e.g. user interface tools, data communication packages, or drawing packages.

■ Systems that model and simulate physical objects, e.g. electronic circuits.

■ Systems that control physical objects, e.g. a network of conveyor belts or a plant with pipes and valves.

In these cases we either model a computer artifact (the IT tools) or we model something that really *is* a collection of physical objects. For good reasons, object people prefer these kinds of systems as examples.

These observations apply to object-oriented analysis and requirements specification. Object-oriented *programming* is another issue. Often it is an advantage to structure the program as objects, and because many programming tools and packages are object-oriented, OO-programming is often a must. These concerns are implementation issues, of course.

Business applications

We have seen many attempts to design and program business applications in an ideal, object-oriented way. Most teams who have attempted this have burnt their hands trying.

What works better is a less ideal way, illustrated in Figure 4.7B. Arrows show that one object calls another one. The application is divided into four layers, and as a general rule, objects only call objects above them. The layers have these functions:

Database. The top layer is a traditional database, which is usually SQL-driven so that the layer below sends SQL statements to it in order to retrieve or update records in the database.

Data objects. The data objects correspond closely to the data model behind the database, but they translate the SQL database interface into an object-oriented interface. The layers below can thus access data in the database as if it consisted of objects. The data objects typically also buffer the records, so that the user interface can access data more quickly. Although the data objects are complex internally, they mainly have trivial operations such as create, get, set, and delete. You can buy software packages (persistency frameworks) that provide such data objects.

Service functions. Below the data objects are objects that perform more complex operations, combining data from several data objects. As an example, the check-out operation would belong here, not in the *stay* data object. Usually, the service objects are more like traditional sub-routines because they contain little data.

Why are the complex operations collected in the service objects rather than in the data objects? Industrial experience shows that if you try to put them in the data objects, each operation is distributed over several data objects, and each data object has many small parts aimed at the many complex operations. As a result, developers lose their overview of the program logic and the solution becomes like "reading a road map through a soda straw" (Maring 1996; Lauesen 1998). Section 3.22 shows an example.

There is a type of data that logically belongs to the layer of service functions: the communication state of each interface. For the user interface, it is the dialog data that keep track of intermediate states of the user dialog, for instance the customer data and the room selected while a check-in transaction is in progress. The alternative is to store dialog data in the database, which is sometimes more convenient because the temporary dialog state now survives log out and even system crashes.

Observer objects. In the same layer, we often find observer objects that help to update data on the user screens whenever it changes in the database. These objects call the 'wrong' way because they have to distribute data down to the user interface objects.

User interface objects. This layer of objects corresponds to the visual objects seen on the user interface. When the graphical user interface (GUI) package opens a window, it creates a visual object for each field, button, or whatever. When a field has to show or update data in the database, it calls the appropriate data objects directly. If a button has to perform a complex operation, it may call one of the service functions.

If a field needs to be refreshed automatically, the program creates an observer object for the field and links it to the appropriate data object. The automatic refresh now works as follows. When some object calls a set-operation in a data object, the data object in turn calls all the observer objects linked to it, and each of the observer objects calls its visual object asking it to update the field. As a result, all the necessary screen fields are updated. This pattern is a slightly sophisticated version of the Model-View-Control (MVC) pattern used for many years in the language SmallTalk.

However, all this is detailed design and programming, not requirements. We have explained the solution in some detail in order to help you avoid disasters if you get involved in object-oriented development.

Advantages of class diagrams

Class diagrams are widely used, and as an analyst, you have to know about them. In some cases, the customer may insist that you use them.

Class modeling – including the operations – is suited to certain technical domains. Class modeling without the operations may be used as data requirements in the same way as data models.

Fig 4.7B Object-oriented business application

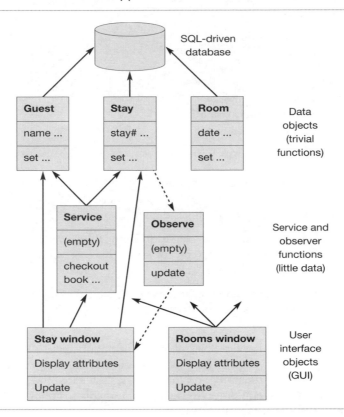

Class diagrams are useful in designing the inner workings of the product, particularly because user interface packages and many other packages are object-oriented. However, this is not an easy job. In particular, be careful with business applications. Don't attempt to combine functions and data in the ideal object-oriented way. Instead use a layered model as shown in Figure 4.7B, where data and complex functions are split into separate objects.

Disadvantages of class diagrams

In business applications, class modeling with operations is not suitable for requirements. As a consultant or developer, you may be requested to make object-oriented requirements. How do you handle that when the object approach isn't suitable? Do what many seasoned consultants do: pretend and succeed.

Use the class model as if it were a data model you created. Be careful with associations and attributes, but gloss over the operations, possibly using as an excuse that there is no time to do it more thoroughly. Then you will see how "object-orientation" can succeed even in business applications!

4.8   Collaboration diagrams

What is it?

A box diagram of how objects call each other.
Good for describing the internal workings of the product.
Sometimes useful for intermediate work products.
Rarely useful as requirements.

A UML collaboration diagram shows how objects co-operate by means of messages. Figure 4.8 shows several hotel system objects co-operating to check out a guest. We have only shown the part that collects data for the invoice.

The figure shows the well-known classes from the hotel system. The arrows show how the classes send messages to each other. In this case, all the messages correspond to simple sub-routine calls.

The story starts when someone outside the diagram calls check-out in the *Stay* class, or rather calls check-out for a particular Stay object. This call is marked as number 1 on the diagram.

The Stay object calls a Service object to get information about a service associated with the stay. Actually, it calls all the Service objects related to the stay. These calls are marked 1.1 on the diagram, and the asterisk shows that the getService operation is called several times. In UML, it is possible to annotate the asterisk with a description of which calls are made.

When getService is called, the Service object calls a ServiceType object to obtain the unit price of that type of service. This call is marked as 1.1.1 to show that it originated in call 1.1. Note that there is no asterisk. Only one call is made for each call of Service.

This done, the Stay object collects information about the rooms occupied during the stay. It calls all the RoomState objects associated with the stay. This is shown as arrow 1.2, indicating that it is the second type of call made by the Stay object.

Finally, each RoomState object calls its associated Room object to get the room price. The arrow is marked 1.2.1 and there is no asterisk because only one call is made for each RoomState object.

This should be sufficient information for the Stay object to produce an invoice. Many other calls are needed to file billing data for the accounting system, clean up room states, etc. These calls are not shown. Furthermore, a good user dialog requires that the receptionist sees a screen corresponding to the invoice before actually printing it. Many hotels even print out a draft invoice for the customer's perusal before printing the final invoice. These issues would need additional operations in the Stay class.

Fig 4.8   A collaboration diagram

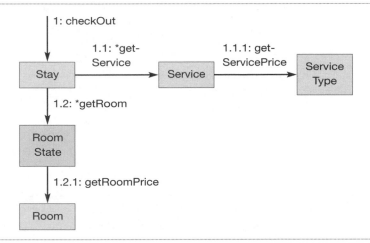

This is an example of a slightly complex function that has to be distributed over several objects. Each object needs some special operation or some special parameter to an operation to be able to handle its part of check-out. As a result, developers lose their overview of the program logic. For this reason we strongly recommend the layered model shown in Figure 4.7B.

Are all these details of the Stay class necessary for requirements? No; what we have described is trivial, and we haven't covered any interesting topics such as VAT, discounts, etc. We could add these things, but this is not a good way of describing requirements.

Would the description be interesting to developers? No. We have only described trivialities, even to a developer with limited domain understanding. Furthermore, the description doesn't match what would take place in a typical program. There the entire extraction of data for the invoice would be done through an SQL statement (database retrieval language) using tables but no objects.

The pros and cons of collaboration diagrams

Since collaboration diagrams are widely used, the analyst should know about them and their limitations. Collaboration diagrams are useful for:

1   Specifying parts of the technical interfaces to the product, particularly the sequence in which things should happen.

2   Describing the internal workings of the program. This assumes that the objects on the diagram correspond to actual objects in the program. This may be relevant as an intermediate work product, but not for the final requirements.

Collaboration diagrams are rarely useful for stating requirements about the user interface. The exception is user interfaces with a very restricted message sequence, for instance those found in an ATM machine.

4.9   Sequence diagrams, events, and messages

What is it?

Time diagram of how objects communicate.
Good for describing simple communication protocols.
Useful as intermediate work products.
Useful as design-level requirements for technical interfaces.

Sequence diagrams are another type of UML diagram. They serve much the same purpose as collaboration diagrams: they show how objects communicate by means of messages. While collaboration diagrams show the sequence of events through the numbering of arrows, sequence diagrams show the sequence graphically because time runs down the diagram.

We will show how to specify interfaces to the product by means of sequence diagrams. We will also use the sequence diagram to explain the relation between events, messages, and transactions. Figure 4.9 shows two examples that illustrate these concepts.

Example 1: Find room

At the top of the picture we see the communication involved when the user asks the product to find free rooms. The user sends the *FindRooms* message, illustrated by the arrow. The product now looks up its database and finds the free rooms. It sends the list of room numbers as a reply message. We will return to the exact meaning of the arrows below.

From the user's point of view, this communication takes place through the computer screen and the keyboard/mouse. The user hits the FindRooms button, which generates the first message. He has entered the room type and the date in fields on his screen, and they become part of the message. He sees the resulting list of rooms in another screen field. Next, the user selects an appropriate room and hits the Select button. This results in a SelectRoom event with an attached room number. The product does not send a reply; it just remembers the chosen room.

Event. An event is the message where the initiative starts. The FindRooms message was an event, because the user took the initiative and sent the message. The black dot where the arrow starts shows that it was an event. The arrowhead is a solid black triangle and shows that it was a *synchronous message*, i.e. that the sender waited to receive a reply message.

The free rooms message is a simple reply message. The line-style of the arrowhead shows that.

Fig 4.9 A sequence diagram

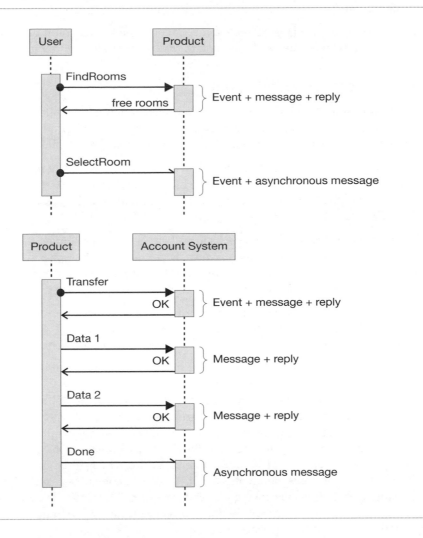

The SelectRoom message is also an event, as shown by the dot. The user took the initiative and could in principle have done all kinds of other things. The message is also *asynchronous*, as shown by the half arrowhead. This means that the sender doesn't wait for a reply but continues immediately.

Messages. A message is some data sent from a sender to a receiver. There are several kinds of messages:

■ A synchronous message with a related reply message, where the sender waits for the reply.

- An asynchronous message *without* a reply, where the sender continues immediately.

- An asynchronous message *with* a reply, where the sender continues after sending the message, and may look for the reply later or ignore it.

Example 2: Transfer accounting data

The next example in Figure 4.9 is the communication involved when the product sends account information to the remote account system. The product takes the initiative, for instance triggered by the computer clock every midnight.

First the product sends the Transfer event. No data is associated with this event. The dot shows that it is an event and the black arrowhead shows that the sender waits for a reply. Next the account system replies with a reply message containing the code OK.

Now the product sends the first package of data, for instance holding the invoice data for the first check-out of the previous day. The account system replies with an OK. The missing dot shows that it is not an event, because the account system expects the data message. The parties are in the middle of a longer handshake protocol.

Next the product sends another package of data and receives a reply, and so on. When all account data have been sent, the product sends a Done message. It is a message without an event, and it is asynchronous because the sender continues without waiting for a reply.

Physically, communication can be achieved in many ways. One way is to use data communication. The hotel system and the account system are in different computers, and a communication link carries the messages. Another way is to use in-memory communication between objects. The hotel system and the account system run in the same computer, and the hotel system has an object that sends messages to an object in the account system. A third way is through file transfer. The hotel system stores the invoice data in a file in a comma-separated form, and calls the operating system asking it to run the account program. In this case, the messages shown on Figure 4.9 are not a correct reflection of what goes on. See section 5.5 on technical interfaces in general.

Notation. The dot, which shows events, is not part of UML, but the author's addition. Sequence diagrams in UML show the messages, but usually only part of the data flow. They don't show the events.

The Sequence diagram uses a special notation to show the life of a component, i.e. an object or actor. Look at the account system component in the lower part of Figure 4.9. Time runs down and the dotted line shows the *lifeline* of the component. The boxes on the lifeline shows when the component is active (busy). Typically it becomes busy when it receives a message, and falls asleep shortly after having sent a reply.

Note that the sender of a synchronous message is busy while he waits for the answer. He cannot reply to other messages sent to him until he has received an answer.

Figure 4.9 shows just two actors, but the notation allows you to show many actors, each with its own lifeline.

Terminology in practice. In object-oriented terminology, objects communicate by sending each other messages. This message concept corresponds closely to the one we used above. However, a synchronous message and its reply message are usually considered one single message. Unfortunately, the terminology is not so clear in practice. Some developers would call the entire account transfer dialog a *single multi-package message*. Other developers might instead call each message an *event*.

Transactions. Sometimes developers use the term transaction, which means a sequence of messages that together achieve a result. All the account transfer messages make up one transaction. Together they complete the transfer of all invoices of the day, involving only one event.

From the product's point of view, each event starts a *transaction*. Two events were involved in the FindRoom dialog and thus we had two transactions from the product's point of view. From the user's point of view, the FindRoom dialog is hardly a transaction. The user wants the entire check-in procedure to be completed before he would call it a transaction. To the user, a transaction serves a domain event, so several product events may be needed for a full user transaction.

From a database viewpoint, a transaction is something else. We want a consistent database. This means that guest data as well as room booking data must go into the database before that transaction is complete. We cannot have a guest without booked rooms or a booked room without a guest.

Timer events. Most events originate in the product surroundings, but sometimes something must be done without an external event saying when to do it.

The transfer of account data is one example of this. It has to be done regularly, but there is no reason why it must be done every midnight; so a requirement saying that it must is arbitrary. Once decided, the product can easily generate a midnight event by means of the computer clock, which can be programmed to send timer events at specified moments or at regular intervals.

As another example, the hotel manager has to draw up a staff roster at regular intervals, for instance once every two weeks. The computer system may remind him to do this, but basically it is his own initiative. He generates the domain event; there is no clock in the domain that drives him to do it at a specific time.

Special events. There are various events that do not occur as part of normal system operation, but are of special importance to requirements. Examples are power failures, disk full, loss of data communication, system initialization, or system re-configuration. For certain kinds of systems it can be important to specify how the product should handle such events. As an example, when creating a process control system for electrical power distribution, a very important feature is that the system should be able to run during a power-cut! This should be stated as a requirement.

Some analysts consider the handling of special events to be part of the quality requirements, e.g. security or availability. Others consider them functional requirements for how to deal with these events. It is not important where they are dealt with as long as they are dealt with somewhere.

Outgoing events. In the product event lists (section 3.3), we only show events arriving to the system. What about outgoing events from the system, i.e. cases where the system takes an initiative? One example is the hotel system asking the accounting system to accept some invoice transactions. Should we list such outgoing events somewhere?

Traditionally, outgoing events are not listed separately in the requirements specification, because it is not part of the requirements to specify how the external system is to handle the events. That belongs to the requirements for the external system. However, if the external system is to be developed at the same time as our product, it is important to specify the outgoing events and how they should be treated in the external product. This part of the requirements would then belong to both products.

The pros and cons of sequence diagrams

Sequence diagrams are widely used and the designer should know about them. They are excellent for discussing and analyzing sequences of events and messages. They correspond closely to use cases where the work is split between human and computer (section 3.12.2), but use a graphical rather than a textual notation.

They can be used as design-level requirements for technical interfaces, and are sometimes useful as design-level requirements for user interfaces, so long as the user interface has a very restricted message sequence.

5

Special interfaces – combined styles

The most important product interface is usually the interactive interface to the user. Most of the discussions in the previous chapter were primarily related to the user interface, although many of the requirement styles could deal with other product interfaces as well. In this section we will look at the other interfaces: reports (usually printed), the platform, and external technical systems.

5.1 Reports

Highlights

Often hundreds of reports.
Specify the clearly necessary reports.
Postpone the rest, but specify the framework for making them.

Reports on screen and paper are a form of one-way communication between product and user. They are usually difficult to specify because there are lots of them in the old system, it is often unclear what purposes they serve, and new report types are needed on demand.

We need several kinds of requirements to cover reports, and it is an interesting exercise to combine the requirement styles in the right way. Figure 5.1 outlines the main types of reports and possible requirements.

External reports. Some stakeholders outside the domain may require reports, for instance checks or pay slips. The reports must satisfy external format requirements. Here is a possible requirement:

R1 The product shall produce pay slips with the layout shown in app. xx. The pay slips should be available on paper as well as in comma-separated files.

This is a typical feature requirement combined with a data requirement (in principle specified as a virtual window).

Specific purposes. Some reports relate to well-defined tasks or other well-defined purposes. Here is an example:

R2 In connection with the monthly roster planning, the system shall print a forecast for room occupation and related staffing, for instance as shown in app. xx. The report shall be available on screen and as a print-out.

As it stands, this is a feature requirement with an example of a solution. However, it might be recast into a Task & Support description (section 3.8). The real requirement would then be to support the planning task described in the left-hand side of that description, while the report requirement would become the right-hand part of the description (as an example of a solution). The advantage of this would be that other solutions might be considered as long as they support the planning task.

Existing reports with vague purposes. Usually the existing system can produce many reports, the purposes of which are unclear. It would be very costly for the customer to specify all these reports, and for the supplier to deliver them all. Costs can be saved here, because many reports are not really needed.

Fig 5.1   Reports

External reports
R1: Product shall produce pay slips with layout as in app. xx.

Specific purpose
R2: Product shall print forecasts of room occupation for monthly roster planning. Format for instance as xx.

Existing reports - vague purpose
R3: Supplier shall provide a list of built-in reports.
R4: Supplier shall develop up to 200 simple reports (like yy) at a price of $_____ per report and up to 50 complex reports (like zz) at a price of $_____ per report.

Reports on demand
R5: Product shall include a report generator. Reports like yy can be developed by:
ordinary user?   yes/no
super user?   yes/no
customer's IT dept?   yes/no

Further, if a COTS-based system is considered, it will most likely have a lot of built-in reports that might be used instead, thus reducing costs. For this reason it is a good idea to decide which reports to develop or modify *after* choosing the supplier. A corresponding requirement could look like this:

R3   As part of the proposal, the supplier shall provide a list of built-in reports together with a sample page for each of them.

R4   The supplier shall develop up to 200 simple reports (similar to report A in app. xx) at a price of $_____ per report, and up to 50 complex reports (similar to report B in app. xx) at a price of $_____ per report.

This is a development process requirement that delays decisions, yet controls the cost. It uses the *open target* approach (section 6.3) where the supplier states what he can offer, both in terms of features (the reports) and in terms of cost (price per report).

Reports on demand. Additional reports may be needed on demand. Usually the supplier offers a report generator, and the crucial point here is how easy it is to use. Here is a corresponding requirement:

R5   The product shall include a report generator, which as far as possible shall be easy to use. If the customer for instance wanted to develop report A in app. xx, could it be done by a typical ordinary user? <u>yes/no</u>

a typical super user? <u>yes/no</u>

the customer's IT department? <u>yes/no</u>

This requirement is partly a feature requirement (the report generator), and partly a usability or maintenance requirement. We assume that the requirements specification gives the profile of typical users somewhere else, otherwise the supplier cannot answer this confidently.

This requirement also uses the open target approach. Can it be verified? Yes, it can, even before the customer decides to deploy the system. However, if we are in a tough contract situation, we should sharpen the requirement and specify the number of test users and the success rate required.

5.2 Platform requirements

Highlights

What the product shall run on, now and in the future.
Dealing with existing and planned platforms.

The *platform* is the combination of hardware and software on which the product must run. The platform comprises hardware, operating system, network system, and sometimes database system and other components. In nearly all cases these components are commercial products.

We have to specify something about the platform on which the product must run, but there are various situations to deal with:

a) We already have a platform.

b) We plan to buy a new platform.

c) We want the platform as part of the product.

Sometimes it is obvious which situation we are in, but at other times it is a strategic decision that should be made before we write the requirements. In some cases the customer wants to delay the decision until he has seen the proposals. Figure 5.2 outlines requirements for the different situations. Let us discuss each of them.

We already have a platform. This is the typical situation for small projects. Requirements could look like this:

R1 The product shall run on Pentium PCs with xx MHz and 128 Mb RAM. Since about 200 older PCs in inventory and production will be used for a few more years, tasks 2.1 to 2.5 must also be supported on 80486 with 64 Mb RAM.

The expression "the product shall run" means that it must fulfill the other requirements when running on the stated platform. This is basically a standards requirement, and it is qualified with reference to task descriptions. Note that we have included the justification for the older platform. This might encourage a potential supplier to suggest more cost-effective solutions than sticking to the old platform.

Here is an example where a specific database platform is required. The justification shows why it is an important requirement.

R2 Since the customer's IT staff have expertise in Oracle, which is used for other applications, the product shall use the same database platform.

The typical way of specifying the software platform on which the system is to run is to specify platform products and release numbers. A special concern is to what

Fig 5.2   Platform requirements

We have a platform

R1: Product shall run on Pentium PCs with 128 MB. Many older PCs still used, so tasks 2.1 to 2.5 must be supported on 80486 with 64 MB.

R2: Our IT staff have expertice in Oracle. Product must use same database platform.

R3: Product shall run on MS Windows release xx.yy. Supplier shall for 3 years port his product to new releases within ___ months from release date.

We want a new platform anyway

R4: Customer expects to switch to client-server running OS zz. Supplier shall specify server memory and server speed needed to obtain capacity and response time for Rxx.

We want software and hardware (maybe)

R5: Supplier shall deliver hardware + software. Supplier shall upgrade if capacity becomes inadequate for the load specified in xx.

R6: Product shall run on Pentium PCs with 128 MB. As an option, total delivery may include the PC's and hardware support.

---

extent the supplier is obliged to update the product for future platform releases. This might be dealt with as follows.

R3   The product shall run under MS Windows release x–y. The supplier shall, for a period of three years, port the product to new Windows releases within ____ months from the release date.

This is a combination of a standards requirement and a maintenance requirement. Unfortunately the maintenance requirement is not verifiable at delivery time. The customer has to look into the supplier's financial situation and track record to assess to what extent he is able to fulfill the requirement.

We want a new platform anyway. This is the typical situation when major changes in IT strategy are involved. The customer wants a new platform for strategic reasons, but he realizes that the new software product may put demands on that platform. A requirement could look like this:

R4   The customer expects to replace his mainframe with a client-server system running Operating System zz. The supplier shall specify the server memory and server speed needed to obtain the capacity and response time specified in requirement xx.

In general the platform requirements are closely related to speed and capacity requirements (sections 6.4 and 6.5). If we for instance require a certain response time, the supplier must know the platform speed and memory size available – or he must specify the assumptions he has made.

We want software and hardware. This is a typical situation if we want a dedicated system for one specific purpose, or if we want a multipurpose system where the supplier also takes care of maintenance and support. Here is an example where the supplier has to take responsibility for response time, etc. of the entire system including the hardware.

R5 The supplier shall deliver the necessary hardware as well as software. If in future the system load increases to the specified maximum, but the delivered configuration cannot provide the specified speed, the supplier is obliged to upgrade the hardware at no cost to the customer.

In principle, the clause "if in future the system load increases to the specified maximum" is unnecessary, because the speed is specified for that load. However, disputes often arise when the system initially works adequately but later performs badly when the load grows towards the maximum. Who is to pay for an upgrade? The requirement above sets this out clearly.

Often the requirements document or the contract has a list of deliverables, and the above requirement might appear there rather than among the functional requirements.

We want software and maybe hardware. Sometimes the customer has not made up his mind. Would he like a combined software/hardware solution or not? Maybe he can get a better deal if the two are combined, maybe he cannot. The solution is to specify the hardware as an option, and decide later:

R6 The client part of the product shall run on Pentium PCs with 128 Mb RAM. As an option, the total delivery may include the necessary PCs and hardware support.

5.3 Product integration – non-technical customers

Highlights

Find someone else to integrate the products.
Specify the user tasks to be supported, or specify the desired commercial products.

In this section we will assume that the customer has little IT skills. The customer might be a user organization such as a hotel, an insurance company department, a government department, or a small factory.

The customer's new product may have to communicate with other hardware and/or software components. We call these components *external products*. The hotel system, for instance, has two external products: the account system and the telephone system. In other applications the customer may want his new product to communicate with external products such as electronic sensors and actuators, front-end computers controlling various devices, remote computers controlled over a standard network, etc. In some cases he has chosen these external products already, in other cases the choice is part of the project. The elevator management system in section 1.5 is an example of this, because it has to communicate with several types of computerized elevator control systems.

Who integrates the products?

From the customer's point of view the situation is complex. Essentially he wants to integrate two or more products. Should he specify requirements for each of them? And what should the requirements say about the other product? Or should he just ask one of the suppliers to take care of it all?

The crucial point turns out to be the integration responsibility. Who is responsible for the adjustments and settings that ensure that the products work together as intended? Figure 5.3A outlines the possibilities. Let us look at the details:

a) The customer might be responsible for the integration. This should be avoided if at all possible. Even simple cases such as integrating the hotel system with the account system can cause endless problems for non-specialists.

b) The customer's IT department might be responsible for the integration. This is fine if they have the necessary technical expertise, but the customer should still make sure that his overall requirements are fulfilled. He should regard the IT department as his main contractor and supplier.

Fig 5.3A Who can integrate?

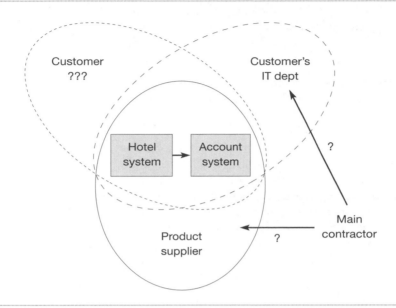

c) An external supplier might be responsible for the integration. This is usually the best choice. The supplier may have a product of his own and he may be used to integrating it with external products. The hotel system supplier is an example; he may integrate his product with the account system. Some suppliers don't have products of their own but are neutral software houses specializing in developing special "glue code" that integrates several products. In all of these cases, the external supplier is a main contractor.

In conclusion, the customer should not do the integration himself, but select a main contractor. The main contractor may be his own IT department or an external supplier.

In his requirements, the customer should primarily care about requirements for the total system. He shouldn't care about which external products are used, but in practice he often does because he may use the external product for other purposes too. In the hotel, for instance, the customer uses the account system for many other purposes than keeping track of guest payments. He may for many reasons favor a particular account system.

We will now look at various ways to specify requirements for integrated products.

Supporting the user's tasks

Let us first look at the requirements from a domain point of view. Figure 5.3B shows a Task & Support description for the combined hotel system and account system. The left-hand column shows what the two systems and the accountant have to do together. On this level we have not split the work between these three parties.

Note that there is a problem of ensuring that everything is posted only once. Also note that some accounting offices actually cover several hotels. The requirement could be:

R1 The product shall support task 5.1, daily accounting.

The right-hand column shows possible solutions. They assume that we have split the work between the hotel system and the accounting system. Obviously we think of an automatic transfer of invoice information, and we also prefer to continue using our existing WonderAccount. Further, we have suggested a way to avoid duplicate or missing transfers. These possible solutions are not requirements, however. We might consider other solutions that support the left-hand side. (In fact, our suggested solution is naive. A more auditor-oriented solution would insist on an audit trail, so that it is always possible to trace a guest invoice to transactions on the accounts, and vice versa. For the sake of simplicity, we ignore this here.)

The solution obviously assumes that the supplier either integrates the two products or delivers a total system. In practice, however, the customer may for various reasons insist on using his present accounting system, or he may insist on using another popular commercial accounting system. Also, if the customer has to use the account system for general financial accounting, we should specify many further requirements about that. In connection with the hotel system acquisition, it would be futile also to specify details of the accounting system.

To handle these situations, we will look at other types of requirements where we specify features or constraints for the integration. Figure 5.3C gives an overview. The Task & Support description may still be a valuable explanation of why we want the features, but it is no longer the requirement.

Integrating with a commercial product

Let us first assume that the customer wants the hotel system to integrate with his existing commercial accounting system. The requirement could be this:

R2 The customer is using WonderAccount *xx* for his financial accounting. The hotel system must ensure that today's invoice transactions are transferred automatically to WonderAccount within the next day. Each transaction must be transferred once and only once.

In this case the hotel system supplier seems to be the integrator, but we might express this explicitly. The requirement is a combination of a standards requirement and a feature requirement, with special concern for unusual events where the

Fig 5.3B Integration requirements, domain-level

R1: The product shall support task 5.1.

Task:	5.1 Daily accounting
Purpose:	Balance with bank account . . .
	Send out invoices to company customers
Frequency:	Daily

Sub-tasks:	Example solution:
1. Get guest invoices	Automatic transfer from hotel system to Wonder-Account xx.yy.
2. Post on accounts	Account numbers defined in a database table.
Problem: Same posted twice or forgotten.	Unbroken sequence of numbers.
3. Send invoices . . .	
Variants:	
1a. We have several hotels and want shared accounting.	Data transmission

communication between the two products fails and causes the hotel system to lose transactions or duplicate them through retransmission.

Integrating with a new commercial product

Another situation arises when the customer wants several new products at once, and he wants to integrate them. Here are two requirements for that:

R3 The customer is considering the purchase of a new system for financial accounting. The hotel system supplier shall list the accounting systems with which his system can integrate. For each accounting system he shall specify the extent to which the solution guarantees that all accounting transactions are transferred to the accounting system once and only once.

R4 The supplier shall integrate his system with the accounting system chosen by the customer, and specify the detailed communication between the products.

Note the additional requirement about specifying the communication in detail. This might later help the customer replace or extend one of the products.

Consortium model: delivering an integrated product

Another solution is to ask a supplier to deliver both products, properly integrated:

R5 The supplier shall deliver the hotel system as well as the accounting system. The accounting system shall provide standard facilities for financial accounting and be integrated with the hotel system.

This kind of requirement is suited for a tender process according to the consortium model, where suppliers are invited to form a consortium that together deliver the integrated product.

The consortium might reduce to a single supplier. He might for instance be the developer of the hotel system, integrating it with a commercial accounting system; or he might be the developer of the accounting system, integrating it with a hotel system. He might also develop the entire combination himself; or he may develop only the 'glue' that combines an existing hotel system and an existing account system.

The main problem with R5 is whether "standard facilities" is a sufficient specification of the accounting system. To guard himself, the customer would have to specify detailed requirements to the accounting system – a futile exercise in this case. In contrast, R3 and R4 allow him to choose the proper accounting system based on informal criteria, recommendations from colleagues, and so on.

The consortium model is the best solution in large systems where many products have to be integrated. An example could be the integration of workflow (keeping track of electronic document flows in a large organization), document handling (scanning and storing massive amounts of paper and electronic documents), and production planning.

When such projects are sent out for tender, we sometimes see the same supplier participating in several consortiums that are competing for the same contract. As an example, supplier D has a document-handling product that includes some workflow management. He may enter into a consortium with W, who has a more ambitious work flow system but no document-handling experience, and P who has a production planning system that interfaces with W's product.

At the same time D may enter into a competing consortium with Q, who has an excellent production planning system. If they get the contract, they will jointly develop an improved workflow management system specially tailored for the kind of production made by the customer.

Fig 5.3C Integration requirements, product-level

We have a commercial product
R2: Customer uses WonderAccount xx.yy. Hotel system shall ensure transfer within next day. Shall transfer . . . once and only once.

We want a new commercial product
R3: Customer wants new account system. Supplier shall specify the systems he integrates with and the degree of transfer reliability.

R4: Supplier shall specify the detailed interface for the chosen account system.

Consortium model
R5: Supplier shall deliver hotel system plus account system. Account system shall provide standard account facilities.

We have a tailor-made system
R6: Customer uses old mainframe system YY for accounting. Hotel system must ensure daily transfers, once and only once.

Let the supplier study YY documentation?
Document the interface?
Let YY developer be main contractor?

Integrating with an existing tailor-made system

When the new product must integrate with the customer's existing system, and that system is a proprietary product, we have a different situation. The existing system could be a legacy system that few people really understand, or a system developed by a third party software house.

Let us assume that the hotel has an old, proprietary accounting system and want the new hotel system to integrate with it. From the customer's point of view the situation is simple. His requirement could be similar to R2, where the accounting system was a commercial one:

R6 The customer is using system *yy* for his financial accounting. *yy* is a tailor-made mainframe system. The hotel system must ensure that today's invoice transactions are transferred to *yy* within the next day. It must be ensured that each transaction is transferred once and only once.

However, the situation is difficult for the supplier because he needs to know how he can interface with system *yy*. In the other cases above, he was asked to interface with a commercial system, and he either knew how to do it or could find out.

So for R6 to be feasible, the customer has to tell the supplier more about system *yy*. How could the customer deal with that?

Co-operate with the supplier. Give the supplier whatever documentation is available and let him explore system *yy*. When he has found a solution, he can quote a price and commit to requirement R6. This is a good approach, but the customer will usually have to pay the supplier for finding a feasible solution before he knows whether he can deliver the solution. The approach is inadequate for a tender process.

Describe the technical interface. If the customer wants a tender process, he might describe the existing product, the platform it runs on, and possible technical interfaces to it (see section 5.5). Based on that description, the supplier may offer a solution. However, the customer may not have the technical expertise or the necessary documentation to do this. Further, he may spend time describing many possibilities, yet fail to describe the crucial one that allows a simple solution from the supplier's point of view.

It might help to let the developer of system *yy* describe the possible interfaces. The developer could be the customer's IT department or the software house that developed system *yy*. They should have the best knowledge available.

Note that if the customer had used a requirement like R4 above when he acquired system *yy*, his situation would have been much easier.

Use *yy* as a main contractor. Let the developer of system *yy* handle the project as a main contractor. R6 is then an adequate requirement from the customer's point of view. The rest is simply design work, for instance carried out jointly by the supplier of the new system and the developer of the *yy* program, who can, as a team, find a good solution. They describe the solution in a design document – the chosen technical interface.

Unfortunately, this approach often fails because the *yy* developer sees the integration as a threat to his own position. Once again, the customer could have prevented this problem if he had got descriptions of the technical interfaces at the time he acquired *yy*.

5.4 Product integration – main contractor

Highlights

Product integration is a main contractor's job.
Technical interfaces are a design issue.
Divide total product into sub-products, using what is available.

In this section we will look at the integration process from the main contractor's point of view. The main contractor may be hired to help a customer integrate some products in an ad hoc manner, or he may develop a new product of his own that builds on other products. The ad hoc integration is simpler than the product development situation, so in this section we will focus on the main contractor who develops a new product.

Product developers use integration with third party products more and more, because third party products can offer increasingly complex and intelligent services. Instead of trying to develop such services as part of their own products, developers try to integrate with third party products.

The main contractor will naturally have the responsibility for the integration. As part of development, he will write requirements together with each sub-contractor. These requirements will specify the technical interfaces between the products, plus all the other types of requirements.

The main contractor himself must fulfill requirements for the total product that he develops. In this respect he is the supplier who tries to satisfy the customer's demands or the demands of the market. To these customers, some sub-products are fully embedded in the main contractor's product and the customers don't see them as separate products. In the hotel system, the database system is an example of this. Other sub-products are visible to the customer, and he may use them for additional purposes independently of the main contractor's product. The hotel system with an integrated accounting system is an example where the customer has additional criteria for selecting the right accounting system, and indirectly this influences his choice of the hotel system. Figure 5.4 illustrates the situation.

The main contractor's job is not simply to write requirements and carry out the integration. His job is very much a high-level *design* job. Essentially he has to divide the total product into sub-products, taking into account existing products, to what extent they are adequate, who is willing to modify their own product and contribute their expertise, etc. It is a question of finding the optimal split of functionality so that the cost is low and the market value high.

Fig 5.4 Main contractor

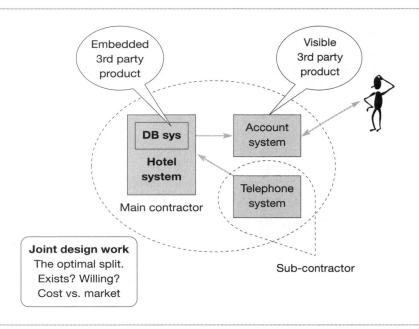

5.5   Technical interfaces

Highlights

Many ways to specify the technical interface.
Prototype and test the communication early.

The technical interface between a product and an external product is always one or more communication channels, and there are many types of channels. From a theoretical point of view, the communication can always be described as messages with associated data sent between the products. To specify the detailed interface, we need several things:

■   **The physical channel:** how is data communicated? As data transmission, inter-object calls, snail-mail or something else?

■   **The messages:** how is the message identity or the event communicated, and which data formats are involved?

■   **The protocol:** what are the possible message sequences, error recovery, etc.?

■   **The semantics:** what do they communicate about?

Examples of channels

A communication channel may take many forms. Here are a few examples:

File transfer. Example: the hotel accounting system. The external product is a separate program that runs in the same computer or remotely. Our product writes data into a local or remote file. In principle, the file holds the data of a single message, which however may comprise data for several user transactions. The user may ask the external product to look at the file at suitable times, so our product doesn't generate an event to trigger the external product, or our product may generate a *run* event after writing the file, for instance by starting the external program through the operating system.

Object calls. Example: a 3D graphics package. The external product is a package of objects (classes) residing in the same computer and called by our product. The messages are the calls and the message identity is the operation (method) called. The data of the message is contained in call parameters. Usually, the two products are bound (linked) together during program installation or during program start-up. Some platforms support object calls to remote objects that are bound dynamically at run time.

Fig 5.5   Technical interfaces

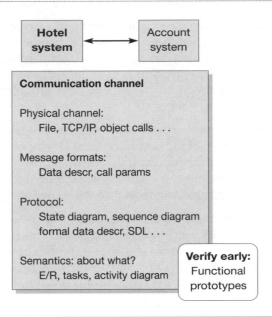

Network communication. Example: remote process control. The external product resides in another node on the network. Our product and the external product communicate by messages sent over the network. The messages contain a tag (a special field) that gives the identity of the message, and other fields that contain the data of the message.

Channel descriptions

We have to specify the physical channel, the messages, the protocol, and the semantics. How can we do that? Figure 5.5 outlines the possibilities. Here are the details:

Physical channel. The physical channel is specified as the platform on which it all runs, or as a communication standard. For telecommunications, for instance, the specification might state that communication is done with TCP/IP, which is a standard for the transmission of data packages. However, this doesn't say anything about what the packages contain. The examples above, file transfer, object calls, and network communication, all use different physical channels. The channel is often given implicitly from the context.

Messages. We can use various types of data descriptions to describe the contents of the messages, for instance data expressions (section 2.4), data dictionaries (section 2.3), or object operations with parameters. In most cases a data dictionary is necessary to explain the message contents and relate it to domain concepts.

Protocol. The protocol is the most complex part of the interface. Essentially it has to describe all legal message sequences and how to handle error situations. Some suitable techniques are state diagrams (4.4), state-transition matrices (4.5), sequence diagrams (4.9), collaboration diagrams (4.8), and use cases (3.12.2). Data expressions may also be used (section 2.4), since they are able to describe the allowed sequences of data or messages.

Many special notations exist for describing protocols. The telecommunications industry, for instance, uses SDL (Specification and Description Language) to specify protocols and data in a standard form (Ellsberger *et al*. 1997). SDL has a dual notation: a graphical notation and a corresponding formal text description. SDL is suited to many other technical interfaces than those used in telecommunications.

Semantics. It is hard to understand message descriptions and protocols unless you know what the two parties are communicating about. This means that you have to know something about the domains in both ends of the channel. There is little tradition for how to do that, but since this book discusses the requirements world, we have a good suggestion: use the various domain descriptions, for instance:

- Data models. They can define which entities the parties talk about, and help the reader understand the various addresses and identifiers communicated in the messages.

- Task descriptions or essential use cases. They can describe what the users or the domain in general do at each end of the channel.

- Dataflow diagrams or activity descriptions (or the SDL equivalents). They can provide an overview of how several products and systems communicate.

The requirements. The "hard" requirements in a technical interface description will usually be the message formats, the protocol, and sometimes the physical channel. The semantics are background information to help the reader. The hard requirements are crucial when two independent organizations develop separate parts of the whole. If they misunderstand the specification, they may end up with sub-products that cannot communicate or cannot achieve the overall purpose.

To avoid such costly mistakes, close co-operation with joint requirements management and joint configuration management is needed during the project. Early functional prototypes of the central parts of the communication are very useful too, and may prevent many misunderstandings.

6

Quality requirements

The quality requirements specify how well the system must perform its functions. How fast must it respond? How easy must it be to use? How secure does it have to be against attacks? How easy should it be to maintain?

Quality requirements are also called *non-functional requirements* to contrast them against functional requirements. However, the term "non-functional" gives many people the impression that these requirements don't "function" and are unimportant. This impression is wrong, so we prefer the term "quality requirements".

In most requirements specifications the functional requirements take up most of the space, while little is stated about the quality requirements.

Many requirements engineers recognize that quality requirements are very important, but they don't know how to specify them, and little help is available in the literature. In this chapter we will discuss various quality requirements, particularly the different styles in which we can specify them.

Many quality requirements are not only software requirements, but requirements for the entire system. Response time, for instance, depends on hardware as well as software. Security depends on hardware, software, people-ware (for instance, management), and physical factors such as building construction.

Some quality requirements are mandatory in the same sense as functional requirements. For instance this is the case with response time requirements in process control and other technical systems. If the system has to close a valve within 0.13 seconds to avoid some critical consequences, it has to do so. Being even a fraction slower would make the system useless.

However, many quality requirements are not mandatory in the same sense. For instance, if we ask for a system response time of 2 seconds to update the customer screen, but the system needs 4 seconds to do it, the customer may still use the system – although at a higher cost. In section 6.3 we will show ways to deal with this issue of soft targets.

The basic difference between the mandatory response times in technical systems and the softer requirements for the user interaction, is that the physical world doesn't wait for the system, while users may do so.

Some authors are more pessimistic about the importance of the soft quality factors. As an example, Spool (1997) reports that the weight between functional requirements and soft quality requirements changes as the market develops. Initially, the functional requirements dominate (the feature competition), and only when the players on the market offer roughly the same features, will customers start looking for the soft qualities.

6.1 Quality factors

Highlights

Many lists of quality factors.
Use them as checklists.
Add your own in light of your own experience.

How many kinds of quality dimensions can we distinguish? Many authors and standardization bodies have suggested answers to this question. Figure 6.1 compares two lists of quality factors. The one to the left is my favorite (McCall and Matsumoto), and it is the basis for this book. Below we will explain this list and later compare it with other lists.

McCall and Matsumoto

The first good attempt at defining a list of quality factors was made by McCall and Matsumoto (1980) at the US Airforce. The list is a two-level taxonomy. At the top level, they distinguish between three major uses of software:

Operation: Daily use by end users.

Revision: Maintenance and extension of the software.

Transition: Use of the software in new technical surroundings.

On the next level, we find these quality factors:

Operation

Integrity: How well the system handles physical disturbances and prevents malicious access attempts, etc. (Today *security* would be a better term.)

Correctness: How many errors there are in the system.

Reliability: How frequently the system malfunctions (MTBF, Mean Time Between Failures) and the percentage of time it is available (availability, e.g. 99%).

Usability: How easy it is to learn the system, how efficient it is for carrying out day to day tasks, etc.

Efficiency: How fast the system responds, how many resources it uses, how accurately it computes values, etc. (*Performance* is another term for this.)

Revision

Maintainability: How easy it is to locate and repair errors.

Fig 6.1   Quality factors

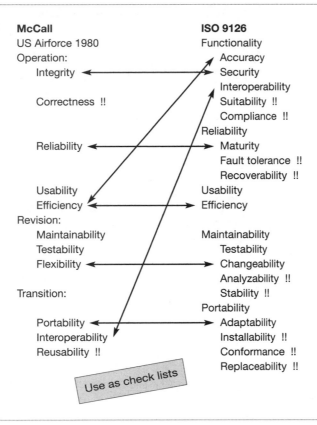

McCall
US Airforce 1980
Operation:
    Integrity
    Correctness !!
    Reliability
    Usability
    Efficiency
Revision:
    Maintainability
    Testability
    Flexibility
Transition:
    Portability
    Interoperability
    Reusability !!

ISO 9126
Functionality
    Accuracy
    Security
    Interoperability
    Suitability !!
    Compliance !!
Reliability
    Maturity
    Fault tolerance !!
    Recoverability !!
Usability
Efficiency
Maintainability
    Testability
    Changeability
    Analyzability !!
    Stability !!
Portability
    Adaptability
    Installability !!
    Conformance !!
    Replaceability !!

Use as check lists

Testability: How easy it is to test the system after a change.

Flexibility: How easy it is to expand the system with new features.

Transition

Portability: How easy it is to move the system to a new software or hardware platform.

Interoperability: How easy it is for the system to cooperate with other systems, e.g. file transfer to spreadsheets, attachment of new hardware units.

Reusability: How easy it is to reuse parts of the software in other systems.

The authors also suggested ideal ways of measuring these quality factors. Flexibility, for instance, could be measured as the *average time it takes to expand the system with a new feature*. The authors recognized, however, that such measurements were unrealistic since it was impossible to define an average feature. Using such measures as targets during development seemed elusive too. In other cases, verifiable measures were easy to define, for instance response time.

ISO 9126

The ideas behind their approach were well received, and soon many other attempts appeared. Committees were set up to define standards, etc. The right-hand side of Figure 6.1 shows the standard ISO 9126, 1991. Exclamation marks show where one of the taxonomies contains something that the other taxonomy doesn't mention explicitly. The arrows show quality factors that appear in both taxonomies, but with different names or positions.

On the top level, ISO 9126 has six quality factors:

Functionality: This is slightly confusing since quality factors are supposed to be non-functional. Several items from the McCall list are included here: security, part of efficiency (accuracy), and interoperability. Presumably the committee believed that these quality factors were better expressed as functional requirements.

Reliability: Similar to McCall's reliability, but also covers fault tolerance and ability to recover from faults.

Usability: Similar to McCall.

Efficiency: Similar to McCall, but accuracy is moved to functionality.

Maintainability: Similar to McCall but includes factors that McCall had listed as separate issues. Makes it more explicit that time to locate an error and avoidance of introducing new errors are important (*analyzability* and *stability*).

Portability: Similar to McCall, but covers some more issues.

ISO 9126 doesn't have an official second level in the taxonomy, but an "informative" appendix with suggested sub-characteristics (those shown on the figure). Without this informative appendix, the top-level factors would be abstract and hard to understand.

Several quality factors have been given new names as shown on the figure. We have already mentioned *integrity versus security*. Further, McCall's *reliability* is more like *maturity* in ISO 9126. The same applies to *flexibility* versus *changeability*, and *portability* versus *adaptability*.

More surprising is that two factors on the McCall list have dropped out: *correctness* (number of errors) and *reusability* (ability to reuse parts of the software).

Several new things have turned up in the ISO 9126 informative appendix:

Suitability: Whether the system adequately supports the user tasks.

Compliance and Conformance: How well the system fulfills domain standards and technical standards.

New sub-factors: *Reliability*, *maintainability*, and *portability* have got new sub-factors on the informative list.

IEEE 830

The IEEE Guide to software requirements specifications (IEEE 830) also mentions quality factors but uses slightly different terms:

Performance requirements correspond to efficiency requirements in the two other taxonomies. IEEE 830 distinguishes between static numerical requirements (capacity requirements) and dynamic numerical requirements (response time, etc.).

Software system attributes correspond to some of the other quality factors. The name indicates that it is an attribute of the entire system, not any particular feature in it. IEEE 830 mentions the following attributes or quality factors:

Reliability: Not really explained, but might correspond to McCall's correctness.

Availability: Corresponds to reliability in ISO 9126, which also includes reliability according to McCall.

Security: Corresponds to Security in ISO 9126 or Integrity in McCall.

Maintainability: Similar to the concepts in McCall and ISO 9126.

Portability: Corresponds to Portability in McCall and Adaptability in ISO 9126.

Ease of use: Mentioned in a parenthesis in IEEE 830 under the heading *User Interfaces*. Corresponds to usability in McCall and ISO 9126.

Which list should you use?

There are many other lists of quality factors, more or less standard, so which one should you use? The answer is simple: None of them gives the full truth, but you can use them as checklists for what to consider. Ask yourself which factors are important in the product you deal with. Then specify something about those. We show an example in the next section.

When I worked as a quality assurance manager, we started with the McCall factors and added more factors to our checklist in light of project experience. For instance we had experienced that installation could be an issue, so we added an installability factor. (This was in the days before ISO 9126, which later included the same factor.)

In some projects, you have to follow a company standard, but even in these cases, consult other lists of quality factors to identify important or risky areas.

The rest of the chapter shows ways to specify requirements for some of the quality factors. We cover the McCall factors as follows:

Operation:
Integrity: Section 6.8 and 6.9
Correctness. Not covered.

Reliability. Some aspects in section 6.8 and 6.9
Usability. Section 6.6 and 6.7
Efficiency. Section 6.4 and 6.5

Revision:
Maintainability. Section 6.10 and 6.11
Testability. Some aspects in section 6.10 and 6.11
Flexibility. Section 6.10 and 6.11

Transition:
Portability. Not covered.
Interoperability. Not covered.
Reusability. Not covered.

6.2   The quality grid

Highlights

Look at all factors on your list.
Assess importance for each of them.
Specify requirements for the important ones only.

In most projects some quality factors are important, while others are unimportant. The essential point is to consider all the factors and consciously assess their degree of importance. For the important factors, we have to specify the quality in more detail. Figure 6.2 shows a *quality grid* that helps you find the important factors in a systematic way. The technique was developed by Jens Brix Christiansen and the author when we worked with software quality assurance. It has been used successfully in many projects.

Select the factors. The grid on the figure has a row for each of the quality factors on our checklist. In the example, the project team started as usual with the McCall and Matsumoto factors. Next they looked at the ISO 9126 factors and noticed that *installability* was a concern in this project, and added a line about that.

Assess importance. For each factor the team now assessed how important it was for the product. The scale on the figure is intended for suppliers and shows the importance relative to what the developers usually do. If you represent a customer, interpret the headings as the importance relative to what suppliers usually deliver.

As shown on the figure, the development team identified four important or critical factors: reliability/availability, usability, interoperability, and installability. Notice that there are two opinions on interoperability: critical and unimportant. This is common and usually reflects opinions about different parts of the system.

Specify concerns. For the important or critical factors, the team wrote down the concern behind the priority, as outlined on the figure. You see some very good business arguments for the high-priority factors. Note also how the two opinions on interoperability have been resolved.

The concerns are not yet requirements, but goals to be translated into requirements at a later date.

Be balanced! When we initially introduced the technique, developers tended to give all factors a high priority. They really wanted to do a good job, but Jens asked them: Do you get more funding than usual in this project? No, they answered. So what makes you believe you can improve all factors? You have to give some factors lower priority than usual *or* get more funding.

Developers were quite surprised to hear this viewpoint from quality assurance. Usually quality assurance people want developers to achieve perfect quality everywhere, but they saw the point and learned to balance their priorities.

Fig 6.2 Quality grid

Quality factors for hotel system

	Critical	Important	As usual	Unimportant	Ignore
Operation					
Integrity/security			X		
Correctness			X		
Reliability/availability		1			
Usability		2			
Efficiency			X		
Revision					
Maintainability			X		
Testability			X		
Flexibility			X		
Transition					
Portability					X
Interoperability	3			4	
Reusability					X
Installability		5			

Concerns:

1. Hard to run the hotel if system is down. Checking in guests is impossible since room status is not visible.
2. We aim at small hotels too. They have less qualified staff.
3. Customers have many kinds of account systems. They prioritize smooth integration with what they have.
4. Integration with spreadsheet, etc. unimportant. Built-in statistics suffice.
5. Must be much easier than present system. Staff in small hotels should ideally do it themselves.

Later, quality assurance learned to be more balanced too. The wisdom today is:

You can improve quality by:

- working harder,
- getting more funding,
- ignoring unimportant things,
- using a better technique.

Sometimes we actually see techniques that improve quality *and* reduce the hard work. Usability techniques is an example where the early design and test of the user interface reduces programming efforts and improves customer satisfaction (see 6.6).

6.3 Open metric and open target

Highlights

Often hard to select a metric for measuring quality.
Even harder to decide the value needed.
Solution: Leave it to the supplier to specify it.

A quality requirement will often have a numerical target to reach. Figure 6.3A shows a simple example from a speed trap system where speed violators are photographed for identification:

R1 The product shall detect a speed violation and take a photo within 0.5 seconds.

The target of 0.5 seconds has a physical explanation. If the trap system doesn't take the photo within that time, the violator will have disappeared from the camera view. Furthermore, a faster system has no extra advantage.

In many cases, however, there is not a similar justification for the target value. Consider the next example in Figure 6.3A:

R2 The product shall compute and show a forecast for room occupation within two minutes.

This requirement specifies the target "two minutes" for the response time. It is easy to specify such a target, but from where do we get it? What would happen if we wrote four minutes? And why not ask for one minute?

This is a typical case where the quality requirement is not really mandatory. Assume that nobody could guarantee a response time of two minutes (at a reasonable cost), but four minutes were available. In this case, the customer would probably accept the four minutes.

The customer might even choose a system with a four-minute response time, even though one with two minutes was available. This could happen if the four-minute system was superior in other respects.

Apparently, the customer can live with the higher limit, so why did he specify a low one? All right, he should specify four minutes, as in R3 on the figure. Unfortunately, this means that the supplier will not try to make an effort to get down to two minutes, so the customer gets a worse system. Furthermore, if the customer specified four minutes, by the same argument he might still accept a higher limit if necessary.

Open target One way out is to ask the supplier to specify what response time he can provide, as shown in R4. We call this the *open target* approach.

Fig 6.3A Open metric and open target

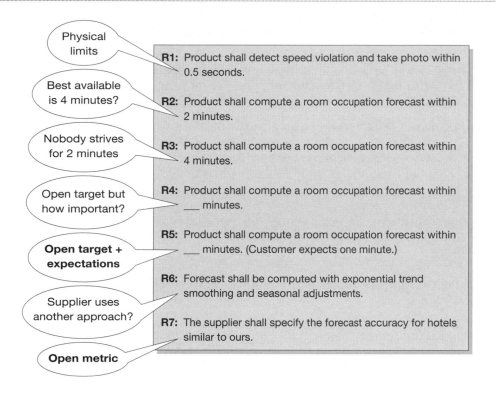

R1: Product shall detect speed violation and take photo within 0.5 seconds. — *Physical limits*

R2: Product shall compute a room occupation forecast within 2 minutes. — *Best available is 4 minutes?*

R3: Product shall compute a room occupation forecast within 4 minutes. — *Nobody strives for 2 minutes*

R4: Product shall compute a room occupation forecast within ___ minutes. — *Open target but how important?*

R5: Product shall compute a room occupation forecast within ___ minutes. (Customer expects one minute.) — **Open target + expectations**

R6: Forecast shall be computed with exponential trend smoothing and seasonal adjustments. — *Supplier uses another approach?*

R7: The supplier shall specify the forecast accuracy for hotels similar to ours. — **Open metric**

There is a problem with that. The supplier has no idea how important the response time is. Some suppliers may suggest a very expensive solution to provide a short response time, others may suggest a cheap solution with a response time they consider adequate.

How do we handle that? We see good results with the approach shown in R5. The customer specifies his expectations and asks the supplier to specify what he can offer. In a contract situation, this will usually start a discussion of what is feasible. In a tender situation, the customer may compare several proposals and select the "best" according to an overall evaluation. Skilled suppliers may even include options with separate prices in their proposal, for instance an option with a fast response time and one with a slow response time.

Open metric In some cases the customer may not even know how to measure the quality of the system. He hasn't defined the metric to be used. R6 and R7 on Figure 6.3A shows an example of this.

In R6 the customer (or his advisor) has specified the algorithm to be used for the forecast. This is clearly a design-level requirement, and it may be adequate in some situations, for instance if we ask for a tailor-made system and we know that the algorithm solves the problem. However, what *is* the problem?

The customer basically wants a solution that gives a good forecast, but as a typical hotel owner, he doesn't know how to measure it. So why not ask the supplier about that too? Most likely the supplier has more experience with forecasts than the hotel owner.

Requirement R7 shows a simple way to do this. We call this the *open metric* approach. The customer will now study the specifications delivered by the suppliers and subjectively assess what is best when all requirements are taken into consideration.

Planguage

Tom Gilb has developed a language and notation for discussing quality factors (Planguage; Gilb 2001). His approach uses these concepts:

Tag. The factor we talk about, e.g. forecast speed.

Gist. What we are after in broad terms, e.g. how quickly the system completes a forecast report.

Scale. The measurement scale, e.g. the average number of seconds from the user pushing the button to the report appears on the screen.

Meter. How we measure this in practice, e.g. measured 10 times by a stopwatch during busy hours in a hotel reception.

Must. The absolutely crucial level (for instance 8 minutes because the competitive system does it this fast). In principle, the customer would reject the system if this level is not reached.

Plan. The level where we can claim success, e.g. 4 minutes for the report. The plan figure is usually what the supplier promises.

Wish. What the user expects, e.g. 2 minutes.

Past. What the old system did, e.g. a batch job taking about an hour.

Figure 6.3B shows how the room occupation forecast could have been written in Planguage. Notice how a lot of the discussion about the open target and the customer's expectations are captured in Planguage. Our concept of *Metric* corresponds to the Planguage concept of *Scale* combined with *Meter*. Our concept of *Open target* is not mentioned in Planguage, but corresponds to leaving the *Plan* value open for the supplier to fill in.

Experts disagree about the advantage of Planguage. As far as I can see, it is a good terminology for discussing quality requirements, particularly for in-house projects or product development. However, for contracts or tender projects, it may raise doubts about the actual requirements.

Fig 6.3B Planguage version of target, etc.

Forecast speed [Tag]: How quickly the system completes a forecast report [Gist]

Scale: Average number of seconds from pushing button, to report appearing.

Meter: Measured 10 times by a stopwatch during busy hours in hotel reception.

Must: 8 minutes, because the competitive system does it this fast.

Plan: ____ (supplier, please specify).

Wish: 2 minutes.

Past: Done as batch job taking about an hour.

Cost/benefit of quality

Let us return to the simple issue of response times. In principle, the proper response time is a matter of cost versus benefit:

Cost. If the response time has to decrease, the system will be more expensive. Typically the customer has to buy more expensive hardware.

Benefit. If the response time decreases, the system will save more money because users can work faster.

Figure 6.3C outlines how cost and benefit decrease with increasing response time. If the response time for instance has to go from 4 minutes to 2 minutes, the computer cost might double. The benefit will typically be saved user time because the users don't have to wait that long. As the response time increases, the benefit will decrease linearly as shown on the figure.

The figure also shows benefit divided by cost. This curve has a maximum where we get most value for money. In the example, the optimal response time is around 2.5 minutes.

In the forecast example, the saved user time is small because the forecast function is used rarely, around once a week. This means that the benefit line tilts very little and the top of the benefit/cost curve is far to the right. In that case, reducing the response time from 4 to 2 minutes would only increase the cost and hardly increase the benefit.

Be warned that the curves on Figure 6.3C are very idealistic. In practice it may be hard to determine the financial figures necessary to draw the curve. Furthermore, the curves don't decrease smoothly. For instance, the saved time varies differently than shown. When a typical user has waited about 20 seconds for a report, he doesn't wait any longer, but starts doing something else. This causes a sudden loss of time due to task switching, for some jobs in the range of 5 to 20 minutes. After that, an increased response time wastes little more user time because the user is busy doing other things. However, other losses may occur, for instance lost business opportunities in the case of very long delays.

The cost curve may also be very different. Figure 6.3C assumes that response time only depends on hardware speed. In practice, clever programmers may sometimes reduce response times by factors of hundred – without changing the hardware at all. In the database area, for instance, proper use of indexes can often achieve such effects.

Response time is a simple quality factor. For other quality factors, the picture my be much more complex and it may be hard to find a good metric for the quality.

Finding the optimal balance for a huge number of interacting factors is impossible in practice. Decision makers have to use more pragmatic approaches, such as open target or open metric.

Fig 6.3C Cost/benefit of response time

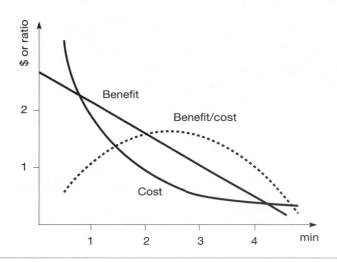

6.4 Capacity and accuracy requirements

Highlights

The simplest quality factor.
Specify worst case data volumes, accuracy, etc.
Trivial, but often forgotten.

Capacity and accuracy requirements are the simplest kind of quality requirements. They specify things such as the number of simultaneous users, number of records in the database, accuracy of numbers. All these things are product related and technical.

Usually the requirements are mandatory in the sense that a smaller target value makes the system useless. As an example, if the system is required to support 200 simultaneous users, it is useless if it only supports 100.

Capacity

Capacities are computer resources that the product can occupy for some time. Figure 6.4 shows some examples.

R1 is from a PC-based system. It recognizes the fact that some programs use whatever memory space is available, thus preventing other programs from giving a fast response.

R2 is from a public administration system with several departments all drawing on the same database. The number of users is essential for how the system is set up, how data communication is handled, etc.

R3 is from a hotel booking system. It specifies the number of records that the system has to store. The specification with a growth factor (20% per year) is typical for this kind of system. The growth factor essentially asks the supplier to be able to scale the system up. It is hard to verify the growth requirement at delivery time, since more hardware than initially installed may be needed for the test, but it is possible.

In principle, the volume of all tables (classes) should be specified, and this is conveniently done in the data model or the data dictionary (sections 2.2 and 2.3). Quite often, it turns out that some unnoticed table is the most space-consuming. In the hotel system, the most space-consuming table is not the guest table, but the table of room states.

The specification also gives the supplier some appreciation of the scale. So hotels could really have 1000 rooms? He may wonder what the free room screen would look like. And with one roomState record per room per day, there would be 360,000

Fig 6.4 Capacity and accuracy requirement

Capacity requirements:
R1: The product shall use < 16 MB of memory even if more is available.

R2: Number of simultaneous users < 2000

R3: Database volume:
#guests < 10,000 growing 20% per year
#rooms < 1,000

R4: Guest screen shall be able to show at least 200 rooms booked/occupied per day, e.g. for a company event with a single "customer".

Accuracy requirements:
R5: The name field shall have 150 characters.

R6: Bookings shall be possible at least two years ahead.

R7: Sensor data shall be stored with 14 bit accuracy, expanding to 18 bits in two years.

R8: The product shall correctly recognize spoken letters and digits with factory background noise ___ % of the time. Tape B contains a sample recorded in the factory.

---

roomState records per year. And hotels may need to keep booking information for five years to satisfy the auditors and to calculate statistics and seasonal forecasts!

R4 is also from the hotel booking system. The requirement came from considering *stress cases* in the Virtual Windows model. Essentially, the analyst asked himself what the Virtual Window would look like in worst cases, e.g. when there were many lines in the guest screen. Analysis showed that sometimes a single "guest" (the personnel manager of a big company), booked 200 rooms at the same time for the yearly sales celebration. Names of the individual guests wouldn't be available until they check in. Most likely, such situations had to be considered in the design.

Accuracy requirements

Accuracy requirements cover both the range and precision of data. How large and small can data values be and how accurate should they be? Figure 6.4 shows typical examples. Some standards for quality factors (e.g. ISO 9126) consider accuracy requirements as part of the functional requirements.

R5 specifies the length of names for persons, a decision which influences database, screen fields, and other things. In many cases it would not be part of enumerated requirements, but would be specified in a data dictionary (section 2.3).

R6 is from the hotel system. It gives the range of booking dates. The developer might translate it to a requirement for the volume of *RoomState*, for instance that 1000 rooms should each have 2×365 room states for booking. However, it is implementation-dependent whether free rooms have a room state in the database, or whether other data representations are used. The customer's demand is not about the volume of the database, but about the range of booking dates.

R7 is from a computerized measurement system. Such systems measure physical things by means of analog-digital (AD) converters. State of the art at the time of the requirement was that an AD converter had 14 bits of accuracy. Many developers were happy for that, because a measurement fitted nicely into a single computer word of 16 bits.

However, rumor had it that a new generation of AD converters were on their way. They would have 18 bits of accuracy. The requirement took that into consideration, leaving it to developers to decide whether to handle it as 18 bits from the beginning, or define data types carefully so that it would be easy to change to 18 bits later.

R8 is from a voice recognition system. The requirement has an open target, but the metric (scale) is specified. The customer has enclosed a sample of the voices to be recognized, recorded in the actual factory environment.

6.5 Performance requirements

Highlights

Many kinds: response time, peak traffic, etc.
Technical and psychological limits.
Risky to mix up average cases, 95% cases, and worst cases.

Performance requirements specify how fast the product shall be, for instance the response time for various functions. The requirements are product-related and technical.

We can also specify domain-related performance requirements, e.g. the maximum time it must take an experienced user to perform a specific task. This is a highly relevant requirement. The total task time consists of product response times and human actions. By convention, such task-related requirements are considered usability requirements (see section 6.7, task time).

Figure 6.5A shows examples of performance requirements specified in various ways.

R1, payment transactions. R1 is from a system that handles credit card transactions. A transaction consists of a few messages. R1 specifies the *throughput*, that is the number of transactions to be handled per unit of time. The specification doesn't say anything about response time, and temporary delays are completely acceptable as long as the average over some longer period is within the specified limit. The term *peak load* should be explained somewhere else. It could be a special setup where no other activities are going on or a particularly busy day of the year.

R2, remote process control. R2 is from a system controlling electrical power in a geographical area. An alarm is a message telling about a power malfunction in the area. The user has to decide what to do when the alarm arrives. In a specific case, the customer expected about 1500 alarms a year, so one second per alarm seemed sufficient.

However, if asked about the real critical tasks, the customer would have explained that those were when something serious happened, like a mast falling in a winter storm. In those cases one malfunction would trigger a few hundred alarms within milliseconds. If R2 didn't mention the 5 seconds for 1000 alarms, the customer might get a system where the operator would have to wait one second for each of the several hundred alarms before he could do anything.

In this case, I was one of the developers involved. We had very little domain knowledge and forgot to ask about the critical tasks. As a result, R2 was not properly stated. Our system handled alarms very reliably, but only one per second. One winter night, a high-voltage mast fell, and about 600 alarms were sent. The operator couldn't see what to do until he had a survey picture reflecting all 600

Fig 6.5A Performance requirements

Performance requirements:

R1: Product shall be able to process 100 payment transactions per second in peak load.

R2: Product shall be able to process one alarm in 1 second, 1000 alarms in 5 seconds.

R3: In standard work load, CPU usage shall be less than 50%, leaving 50% for background jobs.

R4: Scrolling one page up or down in a 200 page document shall take at most 1 s. Searching for a specific keyword shall take at most 5 s.

R5: When moving to the next field, typing must be possible within 0.2 s. When switching to the next screen, typing must be possible within 1.3 s. Showing simple report screens, less than 20 s. (Valid for 95% of the cases in standard load)

R6: A simple report shall take less than 20 s for 95% of the cases. None shall take above 80 s. (UNREALISTIC)

Cover all product functions?

---

alarms, and that took 10 minutes. Then it was easy. He just had to reroute power through other high-voltage lines and everybody would have power again. That night, however, 200,000 people had no power for 12 minutes. The reason for this? We had no domain knowledge and forgot to ask the right questions. Repairing the problem after delivering the system was very difficult because our program logic was geared to the first-come first-served logic.

R3, multi-tasking environment. R3 is from a multi-tasking system that can perform several activities concurrently. The product must not monopolize the CPU. 50% of CPU time should be available for other activities. (Some analysts would for good reasons insist that this is a capacity requirement, because it defines a limit for how much CPU capacity the product may consume.)

R4, shipyard invoices. R4 is from a shipyard. An invoice after a ship repair may be more than 100 pages and it looks more like a novel than a list of items. Editing the invoice is a major task. The requirement reflects the bad experience that the users had with their present invoicing system.

R5, multi-user business system. R5 is from a typical business application. It distinguishes three kinds of functions and defines a maximum response time for each kind. (A more precise specification of the three kinds of functions might be necessary in some types of projects.)

Psychological limits

The three limits, 0.2, 1.3, and 20 seconds, are not chosen at random, but are based on human psychology. An average typist types around 5 characters a second, so 0.2 seconds for moving to the next field allows continuous typing. When experienced users switch to the next chunk of typing, they mentally prepare themselves for 1.35 seconds, for instance to read the next chunk of data. A screen switch of 1.3 seconds will thus not delay users. Read more about this keystroke-level model in section 10.6.

Finally, if the user has to wait more than 20 seconds, he will look for something else to do – even if the system warns him of the likely delay. The result is a significant waste of time because task changes often require a large mental effort (Solingen *et al.* 1998).

R5 solves the problem of specifying response times for a large number of screens – screens that we probably aren't aware of yet. We have also common justifications for the limits in R5. However, deviations from the general limits may be acceptable for some functions that need more time for technical reasons. In such cases, simply state the response time for the functions in question. To avoid apparent inconsistency, add to R5 that the general limits apply where nothing else is stated.

Average and upper limits

Notice that R5 doesn't insist on the stated response time in all cases – 95% is enough. Why is this necessary? Couldn't we just raise the response time a bit and say that it should be valid in 100% of cases? Quite often we see such requirements. R6 is a typical example:

R6   A simple report shall take less than 20 seconds in 95% of cases. None shall take above 80 seconds.

Usually such a requirement would be extremely expensive. Let us see why.

In a multi-user system, response times will vary due to coincidence between user actions. Assume for instance that the system can handle a request in 8 seconds if it has nothing else to do. Also assume that 100 users may use the system and send requests to it every now and then.

If all users by coincidence send a request at almost the same time, their request will go through the same pipeline. The first user will get a response within 8 seconds and the last a response within 800 seconds. Wow, we wanted 80 seconds in all cases! If we really insist on that, we would need hardware that is 10 times as fast to cut the time down from 800 seconds to 80. Such a system would be awfully expensive.

Response time probabilities

However, the worst case is extremely rare. Maybe the customer would be satisfied if we only exceed the 80 seconds very rarely. How often would it happen? We cannot answer this without knowing how many requests the system has to serve. If users send requests very often, a queue of requests will build up and response times increase. If requests are rare, the queues will be short and we will only exceed the 80 seconds very rarely.

Figure 6.5B shows how we can answer the question. In the example we assume that a request arrives to the system every 10 seconds on average – the inter-arrival time is 10 seconds. If all 100 users are equally busy, each of them will thus send a request every 1000 seconds on average (every 17 minutes). We now have this basic data:

Service time: 8 seconds
Inter-arrival time: 10 seconds
System load: 8/10, i.e. 0.8 or 80%

A system load of 80% means that the system in average is busy 80% of the time and has nothing to do for the remaining 20%. Queues build up during the 80% where the system is busy.

Figure 6.5B assumes one more thing: The service time is 8 seconds *on average*. Shorter service times are frequent and very long service times are possible, but rare. (Technically speaking, we assume that the service time is exponentially distributed with mean 8 seconds. The inter-arrival time is exponentially distributed with mean 10 seconds.)

Now look at the graph in Figure 6.5B. The *x*-axis is the system load or traffic intensity, 0.8 in our case. The *y*-axis is the response factor, i.e. the response time for a service time of one second.

The vertical line for system load at 0.8 tells us about the response times in our example. Note that the average response factor is 5. Since we have a service time of 8 seconds, the average response time is $5 \times 8 = 40$ seconds. This far exceeds the 20 seconds we wanted in 95% of the cases.

The 0.8 line also shows that the response factor in 90% of the cases will exceed 12. In other words, in 90% of the cases the response time will be above $12 \times 8 = 96$ seconds. Conclusion: We cannot even satisfy the 80 second limit in 90% of the cases.

What should you do if the users really have a request every 10 seconds on average? The answer is to get a faster system, so that the service time is reduced and the system load goes down. Let us try to double the computer speed. We now have these basic data:

Fig 6.5B Response times M/M/1

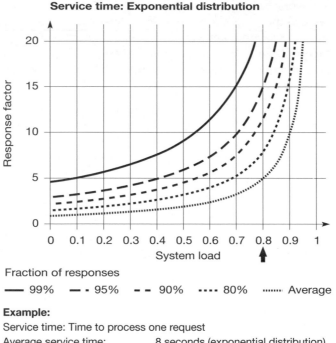

Service time: Exponential distribution

Fraction of responses

— 99% — · 95% — — 90% ···· 80% ········ Average

Example:

Service time: Time to process one request	
Average service time:	8 seconds (exponential distribution)
Average inter-arrival time:	10 seconds (exponential distribution)
System load:	8/10 = 0.8
Average response time:	5 × service time = 40 seconds
90% responses within:	12 × service time = 96 seconds

Service time:	4 seconds
Inter-arrival time:	10 seconds
System load:	4/10, i.e. 0.4 or 40%

For this system load, the diagram shows that the 95% response factor is 5 and the response time will thus be below 5 × 4 = 20 seconds in 95% of the cases. This is exactly what we asked for.

The 99% response factor is 8, so in 99% of the cases, the response time is below 8 × 4 = 32 seconds. The customer ought to be happy. The response time will exceed 32 seconds in less than 1% of the cases. It may exceed also 80 seconds, but only very, very rarely.

Warning: If the users, for instance in an emergency, start to access the system more frequently than the estimated 10 second inter-arrival time, the system load will go up and the response time will increase dramatically. We explain more on this below. If the system has to handle such situations, we should specify the inter-arrival times in these periods or specify the response time for a peak burst of events, such as the situation in R2 in Figure 6.5A.

Fig 6.5C Response times, M/D/1

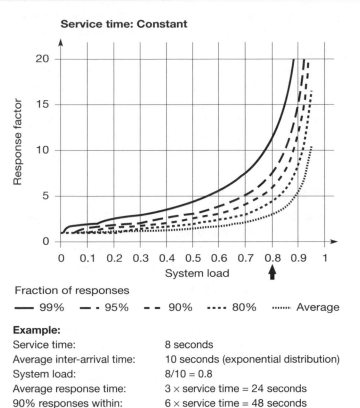

Service time: Constant

Fraction of responses

— 99% — · 95% — — 90% ···· 80% ········ Average

Example:

Service time:	8 seconds
Average inter-arrival time:	10 seconds (exponential distribution)
System load:	8/10 = 0.8
Average response time:	3 × service time = 24 seconds
90% responses within:	6 × service time = 48 seconds

Constant service times

Above we assumed that service times were exponentially distributed, but in many cases they are almost constant, and this decreases response factors. Figure 6.5C shows the response factors when the service time is constant. It also shows the same computation as Figure 6.5B.

Note that the average response time for system load 0.8 is now 24 seconds in contrast to the 40 seconds with exponential service time. In general, the average response factor will be half as long for very high system loads – even though the service time has the same average. For small system loads the average response factor will still be one, of course.

Note also that the 90% response time reduces from 96 to 48 seconds. In general, the 90% curve reduces by a factor two for high system loads. (The other curves behave similarly.)

For small system loads, the 90% curve goes down to one instead of to 2.3 as in Figure 6.5B. Why is that? With a small system load, the system is usually idle and a request will be served immediately. With a constant service time, the response factor will thus be one in all these cases. In contrast, with exponential service time, some requests will have a high service time even at very low system loads.

You may note that the curves are not smooth as in Figure 6.5B. If you look carefully, you will see that for decreasing loads each curve stays around a response factor of two for a wide range and then gradually drops to one. This corresponds to the situation where somebody else is in the queue when our request arrives and his service is more or less finished. The mathematics behind it are complex. See Kleinrock (1975, 1976), Tanenbaum (1988), and Schioler (2001) for more on queuing theory.

The queuing models

The model presented in Figure 6.5C is known as the M/D/1 model. The M shows that the arrivals are exponentially distributed (named after the mathematician Markov). The D shows that the service time is constant (D for Deterministic). Finally, the one shows that there is only one server, in this case one computer, to serve the requests.

Similarly the model in Figure 6.5B is called the M/M/1 model. The only difference is that the service time is exponentially distributed rather than constant.

The models have a common assumption: There must be many users and they must work independently of each other with a steady, average inter-arrival time (exponential distribution). In practice, this assumption is not always fulfilled. For instance, if the system load increases for some external reason, response times may increase significantly and users may believe that something is wrong. They may react in two ways, depending on circumstances: they may be patient or they may panic. Let us look at each of these reactions.

Users are patient. In this case, users are delayed and send fewer requests. Some of them may even stop working and look for something else to do. The result is that system load decreases again so response times will not grow so dramatically. But it slows down users anyway and task times are higher than usual.

Users panic. In this case users try to get the computer's attention by banging the keyboard or using several terminals at the same time. The result is that system load increases further and response times grow dramatically and make it look as if the system is down.

Conclusion

When you specify response times in multi-user systems, never specify maximum response times. The maximum is exceedingly rare and very costly to guarantee. Specifying for instance the 95% limit is okay.

You also have to specify the system load, i.e. the number of requests per second and the kind of requests. You might instead specify the number of users and the kind of tasks they spend their day doing. A skilled supplier should be able to translate this to requests per second.

You also have to specify the hardware speed (or ask the supplier to specify it). Without knowledge of system load and hardware speed, the supplier has no chance of calculating whether or not he can provide the required response times.

Faking the real demands

Be careful not to replace the real customer demands with technical requirements. Customers as well as suppliers may do this without realizing the consequences. Here is a real story to illustrate the point.

In a contract for a national system to support the administration of unemployment benefits and training of unemployed people, the government (the customer) and a large software house (the supplier) had stated maximum response times for switching to the next user screen. It was a national system and thousands of users would work with it simultaneously. The response time was completely unrealistic for the extremely rare worst cases, and the requirements didn't cater for that. When the supplier detected the problem, he suggested that they change the requirement. However, the customer didn't really understand the problem and insisted that the supplier met the requirements – and at the specified price, which also included hardware.

The supplier saw only one way out of the problem: he designed the user interfaces with several screens, each screen having only a few fields for the user to complete. Furthermore, the user had to enter the full client identification on each screen. This slowed down the users so much that the promised response times could be met.

Essentially the supplier traded the product-oriented response times for the domain-oriented ones. The customer hadn't really understood the difference.

When the system was put into operation, users complained, of course, but nothing in the specification could help them. The entire administrative work was slowed down so much that it became a national disaster. It was difficult for the unemployed clients to claim their benefit, and it was even more difficult to get the training that the government funded. The result was that many trainers lost their jobs since they had no clients, in that way increasing unemployment for the clients as well as for themselves.

Which value should you write?

Do you have to specify response time, throughput, etc. for all product functions? In principle yes, otherwise we might have to accept a system with a one-hour response time for some ordinary function that we didn't specify.

For large systems with many functions, this is a hopeless task. Response times for groups of functions, as in R5 on Figure 6.5A, are a solution. In addition, we have to focus on the critical tasks or critical issues where response time is really essential, and then state requirements for them. R1 to R4 are examples of this.

For technically oriented systems, such as process control or embedded software in mobile phones, many of the response times are critical for physical reasons, and thus have to be specified explicitly. Users may wait, but physics won't.

Together, these approaches serve to minimize the risk and reduce the work for all parties involved.

Response time for multi-product systems

In some cases the supplier cannot take responsibility for end-user response times, because other parties are involved. The Internet is a good example. The supplier delivers a server system that has to provide some service to end users sitting with their browser somewhere on the Internet. The customer who buys the server system wants to ensure that the end users experience a low response time.

The problem is that the response time as seen by the end user consists of two parts: the response time from the server and the delay in the Internet. The supplier cannot take responsibility for both.

The solution is for the customer to specify the response time for the server – assuming that the Internet has zero delay. Further, he has to specify the delay on the Internet in his contract with the Internet provider. Both requirements can be measured and verified.

6.6 Usability

Highlights

Usability problems: User cannot figure out . . .
Not technical or functionality problems.
Detect them through usability tests.
In practice only correctable if detected before programming.
Use prototype mockups to detect problems early.

Most of us agree that a computer system should be easy to use – this is important, but how do we define it as a requirement? Quite often we see requirements like this:

R1   The system shall be easy to use.

Yes, we all agree with this, but we cannot verify the requirement as it is. Many developers believe that we cannot define and measure usability, and furthermore we cannot do more about it than we do already.

Nonsense! We can indeed define and verify usability. For instance we can define ease-of-learning for the hotel system in this way:

R2   Four out of five new users shall be able to book a guest within five minutes, check a guest in within 10 minutes, . . .

This requirement is also verifiable – whether we talk about a tailor-made system or a COTS system. In order to avoid too much haggle during verification, it may be useful to specify what "new users" mean, how much training they should have, what kind of booking we are talking about, etc. There are many other ways to specify usability. We look at that later.

We can also *develop* systems so that they get high usability. The basic principle is outlined on Figure 6.6A: make simple prototypes, test them with typical users (usability test), and correct the usability problems detected. However, it is crucial that all this is done as part of design – before a line of code has been written. Otherwise it is too time-consuming to repair the often very serious usability problems.

It seems that these techniques don't slow down development. On the contrary, development seems to become faster and much more predictable. Bruel & Kjaer developed advanced sound measurement products with a traditional approach. To improve product usability, they tried the usability techniques in a large new project. The highly seasoned developers reported:

Fig 6.6A Usability

Usability requirements?

R1: System shall be easy to use??

R2: 4 out of 5 new users can book a guest in 5 minutes, check in in 10 minutes, . . . *New user* means . . . Training . . .

Achieving usability

- Prototypes (mockups) before programming.
- Usability test the prototype.
- Redesign or revise the prototype.

Easier programming.
High customer satisfaction.

Defect types

Program error: Not as intended by the programmer.
Missing functionality: Unsupported task or variant.
Usability problem: User cannot figure out . . .

This is the first time we succeeded in running a project that finished on time – and without stress. The reason? We knew exactly how the user interface should be – and that it was good. The rest was just programming according to the book.

The resulting product had 70% fewer usability problems than comparable products, it sold twice as many units – and at twice the usual price. The method is now used with similar results in all new products in the company (Lauesen and Vinter 2001).

6.6.1　Usability problems

A usability problem is a situation where the user cannot figure out how to carry out his task or finds it too cumbersome. Let us contrast this with other kinds of defects:

Defect types

- If the system doesn't work as intended by the programmer, we have a *program error* – a bug.

- If it is impossible to carry out the task, we have a requirement defect – *missing functionality*.

- If the system works as intended by the programmer and it can support the task, yet the user cannot figure out how to do it or doesn't like the system, we have a *usability problem*.

Here are a few examples of usability problems (Figure 6.6B):

P1　The user cannot figure out how to start the search. The screen says that he should use F10, but for some reason he doesn't see it until he has tried several other ways.

P2　The user believes that he has completed the task and that the result is saved, but he should actually have pressed *Update* before closing the window.

P3 The user cannot figure out which discount code to give the customer, although he knows which field to use.

P4　The user says that it is completely crazy having to go through six screens in order to fill in ten fields.

Usually we classify the usability problems according to their severity to the user. Here is a classification we often use:

Task failure. The user cannot complete the task on his own or he erroneously believes that it is completed. Problems P2 and P3 are of this kind.

Critical problem. Either a task failure or a case where the user complains that the system is annoying or cumbersome. Problems P2, P3 and P4 belong here.

Medium problem. The user finds the solution after lengthy attempts. P1 is this kind.

Minor problem. The user finds the solution after a few short attempts. P1 would have been this kind if the user had found the solution fast.

This is not really a classification of usability problems, but of the observations (occurrences) of the problems. Problem P1, for instance, might be a minor problem to one user, but a task failure to another. If many users have task failures for P1, we might call P1 a task failure, but some judgment is involved. Usually, we cannot ensure that *all* users succeed with everything – even though it would be wonderful.

Fig 6.6B Usability problems

Examples of usability problems

P1: User takes long time to start search. Doesn't notice "Use F10". Tries many other ways first.

P2: Believes task completed and result saved. Should have used *Update* before closing.

P3: Cannot figure out which discount code to give customer. Knows which field to use.

P4: Crazy to go through 6 screens to fill 10 fields.

Problem classification

Task failure: Task not completed – or believes it is completed.
Critical problem: Task failure or complaints that it is cumbersome.
Medium problem: Finds out solution after lengthy attempts.
Minor problem: Finds out solution after short attempts.

6.6.2 Usability tests

The most effective technique to find the usability problems is a usability test. We can also use the technique to measure the usability. There are many variants of usability tests. Below we outline our favored, low-cost, high-effective technique. Figure 6.6C gives a summary of this technique.

During a usability test, we let a user (the test subject) try to carry out realistic tasks using the system or a mockup of it. A mockup may be entirely on paper, and the user would fill in fields by means of a pencil, point at "buttons" with the pencil, etc. The leader of the test (the facilitator) would take paper windows away when they "close" and bring them up when they open.

During the test, we observe which problems the user encounters. The facilitator or the log keeper note down what happens, in particular the problems. There are two important variants here:

Observe only. The facilitator and the log keeper don't interfere with what is going on. They only observe and note the time taken by the user to carry out each task. Mockups are not suited for this. Furthermore, it is difficult to find the cause of the observed problem. For instance, why didn't the user notice F10?

Think aloud. The facilitator asks the user to *think aloud*, or he cautiously asks the user why he did as he did, or what he believes would happen if he did so and so. This of course interferes with time-taking, but it is essential in order to identify the causes of problems.

Before the test, we try to give the user the introduction to the system that he would be given in real life. Usually we repeat the test with one more user, and at later stages with two to four users. We use around one to two hours per user and one to two hours to summarize the problems. After a successful round of tests, we typically have 20 to 50 problems of various severity on our list.

Motivated developers can learn the technique in a day or two, but we strongly recommend that they get an experienced consultant to help them stay on track. Section 10.5 gives additional practical advice. Other recommended guides are Jorgensen (1990) and Dumas and Redish (1993).

What usability tests are not

There are many misunderstandings about usability tests:

- It is *not* necessary to have a functional system. A mockup on the screen or even a paper and pencil version of the screens can reveal most problems.

- It is *not* a demonstration of the system where a developer or a marketing person shows how to perform various tasks with the system. The users and customers may be very excited about the system, yet be completely unable to use it on their own.

Fig 6.6C Usability test and heuristic evaluation

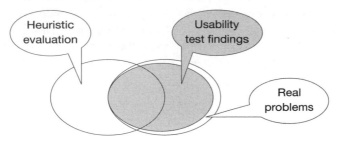

Usability test
Realistic introduction
Realistic tasks.

Note problems.
■ Observe only or
■ Think aloud and ask

Log keeper   User   Facilitator

Heuristic evaluation
Expert's predicted problems ≅ Inspection/Review

Heuristic evaluation

Usability test findings

Real problems

Usability test:
Cover all tasks?
Mockups find same problems as test with final system?

■ It is *not* a test where a colleague is the test user. Most likely he knows so much about IT that he will not encounter certain kinds of problems. And he may know so little about the domain that he encounters problems that real users don't. It is essential to find test users that correspond to the intended audience for the final product.

■ The test does *not* have to take place in a special usability lab with video, electronic log, and semi-transparent glass walls. A desk with a PC, a facilitator, a motivated developer, and preferably a log keeper is sufficient in most cases.

■ It is *not* something you do at the end of development to prove that the system is user-friendly. Most project teams start out with usability testing in that way. They become so scared when they see the user's problems that they don't try again for several years.

6.6.3 Heuristic evaluation

Usability testing may sound cumbersome. Aren't there other ways to identify the usability problems? Maybe we could hire an expert and have him look at the screens and point out the problems? This approach is called *heuristic evaluation* and it is the user interface equivalent to what programmers call code inspection or review.

Unfortunately heuristic evaluation finds lots of problems, but not only the right ones. Figure 6.6C illustrates that even good usability experts detect only half of the real usability problems. Furthermore, half of the "problems" they detect are false in the sense that they don't cause problems to real users. It would be a waste of time trying to correct these false problems. We have often observed this poor hit-rate, and several authors report similar results, e.g. Bailey *et al.* (1992), Cuomo and Bowen (1994), and Desurvire *et al.* (1992).

In contrast, skilled developers can detect most programming errors through a careful inspection of the code, and they find very few "false" problems. What is the reason for this difference? Probably the developers understand the computer far better than the usability experts understand the users. Once you think about it, it is not that surprising.

Usability tests are far better than heuristic evaluation and can find most usability problems, but not all of them. For instance, if the test doesn't include certain tasks or variants, you don't detect problems in that area unless some other task happens to reveal them.

Usability tests with a mockup are almost as good as usability tests of the final system. The main difference is that the mockup doesn't reveal problems with low-level user interaction, for instance that the new system uses the backspace key or mouse clicks in an unusual way.

We don't know of false problems "detected" by usability tests, but mockups can make some usability problems look more severe than with a real system. Users tend not to experiment so much with a mockup, thereby causing a task failure instead of a medium problem. This is probably because each attempt they make means that the facilitator, who plays the role of the computer, has to switch screens, etc. So they give up rather than experiment.

6.6.4 Defect correction

The nature of program errors is very different from usability problems, as outlined on Figure 6.6D.

Programming errors are expected. It is possible to find many of them through inspection or review. You can detect the rest during *program testing* at the end of development. Skilled programmers can easily correct most errors. And finally, test equipment is readily available.

Usability problems come as a surprise to programmers, but not to usability experts. Finding the problems with inspection or heuristic evaluation is not reliable. They must be detected by means of usability tests in the early design stage – not

Fig 6.6D Defects and usability factors

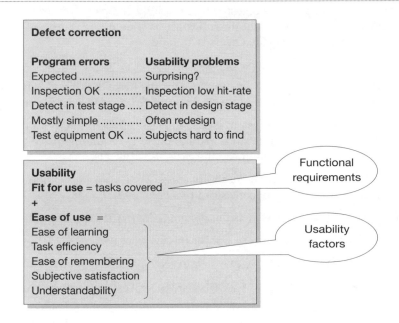

Defect correction

Program errors	Usability problems
Expected	Surprising?
Inspection OK	Inspection low hit-rate
Detect in test stage	Detect in design stage
Mostly simple	Often redesign
Test equipment OK	Subjects hard to find

Usability
Fit for use = tasks covered

\+

Ease of use =
Ease of learning
Task efficiency
Ease of remembering
Subjective satisfaction
Understandability

Functional requirements

Usability factors

during or after program testing. The reason for this is that usability problems often require large changes or the complete redesign of central parts of the user interface. This is not feasible when programming has been carried out, and designers are more willing to do this with mockups. For many usability problems there is no safe cure, so the designers may have to make several attempts. And finally, the "test equipment" is real users, and they are not readily available.

In the Bruel & Kjaer case, the developers first designed a user interface mockup that they were proud of themselves. Unfortunately, a usability test with three potential users revealed that the users couldn't figure out how to operate the product. Developers were disappointed, but recovered and designed a new mockup over the weekend. The new one was based on a very different principle. The first usability test of this revealed several problems, which however were easy to correct. A final test of the mockup revealed only minor problems.

It is interesting that the developers made mockups and usability tests of only a few central screens. The final product had about 23 screens – three times as many as the ones tested. Yet the product had 70% fewer usability problems per screen than comparable products. We don't know this for sure, but we believe that well-tested central screens help the users form a good mental model, causing them to better understand the other screens. Maybe it also helps the developer to find good user concepts that can be used in the rest of the windows.

6.6.5   Usability factors

Above we have implicitly suggested that usability is the absence of usability problems. This is definitely not the full truth, as shown on Figure 6.6D. First of all, the very term *usability* usually covers two things:

> Usability = Fit for use + Ease of use

Fit for use means that the system can support the tasks that the user has in real life. From a requirements viewpoint this is what the functional requirements deal with.

Ease of use means that the system is easy to learn, efficient in day-to-day work, etc. This is what we discuss under the heading usability requirements. When *usability* is used in this book, we usually mean the ease-of-use aspect.

There are many ways to define usability (ease of use), but in the following we will use this definition: Usability consists of five *usability factors*:

1   Ease of learning. How easy is the system to learn for various groups of users?

2   Task efficiency. How efficient is it for the frequent user?

3   Ease of remembering. How easy is it to remember for the occasional user?

4   Subjective satisfaction. How satisfied is the user with the system?

5   Understandability. How easy is it to understand what the system does? This factor is particularly important in unusual situations, for instance error situations or system failures. Only an understanding of what the system does can help the user out.

Developers often say that it is impossible to design a system that scores high on all factors. This may be true, and one purpose of the usability requirements is to specify the necessary level for each factor. As an example, a Web-based system for attracting new customers should have emphasis on ease of learning and subjective satisfaction, while a flight control system should have emphasis on task efficiency and understandability.

The usability factors above are based on Shneiderman's work (1998). We have replaced his factor "few errors" with "understandability". Traditionally, usability experts were reluctant to talk about the user's understanding. You couldn't readily measure it, and what really mattered was whether the user could perform his tasks. Today, understandability is more recognized. It is crucial for mastering complex systems with many tasks and task variants, and you can measure the factor in the same way that you give marks at exams.

6.7 Usability requirements

Highlights

Many ways to measure usability.
Some ways are suitable for new product parts, others for choosing COTS.
Some ways are risky to all parties.

Usability can be specified and measured in many ways. Figure 6.7 shows nine styles for usability requirements. For each style, we have indicated the risk to the customer and the supplier when using the style. The risk to the customer is that although he may get what is specified, he may not get what he really needs. The risk to the supplier is that he may not be able to meet the requirements – or only with excessive costs. Below follow the details of each of the styles.

Problem counts

R1 At most one of five novices shall encounter critical usability problems during tasks Q and R. The total list of usability problems shall contain at most five medium problems. (Critical and medium problems are defined in 6.6.1.)

In a hotel system, tasks Q and R might be booking and checking in. The requirement covers ease of learning quite well. We might include other tasks to cover the system better. If the user is an experienced receptionist (i.e. he has experience from another system), he might also give us an impression of the task efficiency and the ease of understanding.

We should specify more precisely what we mean by *novice*. Novice concerning reception work and/or novice concerning this particular product? We should also specify how much instruction they have been given. (In small hotels there are often temporary staff and night receptionists who get at most 10 minutes of instruction from a more experienced staff member.)

The great advantage of this style is that the requirement can be tested early. For the COTS parts of the system, we can carry out the test before signing the contract. For a tailor-made system, developers can test the requirement during design, and this test is at the same time a natural part of good development. If the requirements are based on task descriptions and variants, they provide excellent test cases (see section 3.6).

The biggest problem with the style is that it is very dangerous to the supplier in the case of a tailor-made product. With the present state of the art in usability, it is hard to know whether the requirement is feasible at all. Another problem is that we are less sure of catching the essence of usability. As an example, we get only indirect indications of task efficiency and subjective satisfaction.

Fig 6.7   Usability requirements

	Risk	
	Customer	**Supplier**
Problem counts **R1:** At most 1 of 5 novices shall encounter critical problems during tasks Q and R. At most 5 medium problems on the list.	▄	▆
Task time **R2:** Novice users shall perform tasks Q and R in 15 minutes. Experienced users complete tasks Q, R, S in 2 minutes.		█
Keystroke counts **R3:** Recording breakfast shall be possible with 5 keystrokes per guest. No mouse.	█	
Opinion poll **R4:** 80% of users shall find system easy to learn. 60% shall recommend system to others.	▄	█
Score for understanding **R5:** Show 5 users 10 common error messages, e.g. *Amount too large*. Ask for the cause. 80% of the answers shall be correct.	▄	▂
Design-level requirements **R6:** System shall use screen pictures in app. *xx*, buttons work as app. *yy*.	█	
Product-level requirements **R7:** For all code fields, user shall be able to select value from drop-down list.	█	
Guideline adherence **R8:** System shall follow style guide *zz*. Menus shall have at most three levels.	█	▂
Development process requirements **R9:** Three prototype versions shall be made and usability-tested during design.	█	

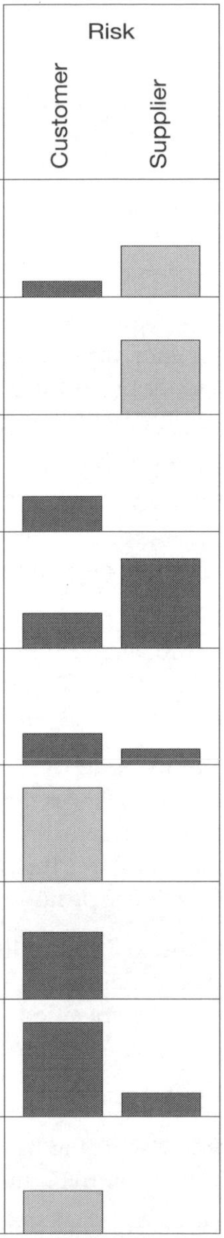

Figure 6.7 shows these problems as a large gray box for the supplier, indicating a large risk for tailor-made parts, and a smaller dark box for the customer, indicating inadequate coverage of all the usability factors.

Task time

R2 Novice users shall be able to perform tasks Q and R in 15 minutes. Experienced users shall be able to perform tasks Q, R, and S in 2 minutes.

This requirement style explicitly covers ease of learning and task efficiency. We can verify the requirement through usability tests. Task efficiency, however, is hard to verify until we have some experienced users to test with.

It is even harder to verify the requirement during development. We need a functional prototype, since mockups give a false picture of the speed. Further, we cannot use think-aloud tests because thinking aloud slows the user down. As a result developers get too little feedback to improve the design.

COTS parts. Surprisingly, the style is low-risk to both parties for the COTS parts of a product. Why? Those parts are finished and the measurements can be made before the buy decision. It may even be possible to find experienced users in another company, in that way measuring also task times for experienced users.

Defining the proper time limits is a problem, of course. However, the open target approach (section 6.3) is suited because the supplier may tell you what is achievable. In many cases, the supplier knows how well his product fares without having to make new measurements.

Tailor-made parts. For tailor-made parts, the style is still excellent from the customer's viewpoint because it can cover important aspects of usability. However, the style is very risky to the supplier. It is not certain that the requirements can be met at all. Furthermore, they cannot be assessed early in development because a functional prototype is needed.

Figure 6.7 shows this as a very large gray box for the supplier, indicating a huge risk for tailor-made parts, and no box for the customer indicating that if he gets what he specified, usability is well covered.

Keystroke counts

R3 Recording breakfast shall be possible with 5 keystrokes per guest, and without using the mouse.

This requirement style covers efficiency for experienced users. If we also require certain response times from the system, we are able to calculate the total task time. We can calculate the user time of the task by means of existing measurements of how fast an average user can press a key, move a mouse, etc. (the *keystroke-level model*, see section

10.6). We further have to add the time for the user to get the data from clients, think about the results, and so on, but this is largely independent of the user interface.

The big advantage of this style is that we can check the requirement early in development. We don't even need access to real users. As a result, the supplier has virtually no risk.

The disadvantage is that we cannot be sure that users find out how to do it in the efficient way, although training may help, of course. Further, this kind of requirement doesn't attempt to cover ease of learning, understandability, etc. If we add usability requirements written in some of the other styles, we can cover these missing points, and still check all the requirements during development.

Opinion poll

R4 80% of users shall find the system easy to learn and efficient for daily use. 60% shall state that they would recommend it to others.

With this requirement style, we ask users about their opinion, typically with questionnaires using a Likert scale. This covers the usability factor *subjective satisfaction*, and it is tempting to believe that it catches the essence of usability.

Unfortunately, users often express satisfaction with their system in spite of evidence that the system is inconvenient and wastes a lot of user time, causes erroneous transactions that IT staff have to deal with, etc. (If the manager knew about this, he would not be as satisfied as the users.)

Satisfaction with the system is heavily influenced by organizational factors, which the supplier cannot control. Another problem with the subjective style is that it is hard to verify the requirement during development. Many usability experts ask users about their subjective opinion after prototype-based usability tests, but it may not correlate well with opinions after system deployment.

The result is that both customer and supplier run a high risk.

Score for understanding

R5 Show 5 users 10 common error messages, for instance

Amount too large [when drawing money from an ATM]
Ask them what the cause might be. 80% shall give the correct answer.

This requirement shows a way to measure *understandability*, in the example error messages from an Automatic Teller Machine. Some subjective assessment of the correctness of the answer may be necessary, but ask a teacher to run the test. He will be able to mark the answer as A, B, C, or D. The requirement could be that 80% get A or B.

When I try the ATM example with people, I get very few correct answers. Few people know that the message may indicate that although they have ample money in their account, they have exceeded their daily cash allowance or their monthly limit. Both limits are there to prevent robberies and fraud but most users are unaware of this.

An understandability test gives us information that is hard to get with task-time measurements or problem counts. The reason is that today's systems have a huge number of error messages. Trying tasks where the user can encounter many of them is extremely time-consuming. Testing as R5 suggests is an easy way out.

On Figure 6.7, the style gets a moderate risk for the customer because it only covers a special aspect of usability. The risk to the supplier is very low because he can test understandability early in development, and he can easily repair the problems – also very late in the project. With COTS parts he can carry out the test even before signing the contract.

Design-level requirements

R6 The system shall use the screen pictures shown in app. *xx*. The menu points and buttons shall work as described in app. *yy*.

This style prescribes the details of the user interface. Essentially it has turned the usability requirements into functional requirements. They are easy to verify in the final product and easy to trace during development. The supplier has a low risk, as shown in Figure 6.7.

Through the design, the analyst has taken full responsibility for the usability. The system designer and programmer can do little to change the usability. If the analyst has done a careful job with task analysis, prototyping, and usability tests, the resulting usability is adequate, and the customer runs a low risk. Otherwise his risk is high – he will not get what he needs. The large gray box on Figure 6.7 shows this conditional risk.

Untested prototypes are risky as requirements, but useful as examples of what the user has in mind and for requirements elicitation (see also prototypes in section 3.5).

Product-level requirements

R7 For all code fields, the user shall be able to type the value directly or select the value from a drop-down list.

This requirement is not a full design, but a required feature. We have a product-level requirement. The purpose of the requirement is usability of course, more precisely the factor ease of remembering.

It is a very reasonable requirement. In other cases, however, we see product-level requirements that reflect a more arbitrary solution to an unstated problem. See also *feature requirements* in section 3.4.

Product-level requirements give the supplier a low risk, because they are straightforward to implement. Although the requirements may be useful, they cannot ensure high usability. Other kinds of requirements are needed too. For this reason, the customer runs a high risk.

Guideline adherence

R8 The system shall follow style guide zz. Menus shall have at most three levels.

The guideline style prescribes the general appearance and response on the user interface. You may think of it as a set of broad functional requirements that apply to every window, etc. Guidelines may be official or *de facto* style guides, or they may be company guides or experience-based rules. It is possible, but cumbersome, to verify and trace these requirements.

Although guidelines usually improve usability, they have little relation to the essence of usability. In other words, you can have a system that users find very hard to use although it follows the guidelines. (Such systems are actually quite common, as demonstrated by the many programs that follow the MS-Windows guidelines, yet are very difficult to use.) As a supplement to other styles, the guideline style is quite useful, particularly to help users switch between applications.

Development process requirements

R9 During design, a sequence of three prototypes shall be made. Each prototype shall be usability tested and the most important defects corrected.

This requirement specifies the development process to be used for ensuring usability. The style doesn't say anything about the result of the development, but the customer hopes that the process will generate a good result. The example specifies iterative prototype-based development since this is recognized as an effective process, but we could specify other more risky processes such as heuristic evaluation and structured dialog design.

How many iterations do we need? We might specify the termination criteria for the iterations, e.g. continue until no serious usability defects are left, but then we would actually have a problem-count style, rather than a development-process style. However, we could specify that more iterations shall be negotiated between customer and supplier after the three iterations. This would still be a development process requirement.

The style is useful in many cases where developers can commit to a specific process, but not to task-times or problem counts. The developer has a low risk.

The customer cannot be sure that he gets what he needs, because much is left to developers. Developers often select the wrong tasks and users for usability testing, or they only make minor changes to the prototypes rather than redesign them. The result may be that usability is still unacceptable after the three iterations.

The customer may cover himself by means of a clause in the contract allowing him to cancel the contract in case the result of the iteration is inadequate (see the shipyard case in 10.4). This is shown on Figure 6.7 as a medium, conditional risk to the customer.

With the current state of the art in usability, a development process requirement is probably the best choice for tailor-made system parts. See also sections 1.7.3 and 3.16.

6.8 Security

What could we specify about security? That we need encryption? Firewalls? Duplicated disks? Yes, we may write all of that, but it corresponds to the situation where we write functional requirements saying that the system shall have screens B and C. In other words, we have asked for a specific solution rather than a solution to a specific problem.

The problem with these product-level requirements is that it is the customer's responsibility that the requirements match his real needs. He has also discarded other solutions that might better solve his problem.

Safeguard the assets. Now, what are the security issues? The answer is that the customer wants to safeguard his assets against threats. The assets are data and process capabilities, e.g. the database and the computer power. There are many kinds of threats, e.g. accidental fires, a cut transmission line, hackers abusing the database, intentional fraud inside the company. For each threat there are ways to prevent it, e.g. smoke alarms, multiple transmission lines, passwords, auditing. Different prevention techniques have different degrees of effectiveness and different costs.

We can state the difference between security requirements and other kinds of requirements in this simplified way:

Security requirements aim at preventing abuse cases. Other kinds of requirements aim at supporting use cases.

Ensure CIA+A. Instead of talking about threats, we can talk about the opposite concept, something we want to ensure. Security specialists talk about the need to ensure four things, easily remembered as CIA+A:

Confidentiality. Ensure that data is used only for authorized purposes.

Integrity. Ensure that data is correct.

Availability. Ensure that data and processing power are available to authorized people.

Authenticity. Ensure that a person who claims to be John Smith really is John Smith.

Fig 6.8A Threats

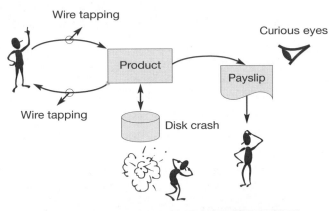

Threats	Violate	Preventions
Input, e.g.		**Examples**
Mistake	Integrity	Logical checks
Illegal access	Authenticity	Signature
Wire tapping	Confidentiality	Encryption
Storing, e.g.		
Disk crash	Availability	RAID disks
Program error	Integrity	Test techniques
Virus deletes data	Availability	Firewall
Output, e.g.		
Transmission	Availability	Multiple lines
Fraud	Confidentiality	Auditing
Virus sends data	Authenticity	Encryption

6.8.1 Threats

The list of threats is long, and as criminals and hackers become more and more creative, more threats are added to the list. Figure 6.8A illustrates the three basic data processes where threats can occur. It also shows examples of threats and ways to prevent them from happening. For each threat there are several possible ways to prevent it.

Input process. Data is created in the domain, typically by a user, sometimes by an external product. Data then travels to the computer (the product) where it is processed by programs and usually stored in a database. Examples of threats during the input process are simple user mistakes, illegal access, or wire tapping, where unauthorized people spy on the data while it is transmitted.

Storage process. While it is stored in the database, data may be processed in various ways, e.g. copied for backup purposes, restructured for better performance, etc. Examples of threats during the storage "process" are disk crashes, erroneous programs that accidentally corrupt data, or virus programs that delete files.

Output process. Output is generated by programs and then travels to a user or an external product. Output may be a reply to data sent by a user, or it may go to other users, for instance as printed data. Examples of threats during the output process are transmission errors, fraudulent use of the output, or virus programs that send data pretending that the user has sent them.

You might expect that violation of confidentiality takes place during the output process and violation of integrity during the input process. However, as outlined on Figure 6.8A, violation of all CIA+A factors may happen during any of the three processes.

6.8.2   Security risk assessment

Since there are so many threats, it is hard to state requirements for all of them. Usually only a few relate to the product we specify. Others have to be handled by the general IT infrastructure, business procedures, or management policy.

In practice analysts identify the more critical threats by means of a security risk assessment, where they estimate the frequency of each threat and the loss if it occurs. Usually security experts use the term *risk assessment*, which may be confusing because there are other kinds of risk, for instance development risks that we discuss in sections 8.2.16 and 9.3.1.

It may be hard to estimate security risks, but it helps to force yourself to choose between a few alternatives. Figure 6.8B shows an example from the hotel system. The table has one line for each threat. The three columns on the left show the estimated number of times this threat will occur. The middle section shows the estimated loss per hit. The column on the right shows the total loss per year. As you see, virus attacks may be very costly. Next comes disk crashes and fraud. It is very important to guard against these threats.

Let us look at the details. Where did we get the threats? Actually, we looked through all the threats from section 6.8.3 below, assessing for each of them whether it was relevant in the hotel case. The result was this list (some threats are left out for space reasons):

Illegal access. We assume that the hotel has online booking over the Web and the guest states his credit card details. If the credit card details are false or there isn't money on the account, the hotel may lose money holding the room for him. How often does this happen? It is difficult to tell, it seems. However, the table forces us to choose between 10, 1, and 0.1 times per year. Well, it definitely happens more often than once a year. Maybe ten times per year is about right. (In large hotels or dubious areas it may

Fig 6.8B Security risk assessment

Threat	Times per year			Loss (in $000) per hit			Loss per year
	10	1	0.1	1	10	100	
Input Illegal access	1			0.3			3
Process Disk crash			3			1	30
Computer crash		1		5			5
Sabotage			1			1	10
Fraud			2			1	20
Virus		1				1	100
Output Printer error	2			0.2			4

Assumptions:
Losing the database with all the bookings: 100,000$
Losing the computer access for one day: 5,000$
Online booking turning out to be false: 300$

be more.) What is the average loss when it happens? Typically two bednights, or $300, resulting in $3000 per year. Safeguards? We leave that as an exercise for the reader.

Disaster, disk crash. If the disk crashes, we lose the entire database. How often does a disk crash? Not once a year, but more than once every ten years. A good estimate is every three years, but the disk supplier can give us more exact figures. What would it cost to lose the database entirely? Of course we lose the customer database, but that might not be a disaster. We also lose the history of previous room occupations, but we could do without it, although less efficiently. The real damage, however, would be to lose all bookings. It might involve all the rooms for many days ahead. We wouldn't know how many rooms we could book in addition. We would either lose customers if they turn up and there is no room for them, although they have booked, or we would lose money by having empty rooms. We have estimated the loss at around $100,000 – depending on hotel size, of course. In total, the average loss is around $30,000 per year.

Disaster, computer crash. If the computer crashes, but not the disk, the hotel staff will have a busy and chaotic day. They have to get a new computer and connect the old disk to it. They must be careful not to book too many additional guests since they don't know for sure how many rooms were booked. It is also very confusing having to rush to each physical room to find out whether it is free. Further, all the potential, new Web bookings of the day are lost. The estimated loss is $5000. The frequency of this is around once a year.

Sabotage. In certain areas, the hotel may be robbed and equipment damaged. If the computer is in the front office, we estimated that this might happen once every ten years in the hotel under consideration. The loss would correspond to a disk crash.

Fraud. Fraud may happen in many ways that the product has nothing to do with. However, the presence of temporary account data on the product exposes a risk. An authorized staff member may delete some check-ins from the computer and cash the money himself. Such events may happen about every five years, and the loss may reach $100,000 before anybody notices what is happening.

Virus. If a virus enters the system through an e-mail, it might erase the entire hard disk. In simple PCs, viruses might arrive once a month, but fortunately only few of them erase databases. We have estimated the risk as once a year, but the database will be lost, costing the hotel around $100,000 a year. Note that this is yet another way to lose the database.

Printer error. A printer error is usually not a serious problem, but if we use it for printing invoices, errors *are* a problem. If the printer runs out of ink, for instance, the computer believes that the invoice has been printed. Printing it once more may cause problems in the audit trail inside the system. We have estimated that the administrative mess caused by such a problem may cost around $2000. With this problem happening about twice a month, the yearly cost is around $4000.

Other threats. We have ignored most threats from the list below because they seem less important in the hotel case. As an example, we have ignored the risk of program errors or programmed crime (apart from viruses). The reason is that the hotel expects to buy a COTS-based system. Although it may have many program errors, they are usually nuisances that have no effect on the database.

6.8.3 Threats and safeguards

Below follows a list of the various kinds of threats. There is a list for each of the information processes, input, storage, and output. We give examples of each kind of threat and mention a few possible safeguards.

As criminals and hackers invent more and more threats, the possible safeguards develop too, and it is hard to follow what goes on in this area. If you are involved in projects where security is an important issue, consult an expert.

A good source for further information is Pfleeger (1997), who covers threats and most technical issues. British Standard (BS 7799) lists the safeguards you should use, particularly in the managerial area. Sometimes it also mentions the threats that the safeguard protects against, in other cases you have to imagine the threats.

Safeguards

There are basically three kinds of safeguards:

Prevention. A technique that reduces the occurrence of the threat. As an example, the use of passwords reduces the chances of illegal access to the system.

Detection. A technique that reports that a threat succeeded. As an example, logging of all log-on attempts may help to identify illegal access. A consistency check of the database may reveal that a program didn't update the database properly.

Repair. A technique that helps to repair the damage after a hit. As an example, a backup copy of data may help a system to recover from a disk crash or a virus. Sending a letter to people who inadvertently had confidential data revealed may help them take appropriate action.

The threats below have examples of all three kinds of safeguards. It is left to the reader as an exercise to classify the safeguards as prevention, detection, or repair.

Input process

The threats in this group occur while data are captured, transmitted to the computer, processed, and sent to the database.

Physical distortion, e.g. messages lost, duplicated, or distorted. Safeguards: the standard transmission protocols detect and prevent these cases to a very large extent by means of parity checks, packet numbers, etc.

Disaster, e.g. a transmission line is broken, a network computer along the path breaks down, the input device breaks down. Safeguards: duplicate equipment and reroute transmission.

Simple user errors, e.g. the user types a wrong item number, forgets to enter a batch of vouchers, or simply misunderstands what he has to enter. Safeguards: for instance check digits, hash totals, bar codes, usability tests, user training and motivation.

Program errors. The program unintentionally distorts, duplicates, or deletes data. Safeguards: testing techniques, configuration management to ensure that only certified programs are installed, audit programs that check results of other programs.

Sabotage, e.g. equipment intentionally destroyed. Safeguards: physical access control, security checks of visitors.

Illegal access. A person sends data pretending that he is someone else. A well-known example is criminals who use stolen credit cards. Safeguards: passwords, for instance PIN numbers, logging of all access attempts.

Stealing passwords. A person might steal someone else's password, for instance by looking over the shoulder of an authorized user, noting which keys he pushes. Or he may look at the "secret" slip of paper with passwords in a colleague's drawer. Or he may try out various likely passwords. Safeguards: frequent change of passwords, logging of access attempts, firewalls that report suspicious log-on patterns, physical security (no unauthorized persons nearby), security procedures such as "never write down your password" or "use a password with at least three digits and three letters".

Fraud. An authorized user sends intentionally wrong data, for instance a bank officer who transfers money from a central bank account to his friend's account. Safeguards: auditing of transactions, required authorization by two employees for large money transfers, personnel policies.

Wire tapping. Someone connects a computer to the transmission lines and taps the data. He might also be a support person who has access to one of the servers and runs his own spy program that taps the data. In any of these ways he may obtain passwords and user IDs from authorized users, spy on confidential messages, etc. Safeguards: encryption of the transmitted data so that the spy cannot understand it, physical security (no unauthorized persons close to equipment), frequent changes of password.

Wire tampering. A variant of wire tapping is wire tampering. The person not only taps data, he also modifies it and passes it on to where it should have gone in the first place. The receiver believes it comes from the person who established the connection. Safeguards: hash totals transmitted for the entire session, electronic signatures using public key encryption.

In public key encryption, the sender uses his private key (secret) to encrypt messages. Anybody knowing who the sender is can use his public key to decrypt the message and read its content. In this way the receiver also tests that the sender is the person who claims to be the sender. Nobody can create messages that pass this test without knowing the sender's private key. In theory it is possible to derive the private key from the public key, but it would take years of computing time even for the fastest computers.

Programmed crime, e.g. the programmer has installed a system program that allows him to log on in the usual way, and then use the program to change data in the database, retrieve internal system data, modify log files to hide what has happened, etc. Safeguards: for instance configuration management, file security checks, internal auditing, personnel policies.

Storage process

The threats in this group occur while data are stored in the system.

Physical distortion, e.g. data lost, duplicated, or distorted. Safeguards: standard, internal checks in computers prevent such errors to a very large extent. Unrecoverable errors will appear as system crashes.

Disaster, e.g. the computer breaks down, a disk crashes, power is cut, there is a fire or an earthquake.

Safeguards against simple breakdowns: duplicate the equipment. The most vulnerable piece of hardware is the hard disk, and there are various standard ways of running two or more disks that mirror each other (RAID disks). If one disk breaks down, the system continues with the remaining disk. Support staff replace the broken disk, and the system automatically initializes the new disk to match the one in operation. The users haven't noticed anything amiss.

For computer breakdowns there are similar, more expensive approaches. A simpler version is to tolerate a short breakdown, connect the disks to a healthy computer, and start it up. In this case the users will notice the interruption, and the latest transactions may be lost.

Safeguards against power loss: backup power supply. If a breakdown period is acceptable, and the database is handled by means of a mature database system, there is no reason to do anything. The database can recover from such breakdowns, but the most recent transactions may be lost.

Safeguards against fire and earthquakes: fire alarms, automatic fire extinguishers, adequate building constructions. To guard against the worst possible, e.g. a nuclear attack, maintain a copy of the database in a very remote location or far underground. In most systems, these extreme threats can be ignored because so many other things would go awry in such cases. For instance, it would not be realistic to attempt to run a hotel after a nuclear attack – even if the database survived.

Simple user errors, e.g. the operator copies the old version of a file to the new version instead of the opposite, makes mistakes during planned reconfiguration. Safeguards: automatic backup procedures, separate test installations for testing new configurations, have two people working on all reconfiguration jobs.

Program errors. Programs that run automatically, for instance periodically, may unintentionally distort, duplicate, or delete data. Safeguards: as for the input process.

Sabotage. As for the input process.

Illegal access, e.g. an unauthorized person tampers with the system. Safeguards: for instance physical access control, logging of all configuration events, personnel policies.

Fraud. An authorized person tampers with the system. Safeguards: logging of all entrants to the computer room, logging of configuration events, personnel policies.

Insufficient protection management, e.g. a program intended for support staff is left for public use. A hacker gets access by disguising as an ordinary user, runs the program and lists system files, e.g. user identifications and passwords. Soon he gets privileged access as a support person and the doors are open to do anything. Safeguards: configuration management and automatic configuration checks.

Programmed crime. As for the input process. In addition cases where a virus program deletes or modifies files. Safeguards: firewalls or virus scanners that detect known types of viruses. Standard procedures such as "never open a program file unless you know what it is and where it came from".

Output process

The threats in this group occur while the results are being produced, transmitted to the receiver, and used by the receiver.

Physical distortion. As for the input process.

Disaster. As for the input process. In addition cases such as the printer being out of ink when printing invoices. Printing the invoices again may corrupt the audit trail, unless special product features can deal with this situation.

Simple user errors, e.g. the user asks for the wrong thing or misunderstands the output. Safeguards: usability tests, user training, and motivation.

Program errors. The program unintentionally computes a wrong result. Safeguards: testing techniques, configuration management to ensure that only certified programs are installed.

Sabotage. As for the input process.

Illegal access. As for the input process.

Stealing passwords. As for the input process.

Fraud. An authorized user receives data and uses it for something that he isn't authorized to do. As an example, in electronic shopping you send your credit card details and trust that they are used for this purchase only. However, the vendor might use them for other purposes and even charge your account several times. Safeguards: logging of all actions, auditing, reclaim policies, third party authorization of payments (e.g. the SET protocol – Secure Electronic Transfer).

Wire tapping and wire tampering. As for the input process. In addition there are risks of disclosing printed output. An example is prints of payslips or PIN codes, where the computer operator shouldn't see them. The standard safeguard is to print on special three-sheet paper with the print between the sheets. The final receiver tears the sheets open to read what is inside.

Programmed crime. As for the input process. In addition there are cases where a virus program sends out messages that purport to come from a friend. A copy of the virus program is attached to the message, and when the receiver – believing that the message is from a friend – opens the program, the virus attacks again. Safeguards: firewalls or virus scanners that detect known types of viruses. Standard procedures such as "never open a program file unless you know what it is and who it is from". Public key encryption to ensure that the message is from the person who claims to be the sender.

6.9　Security requirements

Highlights

Estimate security risks first.
Ask supplier how to protect against high-loss threats.
Avoid asking for features unless you know they will protect you adequately.

Figure 6.8B showed a risk assessment for the hotel. We will now discuss various requirements intended to guard against the risks. Figure 6.9 shows the outline.

Safeguarding the database

The risk assessment showed that loss of the database could be very expensive. The first five requirements in Figure 6.9 deal with that.

R1　The product shall safeguard against loss of the database. The estimated losses shall be <1 per 50 years.

This requirement focuses on the asset to be protected: the database. We could consider it a broad domain-level requirement. The supplier has to find out which threats might destroy the database and propose safeguards that would reduce the risk as required. The calculation of the estimated losses might of course be somewhat subjective, but could also be based on available statistics.

One problem with the requirement is that risks change over time. Crime, for instance, may go up or down. New hacker attacks may be invented. A more serious problem with the requirement is that it cannot be verified at delivery time, although the risk calculation may be checked.

R2　The product shall safeguard against consequences of disk crashes. Estimated losses to be <1 per 100 years.

R2 focuses on a single threat: a disk crash due to mechanical or electronic failure. It is a typical domain-level requirement. We don't ask for a specific solution, but it will most likely be some kind of duplicated disk.

It is easy to calculate the remaining risk with such a solution. If one disk crashes, the other takes over while the faulty one is replaced. Only if the second disk also crashes during the replacement will we lose the database. More than two disks may be used, thus further reducing the risk.

The problem with the requirement is that it only cares about a single threat. The database might also be lost due to other threats, for instance a virus that deletes files.

Fig 6.9   Security requirements

> **R1:** Safeguard against loss of database. Estimated losses to be <1 per 50 years.
>
> **R2:** Safeguard against disk crashes. Estimated losses to be <1 per 100 years.
>
> **R3:** Product shall use duplicated disks (RAID disks).
>
> **R4:** Product shall safeguard against viruses that delete files. Remaining risk to be <_____.
>
> **R5:** Product shall include firewalls for virus detection.
>
> **R6:** Product shall follow good accounting practices. Supplier shall obtain certification.
>
> **R7:** Product shall prevent users deleting invoices before transfer to the account system.
>
> **R8:** The supplier shall as an option offer features for checking and reserving deposits made by credit cards.
>
> **R9:** The supplier must enclose a risk assessment and suggest optional safeguards.

R3   The product shall use duplicated disks (RAID disks).

R3 is a typical product-level requirement that asks for a specific technical solution. It may be adequate, but the analyst should make sure that the required solution reduces the risk sufficiently.

R4   The product shall safeguard against viruses that delete files. The remaining risk shall be < ____.

R4 asks for safeguards against another threat, viruses, in particular those that delete files, for instance the database. The supplier has to suggest a solution. This is okay, and we may subjectively assess the effectiveness of the solution. However, the supplier is also asked to specify the remaining risk of such a virus attack (the open target approach). We doubt that serious suppliers will specify this risk, because it is impossible to calculate the inventiveness of hackers. Fortunately, it will also be very hard to tell later what the risk actually was (unless there are many successful attacks available for statistical analysis).

R5   The product shall include firewalls for virus detection.

R5 asks for a specific way of preventing viruses from entering the system through the Internet. The customer has taken the responsibility for the adequacy of the solution.

Fraud

The next two requirements deal with the threat of fraud – an employee who deletes the recorded invoices and cashes the money himself.

R6 The product shall follow good accounting practices. The supplier shall obtain certification.

R6 is a broad requirement: follow an established standard. Most likely, following the standard will guard against this threat and other related threats, but it might be a good idea to be explicit about it. (See other examples of standards as requirements in section 3.15.)

R7 The product shall prevent users from deleting invoices before transferring them to the account system.

With R7 we explicitly ask for prevention of the threat, and we can more easily convince ourselves that the prevention technique is adequate. As for most domain-oriented security requirements, it is hard to test that the requirement is met at delivery time.

Other examples

R8 The supplier shall as an option offer features for checking and reserving deposits made by credit cards.

R8 deals with another threat: guests who book and pay a deposit, but don't turn up and have no money on their account. The risk assessment (illegal access) showed that the average yearly loss should be around $5,000. Since the customer expects that a solution might be expensive compared to the loss, he asks for a solution as an *option*. This means that the solution has a separate price and the customer may take it or leave it.

R9 The supplier must enclose a risk assessment and suggest optional safeguards.

This is a real, broad requirement of the open metric type. The customer doesn't know about security and simply asks the supplier for help. The customer reserves the right to choose among the various solutions. The requirement is good in case of an analysis project or a contract-based project (all-in-one contract, see section 1.7.4). In tender-based projects it is less suitable because the supplier will have to do a customer-specific investigation before submitting his proposal.

6.10 Maintenance

Highlights

Maintenance: repair defects, extend product, inform, and train users.
Systematically handle problems, defects, and requests for change.
Defect versus change: unimportant.
What to do: important – so do it.

Most products need maintenance. Users encounter errors in them, demands grow, the environment changes. Many suppliers make quite a good business in this area, and customers are more or less forced to pay what the supplier asks, because the alternative is to get an entirely new system with all the implied costs of change. In some cases, suppliers sell the first version of their product cheap, then collect the profit through maintenance.

To the customer the maintenance expenses can become a real burden, both because of fees to the supplier, but also because of disrupted business when program updates are installed. The purpose of maintenance requirements is to guard against both factors.

What is maintenance?

Usually software engineers distinguish between three types of maintenance, as illustrated on Figure 6.10:

Corrective maintenance. Correcting reported defects in the product.

Preventive maintenance. Correcting defects that haven't caused problems yet, but might do it later. The Millennium Bug or Year 2000 problem was a good example. It was expected that many programs would incorrectly decide that a date like 4/23-2000 was before 4/23-1999 because these dates inside the computer were represented as 00-04-23 and 99-04-23. A massive preventive effort was made worldwide, and many defects were found and corrected. As a result nothing serious happened.

Another example is that the supplier corrects a reported defect, for instance discount calculations on invoices, but ignores that it influences something else, for instance credit notes, thereby causing a problem later. Avoiding related defects is essential to both customer and supplier, since additional repairs are costly to both parties.

Perfective maintenance. Expanding the system to meet additional demands.

Maintainability requirements should deal with all these types. Let us first look at the maintenance cycle, i.e. what happens to a defect or a request for change:

Fig 6.10 Maintenance

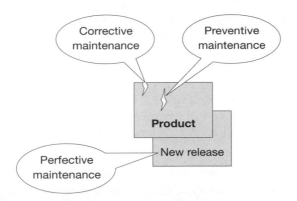

Maintenance cycle:
Report:	Record and acknowledge.
Analyze:	Error, change, usability, mistake? Cost/benefit?
Decide:	Repair? reject? Work-around? next release? train users?
Reply:	Report decision to source.
Test:	Test solution. Related defects?
Carry out:	Install, transfer user data, inform.

Maintenance cycle

1 **Reporting.** A problem is reported to maintenance staff. They record it with date, source, and a short description. If necessary, the source person who reported the problem gets a confirmation.

2 **Analysis.** The report is analyzed. Is it a programming error, a change request, a usability problem, or the reporter's misunderstanding. Where is the defect that caused the problem, or what is the real need behind the change request? What would it cost to repair the problem? What would it cost to the user if nothing is done? Sometimes staff have to make further investigations to complete the analysis.

3 **Decision.** What are the possible actions? Repair it immediately? Include in the next release? Find a work-around (something the user can do to complete his task anyway)? Inform users? Give them a training course? Reject the problem because it isn't worth doing anything? Make further analysis?

4 **Reply.** Report the decision to the source.

5 **Test the solution.** If a repair or a work-around has been decided, try it out and test that it works. Also try to find and correct related defects that might turn up later (preventive maintenance).

6 Carry out the decision. In case of repairs, install the changes and ensure that user data, set-ups, etc. are preserved. In all cases, inform the users.

Many suppliers don't have a well established maintenance cycle, and part of the requirements could be that they shall have one.

What is a defect?

Part of the cycle is to determine whether something is a defect or a change request. The supplier often has to correct defects free of charge, whereas the customer has to pay for changes. The distinction can be quite difficult in practice, but here are some guidelines:

■ If the system doesn't work as intended by the programmer, it is a *programming error*. This is clearly a defect.

■ If the system doesn't meet the stated requirements, it is another kind of defect: a *violated requirement*.

■ If the user has unstated expectations that the system doesn't meet, this is a gray area. In practice it is unrealistic to specify all requirements, so if the user has a *reasonable expectation*, most courts worldwide will consider it a defect (see section 1.1, Court Cases).

■ If the issue was not a reasonable expectation at the start of the project, it is clearly a change request.

■ If the system can do what the user wants, but the user cannot figure out how to do it, it is a *usability problem*. Usually it is not considered a defect unless we have stated some usability requirements. In practice these problems are often rejected, although it might be cost-effective to improve the user interface.

As you see, there are gray areas where disagreements could occur and matters might end up in court. To avoid this, the contract could contain a statement that disagreements about defects shall be decided by an arbiter nominated by both parties.

6.11 Maintainability requirements

Highlights

Many ways to specify maintenance requirements.
Guaranteed time to repair is safe to customer, but risky to supplier.
Supplier can charge high fees for changes. Ask for a price per unit of change.
Don't rely on complexity measures of the code.

Figures 6.11A and 6.11B show 11 examples of maintainability requirements. The figures have space to indicate the risk to the customer and the supplier, but we leave it to the reader to fill these in as an exercise.

Maintenance performance

Examples 1 to 3 specify the efficiency of the maintenance process.

R1 The supplier's hot-line shall analyze 95% of the problem reports within 2 work hours. Urgent defects (no work-around possible) shall be repaired within 30 work hours in 95% of cases.

This requirement limits the time the user has to wait before he knows how to proceed following a problem. In most cases there is a work-around for defects, but otherwise a repair is guaranteed within a specific period. The requirement acknowledges that some problems are more difficult, but limits their number. Requirements as strict as R1 occur for critical systems such as bank networks and process control. Details about what work hours mean, how to reply to the user, etc. may have to be specified for some types of projects.

R2 When repairing a defect, related non-repaired defects shall be less than 0.5 on average.

This requirement deals with preventive maintenance. It encourages the supplier to find related problems instead of just rushing for a simple fix. The requirement assumes of course that defect reports are collected and analyzed. Typically, a financial penalty may be specified if the requirement is not met. (The more modern variant is to give the supplier a bonus if it is met!)

R3 For a period of two years, the supplier shall enhance the product at a cost of ___ per Function Point.

This requirement limits the cost of enhancing the system (perfective maintenance). Essentially, it states that enhancements shall have a cost proportional to their size. The cost per enhancement unit has to be fixed. The example is from a tender process where the supplier is asked to specify the unit cost (open target), so that the

Fig 6.11A Maintainability requirements

	Risk	
	Customer	Supplier
Maintenance performance **R1:** Supplier's hotline shall analyze 95% of reports within 2 work hours. Urgent defects (no work-around) shall be repaired within 30 work hours in 95% of cases.		
R2: When repairing a defect, related non-repaired defects shall be less than 0.5 on average.		
R3: For a period of two years, supplier shall enhance the product at a cost of ___ per Function Point.		
Support features **R4:** Installation of a new version shall leave all database contents and personal settings unchanged.		
R5: Supplier shall station a qualified developer at the customer's site.		
R6: Supplier shall deposit code and full documentation of every release and correction at _____.		

customer can compare suppliers. Stating the cost per unit of enhancement prevents the supplier from exploiting the situation after delivery, when he has a de facto monopoly on enhancements (see section 1.7.4).

Function Points are recognized in some domains as a way of measuring the size of a development job independent of programming techniques and programmer experience. In other domains, the parties will have to agree on other size measures in order to use this style. Some experts find Function Points dubious as cost predictors (see Furey and Kitchenham 1997).

Maintenance performance requirements can get close to what the customer essentially needs. However, only very mature (or very naive) suppliers are willing to commit to this kind of requirement.

Support features

Support features specify things to happen during maintenance, but they don't say anything about how fast they should happen.

R4 Installation of a new version shall leave all database contents and all personal settings unchanged.

R4 deals with a common nuisance. The supplier has installed a new version for a customer, and then every user has to spend hours setting up all the options they set up long ago, but have completely forgotten about. The requirement doesn't say whether the supplier shall deal with it manually or whether his product shall transfer the old settings automatically.

R5 The supplier shall station a qualified developer to perform maintenance at the customer's site.

R5 requires exclusive access to a maintenance person, so that the customer is not dependent on other customers calling for maintenance. Sometimes it may be necessary to specify the qualifications of that person. If the person has to be highly qualified, it may be a problem to keep him motivated day after day away from his fellow developers. Find a reasonable balance.

R6 The supplier shall deposit code and full documentation of every release and correction at _____.

Depositing code and documentation is an emergency precaution in case the supplier stops his business or doesn't fulfill the maintenance requirements. In this case, the customer may find someone else to do the maintenance, and the code and documentation will allow that.

Fig 6.11B Maintainability requirements

	Risk	
	Customer	Supplier
Development process requirements **R7:** Every program module must be assessed for maintainability according to procedure xx. 70% must obtain "highly maintainable" and none "poor".		
R8: Development must use regression test allowing full re-testing in 12 hours.		
Program complexity requirements **R9:** The cyclomatic complexity of code may not exceed 7. No method in any object may exceed 200 lines of code.		
Product feature requirements **R10:** Product shall log all actions and provide remote diagnostic functions.		
R11: Product shall provide facilities for tracing any database field to places where it is used.		

Development process requirements

These requirements specify something about the development process. The intent is to ensure that the product is easy to maintain, but to what extent it really helps is another matter.

R7 Every program module must be assessed for maintainability according to the procedures in app. *xx*. At least 70% must obtain "highly maintainable" and none may obtain "poor".

The assessment specified in appendix *xx* could be a kind of inspection where experienced developers from the supplier's staff and a third party review and score the code. R7 specifies a good way to check that the code is easy to maintain. It cannot, however, guarantee that the supplier later makes the effort needed to actually carry out the maintenance.

The approach is particularly useful if someone else is going to do the maintenance. We have for instance seen the requirement used in a case where a national stock exchange wanted a trading system from abroad, but due to the local language and alphabet, maintenance had to be carried out by local staff. The main criteria in the purchase was the ease of modifying the code, and the local staff assessed that together with supplier staff for each of the potential suppliers.

R8 The development process must have a regression test procedure that allows complete re-testing within 12 hours.

R8 deals with the frequent problem that developers change something, but this change has an unexpected effect on something else. A regression test is an automated procedure that tests the product with earlier test data and reports any deviations in output.

Product complexity requirements

Some developers believe that maintainability can be measured in the code by automatic means, as in this requirement:

R9 The cyclomatic complexity measure of code may not exceed 7. No method in any object may exceed 200 lines of code.

Cyclomatic complexity essentially counts the levels of nesting in the program, assuming that a program with 12 nested loops is more difficult to maintain than one with 4.

If this requirement is met, maintainability is probably increased in many cases, but there is no guarantee that it helps significantly on the real maintainability issue as experienced by the customer. Seasoned developers find such automatic counts of dubious value for predicting maintainability.

Product feature requirements

Experienced developers faced with requirements such as R1 and R2 will try to build features into the product or the support tools to enable them satisfy the requirements with less effort. It could be stated as requirements, for instance like this:

R10 The product shall log all actions and provide remote diagnostic functions.

R11 The product shall provide facilities for tracing any database field to places where it is used.

R10 helps in analyzing error causes, and R11 helps in finding places in the code that might be influenced by a change. Most suppliers are unwilling to commit to the performance requirements in R1 and R2, but would consider delivering product features such as R10 and R11.

7

Requirements in the product life cycle

Requirements play a role in many parts of the product life cycle. We mentioned some of them in sections 1.1 and 1.7. In this chapter we will look at the roles in more depth. Here are the main places where requirements are involved (Figure 7.1 gives an overview):

Project inception

Someone starts a project to get a product. A tentative project scope and business goals are outlined. A project team is formed. Who drives this? In case of product development, the supplier drives the process, but he should involve potential customers and sub-contractors. For in-house or contract-based projects the customer is the driving force, but the supplier may also enter at this stage. We look at project inception in section 7.1.

Elicitation

The team defines the more precise business goals in co-operation with stakeholders. They also outline the requirements. This is a large area, and we have devoted a full chapter to it (Chapter 8). In most projects, the supplier is heavily involved here, the exception being tender projects where the supplier is not usually involved until the requirements are sent out.

Writing the requirements

Someone writes the requirements in a finished form. This is a huge area, and we have devoted several chapters to it (Chapters 2 to 6). Who does the writing? Usually someone in the project team, but although it is a specialist job, we often see it attacked by people without the necessary skills and experience, for instance ordinary users at the customer site, or even suppliers and consultants with insufficient background.

Checking and validation

Before requirements are ready for contracting, they must be checked and validated. This is usually also a specialist job, although the specialist must work with the customer during validation. We have devoted Chapter 9 to checking and validation.

Delivery contract

At a certain point the two parties can sign the requirements and the contract. In many cases the supplier has already become involved, so signing is more or less a formality. For tender processes, however, this is a long process. The customer sends out a request for proposal (RFP), suppliers send in their proposals, the customer compares them and eventually signs a contract with one of them. Section 7.2 explains more on this.

Comparing proposals

In tender processes, the customer has to compare the proposals, and this is not as easy as it may sound. Sections 7.3 and 7.4 show ways to do it.

Writing proposals

What do you do if you are a supplier who wants to send in a proposal? How can you convince the customer to choose you? How can you address various kinds of requirements, and what should you do when the requirements are bad? Section 7.5 can help you.

Design and programming

If development is involved, requirements play an important role. You have to *trace* the requirements into the growing product and *verify* that they are met. Section 7.6 shows ways to do this.

Acceptance test and delivery

When the product is ready for deployment, it is installed and tested in many ways. Among other things, developers must *verify* that it meets requirements. Section 7.7 explains what to do.

Requirements management

Requirements change from the beginning of a project to the end of the product's life. From the customer's viewpoint, the project usually ends after delivery. What comes after this is maintenance and support. Section 7.8 shows ways to manage the changes.

Fig 7.1   Requirements in product life cycle

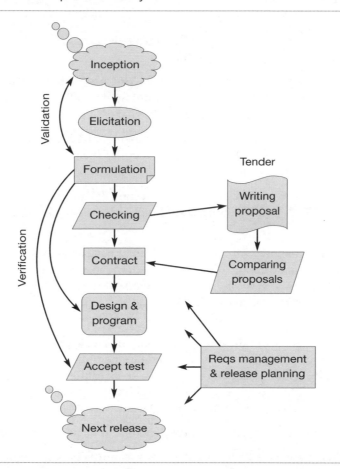

Release planning

From the supplier's viewpoint, the project often continues with new releases, particularly if it is a product for a wider market. Section 7.9 has a short discussion of this.

Tracing and tool support

Tracing of requirements to other information sources is important for a successful product, and requirements tools can be of great help here. We have covered many tracing techniques in other parts of the book, but give an overview in Section 7.10.

7.1 Project inception

Projects may start in many ways. Here are a few quotes from people that helped start the projects behind the case studies:

Immediate need: "Our idea about a Tax Payers' Association has really caught attention. Lots of people are calling us wanting to enroll, and if we don't get an IT-system to support us, we will be in a huge mess very soon."

A bright idea: "We lose too much on our repair contracts. Why not collect experience data to see what things really cost us? It would also be a good opportunity to replace our outdated business applications."

Seeing what others have: "I saw an interesting 3D graphics product yesterday. Maybe we could come up with a sound-measuring system where the results are shown in 3D."

Long-term nuisance: "All this roster planning has been a nightmare for a long time. Staff complain about all the mistakes in the roster. In the old days it wasn't like that, but now it is getting worse and worse. Maybe it is time to see whether we could get an IT system to help us. By the way, why not ask for a better handling of overtime payment at the same time?"

Often people talk about the issues for a long time, collecting evidence for the problems, discussing how much to include in the project, discussing pros and cons. Usually nothing happens until someone takes the leading role and becomes a champion of the project. Typically, he finds someone else to support him and together they manage to get the project started.

During the first part of the project they try to resolve many vague issues such as:

Goals: What are the advantages of a new system? What are the business goals and why would someone like to pay for this?

Scope: What should be included and excluded?

Vision: In broad terms, what might the final system look like? How would the users work with it?

Cost/benefit: Is there a favorable balance between advantages and disadvantages? Does it pay on the bottom line?

Stakeholders: Who is affected by the system and who is critical for its success?

Goals and scope are the first versions of the requirements. If you can state them in verifiable ways, they can serve as high-level requirements.

If it seems realistic to get such a system and the cost/benefit is favorable, the project has a chance to proceed (see examples of cost/benefit in section 8.6). At this stage, a more systematic search for requirements, *requirements elicitation*, is appropriate. The requirements engineers also have to formulate the requirements in a final form and check them for consistency. Usually the goals, scope, cost/benefit, etc. will change during the process. The result of all this is a requirements specification.

7.2   Contracts

There are many types of contracts in the IT world. In section 1.7.4 we discussed contracts for doing the analysis and requirements, contracts for doing development, and contracts for doing the whole job from analysis to development. In this section we will only look at contracts to deliver something according to requirements.

How to define the requirements and the contract depends on the project type. Let us have a closer look.

In-house development

The project is carried out inside a company for its own use. Usually, the customer (typically a user department) and the IT department co-operate to make the specification, and both parties sign off on it. There should also be a statement about delivery time, who does what and who pays what.

As part of the co-operation, the parties have had opportunities to reach consensus and understand the consequences of introducing the new system. In practice, however, this is a weak point. Consequences are rarely clear to either party, and they often sign under time pressure.

Proper choice of elicitation techniques can prevent many problems (section 8.2). In particular, we recommend stakeholder analysis, prototyping, pilot experiments, study of similar companies, cost/benefit analysis, and goal-domain analysis. Some of the requirements styles can help document the consequences of the new system. We recommend Tasks & Support, virtual windows, and at a later stage, prototypes with usability tests.

When disputes arise over the project, whether about requirements, delivery time, or costs, resolution is handled inside the company. This doesn't mean that it is easy. Although the parties should have a higher-level common goal – the benefit of the company – they also have their own interests. For this reason, the conflict may have to be escalated to a higher level, but in many cultures both parties lose face if that is necessary.

Product development

The product is a commercial product to be marketed by a company. The "customer" is the marketing department and the "supplier" the development department. Contract-wise, the situation is very similar to in-house development.

Release planning is particularly important for product development. It is not just a matter of deciding on requirements in the next release, requirements for the following releases must be taken into account as well (section 7.8).

COTS purchase

In this case the supplier just delivers a product off the shelf. The supplier will provide a more or less complete specification of the product.

The customer may get the product on a trial basis, or try it out in some other way. If the customer has made a requirements specification, it is his own guide for selecting between alternative products, or at least find out which requirements can be met and which cannot. The supplier will rarely take any responsibility for fulfilling the customer's requirements.

Tender

The customer starts a tender process and sends out a request for proposal (RFP). The tender documentation contains an elaborate requirements specification written by the customer or his consultant. Usually the documentation includes a contract stating delivery times and other conditions. The product may be a tailor-made system or a COTS-based system with extensions.

When a supplier decides to participate, he sends a proposal to the customer. The proposal must describe how the supplier is going to meet the requirements and at what price (see section 7.5).

Generally, the customer announces the tender to a wide audience, for instance in newspapers or trade journals, and anybody can reply. Some suppliers request the specification, study it, and decide that they want to participate. They write a proposal and send it to the customer, who compares the different proposals and selects one. The parties then set up a contract for what to deliver and how.

Comparing the proposals is often a major task. The customer has to compare prices and business values of the offered solutions. Section 7.3 shows ways to structure the comparison.

Pre-qualification. The tender process can be very time-consuming and costly for both parties. If many suppliers participate, the chance of getting the contract is small, and serious suppliers may decide to ignore the opportunity. To restrict the number of suppliers involved, customers often use a limited tender process. First the customer announces that he is going to make a tender process within area xx, and he invites suppliers to apply for pre-qualification.

In order to qualify, the supplier must document experience within the area, a good track record, and solid financial status for a project of this size. Very little is explained about the project, so interested suppliers can send in an application without too much effort.

The customer selects a limited number of suppliers and sends the full requirements to them. Seeing the details, some suppliers drop out, while others invest time in writing a proposal.

Contract. When the customer has chosen a proposal, he signs a contract with the supplier. The contract has a lot of legal stuff, and the requirements are usually in an appendix. But what are the requirements at this stage? The original requirements from the tender documents or the solution proposed by the supplier?

Let us illustrate the problem with an example. The customer has specified requirements like this in the tender documents:

R1 The system shall support check-in according to this task description . . .

The supplier specifies his proposal in this way:

R2 The supplier delivers his standard hotel application WonderHotel release 3.5, installs it and converts the master files.

If it later turns out that the WonderHotel product cannot support check-in as described, who is right? That depends on what the parties have written in the contract.

One model is that the customer's requirements rule, and that the supplier is responsible for his solution meeting those requirements. Even though the customer has signed that he wants WonderHotel, it is still the supplier's responsibility that the solution is adequate.

Another model is that the supplier's proposal rules. That is what the customer has signed. In this case it is the customer's responsibility that the solution actually meets his needs.

We know of cases where a supplier from another country signed a standard contract from the customer's country without paying attention to which model it used. In the contract a single line said that the customer's requirements ruled in case of doubt. Later the supplier was completely taken by surprise when the customer asked him to modify the product to match the customer's needs. No, why should he change the product? The customer had signed that he wanted the standard product. He hadn't understood that little paragraph. The case ended up in court, but although the customer won, both parties lost a lot of money.

Contract development

The supplier develops and delivers a system to the customer. The requirements specification and the contract specify what is to be delivered, who is to do what, etc. The system may be tailor-made or a COTS-based system with modifications.

The two companies will often work together for some time to write the requirements and the contract. In many ways, the situation is like in-house development, but in case of conflicts the parties have no common goal. The conflict has to be resolved by court or arbitration. For this reason it is more critical to write verifiable requirements and state how to verify them, to be careful to state responsibilities in the contract, etc.

It is often a good idea to make two-step contracts where the first contract deals with making the detailed requirements, while the next one deals with developing the system (see sections 1.7.3 and 1.7.4). According to this model, the parties first elicit domain-level requirements, e.g. in the form of task descriptions, and next they define design-level requirements, e.g. in the form of prototypes.

In this case, there is also a choice of contract model: If the design-level requirements don't satisfy the domain-level requirements, which of them is valid? The answer should be stated in the contract.

7.3 Comparing proposals

In a tender process, the customer may get over ten proposals, while at other times he gets only two or three.

Some customers believe that they can specify all kinds of stringent requirements. The result may be that nobody cares to send a proposal – to the customer's great surprise. In other cases, the customer has specified very design-oriented requirements that he got from looking at a specific product. As a result only one supplier may bid, and he knows that nobody else can meet the requirements, so he can state his price accordingly.

Comparing two proposals is no easy task, and with ten or more it may be a huge task. It is not just a matter of comparing prices, because suppliers may meet the requirements to various degrees. They may even offer several solutions at different prices.

It is common for the supplier and customer to meet when the customer has had a chance to study the proposal. During the meeting the supplier presents his solution and the customer asks questions. These meetings (sometimes called "workshops") are a key activity for exchanging information, but in principle, the supplier has written the necessary information about prices and what to deliver in his proposal.

When the customer organization compares the proposals, stakeholders may start fighting because each of them have their own favorite requirements that are supported in various ways by suppliers. So the stakeholders may rate the suppliers differently.

To create order out of chaos, a structured comparison of the proposals is essential. Figure 7.3 shows one way to do it. We assume that a hotel owner has three proposals, A, B, and C, and we rate each of them according to several criteria. The choice of criteria may vary from one project to another, and during evaluation the parties may add more criteria to the list. Figure 7.3 uses the following criteria:

Normal requirements. This is an average or overall rating of the requirements. Section 7.4 shows ways to compute the rating. Usually, a supplier meets all requirements reasonably – otherwise he would not have sent a proposal – but a few requirements are not met adequately. Completely disqualifying a proposal that fails at a few points, but is excellent in other ways, might be stupid. The customer might reconsider his priorities or find complementary solutions. When rating the overall level, we exclude these failed requirements. In the example, proposal A meets most requirements on a bread-and-butter level, while proposal C has an excellent support of most requirements.

Weakest requirements. For each proposal there are usually some important requirements that are not well supported, but which ones vary from one proposal to another. In the hotel case, proposal B might be too weak in handling discount rules, while proposal C completely lacks support for Web-booking. The result is the ratings shown. Proposal A has no particular weaknesses, so the weakest requirements are rated as the normal requirements.

Fig 7.3   Comparing proposals

Hotel system evaluation 0 (bad) – 5 (excellent)	Proposals		
	A	**B**	**C**
Normal requirements	3	4	5
Weakest requirements	3	2	(0)
Total product points	**6**	**6**	**5**
Understand our problem	(1)	3	5
Track record	4	(1)	4
Solidity	5	4	4
Total points	**16**	**14**	**18**
Base price	25	20	15
Option 1: Floor map	10	6	–
Option 2: ...	8	–	8

If stakeholders don't agree?

Ideal evaluation	Proposals		
	A	**B**	**C**
Business value (NPV)	100	100	90
Supplier's price	25	20	15
Internal investment costs	30	25	10
Net value	**45**	**55**	**65**

Total product points. This is the total of the two points above. In many projects there will be more product criteria to add up.

Understand our problem. Some suppliers just say "yes" to the requirements, without providing evidence of how they are going to meet them. Such proposals make the customer nervous. Has the supplier understood what we ask for? Does he show that he really knows our business and understands our needs? Many customers don't rate this criteria explicitly, but it remains an important, yet subjective issue. Figure 7.3 treats the criteria explicitly. In the example, proposal A is from a supplier that obviously considers himself a master in the IT industry, and he hasn't cared to show that he understands the hotel business too. Proposal C is from a supplier who demonstrates intimate knowledge of small hotels such as the ones run by the customer.

Is this factor really so important? Emam and Madhavji (1995) investigated the factors in the requirements process and found out what customers rated highest. The clear winner was "the ability to see the consequences for our work and business". This result is closely related to the evaluation factor "understand our business".

Track record. It doesn't help that you choose a proposal that promises to satisfy all your needs, if the supplier cannot run projects, either because he is a novice or because something is wrong in his organization. The track record criteria rates that. Supplier A has a good reputation in general. Supplier C is less well known, but has provided good evidence for his past achievements. Supplier B hasn't said much about his track record.

Solidity. The financial status of the supplier. Can he survive a situation where he has misjudged the size of the project and loses money? Can he survive a court case? In the example, proposer A has no such problem (but he might be an expensive opponent in court, so ensure in the contract that conflicts will be resolved by arbitration rather than in court). The other proposers are okay.

Total points. This is simply the total of all the points above. Some stakeholders play around with weights for each criteria, and by cleverly manipulating the weights, they may end up with a top rating for their favorite supplier. Don't participate in that game! The total points – weighted or not – are just a rough guideline to be used subjectively.

In some countries, the weighting game is even used as a vehicle for fraud and corruption. One stakeholder may for instance get commission in the form of a kickback from a specific supplier if he gives him the contract. By manipulating the weights and the individual scores, he may achieve this. Some customers try to prevent this by stating precise rating rules and weights in advance, but a corrupt stakeholder may also influence this process. Furthermore, the stated precise rules and weights may later turn out to be inadequate, for instance because important criteria have been forgotten. Sticking to the wrong rules might lead to selecting an obviously wrong supplier.

Base price. The price for the product in its basic version without options.

Option 1, 2, etc. Prices for the different options. In the hotel case, option 1 could be a floor map showing occupied rooms. Proposal C doesn't offer a solution here. If there are many options, the list may be long, and it may be necessary to bundle the options into groups, for instance according to the user tasks involved.

Stakeholder viewpoints. If stakeholders cannot agree on the ratings, let each stakeholder group make their own rating of the requirements. Ratings for track record, etc. should be the same. Quite often, it turns out that although stakeholders rate the criteria differently, the final conclusion on whom to choose is the same.

Choosing the winner

In the example, which proposal should the customer choose? In this case it is hard because the proposals are close, and their weak points are different. However, in most cases we see, the conclusion is obvious to everybody once the comparison is set up in a structured way as in Figure 7.3.

In the example, proposal C is by far the cheapest. If you consider the price per point, C is even more advantageous, while A and B are about equal. But take care, these are just blind computations. What about the weakest requirements, for instance? They speak against proposal C.

An important thing to do is to look at the weakest points to see whether they are acceptable, and whether the parties could mitigate them. In the example, each proposal has a real weak point, as shown by the circles drawn round their lowest scores. If we reject all the proposals with a serious weak point, there are no proposals left!

Proposal A doesn't give evidence for the solution and gives the impression that the supplier doesn't care about the customer's business. Is this true or has he just underestimated this point? Is he willing to work with our expert users to learn more? A meeting might shred some light on this.

Proposer B has no track record, or rather he hasn't documented it. Could he refer to previous customers where we could learn about their experiences? Are there reasons we might run the risk of giving him the contract if he is new to the market?

Proposal C has no provision for Web-booking. Maybe the proposer could point to an acceptable solution, for instance enter into a joint project with an e-business provider or deliver a version next year? A meeting might shred light on that. And after all, is it worth investing in Web-booking?

Negotiation. In some countries and some situations, supplier and customer can freely negotiate about details in the proposal.

In other countries legal rules forbid customer and supplier from negotiating or from meeting during the tender process. Proposers can ask questions in writing and will receive written replies, but all other proposers will see the questions and answers too. With products as complex as software, the lack of personal communication makes things very difficult. Many reasonable mitigation actions are lost in that way. Fortunately, if no supplier satisfies all requirements, the customer is allowed to bargain and discuss. In the example, we might claim that this is the situation, and that would actually help us out.

Ideal evaluation

When comparing prices and points, bear in mind that they only give some indication of the bottom line. The bottom of Figure 7.3 shows the ideal computation. First we assess the business value of each proposal – how much will we earn or save with each solution? In practice, analysts total the earnings for a few years, computing the net present value (NPV) of the earnings. Proposal A and B are roughly equal because they provide much the same functionality, while C is lower because its lack of Web-booking may lose some guests. The product points above are closely related to the business value.

The supplier's price is the same as above. The internal investment costs include the time to train users, and risks, for instance because the supplier doesn't understand the hotel business. Here proposal A is the clear loser, while proposal C is the clear winner due to their demonstrated understanding of small hotels. The risk points are closely related to the internal costs.

The bottom line shows C as the winner – even though C doesn't satisfy the important Web-booking requirement.

If properly done, the ideal evaluation handles also the stakeholder's individual interests in a fair way – at least as seen from a top management viewpoint. The only problem is that the ideal evaluation is hard to make. However, it can serve as a mental yardstick in many debates during evaluation.

7.4 Rating the requirements

Although many analysts claim that requirements are mandatory – at least the functional ones – this is not quite true in practice. Further, requirements may be fulfilled to varying degrees, and the customer will have to rate how well they are fulfilled.

For the supplier the problem is that it is hard to see how important the various requirements are. There are several ways to deal with the issues:

1 Assign each requirement a priority.

2 State optional requirements that the supplier may fulfill at a separate price or ignore.

3 Use Open Metrics and Open Targets.

4 State requirements as Tasks & Support.

Priorities are widely used for feature-based requirements. The Midland Hospital specification (Chapter 12) is an example. It gives each requirement a priority from 1 to 4, with 4 being a requirement of crucial importance, while 1 is a requirement that is desirable in the long run.

But what is a priority really? Does it mean that all high-priority requirements have to be met before low-priority requirements are considered? No, not in practice. If a high-priority requirement would cost a fortune to satisfy, it may turn out to be less important than the customer thought.

In many cases, the priorities are used as weights. When assessing a proposal, the customer gives each requirement a score for how well it is met. He multiplies the score by its priority to find the weighted sum of all requirements. Since the supplier knows the priorities, he may find ways to satisfy the high priorities well, and the low priorities in a cheap way.

In principle priorities (weights) are a sound approach, but in practice customers tend to give everything a high priority. The consultant for Midland Hospital reported that it took weeks to convince hospital staff to give some requirements a lower weight. The trick was to ask: what would you do if nobody could give you this? Usually the users could find some ways to live without that feature, and the inconvenience was an indication of the weight. Yet, in the final specification, more than half of the requirements have weight 4 and only a few have weight 1.

Options are requirements that the supplier may fulfill at a separate price, or ignore. In the hotel case, the customer might realize that having a floor map showing occupied rooms could be expensive, and he might run the business without it. Thus he asks for a floor map as an option. When he later sees the price, he can decide whether or not he needs it.

Large tender projects are often defined in such a way that all requirements are essentially options. The customer wants to see how much he can get for his money, and he will adapt to what is available at a reasonable price. The Midland Hospital specification is an example. It has more than 700 feature-oriented requirements. The supplier got a list of them in a computer spreadsheet, and he had to mark each of them with an indication of how he would meet them. The marks in the Midland Hospital were something like this:

Mark:

5   A standard feature in the system.
4   Supported by means of a report generator.
3   An added feature that will be supported in future releases too.
2   An added feature that requires special maintenance to transfer to future releases.
1   Supplied as a new customer-specific program, maintained separately.
0   Not offered.

The last possibility makes the requirement optional, although the supplier isn't asked to state a separate price for the feature. The customer computes a total score for the requirements by multiplying the marks with the weights (priorities) and calculating the total.

Open metrics and open targets

A requirement with open metric asks the supplier to specify how he fulfills the requirement. As an example, the hotel owner could ask the supplier to provide forecast functions and specify how he measures their hit rate and what the hit rates are.

In a requirement with an open target, the customer has specified how he measures the requirement, but leaves it to the supplier to specify the actual value. As an example, the customer wants a response time of around 3 seconds, but leaves it to the supplier to specify the response time he can provide (section 6.3).

When assessing the proposal, the customer scores each requirement according to how well it meets or exceeds his expectations. He can total all the scores or weigh them with priorities.

Task & Support requirements

When the customer has specified requirements in Task & Support style (section 3.8), he usually assesses the proposal as outlined in Figure 7.4 with the check-in task as an example.

This figure shows the original Task & Support specification with some modifications relating to proposal B. A team consisting of an expert user and an analyst have tried out the existing parts of the system according to the task description and the variants.

They have noted that there is no floor map at present, but the supplier offers it as an option to be implemented if he gets the contract. They like the bargain price display, but find the user dialog cumbersome if it turns out that the guest hasn't booked. There is no support for electronic keys and none is offered. Searching for a guest by his name is cumbersome. Overall rating: 3.

The advantage of this approach is that the rating is grounded in the tasks. It is much easier to assess advantages in that context than as separate features out of context. Further, there are far fewer tasks than features, so the final list of scores is manageable. We should mention that a feature used in many tasks is implicitly rated several times – once for each task where it is used. This is an advantage, because a feature may appear convenient in one task context but inconvenient in another.

What should you do if no part of the system currently exists? In that case, the assessors have to rely on the description provided by the supplier. A skilled supplier will have filled in the right-hand side of the task form with a short description of how he intends to support the task. He might even have outlined some screens or virtual windows to be used.

Fig 7.4 Customer's rating

Task: 1.2 Check-in Purpose: Give guest a room . . . Frequency: . . .	**Proposal B** **Rating: 3**
Sub-tasks:	**Assessment:**
1. Find room. **Problem:** Guest wants neighboring rooms; price bargain.	*Floor map developed as an option.* *Very convenient display of bargain prices.*
2. Record guest as checked in.	*If guest is not booked, cumbersome* *to switch to that task.*
3. Deliver key. **Problem:** Guests forget to return the key; wants two keys.	*No support for electronic keys.*
Variants:	
1a. Guest has booked in advance. **Problem:** Guest identification fuzzy.	*Tests show no tolerance for spelling errors.* *Very long search time for names.*

7.5 Writing a proposal

In the preceding sections we looked at the tender situation from the customer's viewpoint. We will now consider it from the supplier's viewpoint.

Assume that you as a supplier have got a requirements specification and want to write a proposal. What should you do?

First of all, you have to deliver the information that the customer requests. If the customer asks you to fill in an electronic form with your reply for each of the 1,001 requirements, you have to do it. If he asks for prices for each of 200 options, you have to give them, although you may bundle them into groups covered by a price per group. If he asks for evidence of your track record or financial status, you have to give it.

All of this is just the formalities. If competition is hard, you will not win just by following the formalities, but you will be considered non-compliant if you don't. How do you win, then? Have a look at section 7.3 to see how a customer might rate your proposal. Note that it is essential that you convince the customer, in particular demonstrating that you understand his problems and his specific business.

Just answering yes and no to the questions doesn't sound convincing to the customer. He may doubt that you really know what you are saying yes to. And in fact he is right. Many suppliers don't quite understand the requirements, but they say yes to them anyway to get the contract. "We have to find out about them during the project", they say. Sometimes the project succeeds anyway, but in many cases it ends up as a disaster for both parties.

The other extreme is to flood the customer with information such as piles of colorful screen pictures and lengthy technical descriptions of your products. This will not convince the customer either. He wants you to address his problems – to map your solutions into his picture of the world. He is not able to make that mapping himself, and if you are unable to do this as well, co-operation between you seems unlikely.

You may convince the customer by giving examples (screens, stories, etc.) of how you handled a similar situation in another project. In general, tangible examples are more convincing than general policy statements or general product descriptions.

Usually, the best way to convince the customer is to show how you might solve his problems. Unfortunately, your chance of doing so depends very much on the style used by the customer in the specification. We will look at the possibilities for different styles.

Open metrics and open targets

If the customer has used open metrics or open targets, you have a good opportunity to address his problem. You may even give several replies, if necessary as options with different prices. Assume for instance, that the customer has asked for this:

R25 The response time shall be at most ___ seconds when moving from one screen to another. Valid for 95% of the cases. Customer expects 1.0 seconds.

You may fill in the empty field with 0.8 seconds, but add a note saying that if he can accept 0.8 seconds on *average*, and 2 seconds in 95% of cases, the hardware costs will be halved.

Assumptions

In some cases the customer has given insufficient information for the supplier to give a full answer. For instance the customer may have failed to specify how many users the system will have and what they will use the system to do. In that case, the supplier has no way of finding out whether he can satisfy the response time requirements. He could protect himself by stating an assumption in the proposal:

Assumption: It is assumed that at most 10 users will be working full speed with cost registration.

Tasks & Support

Tasks & Support work remarkably well for you as a supplier. You can much better understand the customer's situation, comment on his example solution, and describe your proposed solution in convincing terms.

Figure 7.5 shows how a supplier might reply in the hotel case to the check-in task. He offers to develop a floor map as an option with a price stated with the other options. He has made an outline of the screen on page *xx*, and he shows the standard room screen on page *yy*.

He has shown the appropriate check-in screens on page *zz*, and he admits that they cannot support electronic keys right now, but plan to do so in the near future. Finally, he describes how they solve the problem of fuzzy guest identification (e.g. misspelled names and addresses).

All of this directly addresses the customer's concerns in a way he can relate to. For comparison, look at Figure 7.4 to see how the customer rated this part of the proposal.

Feature-based requirements

What should you do if the customer has made a traditional feature-oriented specification? If he hasn't given any background information, and you are not a specialist in his business, you have no chance to guess why he needs the system and which tasks he wants to support. How can you convince him that you understand his problem, when you don't actually understand it?

The best thing to do is to find out about his actual tasks. Go and see what his company does, or talk to someone who has worked there. Then write that you assume that his tasks will be so and so and that you can support them so and so. You don't have to do this for all tasks, just a few critical ones to show that you are willing to work in that direction.

Also outline the solution, for instance with Virtual Windows. We have seen that even simple hand-drawn screens can convince customers that you are willing to co-operate and that you are already heading in the right direction to produce a good solution.

High-risk requirements

What should you do if the customer has specified an unrealistic requirement or one that will be unreasonably costly to fulfill? A good example is the unrealistic response time:

R26 The response time shall be at most 0.5 seconds on average when moving from one screen to another. The response time shall never be above 2 seconds.

If this is a multi-user system with 200 users, the worst case is that all of them will send a request at the same time. With an average response time of 0.5 seconds, the worst case might display a response time of 200×0.5 seconds. Guaranteeing the 2 seconds would be very costly, and the customer has probably not realized what he has asked for. (Read more on this in section 6.5.)

Suppliers treat such requirements in different ways. As an example, assume that five suppliers sent a proposal:

- Supplier A. We didn't notice any problem. Our response times are of that magnitude.

- Supplier B. We don't care. We'll find a way out later.

- Supplier C. We state as an assumption that 95% of the cases will be sufficient.

- Supplier D. We fulfill the requirement although it will be expensive.

- Supplier E. We tell the customer what it would cost and why, and then offer a reasonable alternative. Eventually, we offer the full solution as an expensive option.

Supplier D, who carefully met the requirement, doesn't get the contract. An immature customer, confused by all the talk in proposal E, will choose proposal A, B, or C.

In some cases he may never notice that he didn't get what he asked for. In other cases, the parties notice some time after signing the contract, and the customer insists on the requirement being fulfilled. Here supplier C is safe. He stated his assumption and the customer accepted.

Supplier A and B will start the literal requirements game if the customer later insists on the unrealistic response time. The supplier finds a solution that isn't against the literal requirements: he divides all screens into small screens each

Fig 7.5 Supplier's proposal

Task:	1.2 Check-in	
Purpose:	Give guest a room . . .	
Frequency:	. . .	

Sub-tasks:	Proposal:
1. Find room. **Problem:** Guest wants neighboring rooms; price bargain.	*Floor map developed as an option. See outline on page xx. See room screen on page yy.*
2. Record guest as checked in.	*See guest screen and check-in screen on page zz.*
3. Deliver key. **Problem:** Guest forgets to return the key; wants two keys.	*We provide no support for electronic keys. Planned for release 5 in 1.5 years.*
Variants:	
1a. Guest has booked in advance. **Problem:** Guest identification fuzzy.	*User may search for any field using wild-card character(s).*

requiring a key value before they open. The poor user has to go through countless screens to do the simplest things, but it isn't against requirements. Result? The project ends in disaster for the customer.

Supplier C runs a risk because the customer may decide that he is non-compliant.

A mature customer will of course prefer supplier E, who indirectly managed to discredit his competitors A and B by proving them to be unprofessional.

If you are supplier E, and the customer prefers supplier A or B, you shouldn't cry. Don't make business with him. He is too immature and the entire project will be too risky in many other ways.

High prices

Sometimes you know that your price is higher than the competitor's. Convince the customer that he will get value for money with you. Prove that you understand the real problem and that you can solve it for him. Implicitly you indicate that the other suppliers may not understand the real problem, and that although their price is lower, the customer will have to pay later.

Customers consider IT projects very risky, and they may lead to unexpected costs. Dealing with a supplier that eliminates these risks is worth a great deal of money.

Another way to deal with a high price is to find those parts of the proposal that cause a high price, for instance because the technical solution is expensive, or because the risk is high and you want to cover your risk in the total price.

For these requirements provide optional alternatives with lower prices – and explain why. The customer may realize that his requirements were not that important, considering the price, and that a simpler solution may suffice. (We have shown an example above under Open Metrics.)

7.6 Design and programming

If the project includes development from scratch or extensions to a COTS product, design and programming is involved. During these parts of development it is important to ensure that requirements will be met. There are basically three ways to do this:

Direct implementation. Developers implement the system requirement by requirement, in that way tracing requirements to design or code on the fly.

Verification. At suitable moments, developers look at requirements one by one and check that they are met. The check can be done during a design or code review, or the check can involve some kind of testing.

Embedded trace information. For each piece of code or each design artifact, state the requirements IDs that it deals with. This gives you backwards traceability from code to requirements. With a search tool or a requirements tool you can also go the other way and find all the code pieces involved in a requirement, thus getting forwards traceability as well. By going both ways you ensure that each piece of code is justified by some requirement and that each requirement is handled by some code. The forward traceability also helps developers find the program pieces impacted by proposed changes in requirements.

Some requirements are easy to implement one by one, while others are not. Some requirements are easy to verify during development, while others are not. We have discussed this for each requirement style in Chapters 2 to 6.

Embedded trace information sounds easy and useful, but in practice it only works if requirements are easy to implement one by one and easy to verify during development.

Below we will look at the ease of direct implementation and the ease of verification for different kinds of requirements. (Figure 7.6 gives an overview.)

Data requirement

R1 The system shall store data according to this data model . . .

Implementation: direct. Developers can systematically translate each box of the model into a database table.

Verification: simple. Other developers can easily check that it is done properly.

Design-level requirement

R2 The product shall have screen pictures and menus as shown in app. xx.

Implementation: direct. Developers can implement the screens and menu points one by one.

Fig 7.6 Design and program

R1: System shall store data according to this data model . . .

R2: Product shall have screen pictures and menus as shown in . . .

R3: Product shall record that a room is under repair . . .

R4: Product shall support check-in according to task description . . .

R5: At most 1 of 5 novices shall have critical usability problems during check-in.

R6: Storing a booking shall take less than 1 second on average.

R7: Precalculation of repair orders shall hit within 5% of actual costs.

How to trace and verify
these during development?

Verification: simple. Users can check that it looks right and other developers can review the code to see that it works according to the description. If some of the functions behind the menu points are complex, this is more difficult, of course.

Feature style

R3 The product shall be able to record that a room is occupied for maintenance.

Implementation: modest. The developer has to build a screen for the purpose, or more likely add some functions to another screen. He may care about usability, but cannot do much at this stage.

Verification: simple. Other developers can easily review screens and code to see that it works right.

Task support

R4 The product shall support check-in according to task description *yy*.

Implementation: complex. The developer cannot program this directly. First he has to design the user interface – screens and pictures, then he has to program it. A good design of the screens has to take other user tasks into consideration too.

Verification: simple. Once designed and implemented, it is fairly easy to verify the requirement by carrying out the task – either as a walk-through of which screens to use and what to push, or in a partly working version of the product.

In many cases the user tasks are not visible in the program at all. Well, some developers love to create start screens with main menus labeled *Check-in*, *Create guest*, *Update guest*, etc. The user has to choose one of the possibilities and the system guides him through the rest. In our experience, users are often bewildered by these early choices. Tasks rarely have names that the user will recognize. Tasks are artifacts defined by the analyst. For complex tasks, a good design consists of simple functions that the user can combine in many ways to carry out the complex tasks. The issue is closely related to the many-to-many relationship between domain-level events (the user tasks) and product-level events (the product functions) as discussed in section 3.3.

Usability requirement

R5 At most 1 out of 5 novices shall have critical usability problems during check-in.

Implementation: complex. This requirement is even harder to implement. First the developer has to design the user interface, then usability-test it, then revise the design – probably several times – and then program it.

Verification: done already. The usability test has served as the verification at this stage.

Performance requirement

R6 Storing a booking shall take less than a second on average.

Implementation: complex. The developer may know that this requirement is easy with the usual approach and the given hardware, data volume, and expected traffic. But if he isn't sure, the requirement is hard to implement. He has to write small test programs to measure response times, adjust indexes, invent improved algorithms, etc. When it looks right, he can make the real program. If it turns out to be impossible, he should report the problem and ask for a requirements change.

Verification: complex. If someone else is going to verify the response time requirement at development time, he has to set up test situations with realistic data volumes and simulated traffic.

Goal-level requirement

R7 Precalculation of repair orders shall hit within 5% of actual costs.

Implementation: complex. This goal is far away from an implementation. It is not even certain which user tasks are involved, and we might have to design new tasks. The developer cannot do this on his own. A large part has to be done by the customer. The analyst should have transferred this business goal to ordinary requirements.

Verification: Should we verify this goal at development time? In principle, no, because a careful analyst would have traced the goal to requirements to ensure that the product can support the goal.

However, even careful analysts make a slip every now and then. A careful developer or Quality Assurance (QA) person should check that the product can support the goal. Have we implemented the necessary screens for capturing and using experience data? Are they easy to use for the staff involved? We should better make a usability test of these critical screens since the customer's most important business goal may be wrecked by low usability. Have we implemented means for management to check regularly how close the company is to the business goal? No, the analysts forgot that, but it is still easy to include. Submit it as a request for change, and remember to give a cost estimate.

The lessons

Many managers believe that developers can deal with one requirement at a time. The developer takes requirement R1 and implements it. Next he takes requirement R2, and so on. In some cases this is true, for instance for the first two or three requirements above.

However, most development doesn't work that way. Development is primarily driven by intuition. Based on a general understanding of the domain and the technical possibilities, the developers come up with designs and program parts. For this reason, it is important that the developers have a good understanding of the domain in order that their intuition works in the right direction. The skilled developer checks regularly that requirements are met. (The bad developer forgets about it, and doesn't realize that there are problems until acceptance testing.)

During development it often turns out that a requirement is impossible to fulfill – at least at a reasonable price. Or developers may notice missing requirements, or wrong requirements that are actually inconvenient to the user. These issues should be handled by requirements management like other changes (section 7.8).

7.7   Acceptance testing and delivery

When the product is delivered, customer and/or supplier test it. Often the product is delivered in several parts, and then each delivery is tested separately. Testing is usually done in several steps, for instance in this way:

Installation test. The purpose of the installation test is to ensure that hardware and software are available for the later tests.

The supplier installs the product (hardware and software as needed) in realistic surroundings and checks that the basic functionality is available. In some projects installation is trivial, while in others it is a huge job. Networks of computers, external products, and special measurement systems may be needed. Depending on what the parties have agreed, the test installation may or may not be at the customer's site.

System test. The purpose of the system test is to check that the product fulfills all requirements that can be verified before daily operation starts. Tacit requirements about correctness, stability, etc. are also tested as far as possible.

The test team use the installed system for the test. In order to carry out the test, they need carefully planned test data and test databases intended to exercise all task variants, capacity limits, etc.

Some requirements are simple to test, others are complex, just as for verification during design and programming. Verification during design and programming may often be done as reviews of the documents, but in a system test, we have to test that things actually work. As an example, during programming we would verify that the system stored the correct data through a review of the database configuration. During system test, we would have to store data and retrieve it, preferably through the user screens.

In the simplest cases the test team have a list of the requirements and work through them one by one to see that the system works as prescribed. For each requirement they write their comments and observed problems on the list. Requirements in the form of task descriptions are particularly easy to handle in this way (see section 7.4).

For more complex requirements, the team has designed a set of test cases, for instance test scenarios, in such a way that each test case covers many requirements. The team keep a careful trace document that shows where each requirement is tested. Then they perform the test cases and write down comments and defects. As an example, testing that the system stores the right data could be done as a side effect of trying some user tasks. The team has to keep track of which database fields have been tested. As another example, response times are tested with a full database, many users working concurrently, etc. The entire setup is used to test many requirements in the same session.

It is more difficult to test tacit requirements, for instance that the system responds correctly to all user mistakes, computes correct results in worst case scenarios with strange data, etc. If something is wrong in this area, the developer can usually see it without consulting the requirements. We are dealing with programming errors, not requirement defects. Developers have several ways to test for programming errors, for instance stress tests and whitebox tests where each program branch is tried out (see Beizer 1990). Areas that are risky from a business viewpoint should be tested more thoroughly than other areas. These matters are outside the scope of this book, however.

If the system contains COTS parts, they will usually not be tested as part of delivery because the supplier will have tested them already as part of product development.

Deployment test. The purpose of the deployment test is to check that the product can work in daily operation with production data.

Supplier and customer use production data for the test, and they create the necessary database files and convert data from the old system. They will not attempt to try out all functions in all variants. The system test has done that, and usually it is not possible to make the tests with production data. However, the team check that the system correctly supports the user tasks, that the real customer records are in the database, that discount codes are correct, that invoices come out correctly on the preprinted forms, that data communication works with real data, etc.

Acceptance test. The purpose of an acceptance test is to check that the product can handle all variants and is installed and ready for daily operation.

An acceptance test is a system test plus a deployment test. These two tests may be performed at different times – as described above – or in combination.

Operational test. The purpose of the operational test is to check requirements that can only be verified after a period of daily operation. It might be response time under daily load, breakdown frequency, task time for experienced users, qualifications of the supplier's hotline, etc.

For each test, the parties decide whether the product has passed. In practice it is a question of whether the remaining problems can be considered maintenance problems to be dealt with later.

Passing the tests determines when the customer pays. Usually the contract states that the customer has to pay most of the bill when the product has passed the acceptance test. When the product also passes the operational test, the customer has to pay the rest.

Usually passing the tests leads to various legal consequences too. Typically, the customer is not allowed to use the system in daily operation until he has accepted that it passed the acceptance test. This rule puts pressure on both parties, helping them to reach consensus without delay. Usually the customer carries the risk for fire and other accidents to the system from the moment the product has passed the installation test.

The parties play all kinds of games during this period. Traditionally the supplier has to pay a penalty for each day acceptance is delayed (up to a predecided maximum). When the maximum is passed, the penalties have no more effect. If the supplier still has trouble finishing the product because he is busy with other projects, he may suggest delaying development further unless the customer drops the penalty. The customer has few alternatives at that stage.

Other games are contracts where the supplier gets a 10% benefit if he delivers on time. Consultants say that it works much better than the penalties. We have also seen contracts where the *customer* gets a 10% discount if he accepts on time. This has caused some customers to accept a product that passed a simple deployment test but not a system test. The product was not ready for day-to-day operation because it could only handle straightforward cases.

In practice the test terminology is not as clear-cut as above. The system test may be called an acceptance test, or the deployment test may be called so. This is a dangerous terminology, because the customer may believe that one of the tests will suffice, when in fact both are necessary for a safe operation.

Quite often the system test is combined with either the installation test or the deployment test. The parties may also agree that the tests are carried out on a special installation at the supplier's site, for instance if test equipment is available there.

For large systems, acceptance testing may take months, depending of course on the number of problems to be handled.

7.8 Requirements management

Requirements change during the entire project and during maintenance. In theory this shouldn't be necessary, but in practice it is. Requirements turn out to be wrong during development, new demands are discovered, some requirements turn out to be too expensive to meet, sub-contractors don't deliver as promised, the parties agree to implement something simpler than originally described, etc.

The parties can spend oceans of time discussing the issues, particularly when delivery approaches. Should we ignore the request for change? Is it necessary? Whom should we blame? Who should pay?

You can just as well start managing the change procedure from the beginning. And the beginning is early during elicitation. Already at this time analysts will be digging up demands and requirements that may or may not end up in the specification, and meanwhile they need a "parking lot" for these potential requirements. Requirements management is a good place to keep track of them.

Requirements management will have to continue long after delivery of the product, and at that time it will simply be a part of ordinary maintenance. For certain kinds of product development, for instance operating systems or commercial business systems, requirements management is a huge task and crucially important. We will briefly discuss that below under Product Releases.

Requirements changes can be managed like other kinds of maintenance (section 6.10). First of all, it is important to set up a change control board (CCB) with authority to decide on changes to be made or not. The basic change cycle should now work like this:

1 **Reporting.** A requirements issue is reported to the change control board. They record it with date, source, and a short description. If necessary, the source person who reported the issue gets a confirmation.

2 **Analysis.** The issue is analyzed together with other issues. Is it a new demand, a request to change a requirement, or a misunderstanding? What is the real need behind the request? What are the consequences for the customer? What would it cost to fulfill the request? Will we have to investigate it further? This analysis should be made at regular intervals, for instance weekly or bi-weekly.

3 **Decision.** Should we reject the request because the advantages don't match the costs? Should we include it as a new or changed requirement – with which priority or as an option? Should we include it in the next release or postpone it further? Can we find another way to deal with it? Can we trade it with the supplier for some other changes? Can we delay the decision and for how long? The decisions can be made at the same regular meetings, but not necessarily the same day as the analysis is made.

4 **Reply.** Report the decision to the source and other people impacted by it, for instance developers who have to carry out the change.

5   Carry out the decision. Revise the specification, negotiate with the supplier, put it on the list for the next release, or whatever has been decided.

When the process is well organized, parties do not have to discuss and decide different things all the time, but can focus on it in shorter periods. For instance, when a developer notices requirement problems, he will feel he has to resolve them, and this may block his mental effort on other tasks. Reporting the problems to requirements management allows him to forget about them for the time being.

In some projects the process runs wild when the parties have to prioritize a new requirement. People disagree because some want to give it a high priority (typically the users), while others want to give it a low priority (typically the developers). In some cases the conflict is due to misunderstandings and general distrust, but in many cases the reason is that the parties unconsciously compare costs against benefits, but in different ways.

The trick is to separate costs and benefits. What is the benefit to the users? Usually the parties can agree on that. What is the cost to the developers? Consensus is usually possible on that too. Then the parties compare costs against benefits and can more easily agree on the result.

If the net benefit is clearly positive, the change should be made – no matter whether the customer or the supplier has to pay. The team should include the new requirement and leave the issue of who pays to the lawyers.

If the net benefit is dubious, the decision is more tricky, because if the supplier has to pay, the cost/benefit is always positive from the customer's point of view. In these cases you can either wait for the lawyer's decision (which may take a long time) or find some other change that benefits the supplier, and then trade with that.

Revising the specification

In the heat of development, users and developers may decide on many changes, but these may not be recorded anywhere. Is this important? After all, they are busy delivering. But later the developer forgets or builds something that the user didn't expect, and the fights start. If lawyers have to enter the arena, there is no written evidence of what was decided.

The solution to this is always to write down what is decided. There are several ways of doing this:

■   Modify the requirements specification so that it becomes release n+1. Excellent, the purist would say. The only problem is that you have to print it out and distribute it to many parties, and they have some difficulty keeping track of the changes. Letting your text processor mark changes automatically helps somewhat, but it is still difficult to get an overview of changes.

- Maintain a list of changes. This is easier to manage, but the new requirements appear out of context, making them difficult to understand. After some time, the list of changes become so long that nobody can find their way through it.

- Keep all requirements in a database. Everybody can see the history and arrange requirements according to several contexts. The only problem is that the screen gives you a bad overview and doesn't allow you to make scribbled notes, for instance when you use the requirements in a meeting or when developing the product.

The right choice depends on many factors: the project size, the customer and developer culture, availability of good requirements tools, discipline, etc. Whatever you decide, make sure that you keep track of all changes (see Wiegers 1999, for a good overview of requirements tools).

7.9 Release planning

Although many projects start out with a vision of one single delivery of the product, most successful projects end up with a series of releases. Here are some examples:

Surprise (for instance in-house development). During development, the project team realizes that they cannot meet all expectations on time, and some parts will have to wait for a new release.

Risky project (in-house or contract development). Demands are uncertain and they will most likely change as soon as users get their hands on the first version. For this reason, get a release out soon with sufficient capabilities for people to use it on real work tasks. Then gather experience and requirements for a new release. (This is a typical incremental or evolutionary development approach.)

Usually it is much better to treat a project in this incremental way from the beginning, than plan for the big release and run into the surprise version. Planned releases are much easier to handle than cutting out a smaller release during a stressed project.

Iterative development. The project is risky and developers have decided to make a series of prototypes or pilot tests with users to find the right solution. This is not a series of releases – there is only one release, the one put in operation at the end of the experiments.

Product development. It is expected that demands will change over time, for instance due to competitors' moves and changing technology. At the same time it is critical to be on the market quickly. Regular releases, for instance once a year, are planned to handle this.

How do you handle new releases? In principle it is easy. Each release is a project of its own, starting with analysis and requirements, and ending with acceptance testing and deployment.

The main differences are that you already have many software components (from the previous release), you have collected requirements and demands on the way (as part of requirements management), and you are better able to identify the problems in the previous release.

The main advantage compared to projects that start from scratch is that developers have had a chance to design and program the previous version in such a way that it is much easier to develop the next version. The key part of this is often the data model. It is fairly easy to make a data model that can adapt to future demands, while it is harder to design program modules that can adapt. Data models are much more stable than functionality and user tasks.

We will not discuss release planning and other development approaches here, although it is an interesting area. We have somewhat arbitrarily decided that this is an area for systems development in general, and not for requirements. However, we would like to outline release planning for large commercial products, to set things in perspective.

Commercial product releases

Companies that develop large products with many customers have a very complex requirements management. They are constantly planning two or more releases ahead and get a continuous stream of change requests from marketing departments all over the world.

Including the right features in the next release is crucial for competition. Change requests are counted by the thousands and it is a problem to keep track of when something is a new request for change or just a new statement of an earlier change request. Keeping requirements in some kind of database is a must.

Compared to contract development, there is only one advantage: It is not a matter for lawyers to decide who pays. The supplier always does.

To the customers and marketing divisions around the world, the most important requirement is to know for sure which features will be in the next release. Whether a particular feature is in that release or the next is of secondary importance if you just know it will be there. For this reason some product developers divide features for the next release into two groups:

A features. They will definitely be in the next release. They are planned to take at most 70% of the development capacity for that release.

B features. They may be in the next release, but no promise is given. If not, they will definitely be in the release after that. They are planned to take 30% of the time, but may be displaced by urgent, late requests for change.

Finding out which features to include in the A group for a release is an ongoing debate between developers and marketing. But once decided, the A group doesn't change.

See Regnell *et al.* (2000) and Nat och Dag *et al.* (2001) for further discussion of release policies and tools for finding duplicate requirements among thousands.

7.10 Tracing and tool support

Requirements tracing uses several techniques to check requirements against other information. In this book we have covered the tracing techniques in many contexts, which may be confusing to the reader who looks at tracing as a separate issue. In this section we give an overview. Figure 7.10 shows the trace paths and the techniques involved.

Validation

The validation techniques trace between goals/demands and requirements. Customer and users have to participate in order to ensure that the goal and domain aspects are properly understood by the analysts.

Goal-domain tracing looks at the business goals and traces them to domain-oriented requirements in order to ensure that all goals are covered. Section 8.7 shows examples of how to do this, for instance as part of elicitation.

Domain-requirements tracing looks at domain-oriented issues and traces them to more product-oriented requirements or quality-oriented requirements. Section 8.8 shows ways of doing this, for instance as part of elicitation.

Finally there are several review and test techniques that also ensure that goals are covered. They are explained in section 9.3, and are typically used when the requirements are in a more finished form. The choice of requirements style influences options for review and other types of validation, as explained for each of the styles in Chapters 2 through to 6.

Most validation techniques also work in the opposite direction, that is from requirements to goals/domain, so that it is visible whether all requirements have a purpose.

Consistency checks

Different parts of the specification can be "traced" to each other. Usually we call this consistency checking rather then "tracing". Data requirements, for instance, can be checked against task descriptions and other functional requirements (a CRUD check). Section 9.2 explains various consistency checks.

Verification

Verification techniques trace requirements to product design and programming, and later to the operational system. The purpose is to ensure that the growing system and the final, operational system meet the requirements.

Fig 7.10 Requirements tracing

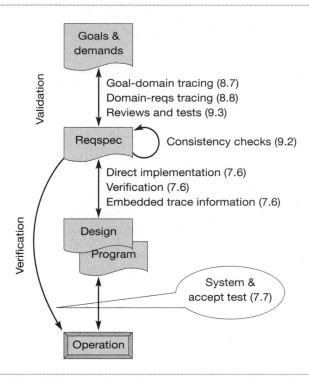

Verification during design and programming can have many forms, depending on the type of requirement and the style chosen by the analyst. Some requirements are easy to implement one by one (direct implementation), while others are not. Some are easy to verify at development time, while others are not. We discuss this for each style in Chapters 3 to 6. In section 7.6 we discuss the same issues for a selection of requirements on different levels.

Another technique is to embed requirements references in each program piece or design artifact. As explained in section 7.6, this allows you to trace both forwards and backwards between requirements and program/design. Unfortunately, this technique works best for simple, product-oriented requirements.

When the system is operational, it is absolutely essential to check that it works as specified and expected. The key test is the system test where developers check that the product meets all stated requirements in addition to tacit requirements about correctness, stability, etc. Another test is the deployment test, which ensures that the product works in its production environment, has the necessary setup and database contents, etc. Section 7.7 explains about these and other final system tests.

Tool support

There are many tools available for supporting requirements specification. They can for instance support requirements management, as explained in section 7.8.

One key benefit of the tools is that they facilitate requirements tracing. Some tools, for instance, can generate CRUD and goal/requirements matrices, or they can generate trace reports between program parts and associated requirements.

Tools are particularly useful for large specifications, of course, where it is difficult to trace information manually. See Wiegers (1999) for a good overview of requirements tools.

All of this comes at a price, of course. The project team has to be disciplined and use the selected tool to record the necessary base data. Many teams believe or experience that the effort of using the tools doesn't match the later benefit.

I must admit that I have visited several organizations that have tried various requirements tools, but few of them have kept using them because they didn't find them cost-effective. Typically, these organizations had found ways of writing short requirements specifications, so tools were not that important. Furthermore, they had developed ways to embed some of the tracing information into the requirements specification. Bruel & Kjaer, for instance, wrote short, yet quite successful specifications where requirements tools would have been overkill (Chapter 14). They also used feature requirements with domain-oriented justifications, and later they used task descriptions.

The companies that I have seen using tools on a regular basis develop ERP products (huge standard business applications) and other huge products with thousands of requirements and a regular release cycle. Often they use their own home-grown requirements tools.

8

Elicitation

The process of finding and formulating requirements is called elicitation. In this chapter we look at various techniques that may be used for elicitation.

Ideally we first elicit overall goals for the system, then information about present work and present problems, then detailed issues that the system shall deal with. Later we look at possible solutions, and finally we transform the issues and possibilities into requirements.

In practice all of this is done, but not in a step-by-step fashion. Studies of present work may cause the goals to change, and looking at possible solutions may change goals as well as visions about the new work procedures.

Choosing techniques. The chapter explains a lot of elicitation techniques, but you don't have to use all of them. Choose the ones that serve the purpose in the specific project. If two techniques serve the same purpose and you have little time, choose the less expensive one. If you want to be sure to cover everything, use both techniques. What one may miss, the other may find.

Use several techniques in parallel in order to save time. There is no reason to wait for the result of one technique before carrying out the next.

Give it a try. We often find that analysts spend a lot of time discussing whether to use a certain technique or not. Stop discussing and try out the technique in small scale. Then decide whether it seems worthwhile. Most of the techniques can be tried out in an hour or two – much less time than you might spend discussing whether to use it. In these few hours you won't get the final results, but you will get a clear indication of whether the technique catches something interesting.

As an example, if you aren't sure whether a brainstorm is worthwhile, find a few users and try it. If you don't know whether a study of similar companies is worthwhile, find someone who knows someone in such a company and arrange a visit.

You cannot be sure that you correctly assess the technique in this way, but the hit-rate is much better than if you just discuss things.

References. Many books and papers cover several elicitation techniques at the same time. To read more, we suggest Beyer and Holtzblatt (1998), Carlshamre and Karlsson (1996), Catledge and Potts (2000), and B.G. Davis (1982).

8.1   Elicitation issues

The purpose of the new system is to serve the various stakeholders, so why don't we just ask them what they need? Unfortunately, it is not that easy. Figure 8.1 gives an overview of the barriers.

8.1.1   Elicitation barriers

1 In most cases, stakeholders cannot express what they need. Sometimes they feel they have a problem, sometimes they don't, although the analyst can see several problems. There is also a tendency to exaggerate today's problem and forget about more serious problems. Even if they see the problem, it may not be easy to express it as a need or a requirement. As a first approach, the analyst could simply formulate the need as "get rid of problems x and y".

2 Many users have great difficulty explaining what tasks they perform, and even more difficulty in explaining why they carry out these tasks.

3 Often stakeholders specify a solution instead of a demand. As an example, a manager might state that "we should have a computer-based decision-support system". It might take the analyst a long time to figure out that the real problem is not to debate and to decide, but to implement what has been decided. The decision-support system wouldn't help with that.

4 Stakeholders find it difficult to imagine new ways of doing things, or imagine the consequences of doing a familiar task in a proposed new way. As an example, it took a long time to realize that the ever-growing problem of getting through to people on the phone could partly be solved through a new technology – e-mail. Later, the introduction of e-mail changed work patterns in a way that nobody had imagined.

5 Often different stakeholders have conflicting views. As an example, in a shipyard the marketing people promise optimistic delivery times to ensure they get the order, while production staff hate this since it means constant stress and overtime for them. A system that makes current work plans visible to everybody could thus be rejected by marketing.

6 Stakeholders will often reject proposals due to a general resistance to change. As an example, when computer-based text processing became feasible, secretarial staff were reluctant to use it. They claimed that it would spoil their good old craft and it was too difficult to learn. However, wherever text processing became available to a few secretaries, all the other secretaries soon insisted on getting it too. Part of the reason for the resistance was simply the difficulty of imagining the new work structure.

Fig 8.1 Elicitation Issues

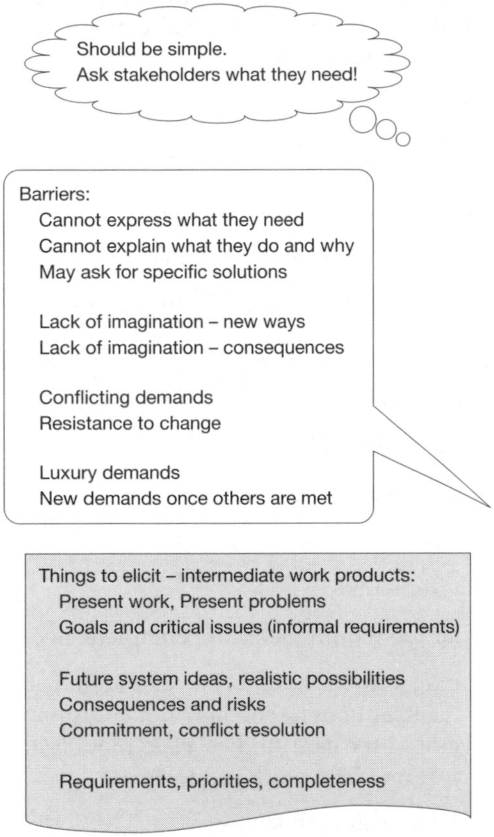

7 Once the analyst gets stakeholders involved in stating requirements, he encounters another problem. Too many requirements come up. Some of them are essential, others are fancy ideas or "nice to have". It can be difficult to have all stakeholders agree on what is essential and what is luxury.

8 Demands change over time. External factors change and priorities change. Once a demand is met, new ones turn up as a result. At the beginning, e-mail helped getting in contact with people when they were not at their office. Next the technology created other needs, e.g. for attaching documents, filing thousands of e-mails, connecting to other systems, etc.

Software houses are happy that demands change over time. That is the whole basis for their business.

8.1.2   Intermediate work products

It is not possible to elicit requirements right from the beginning. The requirements are the end of the elicitation process, and usually many intermediate work products are needed. Here is a list of important work products:

Work products

1   A description of the present work in the domain.

2   A list of the present problems in the domain.

3   A list of goals and critical issues (preliminary requirements).

4   Ideas for the large-scale structure of the future system.

5   Realistic possibilities.

6   Consequences and risks.

7   Commitment from stakeholders.

8   Conflict resolution between stakeholders.

9   Final requirements.

10   Priorities of requirements.

11   Checks to see that the requirements are complete, necessary, etc.

We should add that many of the more technical notation styles from Chapter 4 are useful for work products, although they may not end up as the actual requirements. In several of the case studies, class models and other diagrams played a key role as intermediate work products.

12   Interaction diagrams, class models, etc.

As an analyst, you cannot make these things in a step-by-step fashion. Initially you may find some apparently critical problems and obvious possibilities, but later you may realize that you were all wrong; other things are more important. In practice, all the work products grow in parallel and are constantly modified

A very important work product is the list of *goals and critical issues*. These are the informal requirements that later turn into verifiable requirements. We show examples in section 8.5 and 10.7.

Another important work product is the large-scale structure of the future application domain. It is a vision of how people will work at that time and what role computer products will play.

There are many techniques that can help you make the work products. The best approach is to use them in a team of analysts and users/stakeholders. Many checking techniques are available to ensure completeness, etc. We will discuss these in Chapter 9.

8.1.3 User involvement

Some analysts claim that if you involve the users, the project will be a success. Unfortunately, user involvement is no guarantee of success, as we have seen in several failed projects. True, it is important to involve users in the development process, but how? Here are some roles they can play:

1 Members of design teams or workshops where the user interface is designed.

2 Knowledge sources of how tasks and business procedures are currently carried out.

3 Brainstorm participants who produce ideas and identify problems.

4 Test users who exercise the system at acceptance time to check that everything works.

5 Reviewers who assess the user interface.

6 Test users in usability tests, where they try to carry out tasks with the new user interface.

7 Members of the steering committee for the project.

Users can carry out all these roles, and in roles 2, 3, 6, and 7 they are instrumental in the project's success. The risky thing is if users in role 1 (designers) also handle roles 5, 6, and 7 where they should represent ordinary users. They are no longer typical users and are so absorbed by their design that they may have a problem in seeing its weaknesses.

8.2 Survey of elicitation techniques

Figure 8.2 is a table of useful elicitation techniques. For each technique, we have shown what work products it can produce more or less completely. The darker the shading, the better it is at producing that information.

Fig 8.2 Elicitation techniques

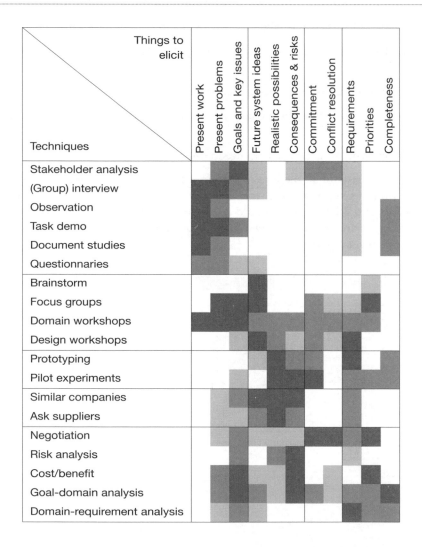

Some analysts use the table to find suitable elicitation techniques in specific situations. For instance they may have a list of wild system ideas, and now want to find realistic solutions. Looking down the column of "realistic possibilities", they get several ideas, for instance make a prototype, or go visit some suppliers of that kind of system.

8.2.1 Stakeholder analysis

Stakeholders are the people who are needed to ensure the success of the project, for instance the future daily users and their managers. It is essential to find all the stakeholder groups and find out their interests.

During stakeholder analysis you try to find answers to these questions:

- Who are the stakeholders?

- What goals do they see for the system?

- Why would they like to contribute?

- What risks and costs do they see?

- What kind of solutions and suppliers do they see?

There are various ways to gather this information. You may call a joint meeting where all the known stakeholders are represented, or you may call several smaller meetings. If everything else fails, you have to go and interview stakeholders one by one.

Sections 8.3 and 8.5 explain more about stakeholders and various kinds of business goals.

8.2.2 Interviewing

As Figure 8.2 shows, interviewing is good for getting knowledge about the present work in the domain and the present problems. It is not quite as good at identifying the goals and critical issues, although we may be forced to use it for that in stakeholder analysis. It can elicit some ideas about the future system.

It can give other information, e.g. opinions about what is realistic and where the conflicts may lie, but other techniques are needed to verify the information and resolve the conflicts.

Many analysts consider interviews the main elicitation technique, and it can of course be used for many things, depending on whom you ask and what kind of questions you ask. The limitation is the elicitation problems we listed above (see also B.G. Davis 1982).

Whom should you interview to get information about current work and current problems? Preferably some members from each user group. Make sure that you interview not only the officially nominated representatives of the user group, but other staff members as well. Often management has nominated a representative (typically a middle-level manager) for a group of users, but experience shows that many representatives don't really know what is going on in the daily business, although they believe they know. Getting information from the real end users can be critical.

What should you ask about? That depends upon when you ask. Initially, you would ask broad questions about day-to-day work, day-to-day problems, and other items on the list of things to elicit. Make sure to ask about *critical tasks*. When does the user work under stress? When is it highly important that things are 100% correct? You can rarely identify these tasks from observation: you have to ask for them. See more about task identification in section 3.10.

You should also try to find out why these tasks are carried out. Sometimes, users are uneasy at being asked such a question, because they cannot really explain properly. If you ask a manager, he may even be directly offensive: I am the manager, don't question why I do as I do. A good idea is to ask *when do you do this* instead of why. People don't feel offended at that. (Thanks to Andrew Gabb for this trick.)

Later, when you have identified critical issues, you ask more detailed questions, e.g. about data volumes, task times, detailed work procedures.

Always prepare yourself by writing a list of questions to ask. Leave ample space at each point for notes during the interview. You don't have to follow the list point by point during the interview. Try to follow the interviewee instead, and consult your list every now and then. Be open to new issues that turn up during the interview, but don't let yourself get sidetracked. I always write my planned list at the upper half of the page with space for notes, and leave the lower half blank for unforeseen issues.

Instead of individual interviews, you can conduct group interviews. A group of users from the same work area can tell you more about the present work, problems, and critical issues than individual interviews. The group inspire each other to remember critical issues, describe day-to-day work, etc. An important thing when conducting such interviews is to keep a balance between participants so that nobody can dominate, and all feel safe at giving their opinion.

8.2.3 Observation

Users are not always aware of what they really do and how they do it. If you ask them, they may come up with logical, but wrong explanations, not because they are lying deliberately – they are doing their best.

As an example, consider a simple task. How do you find a section in a cookbook, manual, or textbook that you know well? Like most people, you would probably say that you use the list of contents or the index. Observation, however, shows that in 80% of cases where this would be a good approach, people start skimming through the book, believing that they can remember or guess where the section is. Only if that approach doesn't succeed do they use the logical approach with indexes, etc.

One way around this mental blindness is to observe what is really going on. The analyst can spend some time with the users, observing their daily tasks. In some cases, analysts use video cameras (with the users' permission) to lengthen the period of observation. This has the advantage that you can later review the tapes with the users and ask what really happened.

Observation vastly improves your knowledge of the current work and some of the associated work problems. It also serves as a check of other information. Unfortunately, the real critical issues and tasks often escape observation. With a power distribution system, for instance, the critical situation is when something goes wrong once a year. The analyst is rarely around at that critical moment.

8.2.4　Task demonstration

A variant of interviewing and observation is task demonstration. You ask the users to show you how they perform a specific task.

In many cases the users cannot explain what they do in their daily work. But they are able to show you how they do specific tasks. Task demonstration is also a way to observe rare, critical tasks.

As an example, an analyst asked a public servant what tasks he had and how he handled them. He couldn't explain, he said, because the tasks were so different. All right, said the analyst, what are you going to do as the next thing today? That was easy to explain, and the user could also explain how he was going to handle that task. What would be the next job, the analyst asked. Oh, something very similar, the user replied. This is quite typical – when asked, the user found it difficult to describe a typical task, but when explaining specific examples, he saw the similarities.

The analyst was also interested in finding out how things had been done before the present computer system was introduced, but the user had not been able to explain this. Now the analyst asked how this particular task would have been done before; and the user could readily explain this to him.

Usability problems. Sometimes you want to identify usability problems in the present system, for instance in order to document how the new system could improve user performance. Mostly, experienced users are not aware of any problems, although there may be serious ones. To identify the problems you need some kind of task demonstration.

The best way in this case is to run a usability test where users carry out frequent or critical tasks by means of the existing computer system. You or a usability specialist observe what the users do, note the time used, errors made, number of keystrokes, etc. You may also ask the users to think aloud so that you understand what they really try to achieve or why they make certain mistakes (see sections 6.6.2 and 10.5). Later you analyze the problems and document the potential for improvement.

8.2.5 Document studies

Document studies are another way to cross-check the interview information. It is also a fast way to get information about data in the old "database".

The analyst studies existing documents such as forms, letter files, computer logs and documentation of the existing computer system. He may also print screen dumps from the existing system.

8.2.6 Questionnaires

The above techniques get information from relatively few users or stakeholders. You can use questionnaires to get information from many people. You can use them in two ways: to get statistical evidence for an assumption, or to gather opinions and suggestions.

In the first case you ask closed questions such as, "How easy is it to get customer statistics with the present system: very difficult, quite difficult, easy, very easy…" You can use the results to see how important the problem really is.

In the second case, you ask open questions. Essentially, you can ask the same questions as during an interview, e.g. "What are the three biggest problems in your daily work?" and, "What are your suggestions for better IT support of your daily work?" It can be quite difficult, however, to interpret the results. The respondents might have misunderstood your questions, and you may misunderstand their answers. During an interview, you can check your understanding immediately and ask questions you hadn't thought of before.

It is difficult to classify the results of open questions since you cannot clearly see whether two issues really are the same. For this reason, open questions should be asked of relatively few people.

There is also a high risk of misunderstanding with closed questions. To reduce this risk, it is essential that you know the domain already. Interviews are a good way to start.

Before sending a questionnaire form to many people, always test the form on a few people from the target group. You will be surprised how much they can misunderstand you. Revise the form and make another test before you send out the final version.

8.2.7 Brainstorming

In a brainstorming session you gather together a group of people, create a stimulating and focused atmosphere, and let people come up with ideas without risk of being ridiculed. The facilitator notes down all ideas on a whiteboard. Soon each idea spawns new ideas, most of them ordinary ideas, some stupid, and some very promising. An important rule of the game is not to criticize any idea. Even seemingly stupid ideas may turn out to have a valuable "diamond" seed in them.

During elicitation, the focus is on goals and requirements for the new system. If creativity doesn't come by itself, the analyst may raise a few issues he has noticed during interviews. Later, during system design, brainstorming sessions focus on innovative ways to meet requirements.

As a result of not criticizing the ideas generated, there will be many unrealistic ideas. The facilitator may finish the session with a joint round where participants prioritize the ideas. Some facilitators insist on not prioritizing at the meeting. They know that if you sleep on it for a couple of nights, some stupid ideas may turn out to be brilliant. If prioritized right after the meeting, they might have been killed.

8.2.8 Focus groups

Focus groups resemble brainstorming sessions, but are more structured. The term *future workshop* is also used to mean roughly the same. A focus group starts with a phase where participants come up with problems in the current way of doing things. Next comes a phase where participants try to imagine an ideal way of doing things. The group also tries to explain why the ideas are good. That helps formulate goals and requirements for the new system.

Several groups of stakeholders should participate, and at the end of the session, each group identifies their high priority issues. When later prioritizing the requirements, it is important that each stakeholder group gets solutions to some of their high-priority issues. If a stakeholder group doesn't get anything in return, they are rarely willing to contribute to the system.

Focus groups also create an excellent understanding between stakeholder groups and often a joint commitment to succeed.

Section 8.4 gives details of how to run a focus group.

8.2.9 Domain workshops

There are many kinds of workshops and the term blends into brainstorming sessions and prototyping. At a workshop users and developers co-operate to analyze or design something.

Here we will describe two types of workshops: domain workshops where the team map the business processes, and design workshops where the team design the user interface.

The result of a domain workshop may be task descriptions, dataflow diagrams, or activity diagrams that describe what goes on in the domain. Later, the analysts turn the descriptions into requirements. The path to requirements is short if task descriptions are used as requirements, but long if requirements have to be in the traditional feature form.

As a side effect of the workshop, the team may specify system goals and critical issues.

It is important that expert users participate in domain workshops. They know all the business details in their own domain. Sometimes, however, expert users know only their own narrow work area and lack an overview of the bigger picture. To gain this overview, experts from several work areas may have to participate, and the analyst will have a fascinating job in trying to make ends meet. Things are much easier if you can find experts with cross-domain expertise.

Managers may participate, but they rarely know the real details of the procedures and cannot replace the expert users. However, they may be instrumental in defining goals and visions.

8.2.10 Design workshops

At a design workshop users and developers co-operate to design something, usually the user interface. The term "co-operative design" means roughly the same.

This form of workshop is widely advocated, but often the result is a disaster. The reason for this is that the users become so absorbed by design and technical issues that they turn into developers and become very committed to the solution they design.

Why is that a problem? Because, in their enthusiasm, they may forget whether all business goals and tasks are covered, and whether other users back in the organization understand the solution.

If you use this kind of workshop, it is crucial that the team every now and then checks the user interface against the tasks descriptions and the business goals (see section 7.6). The team should also usability-test the design with users who have not participated in the design process.

8.2.11 Prototyping

A prototype is a simplified version of part of the final system. Developers experiment with the prototype to get an idea of how it would work in real life. The result of the experiment can be two kinds of requirements:

Product-level requirements. The experiment has shown that the required functionality is realistic (feasible) and useful. The requirements can for instance be stated in feature style or as a task description with an example solution. It is *not* a requirement that the real system has an interface like the prototype.

Design-level requirement. The real product shall have an interface exactly like the prototype. The experiment has shown that such an interface satisfies the goals of the system.

An important kind of prototype is a simplified version of the user interface. The system needs no or little functionality. The facilitator simulates the rest during the experiments. For instance, the system could consist of empty screen pictures and a simple mechanism that allows the facilitator to select the next screen. The facilitator simulates system output by means of yellow stickers attached to the screen and filled out by hand.

If the prototype has been usability-tested against real tasks, it can become a design-style requirement. If not, it is only an example of what the interface might look like. The requirement itself has to be less design-oriented (e.g. features or task descriptions).

Other system parts can be prototyped too. As an example, the product might have to communicate with another, existing product. An experiment where a prototype communicates with the existing product about something in the domain can reveal a lot. What are realistic response times? Is the expected functionality actually present in the existing product? Can we use the results for our tasks?

8.2.12 Pilot experiments

In many cases, the new system will be COTS-based, perhaps with some added functionality. The cost of the system may be high, but the main risk is whether the organization can adapt to the system and use it to improve performance. The organizational changes themselves are often more costly than the product.

In this situation, much of the risk can be eliminated through a pilot experiment. A small part of the organization tries the new system on a trial basis, but with real production data. At the same time they experiment with changed work procedures. The project team observes the results and evaluates the cost and benefits of the new system. Usually they also suggest different ways to use the system if it comes to large-scale deployment.

If the experiment succeeds, it creates a high degree of commitment. It also helps to identify the final requirements and their priorities. The main problem is that the system must be operational to a large extent.

It would be wonderful if we could run pilot experiments with prototypes, and some developers report that they actually do so, but we are not too sure whether they really do this. Maybe they run an extended prototype test where several users play roles during the test – without using the system for production work. Anyway, more experiments in this area are important.

8.2.13 Study similar companies

One of the best sources of realistic ideas is to see what other companies do to handle problems similar to your own. A study of their procedures and comparison with your own can give you many ideas. They may also have experience with the specific product you are considering. Most importantly, a visit to their site makes it easier to imagine how the new system could work.

Aren't other companies reluctant to share such knowledge? Yes, it may happen, particularly if they are competitors, but often the study is mutually beneficial, and they are willing to share experiences.

There are other ways to get information about competitors' procedures. Some international auditing and consultancy companies have a huge benchmark database with performance figures for other companies in your field. Performance is measured for many kinds of internal processes such as recruitment, internal IT support, etc. At least you can find out how your performance compares to others. Improvement is possible if you are not in the top ten – and the consultancy company might give you a clue about how to do this – for a fee, of course.

8.2.14 Ask suppliers

Suppliers of the products you are considering are also an important source of ideas for new solutions. Aren't they just trying to sell their own stuff? Yes, but often they also know a great deal about how others use their product, and they may refer you to some of their customers.

They can also give you a long list of features they provide. Often the customer realizes that he has been much too modest in his initial requirements. State of the art offers much more than he dreamt about.

If you compare features from several potential suppliers, you may realize that many of your hard-derived requirements are useless: every supplier can satisfy them. What makes a difference are two things: the quality requirements (e.g. efficiency and ease of use) and the special features that you haven't thought about (see also Maiden and Ncube 1998).

In this case you should stop worrying about the standard functionality, but pay attention to the quality requirements. You should also consider the special features that you didn't think about initially. If your team can come up with innovative ways of using the special features, you should specify them as requirements.

8.2.15 Negotiation

The purpose of negotiation is to *resolve conflicts*. It can be a matter of conflicts between supplier and customer, but more serious conflicts often arise between various stakeholders inside the customer organization.

Conflicts between supplier and customer are usually discussions about costs, benefits, and who runs the risk. Conflicts inside the customer organization can have many other agendas, e.g. power struggles and conflicts with other projects about resources.

A group discussion with conflict resolution on the agenda has participants from the conflicting parties. To be fruitful, the parties must be willing to talk together and try to understand each other. Otherwise, preparatory work should be done on an individual basis, or the whole issue escalated to a higher level in the organization. (The threat of escalation can often bring the parties to a constructive meeting.)

There are many tricks available for resolving conflicts, for instance to have each party explain what they believe the other party wants and why.

From a requirements point of view, the most important thing is to analyze the goals for each party. Often conflicts are about the solutions, though everybody can accept each other's goals. The trick is to find solutions that don't conflict, but support everybody's goals (a win-win situation). Section 10.3 explains a case where the proper technical solution resolved a national conflict.

8.2.16 Risk analysis

Risk issues play different roles during elicitation and development. The purpose of risk analysis during elicitation is to identify risky areas of the project and find ways to reduce the risk. In the elicitation stage you primarily look at the possible consequences to work procedures, client relations, the customer's IT staff, etc.

You can identify the risks by working with stakeholders. Ask how the work in their area should proceed after deployment of the new system. What kind of changes are needed, and what are the risks that these changes are blocked? Which potential conflicts do they see with other stakeholders? Then try to find ways to reduce the risks, for instance by involving and motivating users, planning training and change procedures, conducting experiments, and defining additional product requirements.

As in other cases, you can work with stakeholders on an individual basis or in joint meetings and workshops. The difficult part is to imagine the future work situations. If stakeholders cannot do that, there is a great risk that the work situation may be unacceptable. It might help to do as with task demonstrations: take specific examples of work cases and imagine how they would be carried out. Or even better, use a mockup system to simulate that you carry them out.

Later, during transition to development, you do risk assessment and risk management. You look at risks related to requirements and technical issues, e.g. can the supplier develop what is required, what happens if a sub-contractor doesn't deliver what you expect? You can manage the risks in various ways. This is a big area in itself. We give an introduction in section 9.3.1. You can read more in Boehm (1989) and Jones (1994).

8.2.17 Cost/benefit analysis

A cost/benefit analysis looks at the entire project and compares the costs of doing it with the benefits resulting from it. Traditionally, costs and benefits are expressed in money terms, and many analysts rightly claim that it is impossible to measure all the relevant factors in such terms.

However, there is also a broader meaning of cost/benefit. When we say cost/benefit we mean both hard factors (money terms) and soft factors (qualities). The terms tangible and intangible benefits mean the same.

Examples of hard factors are: changed revenue, changed costs, product costs, training costs.

Examples of soft factors are: customer satisfaction, employee satisfaction, decision quality, reaction time to external changes. Section 8.6 shows a detailed example.

8.2.18 Goal-domain analysis

A goal-domain analysis looks at the relation between business goals and tasks (or other domain issues).

We might call it a checking technique, but it is an important part of elicitation since it can drastically change requirements. In many cases important goals are forgotten during elicitation. No requirements deal with them, and as a result the final system doesn't meet the goals. You may also see the opposite: a feature or task that doesn't seem to have a goal. The feature may be superfluous or a goal may be missing. Section 8.7 shows ways to deal with this.

8.2.19 Domain-requirements analysis

A domain-requirements analysis is similar to a goal-domain analysis, but works at a lower level. For instance, we could have an issue saying

the system shall be easy to use.

Since this is not a verifiable requirement, we have to do something about it. In many cases we can translate it into good requirements. Section 8.8 shows the principle and a simple example. Section 10.4 gives a complex example.

8.3　Stakeholders

Stakeholders are the people who are needed to ensure the success of a project. It is essential to find out whom they are, what their attitudes are, and what their interests are.

Some of them have to contribute with money and effort, and they must feel they get something in return, otherwise they won't support the project and they may even obstruct it.

During stakeholder analysis you try to get answers to these questions:

- Who are the stakeholders? (Initially you know only a few of them.)

- What goals do they see for the system? (Many stakeholders look not only at their own goals, but also at other stakeholder's goals.)

- Why would they like to contribute? (Their reward.)

- What risks and costs do they see?

- What kind of solutions, suppliers, and resources do they see? (Should we replace the old system or extend it? Make it ourselves or buy it?)

Some analysts call a "blast-off" meeting where all the known stakeholders are represented. They discuss the above issues and try to give the answers. That will be the foundation for the project.

Unfortunately, it doesn't always work out that easily. If stakeholders are not mentally prepared for the project, discussion may not be fruitful. Try to run a brainstorming session or a focus group instead about the same issues (see section 8.4).

Another problem is that it may be impossible to find a time where everybody can participate. Remember we try to reach the important managers and expert users. They are always busy. Sometimes there are serious conflicts between some stakeholders that could wreck the meeting.

There are other ways, however. You can call smaller meetings with only some of the stakeholders. Knowing that the meeting is going to take place anyway may even cause other stakeholders to change their priorities and participate.

If you are not too sure about the situation, don't run the risk of inviting everybody. Play it safe and start by interviewing stakeholders one by one. That only requires that you can convince them to spare half an hour for you – or a lunch meeting. Ask them the above questions. Also ask whether they see conflicts with other stakeholders. If you sell the case well, you might convince them to participate in a joint meeting later.

Who are the stakeholders?

If the product is to be used internally in a large company, stakeholders might include:

1   The sponsor who pays for the product. He wants value for his money.

2   Daily users from various departments. They have to live with the product and, without their support, there will be no success.

3   Managers of the departments. They want business advantages from the system.

4   The company's customers (clients of the system). Often they will see changes too, and without their support there will be no business advantages.

5   Business partners, for instance suppliers, carriers, and banks. If they will see changes, their support is essential too.

6   Authorities, for instance safety inspectors, auditors, local government.

7   IT people and hotline staff in case the product is to be developed in-house.

8   Other people providing resources for the product.

If we talk about product development for a market, some of these stakeholders are not in our own company, but in our client's company:

9   The daily users of the product at the client's site.

10   Managers and sponsors at the client's site.

11   IT people at the client's site.

12   Distributors and value-adders for our product. (Value adders – or VARs – may for instance be software houses that combine our product with other products or services.)

What about competitors? They are definitely influenced by the product, but usually in an adverse manner. If so, they will not be treated as stakeholders. However, in some cases you depend on their co-operation, for instance if you are going to exchange data with them electronically. These situations may be delicate, and your best chance is to create a win-win situation where they benefit too.

8.4 Focus groups

Focus groups resemble brainstorming sessions, but are more structured. They stimulate people to come up with problems in the current work procedures, identify the real needs and the ideal way of doing things. Several groups of stakeholders participate, and high priority issues for each group are identified.

You should run focus groups early on in the project. All you need is a tentative identification of the application area and a tentative list of stakeholders. There are many variants of focus groups. As far as I know, the variant below is not described anywhere else, but I learned it from Edith Luebcke, IBM Corporation, in 1993. Since then it has been one of my favorite techniques, and I run focus groups frequently, not only about IT projects, but also about services and organizational changes. The technique not only creates ideas, but also mutual understanding and commitment between stakeholders.

Organizing a focus group

A focus group lasts between one and five hours. The more important stakeholders should participate in a focus group. If we are trying to gather ideas for a new product, stakeholders could be: potential end users from different work areas, potential buyers (customer's decision-makers), distributors of the product, supplier's staff from marketing, support, and development.

If we try to gather ideas for an inhouse system, stakeholders could be: users from various departments affected by the system, managers from these departments, computer staff and user support.

Figure 8.4 outlines the setup. Here is a rough guide to the steps involved in running a focus group.

1 **Invite participants.** Invite between 6 and 18 people for a focus group. Make sure that all stakeholders are represented and that supplier's staff make up only one-third of the group.

2 **Open the meeting.** When the meeting begins: present the theme, e.g. the ideal e-mail system. Spend some time letting people get to know each other and feel comfortable with how the session will be run.

3 **Bad experiences.** Conduct a roundtable discussion of bad experiences with that kind of product or that kind of work domain. Record the issues on a whiteboard for everyone to see. Ideas and wishes may come up too. Record them as well. Your main role as a facilitator is to ensure that nobody dominates and that everybody gets a chance to tell their story. Your own staff should be particularly low-key.

Fig 8.4 Focus groups

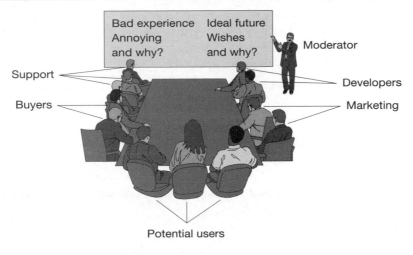

Several stakeholder groups
- Brainstorm – bad experience
- Brainstorm – wishes and ideal future scenario
- Each group selects top ten issues
- A few days later: decide
- Each group must get something

4 **Imagine the future.** Now change the scene to imagine the ideal solution. If you could get what you wanted in this area, what would it be? Allow people to be inspired by each other. Invite wild ideas. Try to get a picture of why people want these things, particularly when an idea seems wild. Ask: why do you want this, or when would you use this? Asking *why* or *when* can bring up the real need behind the idea. Record the ideas and reasons.

Initially, participants tend to come up with ideas that mirror the problems recorded. For instance, you might have recorded that it is a problem that users cannot see who has read their e-mail. Later participants suggest that the product makes it visible who has read the mail. Don't write this down again, but explain that each problem automatically counts as a wish – the wish to get rid of the problem.

5 **List the issues.** At this stage, a lot of issues problems as well as wishes – should have been raised. A good session will produce around 40 issues visible to everybody: ideas, bad things, requirements – and *why*. The next step will be more productive if you edit the list a bit, preferably in front of everyone. Combine similar issues. Group closely related issues. With some practice, you can do this on the fly while you record the issues.

6 **Prioritize the issues.** Ask each group of stakeholders to pick their top ten issues from the long list. The list may comprise ideas, problems to be solved, requirements. New issues often turn up during this step – just include them. The groups shouldn't prioritize among their top ten issues, since this may create unnecessary conflict when some stakeholders later get support for their top priority and others only their third priority.

7 **Review the lists.** Finish off with a round-table discussion commenting on the issues chosen by the other stakeholder groups. Revise and combine issues as needed.

Professional product developers carry out several sessions with different people until the issues seem to repeat themselves. If you cannot do as they do, just hold one or two sessions. This will give lots of ideas and requirements. You can read more in section 10.2, which also give examples of the issues produced by different stakeholders.

Processing the issues raised

During the next few days the project team should select the issues to work with. They should try to come up with possible solutions to difficult problems or "impossible" wishes. It is rarely possible to satisfy all top ten issues, so which are most important?

The crucial point is to satisfy some essential issues for each stakeholder group, since they all have to feel they get something. Otherwise they may not support the project and they may even try to block it. The wrong thing to do is to take average priorities across all stakeholders since that might mean that one group has none of its wishes fulfilled.

The final selection of issues should be based on both the value perceived by the stakeholders and the perceived cost of solving the problem. The QFD technique (section 8.7.1) can assist with that.

The analysts get the list of essential issues, including the whys, so that they better understand the issues. Based on this, they formulate requirements. Marketing or internal promotion staff should also get the list. It can help them develop sales themes, advertising, presentations, etc.

8.5 Business goals

Business goals are the high-level reasons for getting the new product. Although we use the term *business*, this covers non-business cases too. We talk about business goals also for non-profit organizations, government divisions, etc. For a broader perspective on goals, see Cooper (1996).

Figure 8.5 shows examples of business goals for the case studies in Chapters 11, 13, 14, and 15. Let us have a closer look at them.

Shipyard case study

The shipyard specialized in ship repair and wanted a new system for total business administration. Why? Figure 8.5 shows the six reasons – the business goals. In this case, these goals were stated in section 4 of the requirements specification, a section intended to help the reader. On the figure we have shortened the explanation a bit, reordered the goals, and omitted two goals of minor importance.

A1: Replace outdated platform.
The existing system ran on an outdated hardware and software platform. Very few people could maintain the system and the computer was almost obsolete.

A2: Integrate order documents and database.
Order documents include letters about the repair, quotations, technical drawings, etc. For the same order, the information could be filed in many departments and many IT systems. This made it difficult to get a survey of the order, for instance when negotiating additional repairs with the customer once the ship was docked.

A3: Use experience data for quotation.
The estimated cost for an order often differed from the actual cost, causing the shipyard to either lose money on the order – or lose the order because costs were too high. It was expected that the use of experience data, for instance the average hours taken to paint 100 square meters of ship, would increase quotation accuracy.

A4: Support systematic marketing.
Getting an order is a long process. Marketing people have to be aware when ships need to have their certificate renewed, contact potential customers, negotiate orders with them and follow up on proposals. The present IT systems didn't support these processes and orders were probably lost because marketing forgot to do the right thing at the right time.

A5: Faster capture of cost data.
When a ship repair is finished, all cost data has to be collected and used as the basis for the invoice. Cost data include work hours spent on the repair, stock parts used, special parts purchased, and sub-contractor work. Collecting the data at the end is a nightmare. Several kinds of support are needed.

Fig 8.5 Business goals

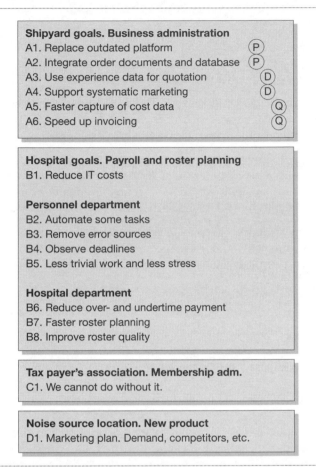

Shipyard goals. Business administration
A1. Replace outdated platform (P)
A2. Integrate order documents and database (P)
A3. Use experience data for quotation (D)
A4. Support systematic marketing (D)
A5. Faster capture of cost data (Q)
A6. Speed up invoicing (Q)

Hospital goals. Payroll and roster planning
B1. Reduce IT costs

Personnel department
B2. Automate some tasks
B3. Remove error sources
B4. Observe deadlines
B5. Less trivial work and less stress

Hospital department
B6. Reduce over- and undertime payment
B7. Faster roster planning
B8. Improve roster quality

Tax payer's association. Membership adm.
C1. We cannot do without it.

Noise source location. New product
D1. Marketing plan. Demand, competitors, etc.

A6: Speed up invoicing.
When a repair is finished, the shipowner's representative inspects the work and scrutinizes the invoice to see that he isn't charged for more work than was actually done. An invoice is often more than hundred pages with detailed explanations of what was done. A delay in invoicing may delay the ship's departure, which can cost the shipping company US$40,000 a day. The invoice task is definitely made under time pressure.

Classes of goals

The shipyard example demonstrates that there are many kinds of goals. We can roughly categorize them as high-level requirements on product level, domain level, or quality level. We can also talk about verifiable and non-verifiable goals.

Product-level requirements: A1 and A2. The customer asks for product features to meet the goal. A1 is easy to verify. A2 may be satisfied by a combination of features, and is reasonably verifiable.

Domain-level requirements: A3 and A4. The customer asks for support of two tasks or activities: quotation and marketing. We can verify that the support is available, but it is a matter of judgement how good it is.

Quality-level requirements: A5 and A6. The customer asks for improved quality and suggests a measure: speed of carrying out the task or activity. If we added some target values for the speed, we could verify the goals.

The business goals are not requirements, because the shipyard doesn't ask the supplier to take responsibility for them. In the specific case, the shipyard asks the supplier to take responsibility for lower-level requirements, while the shipyard has to ensure that the product is used in such a way that the goals are met.

The shipyard might have chosen to specify the goals in more detail, and then use the goals as requirements. If, for instance, we had quantified the speed of invoicing, we would have a requirement. On the other hand, if we quantified A3 as

A3: Quotation costs must match actual costs within 5%

we would have a goal-level requirement, but a typical supplier couldn't take responsibility for this.

Note that none of the business goals are expressed in terms of money. We need a cost/benefit analysis to estimate the value in terms of money.

Hospital case study

The hospital wanted a new system for payroll administration and roster planning. They hadn't written the goals, but could readily explain them when asked. In the requirements specification the goals were completely invisible, and the supplier couldn't guess which requirements were crucial and which were not. Furthermore, several of the goals were not even reflected in the requirements.

B1: Reduce IT costs.
Their present IT system was outsourced and the supplier provided the daily operation according to old agreements. The customer suspected that a tender process would cause him to at least renew his old offer, but at a lower price.

B2: Automate some tasks.
They wanted for instance to automate the transfer of actual work hours from the departments to the central payroll office.

B3: Remove error sources.
Errors crept in because data was distorted in the manual processes.

B4: Observe deadlines.
Some decisions were needed within strict time limits, but data were not available where the decision was taken.

B5: Less trivial work and less stress.
Typing in data repeatedly was annoying. Errors and deadlines created stress.

B6: Reduce over- and undertime payment.
Most staff are employed on a full-time basis. When they have to work overtime they get a higher hourly wage. If they are not really necessary on their duty but assigned anyway to reach full employment, their wage is wasted. One purpose of roster planning is to avoid this, but it is very difficult to do manually and perhaps 10% of wages may be wasted.

B7: Faster roster planning.
Making rosters manually takes a long time.

B8: Improve roster quality.
There were many errors in the rosters, not only needless over- and undertime payments, but also cases where staff without the necessary skills were assigned to duties, for instance two trainees rather than an experienced person and a trainee.

We leave it to the reader to find out which of the goals were product-oriented, domain-oriented, or quality-oriented, and to what extent they could be verified.

Membership administration case study

When the Tax Payers' Association acquired a membership system, there was no explicit business goals. It was one of the many projects where the product was a simple necessity. Nobody would question it. This is completely reasonable in many cases where the product cost is low and the subjective benefits are high.

Noise source location case study

When Bruel & Kjaer started development of their Noise Source Location product, the business goals had been carefully analyzed and reported in a *marketing plan* (*business plan* and many other names are used for such plans).

These plans are top-secret, but typically they contain descriptions of the customer's demands, the expected sales for various prices, the estimated development costs, distributor attitudes, what competitors seem to be doing, planned marketing activities, etc.

A total cost/benefit analysis determines the go/no-go decision.

8.6 Cost/benefit

A cost/benefit analysis looks at the entire project and compares the costs of doing it with the benefits coming out of it. Traditionally, costs and benefits are expressed in money terms, but here we will use both hard factors (money terms) and soft factors (qualities). The terms tangible and intangible factors mean the same.

There are many ways to present a cost/benefit evaluation. Figure 8.6 shows an example from the shipyard case. At the top of the table we have the hard factors, divided between benefits and costs. In the bottom section we have the soft factors. The actual factors on the list will vary from project to project. We will look at the shipyard factors one by one. (There are other cost/benefit factors than those shown, but we ignore them here.)

Hard factors

Avoided losses. One goal of the system was to avoid losing money on orders where the predicted costs exceeded the actual ones. Experience data would help avoiding the losses. A study of loss-making orders suggested that when experience data had been collected for some years, about $4 million might be saved per year. The effect would come gradually.

The table shows that in year 0 (where the new system would be deployed), no effect would occur. In year 1 about $0.2 million would be saved, and from year 3 and on the full $4 million would be saved.

Net present value (NPV). If you total the savings for many years, you would get a very high benefit. In practice analysts look only at the benefits for a few years, because so many other things may happen in the future. If the project doesn't pay in a few years it is very risky anyway.

Analysts also acknowledge that a dollar today is better then a dollar in a year. In calculations, they typically discount the amounts with a fixed percentage per year. In Figure 8.6, we have discounted the values by a factor of 0.9 per year (10% discount). Next we added the discounted values from year 0 to year 4 to get the Net Present Value (NPV). In the case of avoided losses on repair orders, we got:

$$\text{NPV } 6.5 = 0.2 \times 0.9 + 1.0 \times 0.9^2 + 4.0 \times 0.9^3 + 4.0 \times 0.9^4$$

More orders. It is also expected that better follow-up on potential orders will lead to more orders. The effect will occur sooner than the avoided losses because no experience data is needed. On the other hand, the total effect is expected to be smaller. The table shows the expected benefits.

Supplier's price. This is the easiest of all the factors, the price of the system as offered by the supplier. In early stages of the project, you don't have the real figure, of course, but you work with estimates. Note that the entire cost relates to year 0.

Fig 8.6   Cost/benefit analysis

Shipyard	NPV	Y0	Y1	Y2	Y3	Y4
Hard benefits	m$					
Avoided losses	6.5		0.2	1.0	4.0	4.0
More orders	2.5		0.4	1.0	1.0	1.0
Hard costs						
Supplier's price	−0.4	−0.4				
Hardware	−0.6	−0.6				
Staff training	−0.3	−0.3				
Enter exp. data	−0.4	−0.1	−0.1	−0.1	−0.1	−0.1
Net value	7.3	−1.4	0.5	1.9	4.9	4.9

Soft factors	Now	Future	(Scale 0–5)
IT flexibility	0	3	
Customer comm.	3	4	
Stress absence	1	3	
Total points	**4**	**10**	

Hardware. In this project, the new system needed new hardware. This is an easy factor too.

Staff training. In order to utilize the new system, staff need training. We have included the expected cost of the training, both the time spent by the staff and the cost of courses. In this case the cost corresponds to about 50 person-months, because a relatively small number of users are involved. In systems with many users, the training cost may be the dominating factor, and analysts say that this is often severely underestimated.

Enter experience data. The experience data doesn't end up in the system by itself. Whenever a cost item is entered, someone has to attach a description of it saying which physical item was involved and the size of it, for instance in square meters, tons, or kW. The plan is to let the accountants enter it, and that will slow them down, even if the product has high usability in that area. The estimate is to extend the accounting staff by about 20%, giving the estimated costs shown. Note that the costs occur from year 0.

Net value. This line shows the total hard benefits minus hard costs. The NPV shows a very good project. With a modest investment, the shipyard gets a high benefit. Note how the net value for the years starts with a negative value, showing that the company has to pay in the beginning, and get money in later. The net value per year is known as the *cash flow*. If you total the cash flows year by year, you get the accumulated cash flow.

The *payback period* is the time passed until the accumulated cash flow is positive. In the shipyard case, the payback period is somewhere between two and three years. Long payback periods are not accepted by management because the project would be too risky. The maximum acceptable payback length depends a lot on the local culture, Americans being impatient, Asians very patient, and Europeans somewhere in between.

Analysts also use the concept of *Return On Investment* (ROI), which is the interest rate you get for your invested money. In the example, the shipyard invests $1.4 million and get back more than $10 million in a few years. The ROI is 113% in this case. This means that if the shipyard borrowed the $1.4 million from a bank, used the net value each year to pay part of the loan back, and paid 113% interest per year, the loan would have been paid back at the end of year 4. The ROI is complex to calculate. In Excel, you can use the IRR function to compute it (IRR means *Internal Rate of Return* – another term for ROI).

Soft factors

IT flexibility. This is the first of the soft factors, the flexibility of the new IT system. How easy it is to maintain and expand the system, how easy to get qualified staff, how easy to include new technology? The factor is very important for adapting to changes in the rest of the world, but it is impossible to give a monetary value. So we have used a subjective scale from 0 to 5, and show the present level and the future level. The present system is outdated and has flexibility zero. The shipyard hopes that the new system deserves level four. (They will be able to better estimate this when they know the proposals.)

Customer communication. This factor expresses the quality of the communication with the customer; whether drawings and other documents can be transmitted electronically, whether the shipyard staff have all correspondence and drawings ready, whether they can justify the price to the customer, whether they can give him the invoice fast and accurately. Again, this cannot be expressed in money, but we use a subjective scale. The present communication is not that bad, but absorbs some manpower. The shipyard expects a modest improvement from level 3 to 4.

Stress absence. Quite often the work is extremely stressed, particularly in connection with finishing the ship and making the invoice. This is a factor that has a lot to do with motivating staff, attracting staff, improving responsibility and creativity, etc. It would be natural to call this factor *stress level*, but then a high level is bad and a low level good, and the reader would be confused when he scans down a list of factors. For this reason we called the factor *absence* of stress. The present level is one, a lot of stress, and the hope is three, some stress sometimes.

Total points. This line totals the soft factors. Somehow it is meaningless to add them, because it is like adding apples and pears, but it gives you an indication anyway. We can also give weights, as when people compare proposals (section 7.3), but it is no more sensible in this case.

In requirements elicitation we use the soft factors in another way too. If some soft factor decreases, we look at ways to compensate for it. If stress for instance increases, we may define requirements that compensate, for instance usability tests in the stressful areas, or personnel benefits of various kinds.

The bottom line. What is the bottom line in the example? The project team should be happy: There is a hard net value and all soft factors should improve. We cannot hope for more.

In other cases it is not so obvious. What would we do if the net value was zero, for instance? In that case it depends on a subjective assessment of the soft factors. Is it worth investing money just to get IT flexibility, better customer communication, and less stress? Probably, but it depends on the risks too.

What about the case when the net value is negative and the soft factors positive? In other words, is it worth spending say $1 million to improve IT flexibility, etc.? Some managers say it is, because they feel it gives important, yet intangible benefits, but it makes life much more easy for them if they see a positive net value.

Other managers always say no if the net value is negative. If the project team feels it is important to say yes, they may manipulate the figures, or – more honestly – try to translate some soft factors into money, using additional internal data, research statistics on the relation between IT level and profit, etc.

However, some soft factors usually warrant a negative net value, since the life of the company is at stake. One example is the risk of losing reputation. Assume that in the shipyard, the invoices were so inaccurate that the shipyard might get a reputation for trying to manipulate the price. Management would be willing to pay a lot to avoid this.

Choosing the right factors

Which cost and benefit factors should you choose in your project? It varies from project to project, but we suggest that you use three sources:

- The business goals. Each of the goals changes some cost and benefit factors. Identify the factors.

- Factors listed in literature. In particular, we recommend Parker and Benson, *Information Economics* (1988). Appendix C of their book lists important factors for different types of department and different types of industry.

- Your own judgement, for instance exercised in a brainstorming session with stakeholders.

8.7   Goal-domain tracing

Goal-domain tracing looks at the relation between business goals and domain issues, for instance tasks or quality factors. In general, goal-domain tracing answers these questions:

1   For each business goal, which tasks and quality factors ensure that the goal can be met?

2   For each task and quality factor, what is its purpose in terms of business goals?

We might call this a checking technique, but it is an important part of elicitation since it can detect missing requirements, missing goals, and generally change the perception of the entire system. In many cases important goals are forgotten during elicitation. No requirements deal with them, and as a result the final system may not be worth the money.

Figure 8.7A shows a systematic comparison of goals and domain issues in the shipyard case. Each row in the matrix corresponds to one of the business goals from Figure 8.5. Each column corresponds to a domain issue. Most of the columns are work areas, i.e. groups of user tasks. The last two columns are quality areas: usability and response time.

The dots show where a goal requires something from a work area or a quality area. As an example, the experience-data goal requires something from:

a) Quotation. The data must be used in calculating the quotations.

b) Cost registration. The data must be captured during cost registration.

c) Usability. The marketing people don't like IT and need quotation support that is easy to use.

d) Response time. There are lots of experience data and the accountants will record it. They spend much time at the computer and need fast response for the recording.

There are similar justifications for all the other dots in the table.

Goals supported?

Now what can you use this for? You can check that all goals are addressed in the proper places. You can go a step further and check that each work area specifies the necessary support for the indicated goals.

Are there for instance task descriptions for recording experience data? And do they mention the goal and possible ways to achieve it? In the Shipyard case, the answer would have been NO! The analysts had forgotten to mention that task step, and the

Fig 8.7A Goal-domain tracing

	Marketing	Quotation	Production planning	Cost registration	Invoicing	...	Payroll	IT operations	Usability	Response time
Replace IT platform							●	●		
Integrate doc and data	●	●		●						
Experience data		●		●					●	●
Systematic marketing	●	●								
Capture cost data				●	●		●	●		
Speed up invoicing		●			●				●	●

system was developed and delivered without the necessary features. Although the customer carefully verified each requirement, he didn't notice the missing registration of experience data because it wasn't stated as a requirement.

The check would have revealed several other missing requirements, some of which caused problems later, and some of which happened to be fulfilled by the COTS-part of the delivered system.

It is interesting that all the goals were stated in the introductory part of the actual specification. Also, all the work and quality areas had a section. However, the shipyard hadn't compared the two things in a systematic way.

Work areas justified?

You can also use the matrix the other way. Is there a justification for each work area? The matrix clearly shows that no goal requires anything from production planning. This could indicate that this area is of little importance and that there is no reason to support it. In the Shipyard case, however, it was a highly critical area, but nobody had cared to define the associated business goals.

Why had nobody cared about goals for production planning? The reason was that it worked marvelously with the old system. The customer tacitly assumed that the new system would work just as well. It is better not to assume this! Be explicit and also check that the offered solution is as good or better than the existing one.

The shipyard analysts had tried to mitigate the risk by giving the supplier all existing screen pictures, saying "this is what we have at present – please make the new one as least as good". Fortunately, the new system was just as good, but they did not check this during elicitation and contracting.

Goal-task description

Figure 8.7A shows the relationship between goals and work areas. It is sometimes more useful to show the relationship between goals and tasks, in that way highlighting the critical tasks. We could have done that in the Shipyard case, but the analyst hadn't broken the work areas down into tasks. Furthermore, there would have been many tasks and the matrix would be large.

In section 10.7 we show a goal-task analysis for the hospital roster system. The matrix covers only the eight tasks in the most critical work areas, but we could make similar matrices for other work areas.

Verbal goal-domain description

You would often add a verbal description of the relationship between goal and domain. Points (a) to (d) above are an example of a description of a single row in the matrix. The verbal description can give the details of the relationship, while the matrix provides an excellent overview.

8.7.1 Quality Function Deployment (QFD)

QFD is an extended version of the goal-domain matrix. Figure 8.7B shows an example from the shipyard. Due to the "roof" on the matrix, it is often called the *House of Quality*. **Warning:** The example only serves as an illustration of the principles. In the actual case the result is not really meaningful for reasons explained below.

The QFD version adds the following information to the matrix:

Goal value. The business value of meeting the goal. This can be measured on a subjective scale (0–5) or in money terms. In the example, the value of getting experience data is assessed as 5.

Value weights. Inside the matrix, each cell shows the relative contribution of that work area to the goal. For the sake of simplicity, the example shows the weight one for all contributions, except for the value of marketing features in meeting the goal Integrate documents and data, where we have shown the weight 2.

Fig 8.7B QFD matrix

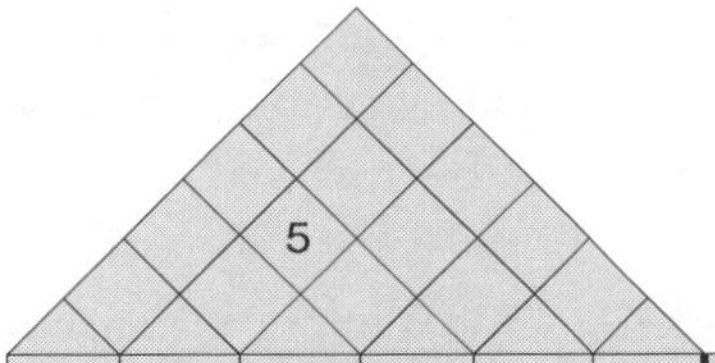

	Marketing	Quotation	Production planning	Cost registration	Invoicing	...	Goal value
				5			
Replace IT platform						−	4
Integrate doc and data	2	1		1		−	1
Experience data		1		1		−	5
Systematic marketing	1	1				−	3
Capture cost data				1	1	−	2
Speed up invoicing		1			1	−	2
Function cost	2	2	10	5	3		
Function value	5	11	0	8	4		

Function cost. The cost of the functions needed to support the work area. In the example, the cost of production planning features is 10, while the cost of invoice features is 3.

Function value. This is a computed business value for the functions in that work area. As an example, the value of the marketing features is 5, computed as follows:

Integrate text documents and data: goal value 1, weight 2, total	2
Systematic marketing: goal value 3, weight 1, total	3
Total function value	5

Computing the function value in this way seems illogical, because the function values become much higher than the goal values. The sum of the function values don't match the sum of the goal values, which I would expect. However, my sources say that this is the way to compute it. I would rather have split the goal values between the functions according to the weights. (Some versions of QFD probably do this.)

Function interaction. The roof of the house shows possible interactions of the functions or features. Functions can support each other so that the cost of providing two functions together is lower than the cost of providing them one by one (a positive interaction). They may also conflict so that the cost of providing both may be higher than providing the two separately (a negative interaction).

In the example, we have shown a positive interaction between quotation and cost registration. The literature is rather vague about how the interaction factors influence the computation of the values, and we have not tried to do this in the example. What we would like to show is that you need both features, but the roof of the house cannot show that clearly. Either one alone makes no sense, so you have to bundle the features into one to deal with it.

Using the QFD matrix

We can use the QFD matrix in similar ways as the simple goal-domain matrix, but we get additional quantitative information. For instance, we can compare the cost of providing the function with the value it contributes.

In the example, quotation support is the most cost-effective function. It contributes a value of 11 and costs just 2 (in whatever units). The other extreme is support for production planning. It costs 10 but contributes nothing. (This is not true in reality, but merely shows that critical goals are omitted.)

We might also notice that the goal *replace IT platform* has a high value, but is not supported at all. This is simply because we haven't shown all the work areas, and the IT work area provides support for that goal.

Why this doesn't work in the Shipyard case

You might have noticed that the argument above sounds rather obscure here and there. The reason is that the shipyard goals are not good goals for a QFD analysis, and the work areas are not good functions.

Some of the goals are really high-level functional requirements, for instance *replace platform* and *integrate documents and data*. According to the QFD principles, these should be functions represented by columns. You should then have higher-level goals in the rows, for instance cost/benefit factors such as IT flexibility and efficient customer communication.

The work areas are not sufficiently function-like. Each of them assumes several functions and features, and the same function may be used in several work areas. If you replace the columns with bundled functions such as capture and use experience data, you would get a better result.

In real QFD, analysts work with a series of QFD matrices. In the Shipyard case, the first matrix could be true business goals in the rows and functional bundles in the columns (not work areas). The next could have the functional bundles in the rows and the tasks in the columns. Finally, the third would have tasks in the rows and task steps or individual features in the columns. This last matrix would provide information similar to Tasks & Support.

Does QFD work in IT projects? QFD has been used successfully in product development, for instance car design and manufacturing. However, we haven't seen the successful use of QFD in IT projects.

Some analysts have claimed that they use QFD, but we have never had the chance to see this. Our example in Figure 8.7B is definitely not successful, due to the confusion of goals and functions.

Personally, I believe that QFD is useful in IT projects. I am just waiting for a convincing example. To see more examples and details of QFD in practice, consult Brown (1991), Rao *et al*. (1996), or Evans and Lindsay (1996).

8.8   Domain-requirements tracing

How do you get from domain-oriented issues such as efficient task support to specific requirements? In principle, it is the same as the goal-domain analysis, just used on a more detailed level, but additional techniques come in. We will look at some possibilities.

Task-feature matrix. You can make a matrix similar to the goal-domain matrix (Figure 8.7A). The difference is that now each task is a row while each column is a feature or a product function. You can apply the same kind of reasoning to find out whether all tasks have the necessary support and whether all features have a purpose.

Features from task descriptions. You can justify each feature verbally by referring to tasks or other domain issues as shown in section 3.7.

Tasks & support. For each task you can describe possible features or functions that would support it. The Tasks & Support technique in section 3.8 is a systematic way to do this.

Quality issue analysis

When the domain issue is a quality factor, the other techniques don't work directly. Instead we have to translate the quality issue into requirements styles, and then add metrics and target values.

Figure 8.8 shows an example from the shipyard project, which was a case of buying a COTS-based product with extensions. One goal was that marketing people should use IT for precalculating orders (job costing). An issue in that connection was that marketing people didn't want to spend time learning IT:

Usability issue: The job costing system must be easy to learn.

This is an informal, unverifiable requirement. Other goals, and studies of frequent and critical tasks, generated more issues.

The next step was to select one or more suitable requirements styles for the issue (section 6.7). One possibility was this:

Style: Task time style.

Now we can outline the requirement corresponding to the issue:

Requirement outline:
R1   After a course of xx hours, marketing people must be able to perform tasks yy in at most zz minutes.

The final step is to select the targets, i.e. decide what to write in place of xx, yy, etc. In some cases we can determine target values through elicitation, while in other

Fig 8.8   Quality-issue analysis

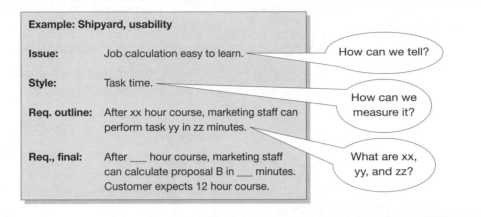

cases it may be better to ask the supplier (open target). We have chosen to specify which tasks to use (*yy*) because we know the kind of tasks involved. We have decided to ask the supplier about *xx* and *zz*, since he knows how difficult his system is to learn, and we as customers have little chance to persuade him to change the user interface.

Final requirement:

R1   After a course of ___ hours, marketing people must be able to calculate a bid as in app. B in at most ___ minutes. The customer expects about 12 course hours.

Real-world cases are slightly more complex, but they follow the same principle. An example is given in section 10.4, where we include all usability aspects in the shipyard and also provide usability requirements that are meaningful whether the function is provided by a COTS part of the product or as a tailor-made part.

Planguage

We could describe the above steps in Tom Gilb's *Planguage* (section 6.3 and Gilb, 2001) as follows:

Usability of job costing: Ease of learning job costing with experience data.

Scale: Average time to calculate a bid as in app. B after an introductory course of xx hours.

Meter: Measured for 3 marketing people.

Plan[course length]: _____ (supplier, please specify).

Plan[bid calculation]: _____ (supplier, please specify).

Wish[course length]: 12 hours.

Wish[bid calculation]: 1 hour.

Past: Manually done without experience data. About 4 hours.

9

Checking and validation

A requirements specification can be a big document with many parts and lots of detail. Behind the requirements are several work products marking the road to the final specification.

Fig 9   Checking and validation

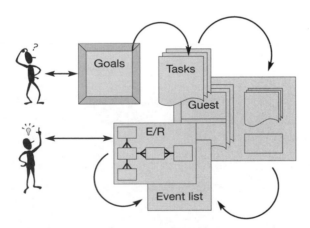

Check that all parts match and everything is included

Validate that stakeholders are happy (customer, user, developer)

Where are the major risks?

Quality product = meeting the spec?

How do you make sure that everything is as it should be? That the stakeholders will get what they expect, that developers can understand the specification, that the different parts of the spec are consistent, and that the major risks have been considered?

There are two ways: (1) close your eyes and pray while the customer and supplier sign the contract; (2) check and validate the whole thing before signing.

The first solution is quite popular. You might believe that everything is fine since the parties have signed, but usually this results in disappointed parties, for instance a customer who threatens that he will cancel the contract, or developers who spend lots of time resolving inconsistencies, meeting all the unstated demands that turn up during development, or fighting the customer to convince him that his new demands have to be priced separately.

It is all very costly to both parties, and if things end up in court, costs skyrocket. Checking and validating the requirements take some time at the beginning but save a lot of time at the end.

Many developers believe that their job is to meet the requirements. That is only true if requirements correctly reflect the customer's expectations.

A supplier who meets the stated requirements but not the customer's expectations may not even win in court. Courts usually acknowledge reasonable expectations from the customer's side (section 1.1).

9.1 Quality criteria for a specification

There is a generally accepted definition of what makes a good requirements specification. It exists in several variants, the one below is a summary of IEEE Std. 830-1998 (version 1993 says exactly the same). Figure 9.1 gives an overview.

A good requirements specification fulfills the *quality criteria* below. For most of the criteria we have added comments to show how the book deals with this.

Correct

Correctness means that each requirement is correct, i.e. reflects a customer need or expectation. Typical correctness problems in practice are that the actual need is something different (the analyst misunderstood) or that the customer doesn't really need the stated thing (a fancy wish). Using tasks or business goals as justifications for the requirements helps ensure correctness.

Complete

Completeness means that all necessary requirements are included, i.e. that all the customer's expectations are covered. Researchers stress this factor a lot, but practitioners realize that it is unrealistic. Most requirements are so trivial that you shouldn't try to specify them. If you tried, the spec would be so long that it would lose more important qualities such as being understandable. The balance in practice is to ensure that all non-trivial requirements are specified, and in particular to ensure that all business goals and critical issues are covered.

However, user interface details are not trivial. Statistics show that requirements concerning the user interface, are the most common source of problems (Lauesen and Vinter, 2001). Unfortunately, it doesn't help to specify something logical about the user interface. You have to specify the user interface indirectly (Tasks & Support) or design and test the user interface carefully (section 6.6).

Unambiguous

If a spec is unambiguous, all parties agree on what each requirement means. This is also a factor that researchers stress a lot, and they suggest formal specifications, sometimes in math notation.

In practice, ambiguity causes few problems. If the developer finds a requirement ambiguous, he will simply ask the customer to clarify it. The risk arises if he believes he understands what the customer means, but the customer actually means something different. Explaining the purpose of each requirement in domainrelated terms is a good guard against this (section 3.4 and 3.7). Definition of domain terms in a glossary is also a help.

Fig 9.1 Quality criteria for a spec

> **Classic: A good requirement spec is**
>
> **Correct**
> Each requirement reflects a need.
>
> **Complete**
> All necessary requirements included.
>
> **Unambiguous**
> All parties agree on meaning.
>
> **Consistent**
> All parts match, e.g. E/R and event list.
>
> **Ranked for importance and stability**
> Priority and expected changes per requirement.
>
> **Modifiable**
> Easy to change, maintaining consistency.
>
> **Verifiable**
> Possible to see whether requirement is met.
>
> **Traceable**
> To goals/purposes, to design/code.
>
> **Additional:**
> **Traceable from goals to requirements.**
> **Understandable by customer and developer.**

Consistent

Consistency means that all parts match in the sense that they don't conflict. Consistency is about the *internal* consistency of the spec. (The match between spec and customer expectations is covered by completeness and correctness.) A typical example of inconsistency given in text books is that one requirement says that a warning should be yellow while another requirement says that it should be red.

In practice this type of inconsistency occurs if the same thing is stated twice, in different parts of the spec. It is recommended that things are stated in one place only, and references are made from other places as needed. However, this often makes the spec difficult to read (the Shipyard case is an example of how to overdo the reference principle). A better approach is to repeat a short version of the requirement and put a reference in parenthesis. In most of these simple cases the developers find any inconsistencies and simply ask the customer for resolution.

A much more dangerous kind of inconsistency is that the combination of one group of requirements contradicts another group. A simple example is that the information needed to support the tasks is not what the data model specifies. A specific check for that can be made, however.

Another example is that the requirements state that the product shall be delivered at a specific date. This may be in conflict with the sheer complexity of the product – nobody can do it in that time, but some adventurous supplier might try anyway. IEEE 830 states that delivery time, etc. should not be part of the requirements spec, although it can be part of the contract. Unfortunately, this rule doesn't remove the inconsistency. It only hides it better.

In general it is impossible to check all combinations of things to see whether they conflict with all other combinations. Philosophically it is a profound question, but mathematics offer an alternative definition of consistency:

A set of statements (e.g. requirements) are consistent if a model exists that satisfies all of them.

Funny, but one of the roles of a prototype is to provide such a model. In other words, if you can make a prototype that satisfies a set of requirements, there is no inconsistency between them. Could you check the consistency of all requirements by making a prototype that satisfied all of them? I hope not, because that would mean that the prototype was just as good as the system to be built, so further development would be unnecessary!

Ranked for importance and stability

Some requirements are more important than others, and some are more volatile than others. Each requirement should state a priority and the expected frequency of changes.

In practice priorities are difficult for several reasons. Customers tend to think that all requirements are absolutely necessary, and it takes a long time to reach consensus about priorities. It is also dubious what priorities mean. Does it mean that all high-level priorities have to be met before a lower-level requirement is met? Or is the customer willing to pay a small amount for low-level priorities and a large amount for high-level ones? See the discussion in section 7.4.

Sometimes requirements must be bundled so that the whole bundle has a common priority. For instance it makes no sense to have a function for using experience data if there is no function for recording it. The two requirements must be bundled into a single feature with a single priority.

The stability ranking is supposed to help the supplier to identify functions that should be easy to modify. He may separate them into modules with a carefully designed internal interface to the rest. This is only possible, however, if the nature of the changes is known or specified. For some parts of the spec we may have an idea that things change, but in most parts we don't know at all. And what does the stability ranking mean to the supplier? Does he commit to making the future changes? In that case, it would be better to replace it with a maintenance requirement.

Modifiable

A spec is modifiable if it is easy to change, and the changes maintain consistency. There are many tricks that help achieve this goal: requirements should be numbered, terminology should be used consistently, there should be an index, requirements should refer to each other rather than repeat each other. (The latter unfortunately reduces readability, as explained under Consistency.)

These days specs can be delivered in electronic form too. This allows the customer to search for occurrences of terms, automatic statistics, cross-references, etc.

In many tender processes, the supplier is asked to fill out various fields in the spec, e.g. whether he can deliver a feature as a standard, as an extension, or not at all, what the product's response times are, etc. In these cases an electronic copy of (parts of) the spec is mandatory.

Verifiable

A requirement is verifiable if there exists an economically feasible way to check that the product meets it. This is a very important criteria, but most specs violate it in many places, particularly for the quality requirements. In this book, we have taken great care to show verifiable requirements for all parts of the spec.

Courts are surprisingly good at deciding whether or not a requirement is met – even if an analyst would say that it is not verifiable. Letting the court do this is very costly, however. It pays to make it verifiable without a court.

In practice it is also important that requirements can be verified tentatively during development (section 7.6). Dealing with an unmet requirement when the product is supposed to be finished may be very costly. In such cases the requirement is often abandoned rather than the product repaired.

Traceable

According to IEEE 830, a spec is traceable if you can see where the requirements come from and where they are used in design and code. In other words, each requirement must be backwards-traceable to goals or domain-oriented documents and forwards-traceable to design and code. You can handle backwards tracing by stating the purpose of each requirement or refer to the purpose in another document.

Sections 8.7 and 8.8 describe various ways of tracing between requirements and goals, and section 7.6 describes pragmatic ways of tracing requirements to design and code. Section 7.10 gives an overview of these and other kinds of tracing.

Qualities in addition to IEEE 830

Traceable from goals to requirements. An important problem in practice is that business goals are forgotten during analysis and never formulated as requirements. Traceability from goals to requirements is thus an important quality. IEEE 830 does not mention this explicitly, but it might be considered part of completeness.

A way to treat it is to state each goal with a list of requirements that relate to the goal. A matrix is a convenient way to show this relationship (see section 8.7).

Understandable by customer and developer. Without being understandable to the parties involved, the spec is not useable as part of a contract. IEEE 830 does not explicitly mention understandability, but ambiguity covers part of it.

Understanding a requirement can have many levels. The customer may understand the words, but not really the meaning. He may understand the meaning, but not the consequences for his business. Domain-oriented explanations or requirements are one way to improve understanding of the consequences. However, seeing a similar system in operation or in a pilot test is even better.

9.2 Checking the spec in isolation

The analyst can check many things in the spec without having to consult other sources. We discuss several checklists below. Now, what happens when a check reveals a problem? Here are some of the possible actions:

- The problem is a simple mistake in the spec: just correct it.

- Some important information is missing. You have to do some more elicitation work.

- Some information is missing, but it is not essential in this project. An example is that the checklist asks for a glossary or for a specification of portability, but it is unimportant in the specific case. Simply ignore it – or write that it is intentionally left out because so and so.

- Some information is apparently missing but given in another form. For instance, the project team has decided to specify requirements on the product-level rather than the domain-level. Simply ignore this.

- Two parts of the spec conflict, for instance there might be some data that isn't used in any task. This may be a simple mistake or missing information that you will have to elicit.

9.2.1 Contents check

This check looks at the contents of the spec to see that everything is there. Figure 9.2A gives an overview. The list below is a checklist. It reminds you of what usually should be there. If an item is omitted, it should be for a good reason. You might rank the risk of omitting that item (see section 9.3.1, risk assessment).

Mature suppliers maintain their own checklists, adding items to them to reflect experienced problems.

Does the spec contain:

Introduction
- Customer and sponsor.

- Background and reason for getting the system.

- Supplier type or project type (in-house, tender, etc.).

System goals
- Business goals.

- Evidence of trace from goals to requirements.

Fig 9.2A Contents check

> **Does the spec contain:**
>
> ▪ Customer, sponsor, background
> ▪ Business goals + evidence of tracing
>
> ▪ Data requirements (database, i/o formats, comm.state, initialize)
>
> ▪ System boundaries & interfaces
> ▪ Domain-level reqs (events & tasks)
> ▪ Product-level reqs (events & features)
> ▪ Design-level reqs (prototype or comm. protocol)
> ▪ Specification of non-trivial functions
> ▪ Stress cases & special events & task failures
>
> ▪ Quality reqs (performance, usability, security . . .)
>
> ▪ Other deliverables (documentation, training . . .)
> ▪ Glossary (definition of domain terms . . .)

Data requirements

▪ Description of data in database or other persistent data. In verbal form and possibly as diagrams.

▪ Description of input/output data formats.

▪ Communication states (temporary data).

▪ Initialization of all data and states.

Functional requirements

▪ System boundaries and interfaces.

▪ Domain-level events on each interface.

▪ Domain-level requirements, e.g. tasks.

▪ Product-level events and functions on each interface.

▪ Design-level requirements, for instance prototype of user interface or communication protocol.

▪ Specification of all non-trivial functions, including their input and output.

Handling of special cases
- Cases that stress the system to its limits.

- Special events such as power failure, hardware malfunction, installation of new components.

- Use cases or variants that deal with special business events or where things go wrong.

Quality requirements:
- Performance, capacity, and accuracy.

- Usability (ease of learning, task efficiency, ease of remembering, understandability, satisfaction).

- Safety and security (handling of physical disturbances, handling of malicious access attempts).

- Reliability (known errors and estimated number of errors).

- Availability (frequency of breakdown, time available for normal operation, recovery).

- Fault tolerance (handling of erroneous input and unexpected events).

- Maintainability (corrective, preventive, perfective).

- Portability (moving the product to other platforms).

- Reusability (reusing components in other products).

- Interoperability (ability to co-operate with other products).

- Installability.

- Other quality factors (see 6.1).

Other deliverables
- Documentation.

- Training.

- Installation.

- Data conversion.

- System operation.

- Support and maintenance.

Glossary
- Definition of domain terms.

- Definition of product terms.

Fig 9.2B Structure check

Does the spec contain:

- Number or ID for each requirement
- Verifiable requirements
- Purpose of each requirement
- Examples of ways to meet requirement
- Plain-text explanation of diagrams, etc.
- Importance and stability for each requirement
- Cross-refs rather than duplicate information
- Index
- An electronic version

9.2.2   Structure check

This check looks at the structure of the spec to see that the "pattern" is correct. Figure 9.2B gives an overview.

Does the spec contain:

- Number or ID for each requirement.

- Verifiable requirements.

- Purpose of each requirement, e.g. relating it to some domain activity or business goal.

- Examples of ways to meet requirement. Should be used cautiously. The purpose is to understand what the user has in mind. Avoid analysis becoming a design discussion.

- Explanation of diagrams, etc. in plain text. Users rarely understand technical diagrams.

- Importance and stability for each requirement.

- Cross-references rather than duplicating information. But don't exaggerate. A bit of duplication helps the reader.

- Index.

- An electronic version.

9.2.3 Consistency checks and CRUD

These checks compare different parts of the spec, looking for missing parts or inconsistencies. Figure 9.2C gives an overview of what is checked against what. Some CASE tools can help organizing the requirements and perform some of the checks.

Here is a more detailed explanation of the checks.

CRUD check

■ Can each entity class in the data model be Created and Deleted by an event or function or user task?

■ Can each field in the data model be Read and Updated by an event or function or user task?

Event check

■ Are all events handled by a function or user task?

Information needs

■ Are the necessary data for each task or message flow available in the data model?

Virtual Windows checks

■ Are all data in the virtual windows available in the data model and vice versa?

■ Are all tasks conveniently supported through few virtual windows?

CRUD matrix

Figure 9.2D shows an example of a CRUD check for the hotel system. The relationship between tasks and entity classes is shown as a matrix. The entities correspond to the data model of Figure 2.2A. Each cell in the matrix shows which functions the user can perform on the data during the task. We use the letters CRUDO as follows:

C: Creation of the entity, including recording and editing the initial values and reading what we recorded.

R: Reading (seeing) the values in the entity.

U: Updating the values in the entity, including seeing the old value.

D: Delete the entity.

O: Overview of several entities or somehow searching for them. The overview function is not traditionally considered in CRUD checks, but we have found it extremely useful when designing user interfaces to support the tasks.

Fig 9.2C Consistency checks

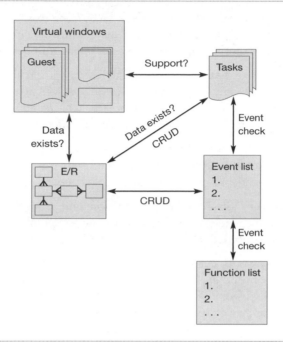

Fig 9.2D CRUD matrix

Create, Read, Update, Delete + Overview

Task \ Entity	Guest	Stay	Room	RoomState	Service	ServiceType
Book	C U O	C	O	U O		
CheckinBooked	R U	U O	O	U O		
CheckinNonbkd	C U O	C	O	U O		
Checkout	U	U O	R	U		
ChangeRoom	R	R	O	U O		
RecordService			O		C	R
PriceChange			C UDO			C UDO
Missing?	D	D		C?UD?	UD	

As an example, look at the first cell: what the Book task can do to the Guest entities. The user can of course Create a guest entity, but he can also Update one and he needs an Overview of many guests – why? The reason is that the guest may be a regular, so the receptionist has to find the guest from earlier recordings, and he may use this opportunity to update addresses, phone numbers, etc.

The bottom line of the matrix is the most interesting part. It shows what is missing in each column. The analyst should look carefully down each column to find things that are missing and consider what to do about each. Usually he will write notes or requirements for each missing point. Here are our notes for the hotel system:

Guest: Missing D. We need to define when guests disappear from the database. They are needed for some time for auditing and statistics, but should be deleted after a couple of years. A retention requirement is needed.

Stay: Missing D. They too should be kept for some time, but there is also a need for deleting them immediately, for instance when a guest phones and cancels a booking. New task needed: change or delete booking.

RoomState: Missing C, U, D. First of all, we assume that a virtual RoomState record exists for each room and each date. Thus no task needs to explicitly create and delete RoomStates. Update, however, is more of a problem. A room can be in many states, but none of the listed tasks can bring it to the Repair state. So a task or a sub-task is missing. Further, several state transitions are not sufficiently covered. For instance the customer may change the booking. (See more about state changes in sections 4.4 and 4.5.)

Service: Missing U and D. There is no task to correct wrong recordings of service. A new task or sub-task is needed.

Conclusion: We need a retention requirement for guest and stay data. We need tasks or sub-tasks for changing/deleting bookings, changing/deleting service records, and setting/clearing the Repair state for rooms. Good catch!

9.3   Checks against surroundings

These checks are based on domain insight and product insight. In practice it means that customer, users and developers make the checks.

Some of the checks are also used as elicitation techniques. It is just a matter of when they are used during analysis. Figure 9.3 lists these checks.

9.3.1   Reviews

Reviews are made by looking carefully at the spec, using judgement, background knowledge, and experience.

Before signing the contract, customer and supplier should carefully review the requirements. In practice they do not do this just before signing, although some developers expect this to be the case. In a good requirements process, the parties have followed the growing specification on the way, reviewed changes, etc. The final check is just a matter of checking the latest amendments.

Review of the specification

Developers and customer review all parts of the spec, reporting any defect they notice. Usually the reviewers do their homework first, and then have a joint meeting with the analyst.

During the meeting, reviewers report the problems or defects they observed. It is allowed to ask questions for clarifying the problem, but it is not allowed to debate possible solutions.

With reviews we have a similar situation as with heuristic evaluation of user interfaces (section 6.6.3). Experts predict a lot of potential problems, but only about half of them cause real problems to users, and half of the real problems experienced by users are not found by experts.

What are the corresponding figures for reviews of requirements? In one project I worked on, a blind review of the spec after project completion revealed about 100 problems, but only 10 of these had caused problems during development. The others were problems of ambiguity and precision and they had been resolved without difficulty during the project (Lauesen and Vinter, 2001). In the same project, about 500 requirement-related problems were reported at the end of development, so the review caught only a tiny proportion of those.

Early in the project, however, it is difficult to know which of the problems needs correction. It is not even certain that it pays to restate requirements for clarity rather than letting the developer resolve the issue later as he digs into the matter and checks other things with the customer anyway. Admittedly, this is a controversial point of view. It is definitely safer to resolve the issues early, but

Fig 9.3   Checks against surroundings

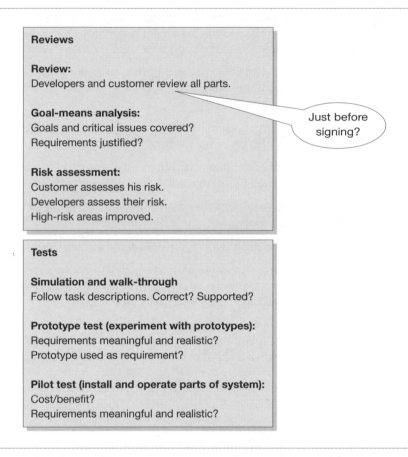

instead of polishing the language, it may work better to describe the task where this requirement is useful (see examples in section 3.4 and 3.7).

Goal-requirements tracing

This is a specialized kind of review where participants look for two things:

■ Are all goals and critical issues covered by requirements?

■ Are all requirements justified by meaningful purposes?

This technique is also used as part of elicitation. See sections 8.7 and 8.8 for a detailed description.

Risk assessment

This is another specialized kind of review, aiming at identifying risky areas of the spec. A requirement that is risky to the customer is often low-risk to the developer and vice versa. For this reason customer and developers work independently initially.

- The customer's staff review the spec and rank each requirement according to their own risk. The typical risk is that the customer doesn't get what he needs even if he gets what is specified.

- They also use a contents check to identify parts that are not well covered in the spec. Then they rank the risk of the incomplete parts.

- Developers do the same, ranking according to their risk. The typical risk is that they are not sure whether they can meet the requirement at a reasonable price.

- A judgement is made to see whether there are areas where the risk is unacceptable to either party.

The unacceptable risks are dealt with, for instance in the following ways:

- Choose another requirements style with lower risk to both parties (see 3.7, 6.7, and 6.11). As an example, choose a development process requirement if you are unsure whether something is technically feasible.

- Elicit more precise requirements, for instance through observations, visits to other companies, tests, and experiments. For example, there may be a risk that users find the product too slow when using it in daily work. A visit to a company using a similar approach may eliminate the risk. As another example, if the possible response time is unknown, make a prototype of central functions and measure the response time.

- Isolate the risk so that it causes less harm to other areas if the accident happens. As an example, if the project is going to use a forthcoming third party package, isolate the parts that use it so that only these parts need to be modified if the package doesn't work as expected.

- Keep the risk under observation so that developers can act quickly if the accident happens. For example, the project may depend on a new standard to be released. Check the status of the upcoming standard regularly.

You can read more about risk assessment and risk management in Boehm (1989) and Jones (1994).

9.3.2   Tests

Tests are the best way to validate the requirements, i.e. see whether the customer gets what he expects and whether it is realistic that he can get it. The tests can also be used as elicitation techniques.

Simulation/walk-through

■ Validate the task descriptions by carrying out the tasks for specific test scenarios. This should be done with expert users. Note any problems with carrying out the task as described. If you make paper slips with the data you use during the task, it is a simulation. If you just check that the steps look right in the test cases, it is a walk-through.

In case the requirements are product-level functions, you may also walk through the tasks, checking at each step whether the necessary functions are specified.

Prototype test

■ Perform experiments with prototypes to see whether the requirements are meaningful and realistic.

■ Test a prototype and use it as a requirement if it is adequate (see section 8.2.11).

Pilot test

■ Install and operate essential parts of the system to observe cost/benefit and validate the requirements (see section 8.2.12).

9.4 Checklist forms

It is convenient to plan and record the checks by means of a form. The next pages show empty forms for that purpose. They cover all the checks mentioned in this chapter.

Figure 9.4 is an example of how the forms were used to review the NSL project (Noise Source Location, Chapter 14). The figure shows only parts of the full forms.

In the left-hand column, you write the factual observations about the spec or what is known from other sources. In the right-hand column, you write whether or not there is a problem. You may emphasize serious problems, and you may suggest actions that should be taken.

As an example, the NSL forms showed that there was no performance figures. Later that turned out to be a problem. An early check might have raised the issue and caused developers to improve requirements elicitation. Another missing point is a specification of the documentation to be provided. This, however, is judged to be unimportant because the company has an adequate standard for documentation.

If you haven't checked a certain point, for instance because you had only part of the spec, you write a note about whether it would be important to perform the check.

Fig 9.4 Check list at work

Project:	Noise Source Location, NSL vers x	**Date, who:** 99-03-15, JPV
Contents check	**Observations – found & missing**	**Problem?**
Customer & sponsor	Missing, OK	
. . .		
Data: Database contents	Class model as intermediate work product	
. . .		
Initial data & states	Missing	Seems innocent, but caused many problems particularly when screen windows were opened.
Functional reqs: Limits & interfaces		
Product-level events and functions	Mostly as features	
. . .		
Special cases: Stress cases		
Power failure, HW failure, config.	Missing	**Problem.** Front-end caused many problems
Quality reqs: Performance	Missing, also in parts not shown here.	**Problem.** Response time became important.
Capacity, accuracy	Missing, also in parts not shown here.	**Problem:** Data volume, etc. became important.
Usability	Missing	Would have been useful
Interoperability	Missing	External dataformats, robot role, etc. caused problems
. . .		
Other deliverables: Documentation	Missing	Hardly important. B&K standards exist.
. . .		

Structure check	**Observations – found & missing**	**Problem?**
Id for each req.	OK	
Purpose of each requirement	Good. Domain described.	

Consistency checks	**Observations – found & missing**	**Problem?**
CRUD check: Create, read, update, delete all data?	Have been made	

Tests	**Observations – found & missing**	**Problem?**
. . .		

Project:		Date, who:
Contents check	**Observations – found and missing**	**Problem?**
Customer and sponsor		
Background		
Supplier type		
Business goals		
Trace goals -> requirements		
Data:		
Database contents		
Input/output formats		
Communication states		
Initial data and states		
Functional requirements:		
Limits and interfaces		
Domain events per Interface		
Domain-level requirements, e.g. tasks		
Product-level events and functions		
Design-level requirements, e.g. prototypes or comm. Protocols		
Spec of non-trivial functions		
Special cases:		
Stress cases		
Power failure, HW failure, configuration		
Use cases dealing with special events or errors		

Contents check (*cont.*)	Observations – found and missing	Problem?
Quality requirements:		
Performance		
Capacity, accuracy		
Usability		
Safety and security		
Reliability		
Availability		
Fault tolerance		
Maintainability		
Portability		
Reusability		
Interoperability		
Installability		
Other qualities		
Other deliverables:		
Documentation		
Training		
Installation		
Data conversion		
System operation		
Support and maintenance		
Glossary:		
Domain and product terms		

Structure check	Observations – found and missing	Problem?
ID for each requirement		
Verifiable requirements		
Purpose of each requirement		
Examples of ways to meet requirement		
Text explanation of diagrams, etc.		
Importance and stability		
No duplicate information		
Index		
An electronic version		
Consistency checks	**Observations – found and missing**	**Problem?**
CRUD check: Create, read, update, delete all data?		
All events handled by task or function?		
Task and message data in database?		
Virtual window data in database?		
Virtual windows support all tasks?		
Reviews	**Observations – found and missing**	**Problem?**
Reviewed by developer and customer?		
Goals and critical issues covered?		
Requirements justified?		
Risk assessment		
High-risk areas improved		
Tests	**Observations – found and missing**	**Problem?**
Simulation or Walk-through		
Prototype test		
Pilot test		

10

Techniques at work

10.1 Observation

Observation of potential users can give significant information that cannot be obtained in other ways. Here are two case stories.

Sound measurement: Bruel and Kjaer

Bruel & Kjaer (B&K) develop and market advanced sound measurement equipment. A development project is always governed by a requirement specification serving as a "contract" between marketing and development.

From studies of an earlier project (NSL, see Chapter 14), B&K realized that task descriptions might be a good way to specify requirements. The first project to use it was the development of a portable sound power meter. The hardware was available – a nice, slim case with a special screen and keyboard, CPU, flash memory, battery, several microphones. Length 50 cm, total weight 3 kg.

Developers expected it to be used when measuring noise levels in houses, traffic noise, etc. Anyone could imagine how these tasks were performed, but just to make sure, they decided to observe potential users and write task descriptions.

To their surprise a major demand was to measure noise levels at the top of tall chimneys or in factory buildings. The user would climb the chimney, carrying the meter, put chalk marks in a carefully measured grid on the chimney, measure the noise level in all grid points with his arm stretched out around the chimney, check that the measurements were of an adequate quality, and climb back down.

This revealed a few problems in the planned design. There was no easy way to carry the sound meter on the ladder, the user had to answer questions in some dialog boxes to start the measurement, and reviewing the measurements for quality was not easy standing on a ladder.

One result of this study was a requirement that described the task and specified that it be supported.

During initial design, the team came up with a slightly revised case for the meter. It should have a carrying strap and a small box for chalk and ruler. The user dialog was changed to allow single-button starting and stopping of measurements with audible signals, etc. The team made usability tests very early, testing the chimney scenario, among other scenarios. The tests made them revise their first design completely, and the next design significantly.

These details made the meter a great success. Competitors did not show the same degree of understanding of the tasks to be supported.

Joystick for ship control

Modern ships have a computerized tiller in the form of a joystick that controls the fine movements of the ship, for instance during mooring along a quay. The control is very advanced, taking into consideration waves, currents, and fluctuations in propeller power. The officer simply moves the joystick in the desired direction and the ship moves steadily that way.

A supplier had experienced that a couple of ships using their tiller control had crashed against a quay resulting in great repair costs. They couldn't understand why, because in the advanced simulators used during training, ship officers could control the ship excellently. The ship officers were accused of neglect, but nothing could be proved.

Usability experts started investigating the system. They videotaped the officers in the simulators and on the real ship. Watching the two videotapes together with the officers, they found the explanation. An experienced officer senses the movement of the ship and the work of the engines through his feet. He unconsciously counteracts the effect of waves and engine fluctuations through small adjustments of the joystick.

Unfortunately, the automatic control also compensated for these effects. The result was a double compensation which in some cases caused a crash. In the simulator, the floor didn't shake like in the real ship, so the same effect was not observed there.

Fortunately, this story is an extreme case. You should not conclude that usability tests with prototypes or simulators in artificial surroundings are a waste of time. On the contrary, they can reveal many, many problems in a costeffective way. This example simply highlights that you cannot find out all problems by means of simulation.

10.2 Focus groups at work

Focus groups can overcome many elicitation problems. They stimulate people to come up with problems in the current way of doing things, expressing the real needs, and imagining the ideal way of doing things. Several groups of stakeholders participate, and high-priority issues for each group are identified.

We have described the basic approach in section 8.4. Here we add some practical details and give examples from real-life focus groups.

Practical details

Usually, the stakeholders are not paid. They may be given a light meal and travel expenses.

It is important that participants don't discuss whether issues are right or wrong, realistic or wild. However, it is allowed to ask questions for clarification, "why" being one of them. Keep the creative, playful atmosphere; the purpose is to gather as many issues as possible. Sorting them and prioritizing them comes later.

Developers and other technical specialists are particularly likely to turn ideas down, arguing, "It is impossible", "We don't have the time", etc. As a facilitator, you must insist that they listen and try to understand the real problem behind the suggestion.

You can record data from the sessions in several ways. The simplest is to use flipcharts which are visible to everybody and which you can carry back to the office later. This is the way we normally do it. Having an assistant keep a log of the issues during the session can be a great help too.

You may supplement your records with audio- or videotapes, but it takes a long time to go through them systematically. However, they can be useful for refreshing your memory or clarifying specific points. Another convenient record is to have participants fill out forms with their own issues, particularly the prioritized ones. GroupWare systems are also useful, mainly to speed up data collection and editing after the sessions.

Handling disasters

Several kinds of disasters may happen. For instance, people may start debating the issues. This is easy to handle. Repeat the rules: no debate, no criticism, all ideas are valuable, no decisions are made here.

The dominant people are more difficult to handle. It may be necessary to use a strict round-table speaking order for a while, which also helps the silent participants express themselves.

A serious problem arises if participants start shooting at each other, for instance because there are real conflicts between stakeholder groups. One group may not accept ideas which appear to threaten their interests. You may handle the situation by insisting that issues are recorded even though others object to them, in that way giving everybody a better basis for resolving the conflicts later. You may also suggest that it is recorded who objects to which issues.

However, it may happen that conflicts are so disruptive that you have to call off the entire session. If you suspect that this could happen, arrange different sessions with different groups and reconcile conflicts later when you can base them on the recorded issues.

Examples

A silly idea? In a focus group about the "ideal washing powder", housewives were asked to imagine the ideal washing powder. A lady said: I want the washing powder to *fly* into the washing machine.

The chemists and technicians frowned at this seemingly stupid suggestion, but the facilitator asked: Why would you like that? I often spill some powder, she explained, it spreads all over and is difficult to remove, and a wet cloth just makes it sticky. This made sense to the chemists, and after a couple of days they invented liquid washing powder. It didn't fly, but it solved the problem. Later they invented the soap ball. It almost made the flying trick too.

Unbelievable demands A big software vendor called major customers and distributors for a focus group on features in their next release. Many features were suggested and developers were figuring out how to squeeze them all into the new release. When the issues were prioritized, it took them a long time to grasp that all stakeholders had the same top priority:

Do as you promise.

This had higher priority than any new feature. Why? The customers explained that they planned their activities based on the promised features. Several times features that had been promised were delayed to the next release. Not getting a promised feature on time was much worse than never having it.

Case study: Focus group on the ideal e-mail system

Participants included users from the engineering field, secretaries of middle-level managers, computer operations staff, and developers from an e-mail vendor. When reading about the wishes below, you will probably notice that several of them have been satisfied in recent releases of e-mail systems. A book cannot keep up with that.

Bad experience. The bad experience step produced the following issues. Some of the discussion is included and facilitator questions are shown in brackets.

B1   Secretary: I never know whether my e-mail message has reached the receiver. Once we lost a big contract that way because my e-mail had been lost.

B2   Secretary: If I distribute an e-mail to several people and the address for one of them is wrong, the system just tells me that it wasn't sent. This is not very helpful. [Why?] I don't know who received it and who didn't, and if I correct one address and resend the e-mail, a lot of people may be disturbed by two mails.

B3   Engineer: Attachments are a problem. [Why?] They come in formats I cannot read. Either I delete them by mistake or they grow into an endless list of strange file names in my attachment directory.

B4   Engineer: The system should show the attachments automatically. Vendor staff: That will be very slow, we cannot identify all formats, and how should we show binary attachments? [Why do you want it?] User: I want to see the attachments at a glance. [Why?] Because otherwise I can't see whether it is something I can just delete. I don't need to see the whole thing – just some of it.

B5   Engineer: People send e-mails without a subject. [Why is that a problem?] I cannot see whether it is a message I want to see now, and when later trying to locate it in the archive, I cannot find it.

B6   Engineer: I always forget how to subscribe/unsubscribe to mailing lists.

B7   Computer staff: Subscriptions give us another problem. When people get a new e-mail address we have a mess because the subscription server identifies them by their sender address, so we get a lot of messages about unknown receivers. They have to subscribe under their new mail address (which they forget) and they cannot cancel the old subscription from their new address.

B8   Engineer: When I am traveling and stay a few days at another site, I borrow a computer there, but cannot get e-mail, mail subscriptions, etc. as I do at home. This is a mess and a waste of time.

B9   Secretary: Editing an incoming message is not allowed. [Why is that a problem?] I want to add or change the subject so that I can better find the message later.

B10 Engineer: People often promise to send me something, but forget. Why can't the system remind them (or me)?

B11 Computer staff: We have too many e-mail products to support. Vendor: Why don't you just use ours only? Staff: People don't want to switch, and even your various versions are not compatible. [Why don't they want to switch?] Because they have become experts with their existing system and it takes a long time to become expert with a new one.

B12 Computer staff: People broadcast mails with huge attachments. [Why is that a problem?] They fill up our disk drives very fast. [How?] Apparently the mailer duplicates the attachments, one for each receiver.

B13 Vendor staff: It is annoying listening to all these complaints without being allowed to tell all of you: The product has many of these features – why don't you read the manual? [The facilitator wrote: Problem: Users cannot figure out what the product can do for them.]

B14 … and about 30 more issues

Ideal future. The step about imagining the ideal future produced these issues/visions:

F1 Engineer: The system is easy to use on all levels of expertise. The novice finds it easy, and the experienced gradually finds new and smarter ways to do things.

F2 Engineer: Seamless interface to all mailers, so that our system can find any address and handle any attachment.

F3 Engineer: Any attachment can be seen. [Note: This is just the reverse of problem B3 mentioned in the *bad experience* step. You may edit B3 and omit F3 to keep the total list of problems and wishes short].

F4 Computer staff: All users must have compulsory training in e-mail concepts, netiquette, etc. [Why?] People cause problems for others when they don't follow the rules of the game.

F5 Engineer: The system should automatically tell me how important and urgent each message is. [Why?] I get too much junk mail, but some e-mails are important. When I get mail from people I know, I always know how important it is.

F6 Secretary: The system automatically files both incoming and outgoing messages according to subject in such a way that I can see the entire conversation at a glance.

F7 Secretary: When I want to see messages relating to a specific subject or a specific person, the system gives me an overview of them very quickly, independent of the folder in which they were filed, independent of spelling errors in the message or headings, independent of whether I put the proper subject on the message when I filed it.

F8 Computer staff: It must be easy to distribute new mailer software to all of our users.

F9   Secretary: I often have to send e-mails to someone on behalf of my boss (or other staff). My boss wants to get the reply – not me.

F10   … and about 20 more issues.

Top priorities. The *prioritize* step produced these lists of top four issues in final edited form:

Engineers

E1   Attachments should follow the message when deleted, filed, or moved.

E2   Using e-mail from two computers alternately, one at office and one at home, should be as easy as using just one. [A new wish that came up during prioritizing].

E3   Help to subscribe and unsubscribe to bulletin boards. Easy to change your address, for instance when you work from someone else's computer.

E4   Retrieval of all messages according to subject, sender, contents, etc. independent of where and how they were filed.

Secretaries

S1   A message should *never* be lost without me knowing about it.

S2   Retrieval of all messages according to subject, sender, contents, etc. independent of where and how they were filed.

S3   The system should be easy to use for novices and still efficient for experienced users.

S4   Possibility of filing messages with user-selected multiple keywords from a thesaurus.

Computer staff

C1   Attachments may be kept at sender's site and retrieved through FTP. [A new idea that came up during prioritizing]. [Why?] Because otherwise broadcast messages fill the disk.

C2   Help to subscribe and unsubscribe to mail lists. Easy to change your address, for instance when you are working from someone else's computer.

C3   All users get compulsory training in e-mail concepts, netiquette, etc.

C4   Ways to find out where people really are (which server) when their address is an alias. [A new idea that came up during prioritizing.]

10.3 Conflict resolution

There are many tricks available for resolving conflicts, for instance to have each party explain what they believe the other party wants and why.

From a requirements point of view, the most important thing is to analyze the goals for each party. Often conflicts are about the solutions, while everybody can accept each other's goals. The trick is to find solutions that don't conflict, but support everybody's goals (a win-win situation).

Does this sound like magic? Well, here is an example where it worked. Denmark was the first country to abandon paper-based bonds and keep track of bond ownership only through computer records. The process of arriving at that system was full of problems and politics. Security was an issue, of course, but IT experts created convincing solutions where records of ownership could survive even a nuclear attack.

The last obstacle was a conflict between the unions and the employers (the credit institutions that issued the bonds). The unions didn't want a centralized registration of ownership, while the employers insisted that this was necessary. The conflict had been on for more than a year, and resolution seemed impossible. An arbiter (Lauesen) was nominated in 1978, and he participated in several meetings, trying to figure out why this was such a conflict.

After two months of heated debate, he realized that the unions wanted a decentralized registration *because* different institutions had different work procedures (based on local computer systems). Unions wanted to keep the old procedures as far as possible, partly to preserve jobs. The employers wanted a central registration *because* millions of dollars worth in bonds were moved around in downtown every day in a hurry (often by bike) to handle the daily trade. A central file of ownership would completely eliminate this. Both parties could fully understand each other's point of view.

So instead of fighting about the requirement that a central computer system be used, the parties should look at two goals:

1 Keep the decentralized administration procedures.

2 Record ownership electronically with immediate update of changes.

It was now obvious to the arbiter that there was at least one solution, this requirement:

R1 The existing decentralized systems shall record ownership through data transmission to a central system. The interface to that system shall be as described in …

It took about ten minutes to explain the parties this solution, particularly that each institution could keep their existing procedures – except that they wouldn't move a paper bond anymore. Next, parties split up for ten minutes talking confidentially with their peers. Then they met again and declared that they could sign an agreement about this requirement. More than a year of fighting had suddenly ended.

The solution carried the project through a lot of public debate and treatment in Parliament. Finally, in 1983, the last paper bond was burned.

10.4 Goal-requirements analysis

Often there is a long way to go from stating business goals to formulating requirements. We have discussed techniques for arriving at functional requirements in many parts of this book, task descriptions being an important intermediate step. In this section we will show a systematic way to do this for quality requirements. We use the shipyard as an example and the quality factor we look at is usability.

In general it is a good idea to first identify the goals, issues or concerns, and later translate them into verifiable requirements. Below we have used this method:

1 Identify the key usability issues by looking at business goals, critical tasks, user profiles, current usability problems, etc.

2 Choose requirements styles to cover the issues.

3 Choose metrics and target values.

Identify key usability issues

Critical tasks. In a complex system, the number of user tasks is very large, and it is unrealistic trying to cover usability fully for all of them. So we have to identify the critical tasks.

Figure 10.4A shows the critical tasks we could identify. The business goal "Use experience data for quotation" gave rise to two critical tasks: recording of experience data and using experience data for quotation. The goal "Shorten administration of ship departure" pointed to invoicing as a critical task.

The original specification mentioned work areas, but not down to task-level, so some elicitation was necessary to find additional critical tasks. We asked about tasks where users spent a large part of the working day at the computer. Accounting was the answer. When we asked about tasks made under stress, invoicing was the answer – although only when a ship departed. Finally two tasks were considered difficult: invoicing and detailed production planning.

Note that invoicing comes up several times since it is made under stress, it is difficult, and it is critical for one of the system goals.

For each critical task we identified the usability factors concerned. The critical usability factors for invoicing are efficiency and understandability. (Understanding what the system does is particularly important under stress.) We have added a non-standard usability factor, *overview*, to denote the need for overview and navigation in long texts. Learnability is not critical for this task, since all invoice staff will have special training.

Fig 10.4A Shipyard, critical tasks

	Critical tasks	Issues
Business goals:		
Use experience data for quotation	Recording experience data	Efficiency
	Using experience data	Learning
Shorten administration of ship departure	Invoicing	Efficiency
Other goals	(No critical tasks)	
Tasks taking much of the working day:	Accounting	Efficiency
Tasks made under stress:	Invoicing	Understanding, efficiency
Difficult tasks:	Invoicing	Efficiency, overview
	Detail planning	Learning, overview

Learnability is critical for some other tasks, such as using experience data, since these tasks might still be performed in the old manual way. Using the system will give better results, however, and it is important that users find it easy to do so.

Similar discussions lie behind the other critical tasks and factors.

User profiles. Analyzing user profiles will often highlight some usability issues. Figure 10.4B shows user profiles and related usability issues for two roles: marketing and accounting. We can make similar profiles for other user groups. Some issues turn up again, other issues are new, e.g. the changeover issue and the switching issue.

Other issues. Some business goals gave rise to critical tasks, while other business goals gave rise to different usability issues. In the shipyard, one of the business goals was "to encourage employees to use computers, e.g. by making the interfaces uniform". This gave rise to this issue:

 Issue: Uniform interfaces.

The issue is closely related to the issue of easy switching between different systems.

Fig 10.4B Shipyard, user profiles

User role: **Marketing**	No. of users: 4
Domain experience	Experts
IT experience	Text processing. Job costing with old system
Domain attitude	Proud
IT attitude	Reluctant
Learning new system	Must use many systems in the future Difficult to take time off for courses Prefer learning gradually on their own
Issues	**Easy to learn on your own** **Easy to switch between systems**

User role: **Accounting**	No. of users: 6
Domain experience	Experts
IT experience	Much, different systems
Domain attitude	Other staff delay things and don't provide correct data
IT attitude	Integrated part of work. Willing to learn
Learning new system	Changeover to new system critical. At most two days
Issues	**Changeover: Short course to learn all basic daily routines**

Current usability problems. Previous experience from text processing suggests that editing of long texts may take an unacceptably long time because the system has a long response time for scrolling and searching. This gives rise to this issue:

Issue: Reasonable response time for scrolling and searching invoice texts.

We have chosen to handle this issue as a usability requirement. Since it is more of a technical requirement, it could also have been handled as a performance requirement.

Fig 10.4C Usability issues and styles

Issue	Style					
	Task time	Problem counts	Process	Opinion poll	Design-level	Guideline
1. Recording experience data, efficiency	X		X			
2. Marketing, learn on your own, particularly using experience data		X	X			
3. Invoicing, efficiency, understanding, overview	X		X			X
4. Accounting, changeover course	X					
5. Accounting, efficiency	X					
6. Detail planning, learning	X		X			
7. Detail planning, efficiency, overview	X		X			
8. Easy to switch between systems						X

If we compile all the usability issues into one list, omitting redundancies and overlaps, we end up with the nine issues shown in Figure 10.4C. The next step is to transform the issues into requirements using an appropriate style.

Choose requirement styles

We don't have to use the same style for all the usability requirements. Some issues are better dealt with in one style, others in another style. Figure 10.4C gives an overview of the possibilities. An X in the table shows that an issue can use a specific style.

Since we assume that the suppliers will suggest solutions based on their commercial product with enhancements, some styles are not useful at all. A prototype (design style), for instance, cannot be used as a requirement since the prototype may not be implementable at a reasonable cost under that standard application.

The table shows that the development process style might be used for several issues. This means that the supplier would have to make a number of prototypes, usability-test them, and improve them. Such a process makes good sense if the supplier hasn't got the feature already and needs to add it to his system. As an example, the supplier might not have a standard solution for the use of experience data.

However, if he has a standard solution, we have to specify the usability requirements in some other way. The table shows that instead of the development process style, we could use the task time or problem count style. That makes sense if the supplier already has a solution.

Why not use the task time or problem count style in all cases? This is not a good idea because it might exclude suppliers that don't have a solution and won't commit to such a risky requirement. The solution is to leave it to the supplier to choose between alternative requirements. We'll show how to do this below.

Figure 10.4C shows that guidelines may be useful for easy switching (issue 9). This is no surprise, since guidelines are particularly useful for that. However, in this case we have shown that guidelines are also useful for invoicing (issue 3). Why is that?

The reason is that it is difficult to specify usability requirements for invoicing, particularly to ensure a good "overview" of the entire invoice. If we use the task time style, we have to specify tasks that reveal whether the user has a good overview, but such tasks are difficult to specify. On the other hand, experience had shown that an overview of 100 invoice pages is barely possible with a good text-processor, but we should accept the text-processor approach as a possible solution since we are not sure that a better solution exists. As a result, a guideline saying that "it shall be possible to edit an invoice in the same way as a text document" might be acceptable.

Some suppliers might have a better solution than the text-processing approach. We could allow for this by leaving it to the supplier to choose between performance, process, or guideline style.

Fig 10.4D Final requirements, issue one

Usability requirements for the shipyard
It must be easy to record experience data. Otherwise it will not be done. This will most conveniently be done while entering or editing job data:

R10.1 When a job has been selected for data entry, it shall be possible for an experienced user to attach experience data within 30 seconds, including lookup of experience keywords. (See task description in App. xx.1.) The vendor may choose R10.6 through R10.8 instead of R10.1 Chosen requirement: _____.

. . .

The vendor may choose an iterative design approach instead of some of the above requirements:

R10.6 During design of non-standard features, a sequence of three prototypes shall be made. Each prototype shall be usability-tested and the defects most important to usability shall be corrected . . .

R10.7 After the last usability test, the customer and the vendor negotiate whether to make additional prototypes for an additional fee, whether to implement the last prototype, or whether to cancel the contract due to insufficient usability.

R10.8 If the contract is cancelled according to R10.7, the customer shall pay $_____ as compensation

---

Metrics and target values

The final step is to write the actual requirements. We have to specify something that can be verified (the metrics) and the target values we require. Figure 10.4D shows the requirements for issue 1, recording experience data. According to this figure, the supplier may choose R10.1, which is in task time style, or R10.6 to R10.8, which specify the development process and conditions for terminating an unsuccessful process.

Figure 10.4E shows the final usability requirements for the first four issues. These are the more complex ones. The usability specification may look long, and it is – compared to most usability specs. However, in total for all nine issues it amounts to barely two pages. Compared to the 40 pages for the rest of the spec (including diagrams), it may be reasonable, given the importance of usability.

In Figure 10.4E we briefly explain why each requirement is necessary. This explanation gives a link to the issues we have identified. It also helps the supplier understand the purpose of the requirement. The requirements themselves are numbered in the typical way used in practice.

Fig 10.4E Shipyard, final usability requirements

Usability requirements
[The requirements below cover issues 1-4. Comments are shown in brackets.]

Section 10. Usability Requirements
Some of the usability requirements below cover the same issue, but in different ways. The efficiency of invoicing, for instance, is covered by R10.3, R10.6, and R10.9. The vendor may choose between the alternatives as shown below.

It must be easy to record experience data, otherwise it will not be done. This will most conveniently be done while entering or editing job data:

R10.1 When a job has been selected for data entry, it shall be possible for an experienced user to attach experience data within 30 seconds, including lookup of experience keywords. (See task description in App. xx.1.) The vendor may choose R10.6 through R10.8 instead of R10.1. Chosen requirement: _____.

Marketing has little time for courses and prefer to learn on their own. The vendor should specify the minimum course time that will allow marketing staff to use the system through their own experiments:

R10.2 After a ___ hour course, marketing staff shall be able to perform 90% of the tasks in App. xx.2 on their own. [*This essentially limits the number of serious usability defects. We don't care about task time. Users are allowed to take the time they think necessary. App. xx.2 has about 20 tasks, two of them dealing with the use of experience data.*] The vendor may choose R10.6 through R10.8 instead of R10.2. Chosen requirement: _____

Invoicing is critical. Invoice staff need an efficient solution that is easy to understand and that has a good overview of the entire invoice:

R10.3 After the changeover course, it shall be possible for an invoice user to edit the invoice printed in App. xx.3 (as shown by the edit markings) within __ minutes. This includes time to verify the corrections without printing the invoice. [*App. xx.3 shows an invoice about 50 pages long with 20 corrections.*] The vendor may choose R10.6 through R10.8 or R10.9 instead of R10.2. Chosen requirement: _____

R10.4 After the changeover course, the invoice user shall be able to explain the effect of editing the invoice text, the cost fields, and the discount fields, for instance what changes this causes in the data base and on the accounts. The user shall also be able to explain what effect a system breakdown has on a partially completed invoice.

Fig 10.4E continued

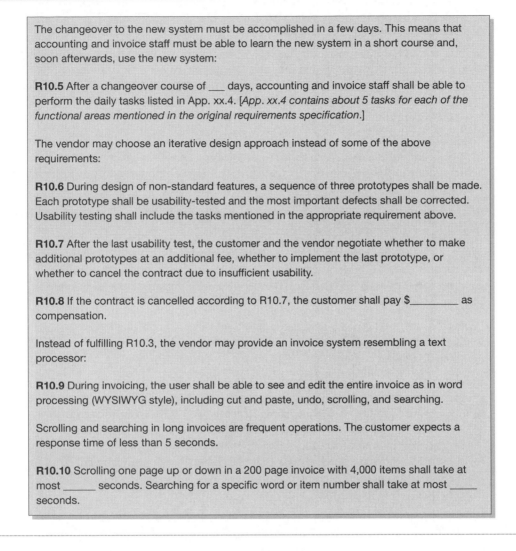

The changeover to the new system must be accomplished in a few days. This means that accounting and invoice staff must be able to learn the new system in a short course and, soon afterwards, use the new system:

R10.5 After a changeover course of ___ days, accounting and invoice staff shall be able to perform the daily tasks listed in App. xx.4. [*App. xx.4 contains about 5 tasks for each of the functional areas mentioned in the original requirements specification.*]

The vendor may choose an iterative design approach instead of some of the above requirements:

R10.6 During design of non-standard features, a sequence of three prototypes shall be made. Each prototype shall be usability-tested and the most important defects shall be corrected. Usability testing shall include the tasks mentioned in the appropriate requirement above.

R10.7 After the last usability test, the customer and the vendor negotiate whether to make additional prototypes at an additional fee, whether to implement the last prototype, or whether to cancel the contract due to insufficient usability.

R10.8 If the contract is cancelled according to R10.7, the customer shall pay $_____ as compensation.

Instead of fulfilling R10.3, the vendor may provide an invoice system resembling a text processor:

R10.9 During invoicing, the user shall be able to see and edit the entire invoice as in word processing (WYSIWYG style), including cut and paste, undo, scrolling, and searching.

Scrolling and searching in long invoices are frequent operations. The customer expects a response time of less than 5 seconds.

R10.10 Scrolling one page up or down in a 200 page invoice with 4,000 items shall take at most _____ seconds. Searching for a specific word or item number shall take at most _____ seconds.

The first three requirements are in task time or problem count style, and many suppliers may be reluctant to accept them, particularly if it is an added feature. For this reason the supplier can choose a process-oriented requirement instead, R10.6, which specifies that iterative design is to be used. For R10.3 (ease of invoicing), the supplier may even choose a guideline style, R10.9, that essentially says that if invoicing looks like text processing, the usability is adequate.

As usual, it is difficult to set target values. In some cases we have defined a value, for instance 30 seconds to record experience data. We based this figure on observa-tions of what people do in similar cases when they are not in a hurry. We also believe that it is quite easy to satisfy the demand.

In general, it is risky to insist on such targets in a COTS-based tender process. If the target is too restrictive, suppliers may decide not to make a proposal. In reality, the customer might be satisfied with a system that doesn't fully meet the target, if the system has other qualities. On the other hand, why set a too pessimistic target if you could get something better (see section 6.3).

The solution is to let the supplier specify the target values. For instance we ask him to specify the necessary course time for performing certain jobs. Experience from actual tender processes shows that the course times recommended by suppliers for their product vary considerably from product to product.

In one case (R10.10), we have given the supplier a clue to what we expect, but leave the actual specification to him.

When the customer later compares the various proposals, he will compare prices as well as performance figures and other issues. The decision of which supplier to choose is always a complex affair where apples are compared against oranges. Section 7.3 discusses these multi-criteria decisions.

When the customer has selected a supplier, they set up a contract based on the tender requirements. In the contract, the requirements show the supplier's choices and target values.

In case the supplier chooses an iterative design, there is a risk that he cannot provide a satisfactory design in three iterations. Customer and supplier might agree to make more iterations according to R10.7. However, if they cannot agree on the price for that or the customer doesn't believe that an adequate solution will be made, he may want to cancel the contract, but since the supplier hasn't committed to any specific usability level, you cannot blame him. A way out is needed, and we have chosen the solution that the customer pays a compensation fee for the cancellation, while the supplier specifies the fee upfront (R10.8).

Which compensation fee would suppliers specify in practice? We have asked a few, and they say they would specify zero. Doing otherwise would indicate that the supplier didn't trust his own abilities. Aha, we said, but what if the compensation clause hadn't been there? Well, we would find it an unfair contract since the customer could unilaterally terminate the project without paying anything. Conclusion: Keep the compensation clause. Although it may not have any financial significance, it has a high psychological one.

10.5 Usability testing in practice

In this section I give some practical advice on how to carry out usability tests and how to deal with typical barriers in the area. The advice is based on my own experience, discussions with developers and usability experts, plus reading a lot about usability testing. I assume that you have read about usability testing in section 6.6.2 so that you know what it is about and why it is used.

Which test tasks?

Developers initially have some difficulties defining good test tasks. Here is a typical badly defined task from a system that can measure and compare sounds and noises:

Task: set sensor sensitivity

1 Open settings window.

2 Select the sensor.

3 Set the sensitivity to 10 mW.

Testing with this task will not find out whether the user is able to perform a real-life task. One weakness is that the task description is a step-by-step instruction that tells the user how to perform the task. But we wanted to find out whether he could do it on his own. Another weakness is that the task is not closed and meaningful to the user. The user would never use the system just to set the sensor sensitivity. He wants to make a measurement, and setting the sensor sensitivity is a necessary step that he might not think of himself. We also want to see if he discovers this step for himself.

A better task would be:

Task: compare the noise at the top and bottom of the dishwasher

Equipment: Sensor supplied in a separate box. Dishwasher is a dummy during prototype testing (a small table will do).

This task is closed and meaningful, and we don't provide "hidden assistance". We also leave it to the user to find the proper sensitivity – just as in real life. My experience is that when developers have seen a few examples of good and bad tasks, they can define good tasks on their own.

Developer in the test team?

Some usability specialists make usability tests without developers on the test team. The developers get the report later and may see the videotape of the session. The reason, say the usability specialists, is that the developer would interfere with the test, discuss issues with the users, or guide the users.

This is a realistic risk, but there is a serious drawback to the approach: It drastically reduces the chance of having the problems corrected. First of all, developers seem to distrust a report stating various problems that they have not experienced themselves and cannot reproduce. (The same pattern is seen when unrepeatable technical errors are reported to developers.) Second, they cannot see what the real problem is, why the user did not see what was at the bottom of the screen, etc. As a result they fail to make a proper correction of the system. If they had been present during the test, they could have asked such questions.

In my experience, many developers are very good participants in usability experiments once they get the idea of the whole thing. With some support during the first session, they find a good balance between inappropriate interference and important information gathering.

Usability test or demo?

I often hear developers say that they made a usability test of their latest product. Great, I say, how many problems did you find? None, they say, the users were very happy with the system. That always surprises me, since we usually find 20 to 30 problems during a one hour usability test. A closer discussion reveals that what the developers did was a demo of the system. They showed the system to the users, walking through typical cases. The users were invited to comment on the system, but did not notice any problems.

In my experience, users can find a system very attractive when seeing a demo of it, yet be completely unable to perform anything with it on their own. The system is thus not easy to learn.

I have noticed several times that developers feel very uncomfortable with the thought of a real usability test, whereas they love to make demos. The reason for this may be their pride in their own work combined with the suspicion that the users will just mess up the whole thing. (This is what we actually expect users to do during the usability test. That is why we make it.)

In early stages of development, a demo may be very useful for finding missing functionality, but this has little to do with usability factors such as ease of learning.

How can you find test subjects?

Maybe the greatest obstacle in usability testing is finding test subjects – potential users of the new system. I have observed several times that this issue blocks serious thoughts about usability testing. The responsibility for finding test subjects usually lies with the developers, but they often don't know how to go about it. They have few social contacts with users, and they are unlikely to approach users or customers whom they don't know. In many product-developing companies they are not even allowed to.

Sales and marketing staff have much better potential for making user contact. I strongly suggest that support in finding test users is planned early and provided from other parts of the company.

Where you find test subjects depends on the kind of product we talk about. If it is a niche product, you will have to find potential users in that niche, and marketing people should be able to help. If we talk about products for a broader market, for instance many Web-based systems, you may find test subjects in public places, even the nearest supermarket. Of course you must get them interested in participating in such a test, but it is possible. Again marketing people may help.

Professional usability experts often use marketing agents to find test subjects over the phone. The developer has to describe the user profile and the number of test users he needs; and the marketing agent finds those people. Many people are willing to participate for nothing if they just have their travel expenses covered and get a free snack. You may use friends, family and neighbors, particularly for the first tests, but make sure they match the intended user profile.

Since test subjects are difficult to find, the same test subjects are often used for testing successive system versions. The result is that the new version seems surprisingly better than the old version. Unfortunately, the reason may be that the users learned the concepts in the first version and successfully transferred the concepts to the next version. New users are more likely to encounter more problems.

A related mistake is to test the system with users who have been involved with analysis or design of the system. They also know too much to be representative users. However, expert users are very good at finding missing functionality as part of a usability test.

If you are to test the ease-of-learning aspect of the system, you should use new users for testing each new version. Testing for performance, however, assumes experienced users, and the same users may well test several versions if you allow them to gain experience with each version.

Problem classification

Usability tests should be made early in the design stage, not in the test stage of the product. Things don't always work as intended, though, and usability tests may be late. But even if there is very little time available, some usability problems can be removed. The question is: which errors? Many development teams try to prioritize the problems, but cannot agree on the priorities. The problem is that they unconsciously mix up the importance to the user with the difficulty of removing the problem. Separating the two factors helps. I have had good results with this approach:

1 **User importance.** On the list of problems, note the number of users that have encountered the problem. Also classify each problem according to its importance to each of the users. For instance, use a scale with the steps explained in section 6.6.1: **task failure, critical problem, medium problem, minor problem**. When classifying the problems it is important not to worry about how to correct the problem, because it influences your judgement of the importance to the user.

2 **Difficulty.** Mull the problem over for at least one night. That often brings new ideas and solutions. Then classify each problem according to how difficult it is to repair. A simple scale could be: **small** effort (change of screen text, etc.), **medium** effort (several modules to be changed), **large** effort (new logic and data structure), **uncertain** how to repair.

3 **Cost/benefit.** Now prioritize according to user importance compared with difficulty of repair (cost/benefit). This can be formalized, but a discussion based on the two factors is usually sufficient.

Low-cost usability testing

Below I have summarized a usability test technique used extensively by my colleagues and myself. It is easy to learn: we practice one or two sessions with developers and help them write the problem list. Then they seem able to do it on their own.

1 Test team: At least one developer and preferably another person knowing the system and the test technique. If the system is a mockup prototype with little or no functionality, the developer is the Wizard of Oz, simulating the system. If there is another person, he keeps a manual log during the test, focusing on the problems encountered by the users. If not, the developer keeps the log.

2 Preparation: Make sure that the system is in the right state, with its database initialized, etc. Have copies available of screens with blank fields. Have a tape recorder and tapes ready (optional).

3 Start of test: Explain the test purpose to the user, the system purpose and the domain, but don't give any more introduction to the system than would realistically be given in real life. (Many developers assume that users will go on a course to learn how to use the system, but in real life users rarely get such courses, or they go on a course only after they have used the system for some time.) Start the tape recording (optional).

4 Give the users exercises with real-life tasks. State the purpose of the task, but don't explain how to perform the task. Give them only one exercise at a time and don't tell them how many you hope to make.

5 Ask the users to think aloud while trying to perform the tasks. If testing with two users at a time, encourage them to discuss what to do and why.

6 During the test, log the rough flow of the dialog (menu points selected, windows brought up). When a user encounters a problem or makes a comment on the system, make a note in the log. If convenient, use blank copies of screens to sketch the situation. Log also the time at various points of the session and at the point where you change tapes.

7 If the users asks for help, encourage them to find the solution themselves.

8 If the users have searched for the solution for some time, help them out, but make sure that you have made a note of the problem. Such a problem is to be categorized as a Task Failure, i.e. the users couldn't complete the task on their own. So make sure that the users have ample time to try to solve problems on their own. By experience, the developer finds ten seconds a long time, while the users finds it a brief moment.

9 If you don't understand what the users are doing, ask cautiously.

10 End of test: Terminate the test itself after roughly one hour. Everybody will be tired by then. Interview the users about what they liked and what they didn't like. To get an impression of their understanding of the system, ask them what they believe the system would do in some specific cases of your choice.

11 Within 24 hours, write a list of the problems detected. This list may include problems from two or more test sessions. Unless you have ample time, don't listen to the entire tape recording, but refer to it in cases where you are not quite sure what happened. Classify the problems as described in section 6.6.1.

A usability test session should last about 1.5 hours in total. The first time we test a user interface, we run only one session. Usually so many problems turn up that it would be stupid to try the system with a new user before correcting the worst problems. Later, we run two or three sessions and then write a joint problem list. It takes about two hours to write the problem list. The report will generally contain 20 to 30 problems of various severity.

Some usability experts claim that you need 10 or more test subjects to get reliable data. Let us look at the consequences of testing with too few users. You will miss some usability problems because the people you have worked with did not encounter them. You may also observe a problem that few other users will encounter. Is this prohibitive? You will find many important problems anyway. It is just a matter of hitrate, just as in other areas of testing. Furthermore, you will have to use your own sound judgement of what to correct no matter how many test users you work with.

10.6 The keystroke-level model

Usability requirements for task efficiency are in principle easy to specify, for instance in the following way:

R2 Experienced users shall be able to carry out task Q in 2 minutes on average.

The only problem is that it is hard to verify the requirement during system design or even at delivery time. Why? Because we don't yet have any experienced users. One way out is to specify the number of keystrokes necessary to carry out task Q (see section 6.7). If we know average user times for keystrokes and the average system response times, we can calculate the task time. We show an example below. In section 6.5 we discuss system response times.

The weakness of the calculation is that we cannot be sure that users in practice find out about the efficient way of doing the task, that they don't make mistakes during the task, and so on. However, we can get some impression of this during ordinary usability tests (section 6.6.2).

Card, Moran, and Newell (1980) measured and analyzed various aspects of user speed. The result is the *keystroke level* model. The model allows you to compute the total time for an experienced user to carry out a task at the computer. Below we have summarized their results in a table. The total time consists of the following parts:

Operation	Seconds
K_a: Keystroke or click, good typist	0.10
K_b: Keystroke or click, average typist	0.20
K_c: Keystroke or click, average non-secretary user	0.30
K_d: Keystrokes in complex codes, for instance product numbers	0.75
P: Pointing with mouse, excluding the click, depending on length moved	0.8–1.5
H: Homing, i.e. moving hand from keyboard to mouse or vice versa	0.40
M: Mental preparation to select a function or start entering a new chunk of data.	1.35
R: System response time. The part of system response time that doesn't overlap mental preparation, talking to customers, etc.	Non-overlapped response time
T: Essential task time to think, get information from customer, etc.	Task-dependent

Let us try to use the model for calculating the time to record breakfast servings in a hotel. We assume that data entry uses the Breakfast screen from Figure 2.5 and that the screen resembles the paper form from the restaurant. The screen has a line for each room, and in the line, the receptionist has to enter the number of breakfast servings in the restaurant and the number of servings in the room. We assume that for most of the rooms one of these fields is blank, and that most rooms have something to be entered.

We also assume that the receptionist can use Tab or Enter to move from one field to the next, and that the system checks line by line that somebody actually is checked into the room concerned. The system doesn't accept input for the next line until it has made the check. The receptionist is an average, non-secretary user. Based on the constants in the table above, the calculation now looks as follows:

	Time	Seconds
One room line: Enter digit and two Tabs	$3 \times K_c$	0.90
User reads data for the next room	$1 \times M$	1.35
System response time to check data. Partially overlaps one K_c plus M	2 seconds	0.35 (non-overlap)
Total time per room		2.60
Time for 100 rooms		260.00 (4 to 5 minutes)

The system starts its check at the moment when the user hits the last Tab of the line. The user will then spend 1.35 seconds as mental preparation (M) to look at the paper form to see the data for the next room. Then he will spend 0.3 seconds in hitting the first key of the new line. If the system makes the check within these 1.65 seconds, the user will not be delayed. If the check takes 2 seconds as in the example, only the non-overlapped time counts as a delay.

Expert users would most likely keep a finger at the paper form and enter data without looking at the screen. They would need no mental preparation time to switch from one room to the next, and most of the two second system response would count as a delay. If the system could accept input for the next room within 0.3 seconds, the expert user would save about 1.35 seconds per room or about 2 minutes a day.

10.7 The story behind Tasks & Support

This section tells the story about how we developed and tested the technique that we now call *Tasks & Support*.

The contact

In September 1998 we (Lauesen and Marianne Mathiassen) happened to get in contact with the IT department of West Zealand County, a Danish local government. They were in the process of acquiring a new payroll and personnel system to support hospitals, rest homes, high schools, etc. in the county. The old system was largely batch-oriented and did not support critical tasks like roster planning. Several local governments were running similar tender processes in that period (Midland Hospital, Chapter 12, is another example.) Our contact persons had acquired a few large IT systems through tenders, but had experienced various problems, e.g. that the supplier failed to deliver.

They agreed to meet with us to discuss their latest requirements specification. They sent it to us under a non-disclosure agreement, and when we met two weeks later, we had studied it carefully.

The start-up meeting

We met with a member of the IT department (Lotte Riberholt Andersen) and an expert user from one of the hospitals (Annemarie Raahauge). They had both been closely involved in the requirements specification for the new system, and they had recently sent the specification out for tender.

After a discussion of the good points in their specification and the major weak points, we showed slides with alternative ways of specifying requirements. When we came to task descriptions in Cockburn style (the hotel example on Figure 3.6A), they were very interested, particularly when we suggested that the task descriptions might be used directly as requirements, although we hadn't tried this yet. In two minutes they understood the idea: "This looks like something we could use!"

Two minutes later, they asked us this nasty question: With the traditional specification, the supplier's proposal specifies what he can supply as a standard feature, what as an extension, etc. With task descriptions, what should he reply?

Our answer was a general statement that he should describe how he would support the task, but, what it meant in practice, we couldn't say at that time.

We suggested that we tried to develop task descriptions for a critical and non-trivial part of the system: roster planning and work registration. First we would gather the necessary information from the staff, then develop task descriptions, and then evaluate the result with users, the IT department, and potential suppliers. We planned another meeting where we should try to gather the task information.

The elicitation meeting

Three weeks later we met again with Lotte Riberholt Andersen and this time Jeanette Andersen, an expert user with experience both as a nurse and as administrator of payroll and personnel. This time they had completed the tender process and just signed the contract with the supplier.

The meeting lasted for four fascinating hours. The expert user, Jeanette, understood the task idea immediately, based on the hotel example. Together we mapped eight tasks that seemed to cover the whole area. We were then going to write the full description back home.

During the meeting, we had noticed several problems with the task approach:

1 Do we describe the present tasks, the imagined future tasks, what the computer does, or what the human does?

2 How do we relate overall project goals to requirements?

3 How do we specify the information aspect, e.g. the necessary information to carry out a task?

4 What is the overlap between the task-based spec and the traditional spec? What should we preserve from the traditional spec?

At that time we couldn't answer these questions, and we decided to go home and work on the problem.

Just before we left we asked about the business goals, not expecting public authorities to have any. But we were wrong. In ten minutes they had explained seven business goals. Together we tried to map them into the tasks, and were surprised to find out that it made sense. With their traditional feature-style requirements it didn't seem possible. In ten minutes we had answered the second question above.

An interesting observation was that the IT person (Lotte) was amazed how much understanding of the user tasks she gained during the elicitation process. As an example, she observed that the system they had just contracted to get would probably lack an essential feature. Nobody in IT had realized that since they didn't understand the user tasks. She also explained that her impression was that suppliers often signed a contract without really understanding the requirements.

Outlining tasks and business goals in four hours was of course only possible because the user (Jeanette) and the IT person (Lotte) had been closely involved in the old spec. Further, the two researchers had studied the existing spec closely.

Homework

Back home we summarized the relation between tasks and business goals as shown in Figure 10.7A. This figure lists the task descriptions needed in the hospital case. Some of the tasks might be automated so that no human action remains (tasks 1.1 and 3.2). One task wasn't carried out today, but had to be in the future (task 3.1). The final, full task descriptions are shown in Chapter 13.

The figure mentions the "120 day rule". It is a Danish union agreement that when an employee has been ill for 120 days within a year, the employer is entitled to dismiss the employee with short notice, assuming that he does so the last of the 120 days. If the employer doesn't observe the deadline, he cannot dismiss the employee immediately, but has to give notice of between three and six months, depending on the employee's seniority. The problem is that decentralized departments know about the illness, but the central personnel department has to start the dismissal action. The proper exchange of information is often forgotten.

Answering the question about present versus future, computer versus human, turned out to be very difficult. We tried many variations of task descriptions, using some of their tasks as examples, and ended up with the idea of Tasks & Support, at that time called Use Cases with Solutions. Below we show some of the thoughts behind the approach.

During these experiments we wrote the full task descriptions shown in Chapter 13. We also made many iterations to find a reasonable grammatical style and template form.

Specify old, new, human, or computer?

The key question was what to write in the task description, the present way or the future way, what the computer did or what the users did. Figure 10.7B illustrates the problem by means of a simple dataflow diagram showing sub-task 3 (*Allocate staff*) of the *Make roster task*.

A bubble is a process that takes input data and produces output data as shown by the arrows (see section 3.14). We might have illustrated the problem with UML activity diagrams (section 4.6), but there would be more to explain.

The upper bubble is sub-task 3. It takes information about regulations, personnel, existing duties and assignments, tacit knowledge about staff preferences, and produces new assignments. The upper bubble corresponds to the joint action of user and computer. The bubble is technology-independent in the sense that the input and output will be the same no matter which technology we use inside the bubble. Thus the bubble models the old way of doing things as well as the possible ways of doing it in the future.

Fig 10.7A Hospital goals and tasks

Business goals \ User tasks	User: Planner in department 1.1 Monthly report to personnel department	1.2 Make roster	User: Staff in department 2.1 Record actual work hours	2.2 Swab duties	2.3 Staff illness	User: Personnel department 3.1 Check rosters	3.2 Payroll amendments	3.3 Record new employees
Personnel department: Automate some tasks	●					●	●	
Remove error sources						●	●	
Observe the 120 day rule	●					●	●	
Less trivial work and stress						●	●	
Hospital department: Reduce overtime pay, etc.		●						
Faster roster planning		●						
Improve roster quality		●			●			

Fig 10.7B Hospital, domain and solution

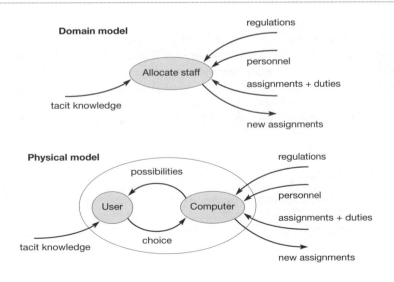

When we ask for an IT system to support the task, we divide the process into two sub-processes, one to be performed by the user and another to be performed by the computer. This is a *physical model* of the process. The figure shows a version where we get good support from the computer. The computer does the hard work of balancing regulations, personnel, etc. and just presents a prioritized list of possibilities to the user. The user makes a choice based on tacit knowledge of staff preferences.

There are many ways to divide the bubble into human and computer part. Some suppliers suggest one way, some another way. The present, old way of performing the task is yet another way of dividing the bubble into a human part and a machine part. What do we describe in the text-based form of the task: the domain model? What the user does now? What the user will do in the new system? What the computer will do?

We experimented with many combinations of these possibilities. We tried versions with several columns, for instance one with the domain model, one with the present way, one with the new user activities, and one with the new computer activities. It turned out that most of the writing was a repeat of the neighboring column, sometimes phrased slightly differently. Only a few fields showed some interesting differences between the old and new way, or between human and computer. Furthermore, all these columns took up a lot of space and we lost the overview that we had tried to gain.

We ended up with the solution explained in section 3.8. Each sub-task has two columns. The first shows the domain-level description. If there is a problem with the old way of doing things, we also explain that part in the first column. The second column describes the physical model, primarily what the product will do, but sometimes also what the user will do. This column may change during the requirements process from the customer's imagined solution to the supplier's proposal, and to the solution they jointly go for.

Complex functions. If you study the detailed description of the *Make roster* task, you might wonder why the regulations are not described in detail. The developer has to know them in order to implement the system. The reason is that the regulations are extremely complex and neither IT department nor the personnel department knows them fully (see complex functions in section 4.1). The customer explicitly stated that they only wanted bids from companies that knew the regulations and had built them into their product.

The information aspect

Task and use case descriptions do not specify the data used in each step. In the Make roster task, for instance, you may notice statements like "system generates a roster". What exactly does that mean? Which fields are involved? What is shown to the user?

As another example, what do we mean by "allocate staff"? Which staff? Staff in the department? Could the same person belong to several departments? In the work area description we have sometimes specified these things, but in a rather arbitrary form.

We feel it is important to specify the information needs for each sub-task, rather than leaving it to the supplier/developer to decide what is needed. On the other hand, it would clutter the picture if we tried to fully specify information needs inside the task description itself. One sign that information has to be specified is that a supplier with expert knowledge in payroll and union regulations, but no experience in hospital rosters, couldn't develop a reasonable roster system based on the tasks as they are. (The existing spec wouldn't help either.)

Today we suggest that analysts should develop a data model or some other data description in parallel with the task descriptions. The data model should be part of the requirements as the specification of data to be recorded by the system. Below we will see that a data model actually helps to cover more of the old functional requirements.

Match with existing spec

The first step in checking that our task approach would be an improvement was to match it against the existing spec to see which parts of the old spec were not covered by the tasks and vice versa.

Uncovered parts of the old spec. We reviewed that part of the original spec which dealt with rosters and time registration, to see whether its requirements were covered by the task model. By "covered" we mean that if the old requirement didn't exist, the task descriptions would give the same effect. One might believe that everything would be covered since the researchers had studied the old spec. Actually, we had based the tasks on the elicitation meeting, and details of the old spec were far back in our mind. This also shows in the comparison. Here are our observations of the existing 42 requirements for roster and time registration:

12 old requirements were fully covered by the tasks. Two of the old ones were more on the goal level, but covered anyway. Example: *All data involved in time registration shall only be recorded once.* (Covered by tasks 1.1, 3.2, and 3.3 for the work area we considered.)

4 old requirements gave additional detail to something covered by the tasks. Example: *All regulations, <u>including individual local agreements</u>, shall be handled by the payroll calculation.*

2 old requirements would have been covered by a data model. Example: *It shall be possible for an employee to work in several roles and several departments at the same day.*

5 old requirements would have been caught if we had made a CRUD check. Example: *If an employee works in more than one department, it must be possible to partition his total pay between the departments.* (We assume that the information model would have shown that cost data related to several departments.)

15 old requirements specified output (reports on screen and paper) that was not demanded by any of our tasks. Example: *The system shall be able to show a vacation account for each employee.*

3 old requirements were strange. We couldn't understand what they meant.

1 old requirement specified something that wasn't a true requirement: *The system shall consist of a planning part and a time registration part.*

42 requirements in total

In addition to these functional requirements, the old spec contained quality requirements in separate chapters. In our case study, we didn't try to cover them with tasks.

The most interesting thing is the 15 output requirements that were not demanded by the tasks. If they are true requirements, there should be tasks that demand them. We know that there are some tasks that we didn't try to cover, partially because the user wasn't too sure about the actual procedures. They involved budgeting and follow-up on the budget. If we had covered these tasks, we might also have covered about half of these 15 output requirements.

However, we also believe that there are a lot of tasks about someone wanting to see how this or that totals, what the history of something is, etc. These tasks are probably quite important, but difficult to get hold of since they don't have a clear operational goal. They belong to a broader class of requirements about *getting an overview* of some (complex) data.

To some extent, a CRUD check might hint at a need to see some of these data. As an example, a CRUD check should ask *who reads the information about vacation days spent*. The answer would include that both employer and employee might want to see them, and it would be reasonable to show also the total number of vacation days and the number of days left. In the counts above, we have not assumed that a CRUD check could reveal the complex output requirements.

New requirements through tasks. We also reviewed the task descriptions to see which requirements were new. We counted eight new requirements:

1 Support needed for vacation much later than the current planning horizon.

2 Automation needed for task 1.1.

3   Need for several temporary versions of a roster and for extensive undo.

4   Need for including people in the roster before they are formally recorded.

5   Need for alerting the personnel department shortly before the end of a 120 day sick leave. (The present spec mentions the problem, but not as a requirement.)

6   Support needed for two people swapping duties.

7   Support needed for an employee falling ill on duty.

8   Need for supervising roster planning and work time registration.

In addition, the tasks added detail and purpose to several existing requirements. The reason we could come up with the new requirements was that working with tasks allowed us to imagine the new work procedures with a degree of clarity that traditional requirements didn't allow us.

We know that the system the customer had contracted to get did not satisfy requirements 1, 5, and 8 above. If these requirements had been stated and checked at proposal time, the customer might well have chosen another supplier or asked for modifications in the system they chose.

We are also quite sure that if the customer had tried to carry out his tasks with the new system before signing the contract, he would most likely have chosen another supplier.

Review with suppliers

The next step was to review the tasks with suppliers to see advantages and disadvantages of the approach.

In the Danish market there are only three suppliers of this kind of system. They had all been involved in the case we studied. We have reviewed the task approach with each of them and asked each of them to replace the example solution with their proposed solution. We had separate meetings with each supplier. Typically we met with two consultants from the supplier.

Advantages. All three suppliers confirmed that the approach favored no supplier, and vastly improved understanding of requirements and customer expectations. The whole idea corresponded to what they usually discussed verbally with customers, but never wrote down. The approach would also allow the customer to evaluate the proposals faster and better.

The tasks were a good basis for demonstration of the product and for acceptance test at the end. One supplier commented that the traditional feature-based requirements could be verified more exactly, but with less meaning to the customer.

They all mentioned the need for a process re-engineering perspective in the customer organization and saw the tasks as a vehicle for that. They also liked the ease with which business goals could be traced to requirements.

One consultant was fascinated with the task goals (Cockburn's idea in his version of use cases), saying that this was essential, but a big problem to most customers. He added that the uncovered requirements (various special reports) were a problem in practice. Often they were a relic of the old system, and the users couldn't explain why they were needed.

Problems and issues. Most of the negative comments related to things we didn't expect to handle with the use-case approach. We agreed to most of them:

Security wasn't covered. Relationships between tasks in different departments wasn't visible (we suggested that a higher-level task might help). The approach couldn't be used for negotiation at top management level.

One consultant felt that the approach couldn't be used with the standard government contract (called K18), but other consultants saw no problem in that area – even if asked explicitly.

All the suppliers believed that customers would take longer to make requirements based on tasks. We have later learned that this is not true. As reported in section 3.8 the same hospital spent 5–10 times *less* time using Tasks & Support in their next tender process.

Some suppliers explained that they often wrote the specification for the customer. At present, large parts of these specs were reused from other specs, so the task approach would take much more time for them, particularly since they had to understand the customer's tasks.

Willing to try? All suppliers were willing to try the approach in practice. One of them was even enthusiastic about the idea, but the initiative would have to come from the customer.

Two suppliers could readily fill out their part of the tasks (the proposed solution), and we had no problem in understanding their proposals. They had described advanced solutions to the various problems, and they explained that this was a very good place to write about the advantages of *their* solution.

The first supplier gave the task of filling their part of the tasks to another staff member. Apparently this staff member wasn't given the proper instructions, so he misunderstood the idea and wanted to correct the description in the left-hand column. As an example, he noticed that the customer in sub-task 3b of Make roster had a problem with access to available staff in other *departments*. "Why didn't the customer ask for access to available staff in the entire *county*?", he complained. (Their product offered that.) The supplier soon learned that he could have written that as a proposed solution in the right-hand column, thereby showing that he had a solution that exceeded what the customer asked for.

Test in a new project. A year later, the county planned to buy another IT system of similar complexity. The new project team had not been involved in the first experiment, but had heard about it. They learned the approach quite fast and successfully used it in the new project. We have explained the details in section 3.8.

11

Danish Shipyard
Contract and requirements for total business administration

Background

In the 1990s, Danish Shipyard (DSY) decided to get a new IT system for all business administration, including marketing support, order handling, production planning, inventory control, and payroll. The name, Danish Shipyard (DSY), is a cover name for a real shipyard in Scandinavia.

Business systems of that kind are often based on commercial products, modified and enhanced for the company in question. The product is selected during a tender process where the proposer will supply the commercial product and develop the modifications.

What should the requirements specification look like in such cases? A central issue is how to describe the functionality of the system. One extreme is the *design-oriented approach*: prescribe the user interface to the product as a set of screen pictures and menus. However, this is really a design issue, and it would exclude a standard system with different screen pictures. A less design-oriented fashion is to prescribe the high-level product functions to be provided. Another extreme is the *domain-oriented*: describe the user tasks and ask for a system to support them.

In the shipyard case a mixed approach was taken: the required functionality was described as a set of *work areas* to be supported and the high-level product functions to support them. For such a system, this is a reasonable level of specification. It allows the customer to validate the specification, and it allows the proposer to estimate the degree of deviation from his standard system.

Jens-Peder Vium worked as a consultant for the shipyard, investigated the demands, wrote the requirements specification, and assisted during the tender process.

A year after deployment of the software, the author (Lauesen) became interested in the project. Together with Susan Willumsen he studied the requirements specification and the actual system. Although the system was successful, it didn't meet all the business goals. One reason was the stated requirements, another reason the way the project was run. We will discuss this further below.

Part of the contract and the entire requirements specification is shown on the following pages.

The documents were written by Jens-Peder Vium (iqm@pip.dknet.dk). The version shown here was translated from Danish by Birgitte Bush and edited by Soren Lauesen and Houman Younessi.

Structure of the case study document

The contract had this structure:

1 Contract, about 30 pages. Below we show about four of them.

2 Appendix 1, one page, time schedule for delivery and installation (not shown below).

3 Appendix 2, the Requirements Specification, about 30 pages. All of them shown below.

4 Appendices 3 to 15, about 10 pages in total. None shown below.

From the contract itself, we have selected only the four pages that are of interest from a requirements engineering perspective.

The original requirements specification used in the tender had several appendices, but they were omitted from the contract. You might notice, however, that the specification still refers to these appendices. We have included one of these appendices: the data model (entity/relationship diagram) and a flow chart.

The requirements specification contains three important parts:

1 Explanation of terms from the user domain in addition to some IT terms, about eight pages in total (section 3 of the specification). When trying to understand these terms, it is useful to refer to the data model, which contains the same terms.

2 System objectives (or business goals). Why does the shipyard want such a system? One page (section 4 of the specification).

3 The real requirements. About 16 pages (section 5 of the specification).

Editorial comments

The editors have felt a need to add comments a few places, for instance to explain what has been omitted, or to explain that strange statements are not mistakes in the translation. Such comments are shown in brackets, e.g.

[**Omitted from the translation:** Section 13 to 29, covering warranties, responsibilities, transferability, signatures, etc.]

In the requirements specification you may notice a few lines with strike-through, e.g.

k) ~~Data capture function for drawings and technical specifications.~~

These occur in the contract version. They are parts from the original tender version which were canceled in the contract. Very little seems to have been added. A noticeable addition is a handwritten note about system performance (section 5.5.2). The contract itself, however, holds several additions and amendments to the requirements.

The researcher's comments

You should recognize that specifications in real life are made under time pressure. Things are not perfect. Resolution of several issues ought to be made in the requirements phase, but sometimes have to be delayed to later stages of development.

In the shipyard case, the specification is quite clear to the customer, but several things are obscure to an ordinary developer. One important purpose of the specification is to make the developer aware that he should ask the customer what this and that actually mean.

Many parts appear to be imprecise, so that it would be hard to verify them in practice. This is often less of a problem than the researcher tends to believe. One example is this statement from section 5.2.2.1.3:

The payroll system shall include the following functions:

…

g) Transfer function for transfer of payments to bank … and other functions, e.g. holiday allowance card and statistics, according to the labor market organizations and public authority requirements in addition to good practice in payroll accounting.

How could you live with a requirement such as "and other functions, e.g."? In practice, if there is a dispute between customer and supplier about what should be covered under "e.g.", they will first seek a peaceful agreement, probably as part of negotiating other issues, extensions to the system, etc. If they cannot agree, they may take the matter to court.

The amazing thing is that courts are excellent in resolving imprecise and ambiguous issues. (All court cases are really of this nature.) If the contract is imprecise, the court investigates what constitutes current good practice, what experts say about the specific case, etc. and they come up with a decision. In many countries, courts tend to rule that what the customer could reasonably expect, for instance because it is practice in competitive products, the customer has the right to get – even if the contract doesn't mention the feature at all!

Unfortunately, going to court is expensive and time-consuming. It is better to be sufficiently precise in the first place so that the issues cannot be debated.

Requirements versus goals

The shipyard system was specified in a domain-oriented way as a list of work areas to be supported. In the shipyard case that was advantageous to product-oriented approaches where screen pictures, etc. were specified.

However, the domain-oriented approach in the shipyard did not ensure that the system would meet the expected overall business goals. But what are the business goals? The answer is in the requirements specification, section 4, The System in Context. It describes concisely what the customer's goals are with the system, and the benefits he expects. Here are some business goals (objectives) from section 4:

a) . . .

e) to strengthen a systematic application of experience data, e.g. in connection with job costing of proposals.

f) to reduce the time from "departure of the ship" to the administrative conclusion of the project: invoicing and cost accounting.

These goals are even more domain-oriented than the work area descriptions. If you could meet these goals without IT at all, such a solution might be as good – or better.

Are these business goals requirements? Is the supplier, for instance, responsible for a better use of experience data when calculating the price in an offer? No, it cannot be his responsibility, since he cannot make all the organizational changes also needed at the shipyard to achieve the goal.

If you look at the contract, you will see that section 4 of the requirements specification is explicitly left out when referring to the requirements. So the supplier is not responsible for the goals. Why are the goals stated, then? They need not be, but in practice they help the developers to understand the requirements, and why they are as they are.

But who is then responsible for meeting the real objectives? In this case it is the customer's responsibility. In principle, the requirements engineer is responsible for translating the technical aspects of the goals into requirements. In practice it is the customer's responsibility to verify that this translation has been properly done. For this reason it is important that the customer can understand the requirements.

In the shipyard case, the requirements do not correctly reflect the goals. The use of experience data (objective (e)), for instance, is not consistently supported by the functional requirements, and the actual system was delivered and accepted without these essential features. Speeding up invoicing (objective (f)) required high usability for the invoice functions. They had to give the user a good overview of invoices more than hundred pages long (typical for ship repairs). No usability requirements were stated, and although the delivered system had the necessary functionality, the user interface was inadequate for this critical task.

The deficiencies in the requirements specification could have been detected early if proper quality assurance had been used. Usually the system owner (the financial manager of DSY) should have ensured it, but in this case he entered into joint development with the supplier. The result was that he became blind to deficiencies and to complaints from employees. Lauesen and Vium (1996) discuss these matters in depth.

Contents, Danish Shipyard, contract and requirements

Contract

between

DSY
Danish Shipyard A/S

(in the following referred to as the customer)

and

Omega•Group A/S

(in the following referred to as the supplier)

about

**delivery and maintenance of systems solution
for administrative data processing**

© 1999 Jens-Peder Vium

5 **2. Terms of Delivery, etc.**

2.1. Scope of Contract

Within the time schedule, cf. Appendix 1, the supplier shall deliver the software specified in appendices 5 and 6 (list of software modules), which shall meet the

10 requirements specified in appendix 2, chapter 5 (Requirements Specification). [Chapter 5 is "systems requirements". Note that according to the contract other parts of the requirements specification, e.g. Section 4.1, Objectives, are not the supplier's responsibility.]

15 ### 2.2. System Description

The supplier shall prepare a system description, which indicates in detail how the requirements in appendix 2 will be met, and how the further expansion potential described in appendix 7 will be considered. The system description shall in full or in

20 part – provided this is convenient – consist of user guides, manuals and other system documentation for the standard system already prepared by the supplier, in addition to a detailed statement on how the standard system will be adapted, changed, expanded or reduced to the effect that it meets the requirements specified in appendix 2.

25 In the event that the supplier, while preparing the system description, becomes aware of errors in appendix 2 or realizes that it will be better to satisfy the customer's stated needs by changing the requirements in appendix 2, the supplier shall point this out to the customer in order that the parties can agree to change the requirements specification.

30

The supplier's proposal for a system description shall be presented to the customer in accordance with the major milestone schedule (appendix 1). The system description must be approved by the customer. However, the customer's approval does not relieve the supplier of any responsibility for the contents of the system

35 description and for fulfilling appendix 2 unless the parties explicitly and in writing agree on specified changes in appendix 2.

When the solutions given in the system description meet the requirements in appendix 2, and the customer has approved the system description, the supplier is

40 entitled and obligated to complete the appropriate parts of the system in accordance with the system description. To the extent that the system description does not comply with appendix 2, including any changes in the agreement, the supplier shall ensure that appendix 2 is complied with and, if necessary, supplement or change the system description.

45

1   Until the system description has been approved, the customer shall be entitled to
     demand that changes are made in appendix 2 in excess of what appendix 7 states
     [appendix 7 is "planned extensions"].

5   Changes of appendix 2 that have been agreed upon or demanded by the customer,
     and which require the supplier to increase or reduce his efforts in excess of what is
     reasonable to expect from developing a system such as the one in question, can be
     conditional on a corresponding and reasonable change in the purchase price and
     the major milestone time schedule. No change that entails an increase in the
10   purchase price or a delay in the time schedule shall be carried out before the
     customer has given his consent in accordance with item 19.

2.3.   Hardware (canceled)
     [no hardware was to be delivered under this contract]

15

2.4.   System Software
     The contract comprises the system software specified in appendix 5.

20   ### 2.5.   User Programs
     The contract comprises the software specified in appendix 6. The software
     comprises partly standard software, partly software developed specifically for
     the customer.

25   ### 2.6.   Changes in Orders for Hardware and Standard Software
         (canceled) [nothing was required]

2.8.   Changes of Specifically Developed Software
30   If the customer, before approval of the system description, makes a request for
     major changes in the specifically developed software in relation to the requirements
     specification, the supplier shall without delay inform the customer how the
     changes will affect time schedule and price.

35   If the customer, after approval of the system description, but within a reasonable
     period of time before the specifically developed software is put into operation,
     makes a request for changes in this software in relation to the requirements
     specification and/or system description, the supplier shall without delay inform
     the customer about possible impacts on time schedule and price.

40
     The price for the changes shall be agreed as a reasonable payment to the supplier, and
     the effect on the time schedule, if any, shall be reasonable compared to the added service
     that the changes reflect. At changes in price and time schedule any savings that are a
     result of the change shall be duly considered. No change shall be carried out before
45   the customer has consented to it in accordance with item 20, paragraph 3.

1

2.9.   Other Services

Agreements on other services (e.g. training of the customer's employees or consulting services) are stated in appendix 8 indicating content and scope, as well as prices for the services.

5

2.10.   Repurchase (canceled) [nothing was required]

[Omitted from the translation:
Section 3 to 11, covering installation, delivery time, prices, terms of payment, test]

10

12.   Availability and Response Times

12.1. Availability

Availability is measured on the basis of the log maintained by the customer, in which system breakdowns, faults, and operational interruptions which reduce the system availability are reported. It shall be logged when the supplier has been notified and when the system is reported available.

15

The cause of each event is traced as far as possible in order that it can be related to a single supplier. The result of the trace is logged too and supporting documents filed.

20

Unavailable time is calculated as the time where key data entry or data capture functions are unavailable.

In case the operational period between reporting the system available and the next unavailable period is less than 60 minutes, and both unavailable periods are related to the supplier, then the entire period shall be counted as unavailable.

25

The customer shall produce monthly reports that show the unavailable time related to the supplier.

30

12.2. Response Times

(See appendix 2, section 5.5.2)

12.3. Ascertainment

35

[Omitted. Deals with using expert appraisement in case conflicts arise over availability and/or response times]

[Omitted from the translation:
Section 13 through 29, covering warranties, responsibilities, transferability, signatures, etc. Appendix 1 with time schedule for delivery and installation]

40

45

Appendix 2

Requirements Specification
for
Systems Acquisition

1. INTRODUCTION

Danish Shipyard (DSY) is one of the few Danish shipyards that has specialized in ship repairs. Compared to shipbuilding, repair work is subject to unforeseeable situations. When a ship returns to land after many years of sailing the seven seas it may show signs of unexpected wear and damage, which naturally are not included in the original proposal of overhaul and repairs. Moreover, it is vital from a competitive perspective that a ship is repaired as quickly as possible.

This implies that management of changes in the agreement between the shipyard and the shipowner is very important. The shipowner must constantly be able to take a comprehensive view of which services have been agreed upon and added to the original proposal, and what the additional services are expected to cost. The shipyard workers and foremen must have accurate and complete instructions about what has been agreed upon and, consequently, what repair work they have to do. If it turns out that the conditions on which the proposal is based have changed, the shipyard must present the shipowner with documentation and settle the matter on the spot.

Since 1978 DSY has used data processing to support such tasks. They began by using the RC8000-based project application, which is still in use today. In 1986 the system was supplemented with job costing, job management and invoicing, based on DDE's Supermax, UNIX and ORACLE platforms.

Today, DSY employs the following sub-systems:

- Contract management: Project application on RC8000 from which data are transferred to the Oracle database for follow-up and cost accounting.
- Accounting system consisting of debtors, credit [creditors] and finance on RC8000.
- Inventory application on RC8000 receiving data from bar code readers via PC and Supermax.
- Payroll application on RC8000.
- Master files of shipowners, ships and projects/orders (Supermax).
- Job costing system on Supermax for estimates and cost accounting; actual costs are transferred from RC8000's project files to Supermax.
- Job creation system on Supermax.
- Invoicing application (Supermax).
- Office system: word processing, spreadsheet on Supermax.

During the last year, a group headed by Orla Skjellerup, DSY's Financial Manager, has examined new systems solutions for Danish Shipyard A/S. The group has visited trade fairs, attended seminars and designed screen pictures – as an outline to a possible solution – in an attempt to show what they want.

1   They have also interviewed a number of employees in order to get an overview of
    the individual tasks, which when combined will constitute the major
    administrative functions of the shipyard.

5   Based on this input we have prepared the requirements specification in an attempt
    to focus and target all the information we have gathered.

2.   ABOUT THE DOCUMENT

10

2.1.   Purpose of Requirements Specification

The basic purpose of the requirements specification is to explicate DSY's
requirements to the information systems that the company plans to acquire, partly
to replace obsolete systems which are no longer maintained, and partly to support
15 new system areas that are relevant in terms of business.

The requirements specification should serve the following purposes:
a) Obtaining a proposal and closing a contract for a total solution meeting the
    specified requirements.
20 b) The chosen supplier's design of solution.
c) Planning of systems test and acceptance procedures by the parties.
d) Clarification of disputes, if any, between the parties during the term of the
    contract.
In order to support these objectives on a daily basis it is necessary to keep the
25 requirements specification up to date during the term of the contract. Therefore, it
must be easy to change, cancel or add items to the requirements specification.

When the supplier has demonstrated by a systems test that the system meets the
requirements specified in the document, and when the purchaser by means of the
30 application test has ascertained that the system can be applied according to the purposes
specified in the document, the buyer is **required** to accept the delivered system.

2.2.   Scope of Requirements Specification

35 This requirements specification covers primarily the functional requirements to a
solution. In addition to the functional requirements, the document also describes
DSY's application of the system in order to make the supplier [solution provider]
aware of all the implied aspects that must also be satisfied if the system is going to
function as an adequate tool, and the investment in the system is going to pay off.

40
It is expected that the following tasks can be performed by available standard systems:
■ Accounts: finance, debtors and creditors.
■ Payroll and personnel.
■ Inventory.
45 ■ Stock ordering.

1 Therefore, the document does not include descriptions of the above tasks, as
investigation has shown that the tasks can be supported efficiently by means of
standard software available on the market.

5 It is expected that the remaining tasks have to be supported by individual systems.
It is therefore essential to describe the aspects that are expected to apply specifically
to DSY and the changes in relation to current systems. To the extent that adequate
solutions can be provided through further use of standard systems, DSY will
positively consider such proposals.
10

Conditions:
a) It is assumed that DSY's present platform, which consists of Supermax
equipment, Unix System V Operating System, Oracle Database System and
Development Tools (TPO, Forms, ReportWriter) would be part of the new
15 systems architecture.
b) The system shall present a multi-company solution with complete separation of
data as seen by the users.
c) PCs shall be able to function as clients in a client-server architecture, as (dumb)
screen terminals to central server systems, and as independent PCs that can
20 operate with or without a disk.
d) The new systems shall be integrated with the systems that survive in an altered
form, cf. appendix 1.
e) It shall be possible to link workshop terminals for data capture directly to the
25 systems.

2.3. Readers' Background

The readers of the requirements specification can be divided into two main groups.
One group comprises DSY's management and employees, who as buyers and users
30 must approve and guarantee that the specified requirements are relevant to and
adequate for their respective areas. The other group consists of systems suppliers,
who must be able to understand and interpret the requirements specification and
use it in preparing their proposals and quotations. The final proposal presented by
the chosen supplier must meet specified as well as implied requirements, which are
35 prerequisites for the reasonable use of the systems in the specified areas.

This is why the language of the document contains as few technical terms as
possible. As it is not assumed that systems suppliers know very much about ship
repairs and related terminology in general, or DSY terminology in particular, the
40 requirements specification contains a separate chapter that defines the most
relevant words and concepts.

45

1 ## 2.4. Keeping the Document Up to Date
It follows from the purpose of the document that it must constantly be updated to ensure that it always reflects what the parties have agreed upon in relation to requirements.

5 A request for a change must be made in writing, and both the change and its consequences for the agreement (time, costs, working hours, detailed specifications) must be approved by both parties.

One of the tasks of project management is to find a procedure for updating the
10 requirements specification and other approved documents and specifications.

3. DEFINITIONS AND TERMS

15 During the development project the definitions and terms ought to be improved and developed.

3.1. Information Model and Information-oriented Terms

Account Cost
20 A quoted job may involve cost entries that must be paid in excess of the quotation. Each cost entry is "earmarked" as belonging to the quotation or to the account part of the job. On a job settled as per account all costs are by definition account costs.

Account Job
25 A job settled as per account is not based on job costing. This may change, however, in which case the job becomes a quoted job.

Account Stipulation
Account stipulations correspond to job costing stipulations and are also used in
30 calculating gross amounts in connection with account jobs and account costs.

Activity
A job can be divided into several activities. Cost types such as payroll, materials and sub-suppliers are registered for the activity.

35
Company
At present, DSY comprises the following companies: Danish Shipyard A/S, Island Shipyard A/S, Hafna A/S, Scandinavian Enterprise A/S [all of them cover names]. In terms of accounting there is no connection between the companies.

40
Contribution Margin
The contribution margin is calculated for each job and divided into a quotation part and an invoice part.

C/M (quotation) = invoiced amount (quotation) – net amount (quotation)
45 C/M (invoice) = invoiced amount (invoice) – net amount (invoice)

1 **Correspondence**
Documents from word processing, such as texts, "box graphics" and in the long
run "real" graphics. The documents may be letters, call reports, etc. The
correspondence refers to one of the following levels: country, shipowner, ship,
5 project. It shall be possible to retrieve documents based on their reference to
country, shipowner, ship, project.

Cost Category
The old system with established cost categories in the range from 9 to 16 shall be
10 replaced by 99 cost categories, which each company can define freely. All cost entries
are related to a cost category. The 99 cost categories are divided into four cost types.

Cost Entry
A book entry referring to a cost (consumption) in connection with a specific project
15 and a specific job on the project. Cost entry is a common term used in connection
with all cost categories, regardless of whether or not the project involves a sales
order or an internal order. Cost entries are specified as separate items on the
contract accounts. The financial accounts only show aggregated entries.

20 **Cost Type**
Cost type is a more general term for cost category. There are four cost types: pay,
materials, sub-suppliers and miscellaneous. The three first types are used in job
costing. The fourth type, miscellaneous, applies to costs that relate to the project,
but are not included in the stipulation. Depending on the particulars of the project,
25 miscellaneous expenses might be re-invoiced to the customer as "outlays".

Customer's Number
The shipowner's position number on his specification of the order – the job to be
performed. [This is admittedly obscure, but closely follows the original. The idea is
30 that the shipowner has made his own enumerated list of things to be done. DSY
documents refer to these "customer's numbers".]

Debtor
A debtor is a natural or a legal entity who at present is a customer of DSY. A
35 shipowner may be a debtor, but need not be. And a debtor may be a shipowner, but
need not be.

Department in Charge
Canceled term
40 **Dock Index**
A collection of job cards that for each department shows the jobs included in a
specific project.

45

1 **Excise Duties**
   Government tax, oil tax, etc. included in supplier invoices, but reimbursable like
   VAT. The excise duties are entered on separate accounts like VAT.

5 **Experience Data**
   See keywords.

   Extra Work
   In connection with quoted jobs it shall be possible to record extra work. Extra work
10 comprises all activities and work that are not included in the proposal. Extra work
   is performed according to open account terms.

   Gross (Amount)
   The term describes the estimated "sales price" as opposed to the net amount
   describing the cost price. For quoted jobs the gross amount is based on a job cost
15 calculation. For extra work performed on quoted jobs and for account jobs the gross
   amount equals the "net amount" _ "the margin factor". The factor is determined
   by the specific project and cost type. The gross amount is only used as a guideline
   for invoicing.

20 **Internal Facility**
   Object on which internal orders can be made, such as building, office, machine.
   Each internal facility has a manager (employee) in charge who is responsible for
   maintenance, etc.

25 **Internal Order**
   An order that applies to a facility at the yard. Cost items that concern internal
   projects must, depending on the nature of the job, be entered on an operating
   account (current maintenance) or on a capital account (investments in
   constructions/improvements). Note that in the current RC8000 system an order
30 that concerns maintenance is called a non-productive order, while an order that
   concerns investment is called an internal order.

   Invoice Amount
   The amount invoiced for a job. For quoted jobs invoicing may include quoted
35 amounts as well as per account amounts.

   Invoice Chapter
   A clustering of jobs for production and invoicing purposes.

   Invoice Outline
40 Print-out from a project showing net amount, gross amount and quotation amount
   at entry level or at higher levels. See e.g. screen picture with print-out conditions in
   appendix 7.

45

1   **Invoice Stipulation**
     Margin percentages (for each cost type) and hourly rates (for each project/sub-
     contractor/performing department) are used in calculating gross amounts in invoicing.

5   **Job Card**
     Work instruction describing what work an employee or a team has to perform on a
     ship. Job cards are printed in a number of copies determined by each job and
     corresponding to the number of employees on the job.

10   **Job List**
     A list of jobs used by the production manager and the shipowner's representative
     during performance of work.

     Job Status
     Similar to project status, job status determines which entries can be made in
15   connection with a job. Job status can be "open" or "closed". By means of job status
     a project can be gradually closed – and finally completely closed by a change in
     project status.

     Job Costing Difference
20   The difference between gross amount and quotation amount. This only applies to
     quoted jobs.

     Job Costing Stipulations
     The stipulations determine, for instance, targets for contribution margins to be used
     with quoted jobs. The contribution margins are quoted as margins for the three cost
25   types: own hours, sub-contractor hours, and materials. The job cost stipulations are
     standard for the company, but it is possible to deviate from/replace them at project
     level. Furthermore, it is possible to depart from the job costing stipulations by
     replacing the calculated quotation price and performing a reverse costing. This will
     result in a calculation difference. Project calculations may be based on several
30   alternative stipulations, but only one set of stipulations will be saved, i.e. the set
     that corresponds to the quotation.

     Job Costing Chapter
     Clustering of jobs for costing purposes.
35
     Keywords
     A job may be given one or several keywords by which experience data can be
     retrieved. There ought to be (at least) two keywords, one describing the part of the
     ship under repair, the other the operations carried out; e.g. auxiliary engine,
40   overhaul; outside hull, painting, etc. The experience data consist of the figures
     which are the sum of the job's cost entries.

     Materials Entry
     A cost entry that indicates consumption of a product carried in stock. The cost type
45   is "materials". Materials entries are recorded by means of bar code readers.

Materials Requisition

A form (in red, yellow, blue, green) that can be used as a base document to record materials entries. The form is used in an emergency, e.g. if the bar code reader breaks down, and when materials are provided for purposes other than a project, e.g. work clothes to the crew on a ship.

Net Amount

The net amount is a term for the cost price as opposed to the gross amount that denotes the sales price. A quoted job involves two kinds of net amounts: the costed amount and the actual amount. When all the costs related to a job have been entered, the actual net amount is the sum of the job's quoted costs. [This is admittedly obscure, but closely follows the original.]

Open Order

An open order is a project where the order has not yet been confirmed. An open order has project status = "open", and the unit holding the project is not "shelved" [apparently "shelved" is a dummy department holding shelved cases].

Order

The words "order" and "project" are used indiscriminately [a word with the same connotation is used in the original], even though an order actually denotes an agreement made with a shipowner about the execution of a project.

Part Payment

Payment from a shipowner "credited on the project account" before the final invoicing of the project.

Performing Department

Reference from an activity to the "department" (e.g. team of workers, supervisor, etc.) that has to perform the work. The performing department does not refer to an organizational unit and should not be confused with the department in charge of the project.

Project

The word is applied as a common term for an external project (sales order) and an internal project (internal order and non-productive order). A project involves a specific piece of work – an order or a contract – on a ship or a facility. The project is the essential object in DSY's financial management. In the old RC8000 system a project was called a ship.

Project Header

Information that relates directly to the project plus milestone dates and who is in charge of the project. The present system stores such information in the project table.

Project Status

Attribute of a project that controls which data processing operations are allowed. Project status is described in more detail in section 5.2.4. and in appendix 2.

1 **Purchase Orders**
Purchase orders are issued in connection with:
- Purchase of materials and services to order (sales orders or internal orders).
- Purchase of goods carried in stock.
5 - Purchase of labor (hours) at a sub-contractor.
Purchase orders are only used as a term for purchase to order. On the purchase order, production management can determine the margin to be applied in calculating the gross amount for the purchased materials and later when the supplier invoice is entered as a cost item.

10 **Quoted Costs**
The costs on a quoted job that relate to the quotation. See also Account costs and Extra work.

Quoted Job
15 A quoted job is created through a job costing calculation. On a quoted job the costs are by default quoted costs. Cost entries concerning extra work on a quoted job are marked as account costs.

Sales Order
20 A project that is related to a ship and can be invoiced to a shipowner. Cost entries are recorded in the contract accounts and the financial accounts as ongoing. At the closing of a project earnings/costs are transferred to sales/purchase.

Ship
25 The ship has a unique ship number. The ship number is a serial number without embedded codes. Every ship must have a shipowner. It shall be possible to change the ownership of the ship, e.g. when a ship is sold.

Shipowner
30 A shipowner is a potential or actual customer of DSY. The shipowner is relevant as a customer in terms of marketing and as a debtor in terms of accounting. The shipowner is given a unique number. The shipowner number is a serial number without embedded information. A shipowner may own or be in charge of one or more ships.

35 **Sub-contractor**
A supplier who provides labor to the shipyard. A purchase agreement made with a sub-contractor is based on the sub-contractor's usual, hourly rate (master file) or a special rate. The sub-contractor's workers fill in time sheets like DSY's own employees.

40 **Sub-contractor Time Sheet**
Form on which the sub-contractor's workers record their hours of work. Corresponds in structure to the time sheet for DSY's own employees.

45

1 **Sub-supplier**
See Supplier.

Supplier
5 Common term for sub-suppliers and sub-contractors. [The distinction between supplier, sub-supplier, and sub-contractor is not followed consistently in the requirements.]

Supplier Invoice
Invoice from a supplier. The supplier invoice has (or ought to have) a requisition
10 number (that is, a reference to a purchase order).

Time Sheet
A base document where own employees (hourly wages) and sub-contractor employees state on which activities and jobs they have worked. See also Sub-
15 contractor time sheet.

Work Hours
Common term covering own hours and hours of sub-contractor.

3.2. Functional Model and Functional Concepts
20 **Breakdown Function**
A breakdown function can divide an element into several sub-elements while preserving the link to the original element: for example, breaking down a job into activities.

25 **Browse Function**
A browse function allows the user to browse through a given text or data set. A bookmark may be inserted where the browsing starts, enabling the user to return to the bookmark by pressing a single key.

Clustering Function
30 A clustering function can gather a range of uniform elements into a group which under given circumstances acts as a unit with its own name and description. Example: invoice chapter where several jobs are gathered into a unit.

Data Capture Function
35 A data capture function can in a fully computerized manner read data from external and internal sources, and update the specified fields in the database. The execution of data capture functions must be done under human supervision.

It shall be possible to read the following external data sources:
40 ■ Bar codes.
■ Text from the word processing function.
■ PC floppy disks with ASCII text.
■ Drawings read by scanner.
■ Typed documents read by scanner and optical character recognition (OCR).

45

1 Examples:
- The shipowner's specifications from floppy disk provided by shipowner.
- The shipowner's specifications from paper document.
- The shipowner's translated specifications from word processing.
5 - The foreman's rough design (drawn by hand) specifying the executed tasks.

It shall be possible to read internal data from the following systems:

- Texts from a text editor.
10 - Texts and figures from a spreadsheet function.

Data Entry Function

In former times data entry was called "punching". Data entry involves reading data, e.g. from a completed form, and entering the data via a keyboard, quickly and 15 without mistakes. The general requirements of data entry are:

- Field type check, text (alpha-numeric), numbers (numeric).
- Field value check, interval, text length, etc.
- Duplicating most recent value.
- Default values that can be overwritten.
20 - Check digit.
- Existence check of elements referred to in the database.

Filing Function
25 Filing comprises:

- Filing of documents with the following detailed functions:
  - Links to structures in the database, e.g. shipowner, ship, project, job.

  - Establishing keywords.
30
  - Write protection, in order to protect against changes in distributed/confirmed documents.
- Regular file where documents are directly and quickly available by means of query functions.
35 - Search function by means of which documents can be retrieved based on lookups in the structured database, by keywords and by time intervals for the document date.
- Transfer function by means of which records/documents of a project can be linked to another item in the database structure, e.g. project documents transferred 40 from one ship to another.
- Cancellation function by means of which experience data in documents can be deleted selectively based on age, project, and cost category.

45

1 **Master File Maintenance**

Master file maintenance keeps track of master data that are part of certain data structures established in the information model. Under conditions that will be specified in more detail later, master data can be created, updated, and deleted.

5 Master data are provided with a unique number according to the number system of the data model. Examples: shipowner file, ship file, project file, goods file.

Print Function

The print function can print data according to a detailed specification, e.g. layout,

10 signs, etc. Consequently, the print function must be seen as a parallel to the query function. Examples: job cost calculations, debtor account statements, purchase orders, invoice outlines, etc.

Project Management Function

The project management function can transfer a project from one organizational

15 unit to another. Example: transfer of a contracted project from the marketing function to the production planning function.

Query function

A query function can:

20

- ■ Define a search area.
- ■ Select candidates within the search area which comply with specified criteria and inform about the number of matches.
- ■ Show an <u>overview</u> of the <u>descriptors</u> of the matches (brief text, note, etc.).

25 ■ Present the <u>matches</u> in a specified level of detail and layout either on screen or on printer in the "report generator format".

Example: search for experience data from completed projects.

Security Function

30 The objective of a security function is to prevent unauthorized persons from creating, reading, updating or deleting certain data. Access attempts which have been refused by the security function shall be documented in a security log whenever and where it is desired. Example: protection of sensitive personnel information concerning payroll accounts.

35

Spreadsheet Function

A spreadsheet function performs computing operations on data arranged in rows and columns. It shall be possible to obtain data from given tables in the central database. After editing/processing in the spreadsheet function it shall be possible

40 to replace the result in the database. Examples: reading account figures from the chart of accounts, preparation and computation of budget, updating budget information on the accounts.

45

1   **Text Editing**

Word processing for keying in and editing letters, proposals, invoices, etc. There are no specific requirements of the word processing facilities which are not covered by the popular PC-based systems, such as WordPerfect. Example: correspondence,

5   editing invoices, translation of shipowner's specification to Danish.

Transfer Function

A transfer function is used to transfer data between two sub-systems. A transfer function is able to write data (that one or several other sub-systems can read and use) according to a defined and documented interface specification. Example:

10   transfer of payroll entries to the payroll application.

4.   THE SYSTEM IN CONTEXT

15   **4.1.   Objectives**

DSY's objectives for the system are:

a) to phase out the RC8000 computer and related systems.

b) to integrate new systems with surviving old systems, cf. appendix 1.

c) to strengthen the topicality of data relating to a project by catching data as close

20   to the source as possible.

d) to strengthen customer service, e.g. by integration of the text-based project administration and other administrative data processing.

e) to strengthen a systematic application of experience data, e.g. in connection with job costing of quotations.

25   f) to reduce the time from "departure of the ship" to the administrative conclusion of the project: invoicing and cost accounting.

g) to strengthen marketing, e.g. by systematic work on potential customers and by following up on present customers.

h) to encourage employees to use computers, e.g. by making the interfaces

30   uniform and by facilitating simple inquiries, e.g. by pop-up windows.

4.2.   The System in the Operational Context

As far as possible the system should be operated from the workplaces where the jobs are performed. The centralized, operational functions should be limited to

35   information system administration and printing of large batches.

All data and programs are stored in the central computer. The common data comprise numbers, text, graphics, and pictures.

The present terminals placed in most offices will gradually be replaced by PCs to

40   the extent and at a pace that makes e.g. introduction of a graphical user interface, graphic data and unloading of "the central CPU" efficient or necessary.

The present communication lines for asynchronous terminals will gradually be replaced by a local area network (LAN) that links local, PC-based systems (clients)

45   and the central database (server).

1   4.3.   Related Development Projects

During the project period, an organizational development project will be carried out in order to strengthen the quality and reduce the lead time in the administrative processes.

5. SYSTEMS REQUIREMENTS

5.1.   System Purpose

The high-level purpose of the system is to record and make it easy to retrieve information concerning all projects from birth to grave. In addition, the system shall meet all regulatory requirements and live up to "generally accepted business practice and accounting principles".

5.2.   Applications and Functional Requirements

5.2.1.   Functions in the Life Cycle of an Order

5.2.1.1 Marketing

Marketing comprises all activities until an agreement has been entered, i.e. when a quotation has been accepted. However, a quotation is not made in all cases. Occasionally, a shipowner sends a ship to the yard per open account. But in such cases a specification will describe the work to be performed.

Marketing is divided into:
- Sales
- Job costing
- Proposal and follow-up activities.

A group of approximately four persons takes care of marketing. It is a very flexible group where things often develop quickly, and where the individual person often switches from one project to another and from one function to another. As a consequence, marketing makes the following demands on the IT systems:
a) Several employees shall be able to work together on the same project, e.g. filing, calculation of jobs in the engine room, calculation of jobs on deck.
b) It shall be easy to learn the user interface.
c) The user interfaces in the systems used by marketing shall be consistent.
d) The query functions shall be fast and perceived as more efficient than the present filing systems which are based on manual letter files.

5.2.1.1.1 Sales and Follow-up Activities

Sales activities consist partly of contacting customers, and partly of answering shipowners who want to obtain a quotation on a given job. The present systems employed by the sales function are based on letter files and word processing. Call reports are kept in a letter file for each country. The memory functions are based on ordinary calendars (Time Manager) and searching a text file where potential projects are recorded. To support sales activities the system shall have the following functions:

1   a) Master file maintenance and query function[1] concerning potential shipowners.

    b) Master file maintenance and query function concerning ships.

    c) Master file maintenance and query function concerning projects.

    d) Query function about the combination of country/shipowner/ship/project.

5   e) Query function about master data of a project (project header).

    f) Query function about documents; narrowed down by means of the functions in items a-e plus g and h.

    g) Query function about job costing and experience data for a project (specified and aggregated) by searching on keywords (place and standard operation).

10   h) Query function about open projects.

    i) Text editing[2,3] for filing documents according to country/shipowner/ship/project.

    j) Filing function for documents related to country, shipowner, ship, project.

    k) ~~Data capture function for drawings and technical specifications.~~

15   l) Query function about shipowners/debtors, creditors, suppliers.

    m) Project management[4] for transfer of project to new unit (including "shelved").

    n) Query function in all screen pictures via pop-up menus about user manual and master files.

20 In all query functions it shall be possible to jump from a screen picture to a master file lookup by applying the current key values from the screen picture and returning the selected values to the screen picture.

5.2.1.1.2 Job costing

25 The job costing function is staffed with experts who have a wide technical/professional knowledge of ship engines, hulls, decks, etc.

The system for the job costing function[5] shall have the following functions:

- from section 5.2.1.1.1: sales and follow-up activities: a, b, c, d, e, f, g, h, i, j, k, m
30   and n in addition to:

    a) Data entry and data capture functions[6] (scanning of text and drawings) for technical specifications and shipowner's specification of the job and the ship (= job text); to be stored in the database as document or job text.

---

[1] The query functions, items a-e plus g, h and I, are placed in some kind of menu.

[2] Text editing is made in Supermax Text. When Supermax Text is activated through Omega•6, the document will be placed in the "right" database table, ensuring it can be retrieved, c.f. item f.

[3] The customer has acquired Supermax Text, and any failure in its functions will therefore be outside the supplier's field of responsibility.

[4] Transfer of project in connection with project management is placed in some kind of menu.

[5] DYS's present C-programs are retained but adapted to the new data model, and changes are specified in detail in the systems description.

[6] Only text can be captured. It is assumed that the shipowner's specification has been prepared by word processing, in which case the task consists of transferring a text file to the Oracle database. The text file must have "recognizable" signs for breakdown into calculation chapters and jobs. It must be possible to identify the customer's number.

b) Data entry for job costing stipulations.

  c) Clustering function for jobs into job costing chapters, where it is possible to reserve a range of job numbers per chapter instead of giving (as now) consecutive numbers to the jobs; the present chapter division with sorting according to

job/customer's number (that is, the shipowner's job number!!) shall be preserved.

  d) Data entry function for job text and keywords (place on ship and standard operation).

  e) Data entry function for calculated hours and net amounts, for three cost types per activity and with instant presentation of totals per job.

f) Browse function for jobs and activities with bookmark and return key.

  g) Job costing function for computing a quotation with the inserted job costing stipulations.

  h) Print function for job costings on job level, including headings and totals for each job costing chapter.

i) Data entry function and print function for obtained quotations; will also be used for purchase orders provided a quotation is accepted.

  j) Query function on sub-contractor and goods table in addition to sub-contractor agreement and internal agreement about the project.

  k) Data entry function for milestone dates about the project (arrival, entering dock,

leaving dock, and departure).

5.2.1.2. Production Planning

The production management is in charge of production planning and any activity in "the yard". While a ship is at the shipyard the production managers act as

project managers and contact persons in relation to the superintendent, who is the shipowner's representative/agent. Therefore, it is the production managers and the superintendent who make all the agreements about extra work, while the ship is at the shipyard. If the conditions for the quotation fail, the same persons must

negotiate the matter.

5.2.1.2.1 Rough Planning

When a quotation has been accepted, the production manager who will be in charge of the project begins to order spare or replacement parts and personnel. In

principle, each transaction with a supplier requires a purchase order. To conform with the present procedure it shall be possible to issue purchase orders as purchasing vouchers from a purchasing voucher pad. The purchase orders are gathered and "punched". But it shall **also** be possible to enter purchase orders directly into the system and make prints of them. The purpose will change

gradually to direct entry into the system.

The supplier shall state purchase order number on delivery note and invoice. The purchase order contains for instance information about project number and job number.

1 However, sometimes the necessary information from job costing will not yet be
   available to the production manager, or the information has not yet been allocated
   to jobs. Therefore, he shall be able to place a copy of the purchase voucher at the
   end of the purchase voucher pad and wait to record the correct job number until it
5 is known. When the number becomes known it must be entered (the purchase
   order is moved from a pseudo-job to the real job).

   The allocation of dock facilities as well as other resources is administered manually
   in a "dock book", and at present there are no plans to change this procedure.

10 The rough planning shall have access to **all** functions from section 5.2.1.1.1: sales
   and follow-up activities, and **all** functions from section 5.2.1.1.2: job costing in
   addition to the following functions:

   a) Clustering of several jobs into an invoice chapter with consecutive job numbers
15   or customer numbers within the chapter.
   b) Print function for various follow-up reports: invoice outline sorted according to
      invoice chapter indicating account/quotation per job number and customer
      number (that is, the shipowner's job number); or merely totals per job, chapter
      or entire order.
20 c) Data entry function for change of project status.
   d) Data entry and print functions for purchase orders.
   e) Query function about obtained quotations, cf. section 5.2.1.1.2: job costing, item i.

   The system description should specify to which extent DSY's existing C-programs
   should be reused.
25

   ### 5.2.1.2.2 Detailed Planning
   The detailed planning is made by a staff member at the supervisor office.
   Sometimes the office may be crowded with supervisors from DSY and sub-
   suppliers [should be "sub-contractors"] who wish to know on which job they
30 should start working, or an acute problem may have to be tackled on a certain job.

   The most important task of the planner is to ensure that the right person receives
   the right work instruction. The instruction consists of a small job card describing
   the job in text format and in the future also as drawings.

35 It shall be possible to print a job card for a worker with his employee number in
   bar code; see registration of costs for further details. In addition to these duties the
   detail planner also functions in part as a secretary for the production management.

   The system for detailed planning[7] shall contain the functions:
40
   ■ From section 5.2.1.1.1.: sales and follow-up activities: a, b, c, d, e, i, j, m and n,

   ----

   [7] DSY's present C-programs are retained, but adapted to the new data model and to changes which will
      be specified in details in the systems description.

- From section 5.2.1.1.2.: job costing: a, c, d, f, i, and k,
- From section 5.2.1.2.1.: rough planning: a and d,

in addition to the following functions:

a) Data entry function for performing department, bonus, if any, plus text and/or supplementary text about the job.
b) Print function for dock index and job lists selected as: all, a specified range of numbers, an invoice chapter, not previously printed (i.e. new since last time).
c) Print function for job cards with bar codes in varying numbers – one card for each person on the job.

5.2.1.3. Registration of Costs

Costs are chiefly recorded in the systems through data entry. However, costs of goods consumed from stock are recorded via a bar code reader by means of a
portable scanner. The scanner data are transferred to and collected on a PC, from which they are transmitted to the Supermax. Then, the inventory account on RC8000 is updated by generating transactions transmitted to RC8000 which updates the accounts during a batch-run.

As mentioned in section 4.1, one of the targets of the new system is to increase the topicality of data. Areas that are relevant to improve are:

- A direct connection from the bar code reader to the inventory system and the contract system.
- Data capture of effort spent per job by means of bar codes on personal ID cards and job cards. The codes are entered via a workshop terminal and directly validated in the contract system.

The system shall include the following functions:

- From section 5.2.1.1.1.: sales and follow-up activities: item d (query about country/shipowner/ship), item e (query about master data of the project), item m (project management), item n (query function).
- From section 5.2.1.1.2: job costing: item i (data entry of purchase orders), item j (sub-contractor agreements about project and internal agreements), item k (data entry of milestone dates).
- From section 5.2.1.2.1: rough planning: item b (printing of various follow-up reports), item c (change in project status) and item d (change in purchase order)

in addition to:

a) Data entry function for cost entries with validation of all information against tables for debtors, creditors, goods, personnel, sub-contractor, sub-contractor personnel, project status, job status (open/closed), performing department and purchase orders; classification as quoted costs or account costs.
b) Transfer function for transferring cost entries from contract system to other systems (e.g. inventory, payroll, accounts).

1 c) Search function for finding/clarifying project, job, performing department. [Point d doesn't occur]

e) Query function for finding/correcting purchase order number; searching among open and/or closed purchase orders.

5 f) Query/browse function for cost entries applying to all cost entries or selected from accounts/quotations or date interval, per project, job, job status, performing department, cost category, cost type, and indicating net amount and/or gross amount on entry level or on various aggregated levels.

g) Query function about financial accounts, debtors, suppliers/creditors, sub-contractors and materials.

10

h) Calculation function for checking requisition amounts of money and hours.

i) Calculation function for determination of pay for cost entry and payroll system.

j) Data capture function for transactions from workshop terminal (time clock).

k) Data capture function for stock consumption via bar code.

15

l) Print function to document all cost entries in the entry book.

5.2.1.4. Closing and Follow-up on Order

5.2.1.4.1 Preparing an Invoice

20 When the ship has departed and the cost entries have been recorded, all entries related to the project are checked in order to ensure that the basis for invoicing is complete and accurate. An invoice outline is printed showing all cost entries of the project, specified per job. Preparing a project involves an auditing analysis of all vouchers and entries. The analysis is made by the staff in the accounts department.

25

The system for preparing a project shall contain the following functions:

- From section 5.2.1.1.1: sales and follow-up activities: item i (text editing), item j (query about sub-contractors, materials, sub-contractor agreement and internal agreement about project), item k (drawings and technical specifications), item m (project management), item n (query function).

30

- From section 5.2.1.2.1: rough planning: item b (various follow-up reports), item c (change of project status).

- From section 5.2.1.3: registration of costs: item e (query about purchase orders), item g (query/browse function for cost entries) [should probably be item f].

35

5.2.1.4.2 Invoicing

The preparation of cost entries completed, the invoice outline is handed over to the invoicing group. Invoicing requires a flair for and knowledge of business matters to ensure that the invoice becomes what it should be, and not an invitation to

40 bargaining discounts or anything worse.

Invoicing involves four steps:

a) Printing of invoice outline

b) Entry of invoice stipulations (margin, etc.) to be used at step c.

45

1   c) Invoice process: jobs are grouped as invoice jobs, which are then invoiced. Totals for invoice chapter are displayed continuously.
    d) Printing of follow-up statement (RESULT LIST).

5   re a: Print function for costs per job; net and gross. Showing job text, quotation/account and specified/totaled per cost type and cost category in addition to project totals. See example of INVOICE OUTLINE in appendix 7 [not part of the contract].

    re b: Entering mark-up percentages and hourly rates for transformation from net
10   to gross amounts. Data which are only valid for invoicing the project in question. Default values can be found at company level.

            Entering print parameters: Job number yes/no, customer number yes/no, etc. Used at display of a job or a clustering of jobs, cf. item c below.

15
    re c: A job or a sequence of jobs appears on the screen with gross amount per cost type calculated according to the rules defined under item b and with selected/relevant information: invoice chapter, job number, customer number, job text, quoted amount, job comments and keywords.

20
            The jobs are grouped as invoice jobs to the effect that several individual jobs occur on the invoice as one job. Entering invoiced amount per cost type; editing the rest of the information, except for job numbers. More detailed information about part invoicing and final invoicing can be found in
25   appendixes 2 and 3.

            Facility for making invoice comments and keyword comments. When step c has been completed, it must be decided whether the invoice is a part invoice or a final invoice. If the function is closed before the task of invoicing is
30   finished, it shall be possible to return, e.g. the next day, and continue where you left off.

    re d: Printing of final invoice and RESULT LIST per invoice job with possibility of showing cost specifications per (individual) job. Totals per invoice chapter
35   and project. For a more detailed description see appendix 6, page 18 [not part of the contract].

    Prerequisite:

40 Purchase orders and account entries for hours and costs must be "ready and checked", for instance as is done when preparing invoices, cf. section 5.2.1.4.1.

    The invoicing system shall comprise the following functions:

    ■ From section 5.2.1.1.1.: sales and follow-up activities: item d (query about coun-
45   try/shipowner/ship/project), item e (master data of the project), item f (query

about documents), item g (job costing and experience data), items i and j (editing and filing documents), item k (data capture of drawings and technical specifications), item m (project management), item n (query function).

■ From section 5.2.1.1.2: job costing: item a (scanning of text and drawings), item d (job texts and keywords), item f (browse function), item h (printing of job costing), item i (quotation), item j (query about sub-contractor and materials).

■ From section 5.2.1.2.1: rough planning: item a (clustering into invoice chapters), item b (follow-up reports), item c (project status)

in addition to the following functions:

a) Master file maintenance of margins, cf. preparation of invoice outline above.
b) Query and job costing functions for printing of invoice outline.
c) Browse, clustering and data entry functions (invoiced amount per job) to support the invoice process.
d) Text editing function, e.g. to change or delete sub-numbers, job texts and totals, and to add comments for internal use.
e) Function for printing the final invoice.
f) Query and job costing functions for printing of result list.

In the invoice process shipowner equals debtor. If duplicate/redundant data occur, the shipowner information shall automatically be valid for debtor. In this way, the user is spared the trouble of maintaining two sets of data.

5.2.1.4.3 Reporting that an Order is Complete

When the invoicing of a project has been completed and all costs have been entered, it shall be reported that the order is finished. This will change the project status and the following process will take place:

a) Costs in the financial accounts, cf. appendix 3 [not part of the contract].
b) List of contribution margin is printed.

Any subsequent cost entries will be printed as an addition to the contribution margin list. It shall be possible to print a new edition of the contribution margin list, if required.

5.2.2. Support Functions

5.2.2.1. The Finance and Accounting Function

5.2.2.1.1 Debtor Management

The debtor management system shall have the following functions:

a) Data entry function for payments received and made in addition to invoicing made outside the contract system.
b) Print and query functions for due date lists and list of balances indicating open entries.
c) Transfer function for transfer of entries to the financial accounts.
d) Master file maintenance for debtors.

5.2.2.1.2 Creditor Management

Most creditor entries (purchase invoices) are recorded as cost entries in the contract system. Other creditor entries are recorded directly in the creditor accounts.

The system for creditor management shall have the following functions:

a) Data entry function for purchase invoices, credit notes, payments made, payments received and various excise duties.
b) Query and print functions for due date lists and list of balances.
c) Data entry function for stopping payments of supplier invoices.
d) Function for printing checks.
e) Transfer function for transfer of entries to the financial accounts.
f) Master file maintenance for creditors.

5.2.2.1.3 Payroll System

The payroll system receives most of its data from the contract system. Wages are paid every two weeks to workers paid by the hour, and salaries are paid once a month to other employees.

The payroll system shall include the following functions:

a) Master file maintenance covering employees, workers and company information.
b) Security function to protect against unauthorized access to sensitive personnel information.
c) Data entry function for pay entries outside the contract system.
d) Browse function to check on pay entries.
e) Transfer function for transfer of entries to the financial accounts.
f) Print function for pay settlements to employees.
g) Transfer function for transfer of payments to bank/PBS [Danish Payment Systems Ltd.].

and other functions, e.g. holiday allowance card and statistics, according to the labor market organizations and public authority requirements, in addition to good practice in payroll accounting.

5.2.2.1.4 Budget and Accounting Function

The system for budget and accounting shall have the following functions:

a) Master file maintenance for company information, accounting periods, etc.
b) Master file maintenance for financial accounts, including either a separate machine master file or references to the contract system's "internal facilities" with rates of depreciation.
c) Data entry function for budget figures.
d) Data entry function for (financial) entries.
e) Data entry function for post-entries at end of an accounting period.
f) Print function for statements of financial accounts.

1   g) Print function for trial balance.
       h) Calculation function for resetting, etc. at change of accounting period.
       i) Print function for budget figures, budget/observed and variances.
       j) Print function for entry journal.
5   k) Print function for interim statements with specifications.

5.2.2.1.5 Internal Audit
It is specifically required that the total system, the part systems and particularly the
links between these are documented and comply with the auditing policies and
10   regulatory requirements.

5.2.2.1.5 Security Function
The security system shall comprise the following functions:

15   a) Security system to protect against unauthorized access to data and programs,
       ~~including infection by PC virus~~.

5.2.2.2 Internal Orders (Internal Projects)
The purpose of internal orders is to record efforts to develop and maintain DSY's
machines and other facilities, such as docks, workshops and cranes.

20   In principle, the internal orders system is similar to the sales order system in its
structure. The following analogies and differences apply:

- "Machine" is analogous to ship.
- "Responsible employee" is analogous to shipowner.
25   ■ Costs covering "operation and maintenance" are entered on (operating) accounts
       in the financial accounts.
- Costs covering "development and improvements" are entered on (capital)
       accounts in the financial accounts.
- Of course, invoices cannot be made on internal orders.

30   Otherwise, the functions are similar to those of sales orders! Internal projects pass
through the same states as external projects, but entries shall be posted at different
account groups in the financial accounts at state change.

5.2.2.3. Inventory Function
35   The purpose of the inventory function is to maintain a service stock of common
parts, such as nuts and bolts, gaskets, fittings, wires, plugs, and work clothes. In
addition to own stock there is a consignment stock comprising, e.g. painting articles.

Besides purchasing, the inventory function includes the following specific
40   functions:

    a) Receipt of goods, applies also to purchase to order.
    b) Delivery of goods from stock.
    c) Monitoring range of inventory goods, e.g. based on inventory turnover ratio.

45

5.2.2.3.1 Inventory Purchase

The inventory purchase system shall have the following functions:

a) Query function on goods that may be ordered or are on order/back order at a supplier.
b) Query function on goods the stock of which is below the reorder point.
c) Data entry function for purchase order.
d) Print function for purchase order to supplier.
e) Query function on suppliers of "difficult pieces".

5.2.2.3.2 Receipt of Goods

Receipt of goods comprises both goods to inventory and goods to order. In both cases quantity and quality is checked at receipt. In case of goods to order, the idea is to have the goods delivered at "the right place" and possibly to have the production manager and/or supervisor informed about the arrival of the goods.

The system for receipt of goods shall have the following functions:
a) Master file function for looking up a purchase order when the purchase order number is on the delivery note.
b) Query function about purchase orders when the purchase order number is not on the delivery note.
c) Combined data capture and data entry function for registration of inventory intake (article number in bar code, keyed in).

5.2.2.3.3 Delivery of Goods from Stock

When goods are delivered to a project (to order), the delivery is recorded directly in a portable scanner where the article number is bar coded, while project number, job, department, and number of goods are keyed in. It shall be possible to place a delivery of goods where the job number does not exist, on a pseudo job as described in section 5.2.1.2.1.: rough planning.

The system for delivery of goods shall have the following functions:
a) Combined data capture and data entry function for registration of delivery from stock (article number in bar code, keyed in number of goods, project number, and job number).
b) Transfer function for transfer of delivery entries to the inventory accounts.

These requirements assume that registration of delivery of goods and the inventory accounts are placed in separate systems linked by means of transfers of account entries.

5.2.2.3.4 Inventory Accounting

The inventory accounting system records supplies to and deliveries from stock, keeps the inventory accounts, and transfers entries to cost registration.

The inventory accounting system shall have the following functions:
a) Master file maintenance for goods.
b) Data entry function for reading and updating supply and delivery plus stock-taking.

1   c) Print function for bar code labels.
    d) Transfer function for transferring stock delivery entries to contract system as
       cost entries.
    e) Transfer function for transferring article numbers to the system's portable
5   scanner for manual stock-taking.
    f) Stock-taking and corrections.
    g) Standard functions for inventory accounting and management, including
       monitoring product range, monthly and yearly inventory statements.

5.2.2.4. Secretariat
10 The secretariat function consists of several groups which carry out the following
    functions with some overlap in activities:

- Switchboard.
- Translation, typing, correspondence.
15 - Handling the mail, incoming/outgoing mail.

The system for the secretariat shall have the following functions:

    a) Editing function for translation, typing, and correspondence.
20 b) Function for filing outgoing correspondence according to
       shipowner/ship/project.

The secretariat makes no other requirements as to the functionality of the system.

5.2.2.5. Computer Service
25 Computer service is carried out by the staff in the accounting department. Most
    employees must know how to start the computers in the morning, shut them
    down, make a batch run at the end of the day, and make backup copies. A logbook
    over the activities is kept.

30 Systems administration beyond the above activities is performed by one employee
    who is better qualified than the rest of the staff, and who has a more thorough
    knowledge of information technology.

Systems administration shall have the following functions:

35 a) Master file for creating and updating company specific data, such as:
      - Various account references (VAT and indirect tax accounts, summary
        accounts, etc.).
      - VAT rates.
      - Standard stipulations for job costing, accounting and invoicing.
40   - Standard mark-up percentages for job costing from net to gross amounts.
      - Standard pay codes for working hours (standard, + 50%, +100%) [i.e. normal
        hours, overtime hours, late overtime hours].
      - Account group references for transfers to other accounts in connection with
        change in project status.
45

1 ■ Accounts period control.
■ Cost types and categories.
■ Foreign exchange rates
■ Various serial number counters.
5 b) Master file and editing function for systems documentation.
c) Master file maintenance for support of systems administration: systems administration (user directories, menus, access protection, etc.).
d) ~~Query function for monitoring disk storage consumption and free resources.~~
e) ~~Query function for monitoring data network.~~
10 f) ~~Program development function for ad hoc programs and minor changes.~~
g) ~~Diagnostic function for identifying the cause of break-downs or reduced performance.~~
h) ~~Master file for administration of hardware and basic software configuration~~.
i) Master file for administration of user program configuration.
15 j) ~~Master file maintenance for administration of data network configuration.~~

In addition, the system is expected to contain the tools that will allow DSY to perform all routines related to an efficient operation. External software assistance should only be necessary in the event of an actual error and changes in system functionality.

20 ### 5.2.3. Functional Relationships between Contract System and Other Accounting Systems
The financial accounts shall show the value of projects in progress in order that accounting can present a true and fair view of the financial position on request. See appendix 3 [not part of contract] for a closer description of accounting relations.
25

5.2.4. Change in Project Status
It shall be possible to make the following state changes:

30

	Change in status to:				
Change in status from:	Created	Open	Closed	Completed	Compressed
Created	–	Yes	No	No	No
Open	Yes*)	–	Yes	No	No
Closed	No	Yes	–	Yes	No
Completed	No	No	Yes	–	Yes
Compressed	No	No	No	No	–

*) Provided that no costs or purchase orders are recorded for the project.
40

For more details on state change, please see appendix 2 [not included in the contract].

45

5.3. Operations

The system operation shall be performed in the following ways:

- Online
- Monitored batch processing
- Non-monitored batch processing
- Back-up copying
- Restoring

It shall be possible to perform batch processing that requires monitoring, while the online systems are open, ~~and in such a way that the response times of the online systems remain acceptable, see section 5.5.~~

Non-monitored batch processing can be performed at night when the online systems are closed. Through appropriate checks it shall in advance be rendered probable that the result of the batch processing is accurate and applicable, e.g. by validating data, balancing totals, etc.

The supplier can choose to make back-up copies with or without monitoring. Depending on the solution chosen, the process times for back-up copying are included for monitored or non-monitored batch processing, respectively.

The supplier can decide whether to restore the systems after a breakdown or system error for a single sub-system, for several sub-systems, or for all the systems together. However, the solution chosen shall comply with the time requirements for restoring specified in section 5.5. If it is necessary or it is chosen to restore individual sub-systems, it shall be ensured through auditing checks that the integrity constraints between the sub-systems are correct. A print-out of the checking data shall be made in order that documentation of accurate restoring can be entered in the installation log.

It shall be possible to restore a system on the basis of a back-up copy and "logged" transactions.

5.4. Interfaces

5.4.1. Interface to the Operating System

The operating system interface shall comply with the UNIX System V standard from UNIX International.

5.4.2. Interface to External Systems

Data communication shall be able to handle the following functions:

a) Connection to Den Danske Banks Dataservice from PC/work station.
b) Transfer via PBS [Danish Payment Systems Ltd.] of creditor payments and pay notices for wages and salaries.
c) Transfer of yearly statements, wages and salaries, including withheld tax to/from the Inland Revenue Department.

1   d) Access to external databases via public data network services.
    The standards relevant to the purpose shall be specified by the supplier.

5.4.3. Database Interfaces

5   It shall be possible to gain access to the database/databases simultaneously from
    mainframe terminals and from PCs that function as "clients" in a client-server
    structure or perform spreadsheet functions, for instance. The system shall comply
    with the standards relevant to this purpose.

5.4.4. Local Area Network Interface

10 The local area network interface shall comply with <u>open standards</u> that allow the
    following:

    a) Connecting additional servers of different makes to the network.
    b) Links to local area networks of subsidiaries via public telecommunication services.
    c) Central control of subsidiaries' local area networks from DSY's data processing
15   function.

5.4.5. Interface between Sub-systems

    The interfaces between sub-systems shall be designed in such a way that they allow
    the staff after restoring a sub-system to verify through simple balancing that the
20 restoring has been completed correctly. For more details see section 5.3.

5.5.   Quality Properties

5.5.1. Availability

25 The central systems, including the central database, shall be accessible (available)
    no less than 98% of the time between 7 a.m. and 6 p.m. on working days. When a
    system is being restored and consequently does not function, the time of restoring
    is counted as unavailable time.

    Each breakdown or the like causing the systems to be unavailable is counted to last
30 at least 20 minutes, regardless of the actual duration.

    The availability is made up each month by DSY based on data from the installation log.

5.5.2. Response Times

    ~~No response times shall be so long that employees find them 'stressful'.~~ There shall
35 be no waiting time at all in connection with data entry ("punching"), data capture,
    and master file maintenance [added by hand:] due to inappropriate programming.

    The response times shall be realized in an operational environment where 20 users
    work simultaneously.

40 ### 5.5.3. Batch Processing

5.5.3.1. Monitored Batch Processing

    It shall be possible to perform batch processes that require monitoring by an
    operator either when the online systems are open or within at most an hour after
    the online systems have been closed down.
45

1 **5.5.3.2. Non-monitored Batch Processing**
It shall be possible to perform all non-monitored batch processes scheduled to run
at periodical intervals (e.g. weekly, monthly, quarterly, annually) in no more than 6
hours for all batches to be run between two working days.

5

5.6.   Documentation
It is part of the systems delivery to provide documentation targeted at the
following objectives:

10
- End user.
- System administration (user catalogue, menus, access protection, company
  information, etc.).
- System operation (open/close, batch processing, back-up, restoring).
- System maintenance (installation, diagnostics, errors correction, system
15   expansion, etc.).

The end user documentation concerning online systems should preferably be
available for online reference.

20 **[Omitted from the translation:**
Appendix 3 to 15, covering prices, possibilities for expansion, maintenance
responsibilities, the customer's responsibilities for making hardware and system
software available, etc.]

25 ## Data Models, etc. (E/R diagrams)
[The following diagrams were part of the original documents sent out for tender. They
were not included in the final contract, but the requirements still referred to them.

We have included all E/R diagrams, but only one of about 15 flowcharts and
30   dataflow diagrams. The E/R notation corresponds to the one in Figure 2.2C.]

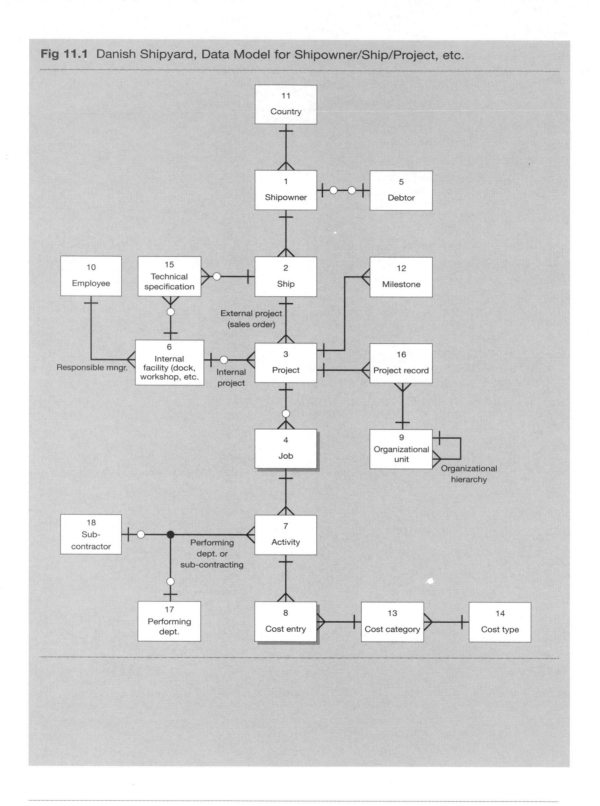

Fig 11.1 Danish Shipyard, Data Model for Shipowner/Ship/Project, etc.

Fig 11.2 Danish Shipyard, Data Model for Purchase Order

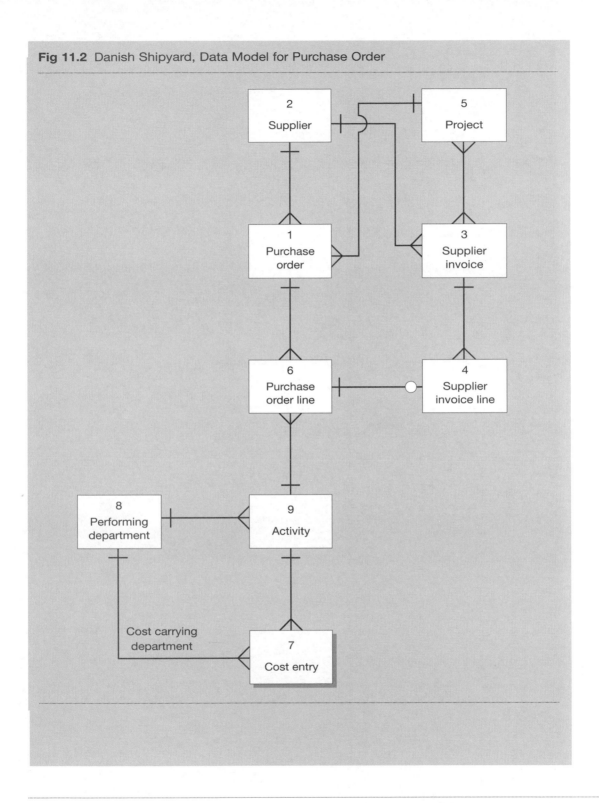

Fig 11.3 Danish Shipyard, Data Model for Experience Data/Keywords

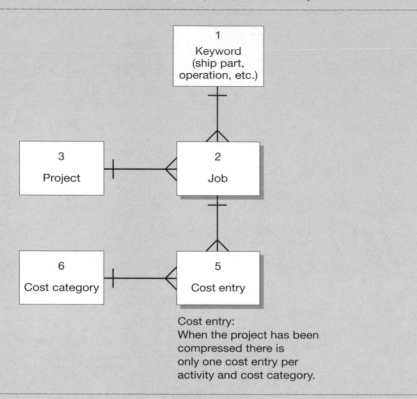

Cost entry:
When the project has been
compressed there is
only one cost entry per
activity and cost category.

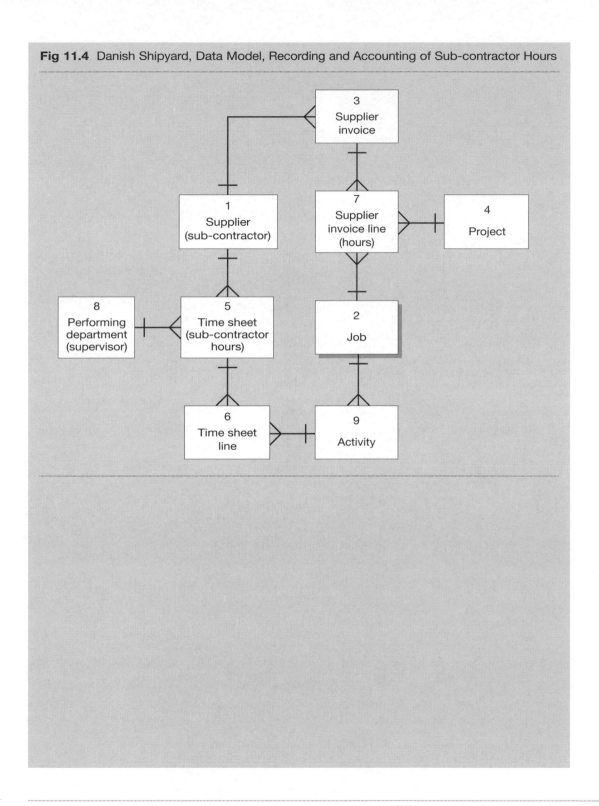

Fig 11.4 Danish Shipyard, Data Model, Recording and Accounting of Sub-contractor Hours

Fig 11.5 Danish Shipyard, Data Model for Job Costing

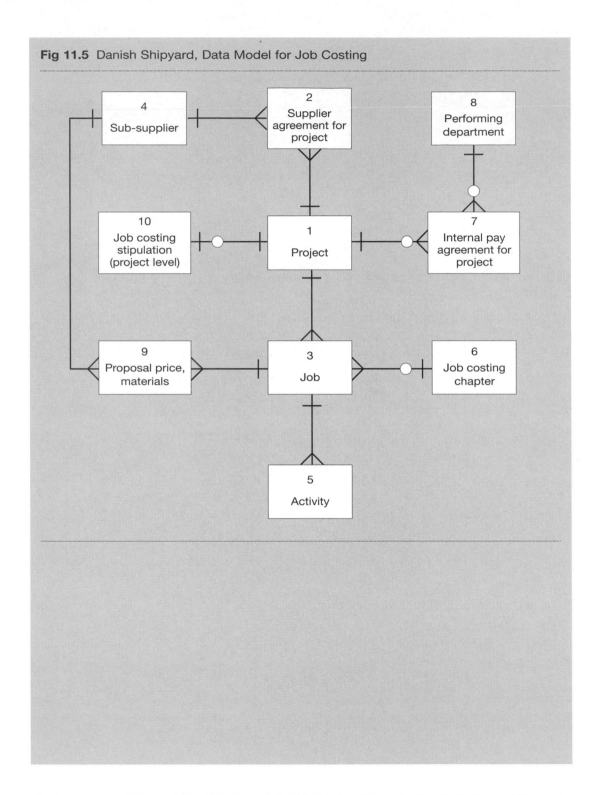

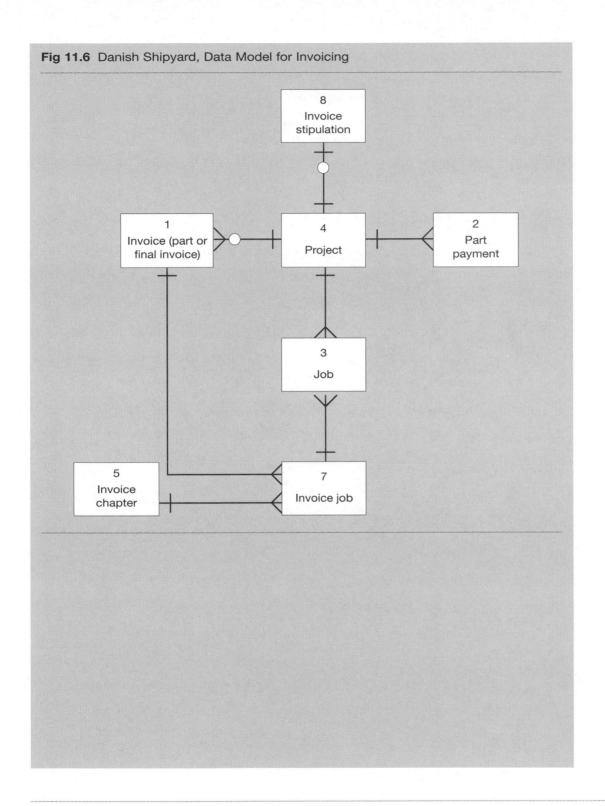

Fig 11.6 Danish Shipyard, Data Model for Invoicing

Fig 11.7 Danish Shipyard, Data Model for Materials Entry

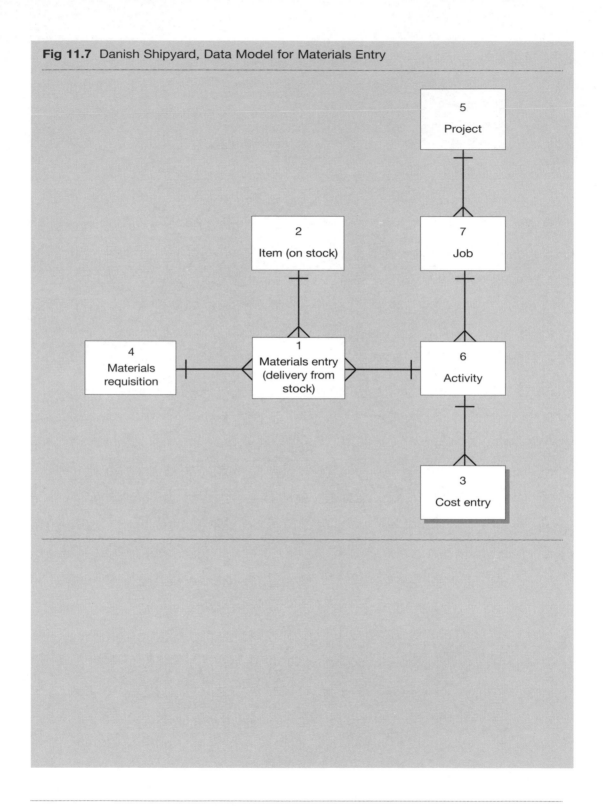

Fig 11.8 Danish Shipyard, Data Model for Rough Planning

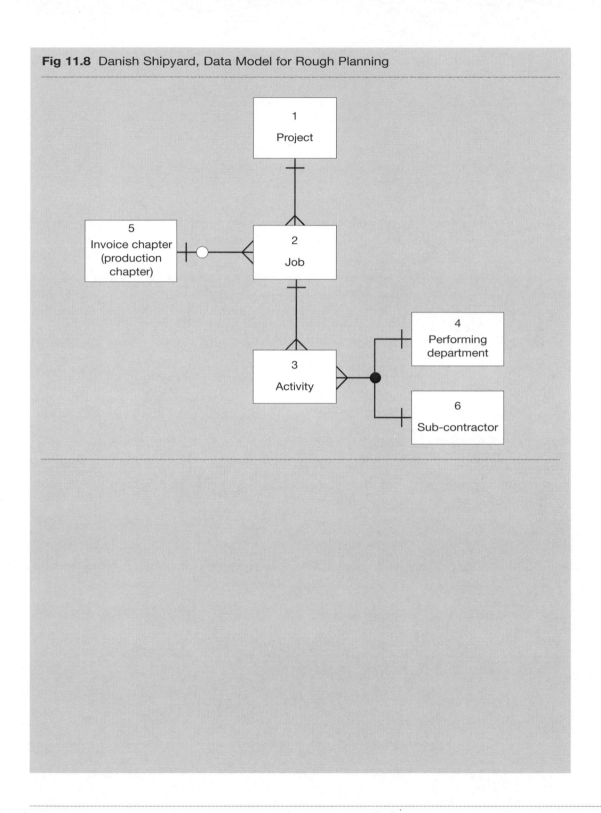

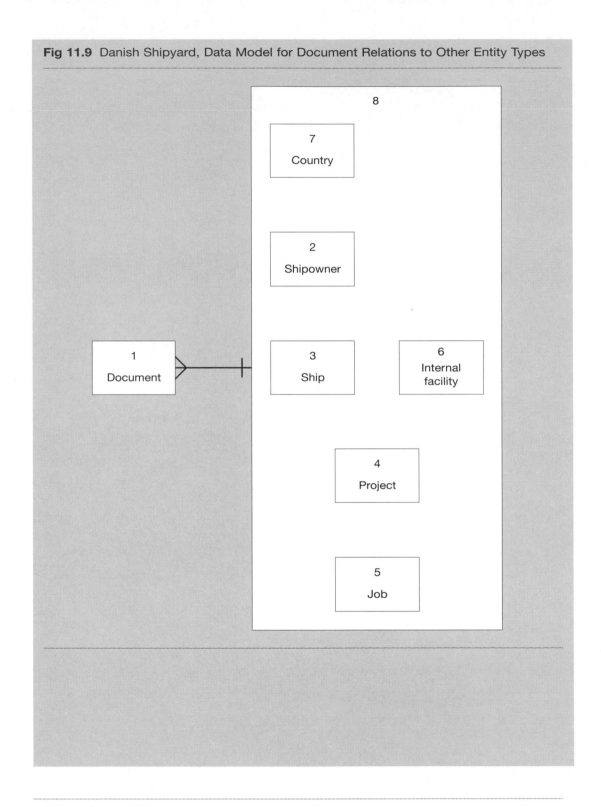

Fig 11.9 Danish Shipyard, Data Model for Document Relations to Other Entity Types

Fig 11.10 Danish Shipyard, Flow Chart for Job Costing, Hourly Rates

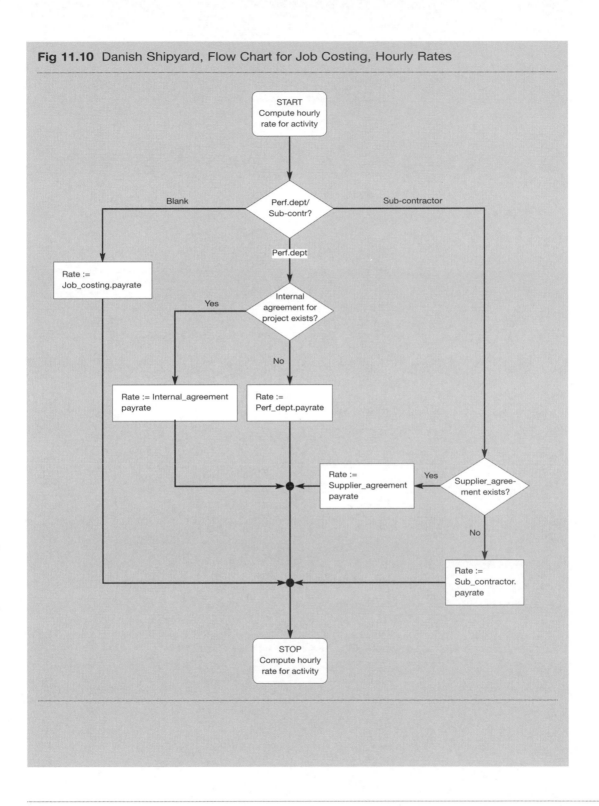

12

Midland Hospital
Requirements for payroll and roster planning

In the late 1990s, many Danish county hospitals replaced their old IT systems. Usually the county was responsible for the larger IT systems and handled the tender processes in co-operation with expert users from the county hospitals. Some counties had several hospitals and other health institutions.

In the case study in this chapter, the county wanted a system to support payroll and staff planning (duty roster) for all health staff. The county name is fictitious as the real county wants to be anonymous. At the time of the tender, they used two systems, one for payroll and one for staff planning. The two systems didn't integrate well, the usability was inadequate, especially for temporary staff, and they were expensive. Several suppliers made a proposal, but one of the requirements essentially prevented any other suppliers than the two present ones from being considered. The crucial requirement is part of the sample below, and we leave it as an exercise for the reader to locate that killer requirement.

Deloitte & Touche helped the county write and edit the specification and the contract. The specification is particularly interesting for its consistent use of options. The supplier has to specify which of the many functions he can supply as a standard, as an addition, etc. The specification also uses open targets, such as the training time needed to use the system.

The specification uses primarily feature style. The features are enumerated and each has a weight reflecting its priority. There is little, if any, description of purposes of the requirements, and the business goals are kept on a very general level. We consider the example a well-written, classical example of a requirements specification.

The sample below corresponds to 16 pages out of about 110. The pages are a fair representation of the full specification. The full spec is just "more of the same".

The parts below are reproduced with kind permission by Karin Lomborg, Deloitte & Touche, Copenhagen.

Midland County
Payroll and Roster Planning

Tender Conditions

1. Introduction [About half a page]

2. Scope of Proposal [About half a page]

3. Criteria for Selecting Supplier [About half a page]

4. Structure of Proposal

4.1. Proposal Format

To facilitate the County's examination of the proposals, the proposal must be structured as shown in section 4.9.

Any reservations that the suppliers may have in connection with the present call for proposals, including proposal and contract conditions, must be clearly stated in a separate section of the proposal.

Evaluations will be based on the submitted documents, which therefore must be adequate.

In order to support the County's assessment of the proposal, the supplier must specify the following codes for each functional requirement in sections 2–13, and as needed give explicit references to additional comments:

S   Standard solution in the offered version.

SE   Standard solution in the offered version. However, the solution must be explained because it works differently than specified in the requirements.

RG Supported by means of a report generator.

M   Requires modifications, but in such a way that updates to future releases will be part of a standard maintenance contract.

MP Requires customer-specific program modifications that have to be transferred to future releases outside the standard maintenance contract.

SD Special development of new customer-specific programs.

N   Cannot be supported and therefore is not offered.

An enclosed disk contains a spreadsheet in Excel format which must be used to complete this part of the proposal.

The replies to sections 14 and 15 in the user requirements must be made in the sections specified in section 4.9.

4.2.–4.8. Alternative Proposals, Contractor Co-operation . . .
[About six pages. The County encourages a consortium model, where several suppliers make a joint proposal]

4.9. Contents of Proposal [Required list of contents. About 2 pages]

5. Tender Process

[When, where, and contact persons. About two pages]

6. Contract and Possible Reservations [One page]

Midland County
Payroll and Roster Planning
User Requirements

[Actually, the term *Statement of Demands* was used rather than *User Requirements*]

1. Introduction

The customer wants one or more integrated systems for payroll and personnel administration specified in the following main functional areas:

- Salary calculation and payment
- Pension calculation and payment, plus imaginary pension
- Personnel management
- Salary budgeting and position management, including management of new pay forms, decentral salary and salary pools, etc.
- Duty roster

[Some elaboration of these points, about one page]

1.1. High-level Requirements

[Some visions, organizational changes, and system goals (e.g. "simplify present administrative processes"). Two pages]

1.2. Specific Functional Requirements

The requirements are divided according to the main functional areas. The division does not reflect the precise expectations to the modular program structure, but indicates the functional areas that the County will use for prioritization in case of restrictions on time or finance. [This is admittedly rather obscure.]

The functional requirements are based on the following assumptions:

- Those parts of the system where the County's functional requirements correspond to a well-defined market standard are only described briefly. Where the functionality is expected to deviate from the expected market standard, the functional description goes into detail. This means that the level of detail varies.
- The system has a design which as far as possible caters for ease of use.
- All procedures/lists/screen pictures, etc. that are necessary for support, maintainance, operation, and check of data bases and files are taken for granted and consequently not mentioned separately.

For each requirement the County has stated a weight that indicates the priority of that requirement. The following weight scale is used:

4 A feature of crucial importance for support of basic tasks in the County. If the feature cannot be offered directly, alternative solutions should be suggested as far as possible.

3 A very important feature for support of essential tasks in the County. If the facility is not available, it is not critical, but it will impair the application value of the system.

2 An important feature that can be used to advantage.

1 A feature that may be desirable in the long run, and therefore must be implementable.

Since the County hospitals have other recording and management needs than those in other parts of the County, it has been necessary to differentiate the requirement priorities in certain areas. Therefore, the hospital priorities are indicated with an H-prefix, while priorities for other County parts are indicated with an O-prefix.

2. Master Data

The system will store data on people and positions that are cross-functional relative to the five main functional areas. These data can be viewed as the system's master data and only have to be entered once.

Below, we have specified data that are more or less cross-functional relative to the main functional areas:

2.1. In General

1 All entered data must be date controlled both in relation to the individual employee, groups of employees, and in general, i.e. for all employees. [Editor's comment: *Date controlled* means that the data, e.g. a pay rise, is to be valid from a specified date.] (Weight: 4)

2 It must be possible to post-date the activation of all entered data and backdate the activation [Editor's comment: e.g. handle salary differences, for example, in the case that a pay rise should have taken place some months earlier]. (Weight: 4)

3 It must be possible to enter a future expiry date for all entered data. (Weight: 4)

2.2. User/Organizational Data

4 The system must have features for entry of global user information that applies to all parts of the system. The information comprises for instance:

    a   Name and address of county.

    b   Tax registration number.

c The county's bank account number.

d Ordering and sorting of output data.   (Weight: 4)

2.3. Employee Data

The system must allow registration of the following employee data:

Name, home address, etc.

5	Civil registration number	(Weight: 4)
6	Name.	(Weight: 4)
7	Address.	(Weight: 4)
8	Municipality of residence (municipality code).	(Weight: 4)
9	Telephone number # 1.	(Weight: 4)
10	Telephone number #2 (e.g. mobile phone number).	(Weight: 2)
11	Fax number	(Weight: 2)
12	e-mail address.	(Weight: 2)
13	Using the civil registration number, it must be possible to retrieve and update master data (full name, address, and other personal data) from the National Register.	(Weight: 4)

Family-related data

14	Marital status.	(Weight: 2)
15	Spouse's civil registration number	(Weight: 3)
16	Birth data of children.	(Weight: 3)

Location in county

17	Office location (location/office number).	(Weight: 2)
18	Telephone extension.	(Weight: 2)

Taxes, bank, pension, etc.

19	Tax data.	(Weight: 4)
20	It must be possible to update tax data through yearly transfer of data from the Central Customs and Tax Administration.	(Weight: 4)
21	Bank data: Bank registration number and account number.	(Weight: 4)
22	Data on retirement pension fund.	(Weight: 4)

Employment

23	Employment status/terms (e.g. employed according to the Public Servants Act or under a collective agreement).	(Weight: 4)
24	Provided nothing is entered on employment status/terms, the system must automatically insert the value for 'employed under a collective agreement'.	(Weight: 4)
25	Pay form.	(Weight: 4)
26	Date of employment.	(Weight: 4)
27	Date of retirement.	(Weight: 4)

28	Recall dates (minimum 6), manual (entered by users with text) and automatic (i.e. derived from other data).	(Weight: 4)
29	The system must be able to calculate term of notice for resignation/ dismissal.	(Weight: 2)
30	It must be possible to record seniority of service, such as important milestones in length of service like 25 or 30 years. If nothing is recorded, it must be set to the date of employment.	(Weight: 4)
31	For employees employed according to The Public Servants Act, the system must be able to automatically record the pay level as of 31 March 1998. The data will be used to calculate the expected final pay level (for pension calculations) under the present agreement for employees who transfer to new pay forms.	(Weight: 4)

Pay seniority

32	It must be possible to record the calculated pay seniority date.	(Weight: 4)
33	If no date is entered, the system must be able to automatically insert the employee's employment date.	(Weight: 4)
34	The system must be able to calculate the promotion date automatically according to entered and transferred data.	(Weight: 4)
35	At return from leave, the system must be able to adjust the pay seniority according to applicable law (cf. section 11 (6) of the Consolidated Act on Leave, the Ministry of Labour, no. 5 of 8 January 1998, published in the Association of County Councils, no. 11.07.1).	(Weight: 3)

Periods of leave

36	Leave with specified kind (educational, maternity/paternity or sabbatical).	(Weight: 3)
37	Military service.	(Weight: 3)
38	Leave of absence (with and without pay).	(Weight: 3)

Education

39	Basic employee education (selection must be possible from a predefined list).	(Weight: 3)
40	Graduation year.	(Weight: 3)
41	Supplementary training, further education, and specialist training.	(Weight: 3)
42	Educational wishes/needs.	(Weight: 2)
43	Job rotation wishes.	(Weight: 2)

External obligations, representation duties, etc.

44	External jobs (mandatory for some employee groups).	(Weight: 4)
45	Humanitarian obligations (e.g. Red Cross).	(Weight: 3)

| 46 | Representation duties, e.g. shop steward, safety representative, member of joint consultation committee, central consultation committee. | (Weight: 3) |

Duty related data

47	It must be possible to attach a duty type code (first duty, end duty, etc.) to the individual employee.	(Weight: 3)
48	It must be possible to attach a rotation code/duty roster number to the individual employee (in order to rotate duty rosters).	(Weight: 4)
49	It must be possible to specify a code for each job type which causes values to be inserted automatically for e.g. payment/time-off in lieu according to the agreement in force.	(Weight: 4)
50	Due to local agreements, it must be possible to change the standard values for payment/time-off –in lieu associated with the various job categories.	(Weight: 4)

Other data

51	It must be possible to record whether an employee is included in the Occupational Health Service.	(Weight: 2)
52	It must be possible to record school code for teachers employed under the Public Servants Act in primary and secondary schools (a school code consists of 6 digits).	(Weight: 4)
53	It must be possible to record whether an employee's residence is owned/managed by the County, by means of a code referring to a file of residences.	(Weight: 4)
54	It must be possible to record information about free residence.	(Weight: 2)
55	It must be possible to record mileage allowance.	(Weight: 1)
56	It must be possible to record free telephone allowance.	(Weight: 2)
57	It must be possible to record a reference to the act which is valid for the telephone allowance, and whether the telephone is owned by the County or the employee in question.	(Weight: 2)
58	The system must include features that enable registration of whether and how employees in the County have been assigned to tasks under reinforced alert.	(Weight: 4)
59	The system must – via codes related to the individual employee – be able to generate a prioritized emergency list for calling personnel in special situations. It must be possible to record the method of alerting through a code that reflects the selected method among a limited set of alternatives.	(Weight: 4)
60	It must be possible to record text strings in at least five comment fields.	(Weight: 4)

2.4. Position data

In addition to data relating to the individual employee, it must be possible to record data relating to the individual job position. The data must be available across the system's main functional areas.

Position designation

61   It must be possible to enter position designations manually
(e.g. indicate that the job is temporary).   (Weight: 4)

62   It must be possible to retrieve the position designation from
the system files according to the recorded agreement/pay scale.   (Weight: 4)

63   When retrieving information on a person, it must be clearly
indicated whether the position designation has been entered
manually and thus may deviate.   (Weight: 4)

[Requirements 64 to 142 deal with more position data, pension, special allowances and deductions, externally funded pay, etc.]

3.   Salary Calculation and Payment

[A one-page introduction summarizing the sections of chapter 3]

3.1.   Collective Agreements, Rules, etc.

Pay calculation is based on registration of calculation rules, pay rates, etc. that follow from collective agreements, contracts, etc.

143   The system must be able to handle all collective agreements and
contracts under the National Association of Local Authorities and
the Association of County Councils, in addition to collective
agreements with the government that apply to personnel groups
in the County, and other relevant regulations, including those
concerned with political duties.   (Weight: 4)

144   The supplier of the system must ensure that all tables and pay
rates are updated according to the collective agreements, legislation
and other agreements. Changes must be updated no later than a
month after release [Editor's comment: this odd sentence is not
a misprint, but the original requirement].   (Weight: 4)

145   It must be possible to supplement with individual agreements/
classifications and collective agreements from the private
labor market.   (Weight: 4)

Creating new pay scales

146   When new pay scales are introduced, the system must be able
to automatically move the persons affected from the old pay
scale to the new scale in accordance with the agreement.   (Weight: 3)

147   If the system cannot automatically move employees from an
old to a new pay scale, the system must have features that ensure
that all affected employees are listed.   (Weight: 4)

3.2.   Operational Data Entry

This section covers the daily entry of data on non-attendance and actual attendance
which affects pay calculation, holiday allowance, days off in lieu, etc.

In the following, requirements are specified for different data entry methods that
reflect an adaptation of the level of registration detail to the need for control and
follow-up. For instance, a feature is required for entering accumulated data for
entire periods by direct entry of a number of units (non-attendance hours, etc.). In
addition, a feature is required for data entry based on daily registration of
arrival/leaving times, and furthermore by means of transferring the corresponding
data from the system's duty roster module.

148   It must be possible to record operational data about overtime, non-attendance, etc. in the following ways:

    a   Direct reporting, cf. section 3.2.1   (Weight: 4)
    b   Recording of arrival/leaving times and deviations from
       these, cf. section 3.2.2.   (Weight: 4)
    c   Recording of duty rosters and deviations from these, cf.
       section 7.   (Weight: 4)
    d   Recording in a flexitime system with automatic transfer of
       registrations to the pay system, cf. section 13.   (Weight: 3)

149   The system must have built-in, logical checks that make it possible
to validate entries of single values against permissible values.   (Weight: 4)
150   The system must have built-in, logical checks that make it possible
to validate combinations of single values against permissible
combinations.   (Weight: 2)
151   It must be possible for the individual user to design his own data
entry screens.   (Weight: 2)
152   It must be possible to create templates with pre-entered field
values in the various entry screens in order to facilitate the entry
of data that are roughly identical.   (Weight: 3)
153   It must be possible to correct and delete entries in isolated fields
before payroll production regardless of the entry method used.   (Weight: 3)
154   Data entry must be possible until the end of working hours at
the day before the payroll run.   (Weight: 4)

3.2.1. Direct Entry

We understand 'direct entry' to mean the entry of data on non-attendance and activities, based on manual registrations and calculations of working hours outside the system boundaries.

The requirements in this section are not relevant for the County's hospitals where entries are not based on this method.

155 The system must be able to handle registration of all types of non-attendance in order to calculate pay and the total amount of holiday allowance, days off in lieu, etc. (Weight: 4)

[Editor's comment: Requirements 155 to 163 relate to activity types, overtime pay, days off in lieu, and various reports.]

3.2.2 Check-in-check-out Recording

This kind of entry is currently used in the County's hospitals and to some extent in other parts of the County. It is expected that in the future these entries can be made through the duty roster system. [Editor's comment: Requirements 164 to 176 relate to this.]

[Requirements 177 to 260 relate to vacation records, time off in lieu, payroll calculation, tax, data transfer to the accounting system, query possibilities, reports.]

4.   Personnel Management

[Requirements 261 to 302 relate to online access to personnel policies, position descriptions, individual cases (e.g. duty-related offences), application management, training, queries and reports.]

5.   Salary Budgeting and Norm Management

[Requirements 303 to 375 relate to budgeting for the number of positions and the salary, predicting total salary in response to various factors, comparing budget against actual spending, paper and screen reports, and data transfer to the accounting system.]

6.   Pension Calculation and Payment

[Requirements 376 to 446 relate to various kinds of pensions and various ways of paying the pension.]

7. Duty Roster (Registration of Work Hours)

[Definition of various terms, e.g. rolling roster, duty, duty team, duty layer, task. About one page.]

447 The system must include all relevant collective agreements/ contracts (as mentioned under general conditions) and ensure that the rules of these are observed. (Weight: 4)

7.1. Data Entry, Registration
7.1.1. Budget module
448 It must be possible to use the budget entered in the budget/ norm prescription (see section 5.1.2), directly in the roster planning in terms of hours or cost. (Weight: 3)

449 It must be possible to record filled as well as planned positions. (Weight: 4)

450 It must be possible to insert and maintain a bar graph (statement of demand for number of resources/persons per day/ duty) by means of graphics, making the system user-friendly and easy to use. (Weight: 4)

451 This bar graph must be available in the planning module. (Weight: 4)

7.1.2. Personnel module
452 It must be possible to record dates and hours where an employee is unable to work (due to holidays, days off, sickness, days off in lieu, maternity leave, leave of absence, etc.). (Weight: 4)

453 In the individual employee's calendar, it must be possible to see the category of non-attendance that applies (holidays, sickness, leave, etc.). (Weight: 4)

454 It must be possible to record an employee's qualifications by means of categories and free-text fields. (Weight: 3)

455 It must be possible to create students, who are not in the pay records, as resources that can be used in the planning – with name and possible duty assignments. (Weight: 3)

456 It must be possible to create foreign doctors (who do not have a Danish civil registration number) as resources that can be used in the roster – with name and possible duty assignments. (Weight: 3)

[Requirements 457 to 473 relate to data for planning the roster and recording deviations from the planned working hours.]

7.2. Functionality
7.2.1. Calculation
474 The system must be able to prepare a roster proposal that respects:
  a Bar graph.
  b Available resources.
  c Collective agreement rules and other regulations.
  d Separate agreements and local agreements.
  e The department's defined level of activity
  (e.g. closed on holidays). (Weight: 4)
475 The system must be able to calculate the financial consequences
of a given duty roster:
  a In hours. (Weight: 4)
  b In units of currency. (Weight: 3)
476 The system must be able to calculate the consequences of a
given duty roster:
  a In hours. (Weight: 4)
  b In units of currency. (Weight: 3)
477 The system must be able to calculate the cost, if any, of ordering an
employee an extra duty beyond the planned (based on the collective
agreement under which the employee in question belongs):
  a In hours. (Weight: 4)
  b In units of currency. (Weight: 3)
478 The system must be able to calculate the consequence of a
rolling roster for an employee's generated lieu days. (Weight: 4)
479 The system must give notice if a duty roster implies use of a
temporary worker for more than three months.
[The Danish legal limit for temporary employment.] (Weight: 3)

[Requirements 480 to 494 relate to rolling rosters, manual changes to an
automatically generated roster, acute absence due to illness, and validity checks.
Requirement 495 to 512 relate to printed reports in the roster area.]

8.   General Requirements to Printed Reports
[Requirements 513 to 532 state requirements applicable to all reports, e.g. availability
of both internal and external reports, reportable master file data, requests for
periodic reports, tailoring standard reports, defining scope of reports (e.g. individual
level, department level, county level), preview, electronic form for later PC use.]

F9.   Present IT Usage
[Sections 9.1 to 9.4 contain no enumerated requirements but specify present
hardware (detailed in an appendix), software, and service providers.]

9.5. Present IT Organization

Today, the County has many different IT resources. It has its own computer center, which develops, maintains and operates several county mainframe applications, e.g. within the areas of finance and health. Organizationally, the computer center is placed in the County's central IT unit, the IT office. The IT office also includes a planning function and an IT service function that operates the local network at the County council offices. In addition, the Central Hospital and the University Hospital have set up their own IT units. The table below shows the number of IT staff in the different areas:

Area	Number of employees
IT office	37
– Computer center, operation	11
– Computer center, development	11
– Computer services, County council offices	8
– Planning	6
The Central Hospital	15
The University Hospital	10

9.6. Data and Transaction Volume

The table below shows data and transaction volumes for 1998. The supplier should expect future transaction volumes of the same magnitude [KMD and SD are two IT service providers that run the heavy applications at present].

Data/transaction	KMD	SD pay OUH	SD pay SHF	SD pay Beach lane	In total Approx.
Number of tax reports for 1998	13,400	10,000	4,500	760	28,000
Number of pay slips in May 1998	8,250	7,000	4,100	600	20,000
Number of new employees in 1998	1,535	1,530	1,270	200	4,500
Number of queries about personnel data in 1998	100,000	133,000	78,000	11,000	+300,000
Total number of queries	300,000	1.1 million			

9.7. Data Conversion

[Requirements 533 to 535 ask the supplier to specify what to convert and how to do it.]

10. Required Deliverables

[Hardware is not part of the tender. Requirements 536 to 564 ask the supplier to specify the required hardware, stress that the existing hardware should be used as far as possible, that open standards are to be used, a modular design is required, certain date formats are required, certain program and data transfers are required in case a three-tier architecture (mainframe, server, PC) is proposed.]

10.7. Requirements to the Suppliers Development Environment

[An introductory section defines the terms *Standard System*, *System*, *Modification*, *Special Development*.]

System modifications

565   Must be made in a development environment which ensures
that modifications are included in new releases.   (Weight: 4)

566   Modifications and extensions must be developed according to
the County's directions and approved by the County as correct
at delivery time before being transferred to the County's
production system.   (Weight: 4)

567   Documentation of modifications is submitted to the County.   (Weight: 4)

Special system development, if any

568   It is required to use a program development tool that allows
co-operation between supplier and County about prototyping
with several iterations, to determine the GUI [graphical user
interface] standard, screen picture and report design. The supplier
is asked to explain the use of program development tools.   (Weight: 3)

Programming standard

569   The program design must comply with design principles and standards
which ensure that the developed program is:

a   portable.   (Weight: 3)
b   easy to maintain.   (Weight: 3)
c   testable.   (Weight: 3)

By portability we mean that the server software can be transferred between platforms of the same type (e.g. server to server – horizontal portability) and between different types of platforms (e.g. PC to server – vertical portability).

By "easy to maintain" we mean that parties other than the supplier are able to correct and extend the software, and that it is easy to add new functionality.

570   The supplier must specify the program's degree of portability.   (Weight: 4)

[Sections 10.8 to 10.10 (requirements 571 to 598) relate to user and system documentation, review documentation for modifications and special development, quality assurance activities, availability and operational requirements.]

10.11. Measuring the Operational Time
[A short introductory section defines the term availability.]

599 The supplier must guarantee an availability of 99.5% in the specified operational periods. The supplier must explain and guarantee the necessary hardware requirements for this. (Specified in the contract, see appendix 3.)   (Weight: 4)

10.12. Response time Requirements

Definition
We understand "response time for online transactions" to mean the time that passes between the user issuing a command (by activating a key) and the complete screen picture appearing on the screen and the system being ready for new entries.

We understand "response time for print of reports" to mean the time that passes between the user-specified start time and the last character in the report being printed. We assume that the printer is available when the report is ready for printing.

Specification of response times
For all functions in the sub-systems, the following general response time requirements apply:

	Type of function	Response time in seconds	
600	Function switch within one sub-system	1	(Weight: 4)
601	Function switch between two sub-systems	2	(Weight: 4)
602	Simple lookups	0.75	(Weight: 4)
603	Routine lookups	1	(Weight: 4)
604	Routine updates	2	(Weight: 4)
605	Requesting a printed report	5	(Weight: 4)
606	Printing of simple reports, per page	60	(Weight: 4)
607	Printing of complex reports, per page	300	(Weight: 4)
608	Log-in, timed from completed entry in the log-in screen to the first function being ready for use (Quick log-in)	5	(Weight: 4)

By simple lookups, we mean functions where the user makes an entry in one field in order to complete another field, e.g. at entry of code and lookup/display of the related name.

By routine lookups and routine updates, we mean functions that are expected to be used at least 20 times a day in the application areas described in the user requirements [Editor's comment: there is no specific reference, so this is a broad requirement].

For online functions that cannot be classified as one of the above types of functions according to the County's fair assessment, the specified response time is 6 seconds.

It is assumed that the table is completed/adjusted prior to conclusion of the contract. In addition, the County is entitled to require an adjustment of the table when a system description is available.

System load
The specified response times must be met under a maximum load as described in section 9.6 on data and transaction volume, i.e. with a maximum volume of data and transactions corresponding to peak load. [Peak load is not specified anywhere, but sections 4.6 of the tender conditions and section 9.3 of the user requirements contain some hints about it.]

Complying with requirements
The response time requirement for a single function has been met when at least 95% of the response times for the function are less than or equal to the specified response time, including any transmission time, and none of the remaining 5 per cent of the response times are longer than 5 times the specified response time (including any transmission time).

The response time requirements of the sub-system/the total system have been met when the requirement for each of all the functions has been met at all connected workstations.

609	The supplier must specify which tasks will normally be subject to batch processing and specify the completion time for these.	(Weight: 4)
610	When typing a text with up to 300 characters a minute, there must be no observable delay between entry and display of the corresponding character.	(Weight: 3)
611	If there is online validation of completed fields or zones during entry, the validation must not be "overtaken" by users typing up to 300 characters a minute.	(Weight: 3)

10.13. Updates and Maintenance [Requirements 612 to 624.]

11. Security [Requirements 625 to 663]

12. Usability Requirements

12.1. General Requirements

664   Updating the system with recorded data must be online.   (Weight: 4)

665   It must be possible to query entered data in the same screen as those where the entries have been made.   (Weight: 4)

666   At all code entries, classifications or the like, screen-based lookup and search among the possible values must be possible, including choice of values without typing.   (Weight: 3)

667   The system must include (or make it possible to define) validations (logical checks) of entered data, and, in case of errors, provide the user with an explanatory error message in text form.   (Weight: 4)

668   The system must not place unnecessary restrictions on the order in which the user performs functions and enters data.   (Weight: 3)

669   The system must give understandable messages in text form in the event of errors, and instruct the user on what to do.   (Weight: 4)

670   In addition the system must provide the user with an understandable message on the status of the last transaction in case there are any doubts about it.   (Weight: 4)

671   The supplier is asked to explain whether the user interface for all application software follows a uniform standard including e.g. layout of screens and prints, use of function keys, selection of functions, and use of messages. Information on the standard or standards is requested.   (Weight: 4)

672   The supplier is asked to explain his plans for following current and forthcoming user interface standards, in particular plans for graphical user interfaces, including the CUA standard.   (Weight: 4)

673   It must be possible to review – and possibly edit – prints on the screen before they are printed on paper.   (Weight: 4)

674   Users must be able to conduct several parallel dialogs from the same workstation (e.g. via hotkey functions) and, if necessary, transfer data between the dialogs (e.g. search criteria or results).   (Weight: 4)

[Requirements 675 to 688 deal with further requirements to the user interface, e.g. shortcut keys, possibility for adapting screen texts to the County terminology and with variations for different user groups, and individually defined additional online help (comments and notes).]

13. Integration with Other Systems

[Requirements 689 to 709. The existing systems to communicate with – public as well as County-operated.]

14. Implementation

[Requirements 710 to 720. Required project organization. Required supplier activities. The supplier is requested to submit a project plan.]

15. Training

[Requirements 721 to 730. Required training for various user groups.]

13

West Zealand Hospital
Requirements for roster planning in
Task & Support style

West Zealand County is part of the largest Danish island, Zealand. They have several hospitals and other health institutions, which together spend $200 million per year.

Like Midland County, West Zealand County bought a payroll and roster planning system in the late 1990s. Central IT staff in the county handled the tender processes in co-operation with expert users from the county hospitals.

The County wrote the requirements specification themselves without outside consultants and, although the user tasks were the same, the specification was very different from the Midland one. For instance, the requirements were not enumerated and prioritized, and they were also harder to verify.

Due to a coincidence, the County invited me (Lauesen) to discuss better ways of writing requirements, and that was the start of a longer co-operation. During the co-operation we invented the Task & Support style, tried it out on roster planning in a simulated way, and later tried it in a tender process for another kind of application. Sections 3.8 and 10.7 explain more about the work.

Below we show the very first requirements specification made with Tasks & Support. It covers the most critical parts of the payroll and roster planning system. The Midland requirements cover the same area through requirements spread over many parts of the specification, but the most critical parts are covered by requirements 474 to 494. If you try to compare the two, you will see how differently requirements can be expressed.

When reading the West Zealand requirements, you may wonder about the "120 day rule". It is a Danish union agreement that when an employee has been ill for 120 days in one year, the employer is entitled to dismiss the employee with short notice, assuming that he does so on the last of the 120 days. If the employer does not observe this deadline, he cannot dismiss the employee immediately, but has to give notice of between three and six months, depending on the employee's seniority. The problem is that decentralized departments may know about the illness, but the central personnel department has to start the dismissal action. The proper exchange of information is often forgotten. For the sake of completeness, we should mention that this rule has relatively little economic impact on the hospital, but forgetting to observe it is a regular annoyance.

West Zealand County
Requirements for Roster Planning and Time Reporting

R3: The product shall support the following user tasks.
To the supplier: Please edit the right-hand side of the sub-tasks to show how your proposed solution works. Feel free to insert references to screen dumps, etc. that illustrate your solution. We prefer that you make the changes in Track-change mode to help us see what you changed.

Work area:	1. Management of duty rosters
General:	The duty roster is planned and updated in the department. The roster covers staff within a certain area of competence. Staff may have different levels of competence within the area, for instance novices and experts. Usually a person in the department is responsible for the roster. Some departments have several duty rosters, e.g. one for nurses and another for surgeons. The same person may work in several departments and thus appear on more than one roster. Each roster may have its own planner. A typical large roster covers 20 persons, but rosters of 60 persons should be possible.
Users:	The planner has experience with duty planning, but is an IT novice. The goal is to make the planner a regular IT user. The planner has knowledge of some of the regulations, but not expert knowledge.

Task:	1.1 Monthly report of illness and actual time worked
Goal:	Ensure that the personnel department knows about deviations from the plan. This is necessary for salary and flexitime purposes.
Frequency:	Once every month.
Critical:	When a person has been sick for 118 days, possible dismissal procedures have to be started within 2 days.

Sub-tasks:		Example of solution:
1	**Report deviations** **Present problem:** Deviations are written in the roster on the noticeboard, and sent to the personnel department early next month. Often the handwriting is difficult to read. Furthermore, if any illnesses last for over 120 days, the personnel department has to know about them within two days. Often they get this information too late.	The monthly reporting disappears. Staff record deviations online on a daily basis and the system sends them to the personnel department within a day.

Variants:		Example of solution:
	(none)	

Task:	1.2 Make roster
Goal:	Staff all duties with competent people. Ensure that regulations are fulfilled and leave requests are respected. Ensure low cost, e.g. avoid overtime and unused staff.
Frequency:	Once every two weeks. In some departments less often. A round of planning is a complex process that may be done over several days.
Critical:	Vacation periods where many regular staff is off. Vacations are allocated several months in advance.

Sub-tasks:		Example of solution:
1	**Initialize new roster period** Typically, planning done in week x covers week $x + 5$ to $x + 8$ for nurses, week $x + 7$ to $x + 32$ for surgeons.	System generates a roster (duties and assignments) for the new period, based on a standard roster template. User can modify the roster as well as the roster template.
2	**Record staff leave** There are two kinds of leave: 1) promised leave, e.g. vacation and maternity leave; 2) requested leave, e.g. flexitime. Promised leave has to be respected by the planner, while requested leave need not be. **Present problems:** Leave requests are kept on a separate calendar or manual notes, often going months into the future. Requests are sometimes forgotten when the plan for that period is drawn up.	System can record leave one year into the future, although no roster has yet been made for that period. System warns if leave is against regulations. It must be easy to record a long period of leave (several months).
3	**Allocate staff for unstaffed duties.** Staff may be regular or temporary. Ensure level of competence, regulations, leave days, and minimal overtime pay, etc. **Present problems:** With the manual method, it is difficult to ensure this. Costs are higher than necessary, and errors often occur.	System shows unstaffed duties and suggestions for staffing. User selects the actual staff. System warns if duties are unstaffed, leave or regulations violated, or unnecessary costs. Warnings must be immediate to support the "jigsaw puzzle". System supports extensive undo of user actions and allows several temporary versions of a plan.
4	**Send roster for internal review**	A print of the roster is sufficient.
5	**Modify roster**	The steps above suffice.
6	**Authorize roster**	User selects one of the temporary rosters as the authorized one for salary and flexitime purposes. A print of the roster is made too.

Variants:		Example of solution:
3a	Staff not yet recorded in the staff file	User enters preliminary data for new staff. Later, the personnel department creates the final record.
3b	No staff available with the necessary competence **Present problem:** User has no information about available staff in other departments.	System suggests staff from other departments based on their authorized rosters.

Work area:	2. Daily changes
General:	When members of staff don't work as planned for one reason or another, they have to record the time they actually worked. Staff may also decide to swap duties (with certain tacit restrictions, e.g. similar levels of competence). When staff are sick, replacements have to be found. These activities may take place at any time during the day or night.
Users:	Most staff are IT novices, and will in many cases never become regular IT users. Supervisors handle re-staffing when staff is sick. Supervisors are IT novices but should become regular users.

Task:	2.1 Record time actually worked
Goal:	Provide basis for calculation of salary and flex time.
Frequency:	Most work is done according to the official plan. Deviations from the plan may happen every two weeks for each person.
Critical:	Nothing really. The recorded times are used once a month for payroll calculations, but corrections made later can be included in the pay slip for next month.

Sub-tasks:		Example of solution:
1	Record work time	Staff record deviating work time in the online roster. Alternatively, time is recorded with time stamps.

Variants:		Example of solution:
1a	Work time recorded the month after the work day	User records the time in the roster from the previous month. Is automatically included as a correction in the payroll. When time stamping is used, the same procedure is used to handle missing or erroneous time stamps.

Task:	2.2 Swap duties	
Goal:	Change the authorized roster to show that two people plan to swap duties on specific days.	
Frequency:	About once every two weeks for each person.	
Critical:	Nothing really. Recording can be done after the fact as in task 2.1.	
Sub-tasks:	Example of solution:	
1	**Modify roster** roster. System may print changed	Staff record changes in the online roster for display on noticeboard.
Variants:		Example of solution:
	(none)	

Task:	2.3 Staff illness	
Goal:	Find a replacement and record the sick person for payroll purposes.	
Frequency:	Almost daily for large departments.	
Critical:	Replacement is critical, but reporting is not. Reporting is critical if the absence has lasted almost 120 days.	
Sub-tasks:		Example of solution:
1	**Record illness**	Supervisor records the illness in the computer roster.
2	**Find replacement** **Present problems:** User has no information about available staff in other departments	System suggests persons from same or other departments according to regulations and cost.
3	**Record replacement**	Supervisor records the chosen replacement. If it is a long-term illness, the user may print out a new roster for display.
4	**Report staff back**	Supervisor assigns the person to a duty. If the illness has lasted more than 118 days, the personnel department is informed within two hours.
Variants:		Example of solution:
1a	**Illness during duty**	The supervisor enters the actual length of illness.

Work area:	3. Personnel department
General:	The personnel department handles employment, salary, dismissal, etc.
Users:	Solid personnel experience. Regular IT users, both with MS Windows and mainframe systems.

Task:	3.1 Check rosters
Goal:	Check that rosters are maintained and daily changes reported. Check whether long-term illness extends over 118 days.
Frequency:	Once a week. If a period of illness is approaching 120 days, once a day.
Critical:	When illness approaches 120 days.

Sub-tasks:		Example of solution:
1	**Check roster** **Present problems:** Not done systematically because rosters are only submitted once a month. Supervision of long-term illness done on ad hoc basis and often forgotten.	System provides a daily report with a line per roster in the entire hospital. Unusually low change rates are flagged. Long-term illness exceeding 110 days is shown in a separate heading of the report.
2	**Act on exceptions** In case of low change rates, personnel staff contact the department to find the reason. In case of 120 days of illness, the department is contacted and legal actions begun.	No system support is needed for this sub-task.
Variants:		**Example of solution:**
	(none)	

Task:	3.2 Payroll amendments	
Goal:	Record payroll amendments corresponding to overtime, late duty warning, etc. Keep track of flexitime status for each employee.	
Frequency:	Monthly.	
Critical:	Nothing. Amendments arriving too late for the monthly payroll are simply included in the payroll for the next month.	
Sub-tasks:		**Example of solution:**
1	**Collect work time information** **Present problems:** Collection is cumbersome, handwriting illegible, etc.	The system automatically transfers the daily registrations.
2	**Enter payroll amendments and update flexitime status** **Present problems:** Difficult and time consuming to calculate the amendments and flexitime according to the various regulations. Many errors occur.	The system computes most of the amendments and flexitime changes based on the daily work time registrations. The system transfers them to the payroll application. Personnel staff are presented with exceptional cases and summary data.
Variants:		**Example of solution:**
	(none)	

Task:	3.3 Record new employees	
Goal:	Record new employees for salary and duty roster purposes.	
Frequency:	Weekly. Typically 20 per week for the entire hospital.	
Critical:	None.	
Sub-tasks:		**Example of solution:**
1	**Record employee data**	
2	**Transfer status information** In case the employee has worked in other institutions in the county, flexitime and salary status from earlier employment must be transferred.	The system transfers all data automatically whenever the person is accessible in the database. In other cases, manual transfer is needed.
Variants:		**Example of solution:**
1a	**Employee recorded preliminary** In urgent situations, employees may start working before they are properly recorded in the payroll system. In order to include them in the roster, only a preliminary record is made.	The system accepts an incomplete registration, but insists on full data before pay can be computed.

14

Bruel & Kjaer
Requirements for a Noise
Source Location System

Bruel &Kjaer (B&K) manufactures professional equipment for sound and vibration measurement. B&K has 700 employees, of which 70 develop software while 55 develop hardware and sensors. Today most of the development effort for such products is in software, and the software part is becoming more and more complex. Although the products use third-party software components such as MS Windows, 3D graphical packages, and communication packages, the B&K software effort is still more than half of the total B&K development effort.

The product described in the requirements is a Noise Source Location system (NSL). It allows engineers to measure the sound field around an object, for instance a washing machine or an airplane, and shows the sound field in three dimensions. This is helpful in locating noise sources. As an initial step, the engineer defines a set of grids surrounding the object. Next he measures the sound at each grid point. The results can be shown in many ways: as three-dimensional contour maps, as spectra, as noise power, etc. The system can also control a robot that moves the microphone and makes the measurements.

The system is based on a PC running MS Windows. It connects to various front-end equipment, e.g. a computerized sound measurement unit with calibration and filtering for several microphones. The source code consists of about 90,000 lines of C++, and the total software development took about 12,000 hours.

The requirements specification consists of 20 pages with 107 enumerated and annotated requirements. Each requirement has a priority indicated by + for a low priority and +++ for a top priority. The parts shown below correspond to about four of the original 20 pages. They are a fair representation of the full spec. The full spec is just "more of the same". The project team used a feature style with domain-oriented justifications of each requirement. They had experienced that it worked much better than previous specifications.

The analysts used a data model (a class diagram) as an intermediate work product. It served as a cross-check of the requirements.

In addition to the 20 pages of requirements, there is a generic requirement specification for all B&K applications running under MS Windows. It consists of 18 pages with 94 enumerated and annotated requirements.

The parts below are reproduced with kind permission by Otto Vinter, Bruel & Kjaer, Naerum, Denmark.

Experience-driven process improvement

B&K routinely records all defects from the later stages of system development. Testers, developers, and customers report all defects they note (problems, errors, and requests for change). When the NSL product was released, about 800 defects had been reported. More than half of them were classified as requirements-related. About two-thirds of these related to usability (ease of use). So although the project team used a requirements style they were experienced in, there were many requirements-related defects.

B&K used the experiences from this project as a basis for a systematic process improvement. The new development process included close studies of potential users, early prototypes of the user interface (mockups), and usability tests. The analyst team had selected these three techniques from about 40 requirements techniques because they promised to prevent more of the observed problems than the other techniques.

When a development team used the process in a new project, the results were remarkable: The product had 70% fewer usability problems and sold twice as many units as similar B&K products – and at twice the usual unit price. Further, the development process proceeded much more smoothly than usual. The developers said that when the user interface was defined and usability-tested, the rest was straightforward programming. See Lauesen and Vinter (2001) for a detailed report of the improvement project.

Requirements Specification for Noise Source Location

1.   Introduction
[Omitted]

2.   General Requirements

2.1.   Description of the application

The Noise Source Location application is used to process sound intensity and sound pressure spectra. The spectra are measured at different positions around a device on which the noise sources are to be located. This is done by setting up a surface containing the measurement positions, by measuring the spectra at these positions, analyzing them to sound intensity vectors or pressure levels, and displaying the results on a picture of the surface or a fraction of the surface. The results can be displayed as a numeric map, as a vector map, or as an iso-contour plot. For plane surfaces the results can be displayed as a 3D-landscape. When the noise sources have been identified the sound power from these sources may be calculated and ranked to determine which parts of the device are of greatest interest.

2.2.   Language

As English is the most common language of our potential customers, the first release of the program will be in English.

(R-1 +)   **The language of this application will be in American English.**

2.3.   Surface

The surface defines the exact places where the sound intensity is measured. The surface therefore has to be defined before any measurement can be performed. It is also used for presentation of the measurements. The surface is described using grids, which for manual measurements are typically built with wood and wires.

2.3.1.   Grid

A grid is a plane rectangle containing m rows and n columns in a right-angled co-ordinate system. Definitions of the grids are a trade-off between accuracy of the measurement and time: Many measurement points give better accuracy but this is more time-consuming. From customers, we know that a noise location application must accept grids with a minimum of 50×50 points.

(R-2 +++)   **The application must support grids of minimum 50×50 points, but ideally the grids should be boundless.**

(R-3 +++)   **The application must be able to hold at least 2,500 measurement points, but ideally should be boundless.**

(R-4 +++)   **It must be possible to construct a surface consisting of at least 50 grids.**

Each grid has its own co-ordinate system.

(R-5 +++)   **Each grid has its own co-ordinate system. The co-ordinate system for each grid must be defined as a right-hand system where the z-axis is parallel to the surface normal vector, and the x- and y- axes are parallel to the gridlines.**

(R-6 +++)   **If only one direction is measured, the direction must be the z-direction.**

(R-7 ++)   **If only two directions are measured, the directions must be the x- and the y-directions.**

As mentioned above, the grids define the measurement points. This can be done in two ways: the intersections of the grid-lines or the center of the squares they indicate. The first method has the advantage that the measurement points are given very precisely, but the disadvantage that the area associated with each measurement point is not as well defined and actually exceeds the defined grid. The second method has the advantage that the areas are well defined and match the grid exactly, but the disadvantage that the measurement points are not as well defined as in the first method. The disadvantage of the inaccurate indication of the measurement point with the second approach disappears if the probe is controlled by a robot.

(R-8 ++)   **The user determines whether the measurement positions are located at the intersections of the grid-lines or at the center of the squares they form.**

Logically the measurement points are always positioned in the center of the squares. This implies that the grid will be changed when the user shifts to and from locating the points at the intersections. The physical positioning of the measurement points will not be changed. It also implies that it will not be possible to take measurements at the edge of the surface.

(R-9 -)   **It is not possible to position a measurement point on the edges of the surface.**

As described above, this implies that the area of the surface exceeds the grids. The sound field will be undefined in the part of the surface area from the outer measurement points to the edge of the surface. In contour map this will be solved using extrapolation.

(R-10 +)   **The contour lines will be extrapolated from the outer measurement positions to the edge of the surface.**

In some cases the resolution of the x-axis and the y-axis is different. This could be in a case where one of the co-ordinates of the position of the noise source is more interesting than the other.

(R-11 ++)   **The two axes of a grid may have different resolution.**

Fig 1   A surface constructed using nine grids (of which only six are visible)

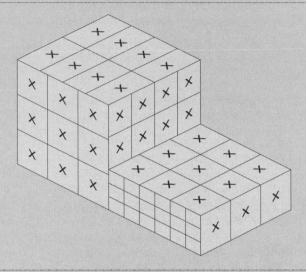

The measurements are preferably made close to the measurement object and at constant distances from it. It must therefore be possible to construct a measurement surface that follows the surface of the measurement object. Therefore it must be possible to build a measurement surface using several grids.

The purpose of the Noise Source Location application is, of course, to find the main sources of noise from the measurement object. This will often be done on machinery standing on the floor (e.g. in a factory). Measuring the entire sound intensity radiated from the machine then requires the construction of a closed measurement surface around the machine. Typically the measurement surface is simply a box.

(R-12 ++)   **The application must contain a function that creates an open box, where each of the five sides is a grid.**

When a measurement has been completed, it sometimes shows that parts of the grid area have an interesting behaviour. To examine these areas more closely they have to be measured with a finer-grained grid, i.e. a smaller distance between the measurement points. On the other hand it would be a waste of time to measure uninteresting areas with the same fine-grained grid; therefore it must be possible to insert a small fine-grained grid into the larger grid.

(R-13 ++)   **It must be possible to insert a smaller grid into an existing (possibly already measured) grid.**

[R14 to R19 omitted]

2.4. Measurement

The application sets up the system ready for the first point when the user initiates a measurement. Then it opens a window containing the measurement surface with all the points drawn on it. To help the user positioning the probe, the application should highlight the measurement point, e.g. give it a different color or show an arrow pointing at it.

(R-14 ++) **During the measurement the application must show the measurement surface highlighting the point that is going to be measured.**

(R-15 ++) **If the point to be measured is hidden by the surface, the application must turn the surface making the point visible.**

[R22 to R24 omitted]

A good way of assuring that the measurement is accurate is to examine the measured spectra. If you present the measured spectra to an experienced user, he will easily be able to determine the quality of the measurement.

(R-16 ++) **During the measurement the application must show the latest measured spectra.**

2.4.1. Data types

The traditional types of data are the sound intensity spectrum and the mean pressure spectrum. You can calculate sound power directly from these types, but for some kinds of measurements the mapping of particle velocity, reactive intensity and P-I index is of high interest. Ideally it should be possible to map any function that is supported by the analyzer.

(R-17 +++) **The application must support active sound intensity spectra.**

(R-18 +++) **The application must support pressure spectra and be able to calculate the mean pressure spectrum.**

The P-I index describes the reactivity of the sound field. The P-I index equals the mean pressure minus the intensity.

(R-19 ++) **The application must support P-I index spectra.**

(R-20 +) **The application must support particle velocity spectra.**

When measuring intensity, you measure only the noise coming out of the source. Sometimes the noise pumps from one part of the test object to another. This kind of noise is called reactive, and it is invisible to the intensity measurement. Reactive intensity makes the reactive noise visible, and it is the best parameter to choose in these cases.

(R-21 ++) **The application must support reactive sound intensity spectra.**

The 2144 delivers CPB spectra. This includes the types 1/1, 1/3, 1/12 and 1/24 octave spectra.

(R-22 +++) **The application must support 1/1, 1/3, 1/12 and 1/24 octave spectra.**

2.4.2. Data transfer paths

You can control the analyzer type 2144 by either the IEEE-interface or the RS-232 interface.

(R-23 +++) **The application must be able to control the front-end via all relevant interfaces.**

Some customers acquire data using only the 2144 analyzer not connected to any computer. They measure into a multispectrum, which they store on the internal floppy disk or hard disk of the analyzer. Then they send the disk or analyzer back to their office, where an engineer will analyze the data using the application.

(R-24 ++) **The application must accept a multispectrum as input.**

Sometimes the user wants to keep some of the grids of a surface in one file and some in another. If he wants to calculate the total sound power, he must merge these grids together.

(R-25 +) **It must be possible to merge two measurement files into one file.**

It is sometimes impossible to measure some of the desired points. It may be too hot in the environment or there may not be enough room to position the probe. The application must therefore be able to display all types of results even if some of the points have not been measured.

(R-26 +++) **The application must be able to display all results, even if some of the points have not been measured.**

(R-27 ++) **The application must be able to calculate a measurement point as the mean value of its (eight) closest neighbours. The user selects whether the average must be calculated using the dB values directly or via a conversion to engineering units.**

To cover any situations where our customers will use the application in a way we have not foreseen, we must support manually entered data. Please note, that there is essentially two kinds of data, spectra and scalars. However, it is sufficient only to accept spectra, as the user can specify a spectrum with only one frequency if he has only one value per point. Very often the user knows something about the sound field which is unknown to the application. If he discovers a measurement point with a value that is clearly wrong, he should be able to adjust this value.

(R-28 +++) **The application must allow the user to alter the value of a measurement point.**

(R-29 ++) **The application must be able to visualize all unmeasured points, when the user requests it.**

When the system overloads, the normal thing to do is to reject the measurement and try again. This is however not always the case, and sometimes the user may judge that the result is useful anyway.

(R-30 ++)   **It must be possible to set up the application to accept overloaded data, and to visualize all results affected by an overload.**

2.4.3. Recording sequence

The recording sequence is very important, but at the same time difficult to communicate. The primary parameters describe if row numbers should be updated before columns and directions or vice versa, or if the measurement path from row to row must follow an S-shape or a Z-shape. Other parameters are the number of probes, the number of channels, if the user wants to include intensity derived functions (two channels per point), or if he only wants pressure spectra (one channel per point). The recording sequence is especially important when dealing with robot controlled measurements or if you perform the measurement without application control.

(R-31 +++)   **The application must support the Z-shape recording sequence**

(R-32 ++)   **The application must support the S-shape recording sequence**

If for some reason the user cannot or will not measure some of the points, he should be able to cut these points out before he begins measuring.

(R-33 ++)   **It must be possible to mark out points in the grid which must not be measured.**

The obvious recording sequences are all six permutations of the three parameters of a grid, Row, Column and Direction. The parameter mentioned first is the one updated first, when going from one point to the next. The next to determine is the sequence of the grids. Ideally, a totally free recording sequence is desirable.

(R-34 +)   **The application must support the totally free recording sequence, where the user determines where to put each measurement just before it is measured.**

A door slamming or an aeroplane flying overhead can lead to inaccurate measurements. In these cases it is necessary to be able to redo just that point instead of having to start all over again. If the user discovers a bad or atypical measurement during post-analysis, it must also be possible to remeasure and replace the bad point.

(R-35 +++)   **It must be possible to repeat the measurement of a point at any time.**

2.5. Post processing

The most commonly used data type is 1/3 octave. In some cases however you may want the higher resolution of 1/12 and 1/24 octave or narrow band. If measurements of these kinds are to be compared with 1/3 octave measurements, a synthesis is required. A further data reduction into 1/1 octave could also be desirable, as it saves storage space.

(R-36 +++)   **It must be possible to synthesize data-types into 1/3 or 1/1 octave where possible. This must be done on all the spectra.**

It must be possible to add and subtract the A-weighting curve. A-weighting a noise signal is a good way to visualize how the human ear interprets the noise.

(R-37 +++)   **It must be possible to A-weigh or un-A-weigh the measured spectra. This must always be done on all spectra.**

[R47 to R107 omitted]

15

Tax Payers' Association Requirements for membership administration in a political association

Many analysts ask: Which of the many requirements styles should we use in a small project, for instance one where the customer expects the whole development to take 2–4 weeks?

The case story below shows the requirements for one such small project. Here is the story behind it.

A new political organization started as a cross-political group among politicians in the Parliament of country X. The name of the group became the *Tax Payers' Association*, and soon it caught a lot of attention. People wanted to enroll, and Parliament secretaries used their spare time to manage the growing association.

When there were 300 members, the secretaries decided that it was time to get an IT system to support them. One of the secretaries, Martin Ipsen, had experience as administrator of other associations and also some knowledge of MS Access. He volunteered to make a small system to keep track of the members. He asked the administrator of the association about the requirements, and initially they were just a matter of recording members and their different interests and roles in the association.

Two days later the administrator of the association said: "Oh, by the way, I would like to see who has paid the yearly fee and who hasn't. And while we're on the subject, we are going to make a lot of courses and conferences. We should also keep track of fees paid for those."

This may sound easy, but these additions made the project grow immensely. Experience from other places is that there are lots of problems with payments. People send checks for the wrong amount, they pay for courses even if they are not yet members, and they may pay for several things at once.

Martin realized that requirements were necessary. He wasn't experienced with requirements, but had heard about user tasks as requirements and tried that approach on his own. The author (Lauesen) happened to read the draft and saw it as a good opportunity to write a small, but careful specification. Martin had the domain experience and I had the requirements expertise.

Based on Martin's outline and talks with him, I wrote the specification below. We both thought that the domain was reasonably well understood when we started the joint work, but when I began describing user tasks in detail, many new aspects came up. Since there were no existing tasks to support, we had to design reasonable manual processes, based on Martin's experience from similar jobs.

When I made detailed descriptions of data, further problems turned up, particularly when I made CRUD checks of data against user tasks. We also started to doubt whether this really was a development job for a parliament secretary. In particular, the maintenance issue was serious. So we decided that requirements should be made in such a way that they could also be used to check whether a COTS product was sufficient, and to get a proposal from a software house which made that type of system. So the project type had to be kept open.

The specification follows the rapid approach described in section 1.7.2. We used several intermediate work products: an E/R model, a context diagram, and a quality grid. They are not shown in the final specification, which is solely textual: a list of the interfaces, task descriptions, data descriptions, and a list of the quality factors with open metric requirements for the critical ones.

Although I favor Tasks & Support, they seemed irrelevant in this case. So I wrote simple task descriptions and didn't even use the table templates.

When I had written the first version, Martin reviewed it and pointed out 14 serious problems that I had to correct. The problems related to task descriptions as well as data descriptions.

Our joint work took about 14 man hours. This was the price for rewriting the draft to a more useful specification, including our time for resolving several domain problems.

Requirements for Membership Administration

Customer: The Tax Payers' Association

Background: The Tax Payers' Association is a newly established political association. Currently it has about 300 members, but experience from a neighboring country suggests that this may grow to more than 50,000 members within a few years. The administrative support is provided by some of the Parliament secretaries in their spare time.

Purpose: The system shall support the secretaries in keeping track of members, their participation in various activities, distributing mail, and keeping track of payment of fees.

Supplier type: Three possibilities are considered. (1) An in-house system developed by one of the secretaries who has much experience with membership administration and some experience with Access development. (2) A tailor-made system provided by a local software house that develops similar applications. (3) An off-the-shelf system for membership administration. The customer wants to choose the supplier later when the requirements are have been made.

Technical interfaces

R1: The system shall use the following technical interfaces:

Platform: The system shall run on a PC running Windows 98. Data files are stored in an existing file server with existing backup facilities. Development tool: MS Access 97. Preferably the system should allow a few simultaneous users (see risk areas below).

ZIP code files: The system shall use the standard ZIP codes and country codes provided by the Postal Office. Might for instance be transferred manually as a comma-separated file.

Payment files: The system shall efficiently support the payment registration formats provided by the Bank Association. In the long term, computer files with payment data must be used. See the task descriptions below.

Word and Excel: The system shall allow transfer of member lists and search results to Word and Excel. See the task descriptions below, e.g. tasks 2, 5, 6.

Tasks to be supported

R2:   The system shall support the following user tasks:

Task 1, Handle a member call

Purpose: Service a specific member in various matters, e.g. enroll as a
                           member, enroll for a course, review the member's payments.

Trigger: A member phones, sends a letter, or sends an e-mail.

Frequency: Usually at most 10 times a day by phone. Up to 50 by mail, but
                           they may be batched by the secretary.

Critical: When the deadline for a conference approaches. May cause 150
                           phone calls per day.

Sub-tasks:

1.1   Look up the member by means of member code, name, or
                           sometimes address.

1.2   Review and modify address and other membership data
                           (optional).

1.3   Enroll the member in an activity (e.g. a conference) or modify
                           the enrollment (optional).
                               Specify the fee to be paid by the member. Usually it is a
                           standard fee for that activity, but individual fees are possible.
                           The fee for the activity is not posted on the member's account
                           until it has been decided that there are enough participants to
                           run the activity (see task 5).

1.4   Review and modify the member's account, e.g. to see whether
                           payments have arrived or amounts are due, add transactions,
                           etc. (optional).

Variants:

1.1a   A new member wants to enroll.

1.1b   A person who is not a member wants to enroll on an activity.

1.3a   The activity is fully booked, so the member may have to go on
                           a waiting list.

1.3b   Sometimes convenient to check the waiting list before looking
                           up the member.

Task 2, Extract member lists

Purpose: Find lists of members according to various criteria. Use the lists
                           for general information, mail merge, spreadsheets, etc.

Trigger: Many types, e.g.
                           – a member calls to get assistance from another member in
                              the same geographical area and with knowledge about
                              income tax.
                           – the chairman wants a letter to be sent to all members
                              interested in energy taxes.
                           – the list of participants on a conference is to be printed.

	– the chairman wants to send a "thanks for your contribution" letter to all members who have paid a gift, supported a conference, etc.
Frequency:	Probably less than 10 times a day, but difficult to estimate at this point.
Critical:	(none)
Sub-tasks:	
2.1	Specify any member data or combination of data as the search criteria.
2.2	See the result and modify it manually by deleting or adding members, and by hiding or showing fields (columns).
2.3	Select any member on the list and see the member details.
2.4	Transfer the list to Word or Excel (optional).
Variants:	(none)

Task 3, Record payments manually

Purpose:	Record payments received from members, e.g. yearly membership fee, fees for activities (e.g. conferences), gifts to the association.
Trigger:	– a payment list arrives from the Bank Association. The list is a photocopy of the pay slips.
	– a check or cash arrives by mail.
Frequency:	Up to 50 per day, typically when a conference takes place.
Critical:	At the beginning of the year when the annual invoice has been sent to all members. Will be handled in batches.
Sub-tasks:	
3.1	Lookup the member by means of member code, part of the name, or sometimes address (data in the payment list may be hard to read). Sometimes name etc. is missing entirely and you have to call the bank to trace the payment.
3.2	Post the paid amount with the proper text. The user should be able to set a default text and change it during the task. Selection from a list of standard texts may be convenient.
3.3	Review and modify address and other membership data (optional).
Variants:	
3.1a	A new member enrolls by sending the yearly fee along with a note. Similar to Task 1.
3.2a	A person who is not a member enrolls on an activity by sending the payment with a note on. Similar to task 1.

Task 4, Record batch payments

Purpose: Record payments received on a computer medium.

Trigger: A payment file arrives from the Bank Association. The file is a comma-separated file from an OCR-scan of the pay slips sent out by the Association, e.g. through task 5.

Frequency: Once per month.

Critical: At the beginning of the year when the annual invoice has been sent to all members.

Sub-tasks:

4.1   Specify the text to be indicated on the account transactions. Start the computer handling of the payment file. Selection from a list of standard texts may be convenient.

4.2   Manually handle any payments that the computer couldn't post on a member account.

4.3   Verify that everything is handled, e.g. by means of hash totals.

Variants: (None. Enrollment cannot occur here since the pay slips are sent out by the Association)

Task 5, Invoice and post fees

Purpose: Record that a fee is due and send an invoice with an attached letter.

Trigger:
– the annual fee has been determined.
– it is decided to run an activity (there are enough participants).

Frequency: About twice a month.

Critical: (none)

Sub-tasks:

5.1   Specify search criteria for the members who have to pay (any member data or combination of data may be used as search criteria).

5.2   Specify the fee and the text for the account transactions. Selection from a list of standard texts may be convenient.

5.3   See the resulting list of members and fees. Modify it manually by deleting or adding members, modifying fees, and hiding or showing fields (columns).

5.4   Perform the automatic posting for the members on the list.

5.5   Print letters and invoices. Possible solution: transfer the member list and the fees as a mail-merge to Word, where the cover letter and invoice are printed.

Variants:

5.1a   Select the members enrolled on an activity. Members who have already received an invoice shall be excluded.

5.2a   When an activity is chosen, take the text from the activity list and the fee that was determined at the time of enrollment (see subtask 1.3).

Task 6, Review accounts

Purpose: General accounting for the Association is manual for the first period. The Membership system shall provide summary data of fees and payments for posting in the manual accounting system, and the auditor shall be able to check them. Furthermore, it shall be possible to send reminders to members who haven't paid.

Trigger: Any time.

Frequency: A few times a year.

Critical: (none)

Sub-tasks:

6.1 For a specified period of time, compute totals of all amounts paid, all fees charged, and the balance of all member accounts (optional).

6.2 Print the totals (optional).

6.3 Show a list of all members that have a net debt above a specified limit (optional).

6.4 Select any member on the list and see his member details (optional).

6.5 Transfer the list to Word or Excel for printing of reminders or further analysis (optional).

Variants:

6.1a For special reports, e.g. summaries of fees charged for an activity, the auditor is expected to use the basic queries and report generators in Access.

Task 7, File maintenance

Purpose: Create, update and delete activities (e.g. conferences), member categories, and maybe standard transaction texts.

Trigger: Any time.

Frequency: About once a month.

Critical: (none)

Sub-tasks: Trivial create, update, and delete operations.

Variants: (none)

Data to be stored

R3:   The system shall store the following data:

Data about members

Member is a generic term that covers real members who pay an annual fee, *observers* that don't pay fees but receive information from the association, and *temporaries* who participate in activities, but don't pay the annual fee (usually they pay a higher price for the activities).

For each member the system shall keep track of these data:

Data volume:	Up to 100,000 members.
Member code:	May be a simple sequential number, but the customer would prefer the enrollment year as part of the code.
Person, company, or employee:	The system must handle personal membership, company membership (at a special fee), and membership for employees in the company (covered by the company's fee). The system must keep track of the relation between company and employees.
Name, address1, address2, address3, zip, country:	Usual address fields.
Home phone, mobile, work phone, fax, email, URL:	Usual phone, e-mail and Website addresses.
Delegate:	Member of the board of delegates.
Executive:	Member of the executive board.
Previous member:	Resigned members. Also set by the administrator when a member hasn't paid for some time.
No ads:	The member doesn't want information from the association.
Observer:	The person or company is not a true member and doesn't pay membership fees, but the board has decided to send informative material anyway.
Temporary:	The person or company participates in an activity, but doesn't pay membership fees and doesn't receive information.
Date created:	The date the membership was recorded.
Last changed:	The last date where the member's data was changed.
Comments:	Free text.

| Categories: | A list of the categories to which the member belongs, e.g. interested in energy tax, willing to help at meetings, willing to distribute letters. The member may belong to several categories. The categories are selected from a table of categories (see below). |

Account transactions

Each member has an account where account transactions are kept. The system shall keep track of these data:

Data volume:	400,000 per year (about four transactions per member per year).
Date:	Date posted.
Activity code:	Used only for fees associated with an activity.
Text:	A descriptive text. If there is a fee for an activity, the text is generated by the system from the activity list.
Amount:	The amount paid (positive) or the amount due (negative). In case of an activity, it is generated by the system from the activity list.

Activity participation

Each member may participate in a number of activities. The system shall keep track of these data:

Data volume:	100,000 per year (in average at most one per member per year).
DateTime:	The date and time when the member enrolled on the activity. Priorities on the waiting list are given by the DateTime, thus time is needed too.
Activity code:	The activity in question – selected from the list of activities.
Waiting:	On a waiting list to that activity.
Fee:	The fee to be paid for the activity. Selected from the activity list at the time of enrollment, but may be modified manually.
Invoiced:	The member has got an invoice for the activity. Necessary in order to avoid members being sent an invoice twice if invoices are sent out in several batches.

Activity list

For each activity, the system shall keep track of these data:

| Data volume: | About 30 per year. |
| Activity code: | Any unique number will do. Essential when posting fees for the activity in order to review the income for the activity. |

Name:	Name of the activity, e.g. "Basic course in investment taxation".
Start:	The start date of the activity. May be blank.
End:	The end date of the activity. May be blank.
Price1:	The fee for members.
Price2:	The fee for non-members.

Member categories

For each member category, the system keeps track of these data:

Data volume:	Around 100.
Name:	A descriptive name, e.g. "Willing to help at meetings".

ZIP list and Country list

The system shall contain lists of zip codes and country codes as provided by the Postal Office.

Quality requirements:

Response time:	Not critical. Usual Access performance seems sufficient, but a risk to be considered when the data volume grows. See below.
Data volume:	100,000 members. See details under the data requirements.
Usability:	Not critical. There are just two to three users, and they will be given individual instructions on how to use the system.
Maintainability:	Critical. High-risk area. See below.
Reliability:	As usual.
Availability:	As usual on that server.
Fault tolerance:	As usual.
Safety & Security:	As usual on that server.
Portability:	Unimportant.
Reusability:	Unimportant.

High-risk areas:

Maintainability has to be considered as part of selecting the supplier.

R4:	The supplier must specify to what extent he can support the system, i.e. provide help hotline, help with ad hoc reports, correct problems, extend the system. Prices for the services have to be specified.

The database may grow to 100,000 members. The customer is not sure whether this is feasible with a reasonable response time.

R5:	The supplier shall specify the lookup time to show a member screen when the database contains 100,000 members. (a) When the user specifies the member code. (b) When the user specifies part of the name or the address. If necessary, a simple prototype should be made to actually measure the response time.

The assumption is that one secretary (plus a backup person) will be able to handle the administration. Thus the system may be designed for a single user. However, the possibility for multi-user access should be considered when selecting the supplier.

R6:	The supplier shall specify to what extent the system may be used by several users simultaneously.

16

Exercises

The discussions and exercises below cover all the book chapters, and are arranged with a section for each chapter. In addition there are five case studies, shown as Figures 16.1 to 16.5. An exercise for each chapter asks you to work out something for one of these case studies, for instance identify the type of project, make a data model, then write task descriptions, suggest elicitation techniques, and so on.

When we use the book for running courses, we divide participants into groups and assign a case project to each group. The group has to work on this project during all stages of the course. Sometimes they may have to serve as reviewers of work products from other groups. If the course is run with a tight schedule, for instance professional courses, we usually assign the same case project to all groups, and cut down on the reviews. With more time, for instance university courses, we use two case studies and cross-reviews.

In addition to the project-oriented exercises, there are other, more independent, discussions and exercises. Discussions are small exercises, useful for classroom discussion. They may also be used for homework. For some of the discussions, the answer is in the text, and in other cases participants have to apply the principles of the text to find the solution. Exercises take more time and are suitable for homework (university courses) or for group work (professional courses). For most of the exercises, there are several questions, identified as (a), (b), etc. Depending on the audience and the circumstances, we select a few of these questions for homework or group work.

The case studies are not just textbook examples, but originate in real, industrial projects. However, we want to emphasize that, as used here, they are only for simple training. You cannot get genuine industry experience in a classroom setting. For university courses we strongly recommend that course participants at the end of the course run a requirements project in a real company or organization. During the project they should produce written requirements for something that the customer actually needs.

Fig 16.1   Case study: Journal circulation

An insurance company with about 1,000 employees subscribes to about 50 periodicals (magazines and journals). The periodicals are circulated in-house and employees can subscribe to the circulation. At present subscription works in this way: When a periodical arrives to the company, it goes to the library where it is registered. Next the librarian attaches a list of the subscribers to it, and sends it to the first employee on the list. The internal snail-mail distribution is used to transport the journal round the building. The employee is supposed to read it within three work days, sign off on the list with name and date, and send it to the next employee on the list. When the last employee on the list has read it, he returns it to the library, where it becomes available for common use.

Unfortunately, employees often forget that they have received the journal and they don't pass it on to the next person on the list. After a while nobody knows who is supposed to have the journal. It is difficult to keep track of the whole thing, and employees keep accusing each other of being forgetful, careless, etc.

The company has an IT department that develops business applications for in-house use. The department suggests that they create a computer-supported system that can keep track of where the journals are. When an employee has finished reading a journal, he tells the system, and the system tells him where to send the journal in the internal snail-mail system. The next reader has to acknowledge that he has received the journal. The system should of course warn people when they have forgotten to pass a journal on.

The personnel department, where the library belongs, thinks this is an excellent idea. In particular, they would like to prioritize people on the circulation list according to vacation (people cannot read journals when they are on a two-week vacation) and according to their ability to observe the circulation deadlines (the three work days for passing the journal on). However, they have experience of such systems dragging on for years while the IT department and the user department fight about what the system is supposed to do. For this reason they want a requirement specification as basis for the study.

Imagine that you are a consultant from the IT department.

Note: This project is relatively small and well-defined, yet has several surprises. Course participants with some general background understanding of 'office work' are needed to make the project a success. It is realistic to make a complete requirement specification during a course.

Fig 16.2 Case study: Ticket machine

The state railway in country C also operates bus routes and is involved as an international travel provider. They have an ambitious plan to develop a system where you can find the fastest and cheapest connection from street A in city X to street B in city Y, using bus, train, aeroplane, and ferry as needed. Of course customers should also be able to buy tickets and make bookings for their selected journey.

At present the state railway operates a simple version of such a system on the Web, covering only local transport in the capital city. The system allows you to find the connection, but not to book or to buy a ticket.

As a central part of their plans, they want a machine to be installed at railway stations, airports, and other transport hubs. From these machines you should be able to find the right connection, book tickets, pay, and receive ticket and reservation. You should of course also be able to get a printed travel itinerary. They envisage that you should also be able to pick up the ticket and reservation for a booking that you have made on the Web.

They have decided that they are not going to make the system themselves – they want someone to deliver the entire system – hardware and software. However, they are willing to contribute their present software for the Web solution. They envisage that several existing systems are close to what they want, but they are not sure.

The state railway has already experienced the difficulty of getting transport schedules from several transport providers, particularly in a uniform format so that they can put the data into their own database. Expanding the system to an even larger set of transport providers will be one of the problems.

Imagine that you work for a software house which has got a three man-month contract to prepare a request for proposal (RFP) for such a ticket machine. In full agreement with the state railway, the software house may later become the software supplier for the system, working as a sub-contractor for the main contractor. They might also enter into a consortium with a hardware supplier, and submit a joint proposal with him.

Note: This project is surprisingly open-ended and its limits are not easy to define. Since you don't have the customer at hand, you have to make preliminary choices on your own. In real life you would have to resolve the issues with the customer. Communication with other systems is a prime concern, and some domain knowledge from, for instance, a travel agency is an advantage. It is realistic to make a complete requirement specification during a course.

Fig 16.3 Case study: E-mail system

A large company with many departments, and scattered use of e-mail, decides to invest in a carefully selected e-mail system for global use in the company. Since they are not going to develop it themselves, they plan to run a tender process. They prefer a commercial product, but might consider a commercial product with tailor-made extensions.

Because of the scattered use, different systems are used at present. Every person using e-mail is likely to fight for his or her system becoming the standard.

The main reason that the company wants everybody to use the same system is that they want to focus their support effort on one product only, and allow staff to easily move from one department to another. Furthermore, they realize that archiving e-mails is becoming a company concern, and they want to make it more easy to connect the e-mail system to a large-scale document filing system.

Imagine that you are a consultant helping the company in the purchase process. The company could, for instance, be the State Railway or the State Postal Agency.

Note: Most of this project is quite well defined, but there are open ends. Most course participants will have domain knowledge that makes the exercise fruitful, although some IT-support background is an advantage. An interesting issue is the tasks to be supported and to what extent they are common across user groups. It is realistic to make an almost complete requirement specification during a course.

Fig 16.4　Case study: Project management

The company WonderCASE develops and markets tools for Computer Aided Software Engineering. For a long time they have focused on providing tools for the many types of diagrams used in software development, ranging from dataflow and data modeling to UML diagrams, and requirements tools. Their customers are software houses doing many kinds of projects.

WonderCASE have realized that there is a potential in also providing project management tools that can assist in giving an overview of the current project status, showing who is supposed to do what, identifying project risks and following up on them, remembering to bill the customer for work an a time-and-material basis, remembering also to charge the customer for travel expenses, etc. It would be nice if these features could somehow integrate with the traditional diagram stuff, so that users felt that they didn't have to record ever more information, but could use what they already record for other purposes.

Imagine that you are an analyst working in WonderCASE and trying to come up with requirements for this new product.

Note: This is a very open-ended project, and the course team must choose the project scope on their own. (This should be checked with the customer in real life, of course.) Some team members should have a good background in software development to make the project succeed. Even then, a focus group with other software developers will significantly change the initial scope imagined by the team. If a reasonably complete requirements specification is to be made during a course, the team must set a very limited scope for the project.

Fig 16.5   Case study: Education management

The Midland University has about 5,000 students and 500 staff, including students that also serve as staff. They have several old IT systems for payroll, exam registration, student records, and so on, but the systems are not integrated and there are many activities without adequate IT support. In particular, the on-line services to students are poor. Small Web applications grow up in individual departments to serve their students, but in an ad hoc manner.

This is the time to create a new, well-planned system for managing university courses, keeping track of students and what could be done to help them succeed, providing support and help to the students, recruiting teachers sufficiently early, and so on. The IT department of the University, which is partially staffed with IT students, is excited about the plans. They suggest that 'we just put all the information on the Web for students and staff to use'. More seasoned developers say that this is not the right solution, because some administration staff will need much faster access and response, particularly for accounting, schedule planning, room allocation, and other critical things.

Imagine that you are a consultant working for the university, and trying to help them find out what to do.

Note: This is a very open-ended project, and the course team have to choose the project scope on their own. (This should be checked with the customer in real life, of course.) Some team members should have a reasonable understanding of university administration to make the project succeed. If a reasonably complete requirements specification is to be made during a course, the team must set a very limited scope for the project.

Chapter 1 Exercises: Introduction and basic concepts

Discussions

1.1 Give examples of the various project types from your own geographical region.

1.2 For each project type: Who has the IT expertise? Who writes the specification? Who should be blamed if requirements are not met? Who should be blamed when demands are not met? How easy is it to change the specification?

1.3 Assume that the system is to run under MS Windows. We should then specify the interface between the system and MS Windows. Which functional requirements should we specify about that interface?

1.4 Assume that the shipyard selected R2 as their requirement to the business system vendor. Who is responsible for R1? Who is responsible for R2? Who is responsible for R3?

1.5 Assume that the shipyard selected R4 as their requirement to a *programming* team, rather than a business system vendor. Who is responsible for R2? Who is responsible for R3? If the system is difficult to use (low usability), whom can be blamed?

1.6 Outline a context diagram for the shipyard (such as in Figure 1.5A). What are the inner and outer domains?

1.7 Which project model should the shipyard have used? Which one did they actually use?

Exercises

1.8 Case project
For one of the case studies (16.1 to 16.5) do the following:
a) Identify the project type (in-house, COTS, etc.).

b) Outline a relevant requirement in the specific project for each of the four levels (goal, domain, etc.).

c) Suggest a project model to use.

1.9 Study existing requirements specifications
Study the following pieces of the specifications in Chapters 11 and onwards:

Midland Hospital (Chapter 12):
Section 2.3 Employee data, requirements 5 to 18
Requirement 144
Requirement 475
Requirement 666
Requirement 669

Danish Shipyard (Chapter 11):
Detailed planning (entire section 5.2.1.2.2)
Objectives (entire section 4.1)

Bruel & Kjaer (Chapter 14):
Requirements R-35 and R-36, including the three-line introduction to these two requirements.

For each of these specification pieces, answer the following questions:

a) Is it a functional requirement?

b) A non-functional one?

c) Something to help the reader?

d) Something about the domain or the product?

e) A system goal?

f) An example?

g) Is it verifiable?

Note: The same piece may be several of these things at the same time.

h) Among the Midland Hospital requirements mentioned above there is a "killer requirement", that is a requirement that looks innocent but could cause disaster for the unwary supplier. Which requirement is it?

Chapter 2 Exercises: Data requirement styles

Discussions

2.1 Some analysts say that a data dictionary, such as Figure 2.3, lacks precision, while a data model, such as Figure 2.2A, is more exact. Other analysts say the opposite. Who is right?

2.2 How are data described in the specifications in Chapters 11, 12, and 15?

2.3 Would it have been suitable to use Virtual Windows for the Shipyard?

Exercises

2.4 Case project
For one of the case studies (16.1 to 16.5) do the following:

a) Specify a data model for the system (for case studies 16.4 and 16.5, make only part of the data model).

b) Write a data dictionary part for an interesting part of the model.

c) Outline virtual windows for an interesting part of the system.

d) Which data requirements styles would you suggest using in the case project? (Don't just propose all of them – time will be scarce in the project; so select the best for the specific project, ignore the rest.)

2.5 Hotel system, data dictionary

For the hotel system, do the following:

a) Complete the data dictionary to cover all classes of Figure 2.2A. You should encounter several parts where you don't think you know enough to complete this part, and where in real life you would have asked the customer. In these cases, write your best guess but add "Check with customer".

b) The data model in Figure 2.2A is too simple. In most hotels, rooms are not booked by room number, but by room type (single, double, deluxe, and so on). When the guest turns up to check in, the receptionist assigns him a physical room with a room number. Furthermore, many hotels overbook, in the sense that they book more rooms than the hotel actually has. In practice some guests don't turn up, so there is no real problem. In case too many guests turn up, the staff find an emergency solution in neighboring hotels or private rooms. In some cases they tell the guests that they have arrived too late – the last room is gone! Or: Sorry, there must have been some mistake, we have no record of your booking. Extend the data model to cover these additional requirements. Write a short data description to explain how the new parts work.

Chapter 3 Exercises: Functional requirement styles

Discussions

3.1 Is the receptionist part of the product? Is he part of the inner domain? Answer the same question for the waiter. Suggest different system limits so that we get another answer.

3.2 Which functional styles were used in the Shipyard (Chapter 11, note also all the diagrams of the chapter), in the Bruel & Kjaer case (Chapter 14), and in the Tax Payers' case (Chapter 15)?

3.3 Can you derive tasks from dataflow diagrams?

3.4 Can you derive tasks from the style used in the Shipyard case (Chapter 11)? Does the Shipyard specification have domain-oriented descriptions?

3.5 Compare dataflow diagrams and task descriptions, for instance based on these factors:

- Precision of input/output
- Precision of function
- Precision of user tasks
- Customer understanding
- Developer understanding
- Problem description
- Design independence
- Verification

3.6 Workflow systems support clerical procedures in large companies. With a manual system, paper documents move from department to department for investigation and sign-off. A computerized workflow system stores the documents in electronic form, and sends electronic copies from department to department. The parties involved can always see how the business case is progressing and who has the case right now. The system also reminds people of steps they have to take in order to pass the case on, etc. When designing workflow applications, analysts often use dataflow diagrams on the domain level. Usually, domain-level dataflows are not useful as requirements. Why are they useful for workflows? (Hint: What is the relationship between the existing flow of paper documents among the departments and what the computer system should do? Compare it with the same domain-computer issue for data and for functions.)

Exercises

3.7 Case project

For one of the case studies (16.1 to 16.5) do the following:

a) Specify a context diagram. If you feel you don't know enough, make your best guess and state what you would like to discuss with the customer.

b) Write task descriptions for all user tasks (for case studies 16.4 and 16.5 select about five good tasks). If suitable, write Tasks & Support rather than simple task descriptions.

c) Specify at least one high-level task for the system. (This is somewhat artificial for case studies 16.1 – journal circulation – and 16.3 – e-mail. You could use one of the other case studies for this question.)

d) Take one of your task descriptions and rewrite it in one of the use case styles. Discuss the differences between the task description and the use case in this specific case.

e) Make a dataflow diagram for part of the system (choose an appropriate level). Discuss the differences between the dataflow diagram, the use case, and the task descriptions.

f) Which functional requirements styles would you suggest using in the case project? Consider all of the styles mentioned in Chapter 3, not only the ones you used above. (Select the best for the case project, ignore the rest.)

3.8 Hotel system, check-out task
a) Describe the check-out task in Task & Support style.

3.9 Hotel system, check-in task
The check-in task in Figure 3.6A handles two situations: (1) the guest has booked in advance, (2) the guest has not booked, but hopes there is a free room at a reasonable price. Do the following:

a) Split the task description into two task descriptions: (1) check in a booked guest, (2) check in a non-booked guest.

b) Discuss the difference between the one-task solution and the two-task one. Also discuss the suitability as requirements.

Chapter 4 Exercises: Functional details

Discussions

4.1 Why do many analysts spend much time describing the simple functions of the system?

4.2 The decision table in Figure 4.2B suggests that the manager can modify the rules and specify other discount percentages. What are the risks involved in letting him do this? What could you suggest to decrease this risk?

4.3 An activity diagram, such as Figure 4.6A, combines dataflow diagrams, flow charts, and synchronization (Petri-nets). Make two new versions of Figure 4.6A: one with only the dataflow parts left and one with only the flowchart parts left. Make a real dataflow diagram for the same area and compare the notations. Why does an activity diagram look overwhelmingly complex to most expert users?

4.4 UML class diagrams and E/R diagrams are competitors. Try to summarize the advantages and disadvantages of the two approaches, not only from a requirements viewpoint, but also from a developer viewpoint and a sales viewpoint.

Exercises

4.5 Case project
For one of the case studies (16.1 to 16.5) do the following:

a) Identify some semi-complex or complex functions in the product, and suggest ways to specify them. Specify some of them in the way you suggest.

b) Specify a state diagram and a state-transition matrix for an interesting entity.

c) Take one of your task descriptions and rewrite it as an activity diagram. Discuss the differences between the task description and the activity diagram in this specific case.

d) Take one of your task descriptions and rewrite it as a sequence diagram. Discuss the differences between the task description and the sequence diagram in this specific case.

4.6 Hotel system, stay states

Figure 4.4 and 4.5 show state diagrams and state-transition matrices for a room state entity. The stay entity has another interesting life cycle. It can be a booked stay, a checked-in stay, etc. However, there is little state information in the stay record itself, but additional information about the stay is available in the associated room state records. Consider the stay a composite logical entity. Now do the following:

a) Specify a state diagram for the logical stay entity.

b) Specify a state-transition matrix for the logical stay entity.

c) Find out whether the necessary data fields are available for the system to figure out the current state of the stay.

d) Write a textual process description (pseudo-code) for one of the interesting state changes (for instance the check-out action).

Chapter 5 Exercises: Special interfaces

Discussions

5.1 Mention some reports that might be useful in the hotel system. How should we specify them?

5.2 Which of the platform requirements would be relevant in the hotel system if we look at the situation from the customer's viewpoint?

5.3 Figure 5.2 shows three basic ways to specify platform requirements. In principle, a platform is just a special kind of external product, so the same basic ways to specify requirements should apply to platforms and other external products. Do they? Which ones? Are there good reasons for any differences?

5.4 Assume that you work for a manufacturer of medical equipment. You are going to contract on delivery of a system for measuring neural signals in human patients (see Figures 1.6B and C). The contract will comprise the software system and a special sensor of neural signals to be selected by the supplier so that it matches his software as well as possible. What should you specify about the interface to the sensor?

5.5 A local government in country Z provides electric power, water, garbage collection, etc. to citizens. For historical reasons, each of these suppliers had their own business administration for purchase, billing, etc. There were good reasons for this, since the nature of the different services was different. Reading the citizen's electricity or gas meters, for instance, was different to keeping track of garbage collection. Other parts of the administration, however, were similar. Operating many different systems was costly, and the local government wanted to purchase a new system that could handle administration for all of the suppliers. They envisaged that they would write requirements that specified the detailed interfaces to each of the supplier's base systems. Then they would start a tender process for a system that interfaced to all of these. What would you advise them to do?

Exercises

5.6 Case project

For one of the case studies (16.1 to 16.5) do the following:

a) Specify requirements for reports.

b) Specify platform requirements. (This question is trivial for Journal Circulation; you might use the Ticket Machine project instead.)

c) Specify the technical interfaces to other products. Take care to resolve the integration issue before doing this. (This question is trivial for Journal Circulation; you might use the Ticket Machine project instead.)

Chapter 6 Exercises: Quality requirements

Discussions

6.1 Outline a cost/benefit graph (similar to that shown in Figure 6.3C) for the speed trap response time (R1 in Figure 6.3A).

6.2 Which of the performance requirements on Figure 6.5A are mandatory? Which are flexible?

6.3 Assume that 100 users, five times a day, ask the system to compute and show a report. At present, the response time is around 30 seconds. Cutting it to 15 seconds would cost around $20,000 in additional hardware costs. Cutting it to 8 seconds would cost another $20,000. Outline a cost/benefit graph (similar to that shown in Figure 6.3C) for the situation. What would be a good response time requirement? (Remember the magical limit of human patience. Also remember that average response time and maximum response time are two different things.)

6.4 Which of the five usability factors are most important for a flight control system, for a Web-based system for attracting new customers, for a hotel system, and for an accounting system?

6.5 Figure 6.8B mentions the threat of illegal access to Web-booking. An example of 'illegal access' is that the guest has booked a room and stated a false credit card number, or he has no credit on his account. The hotel loses money holding the room for him if he doesn't turn up. Which safeguards would you suggest? What should the hotel owner write in the requirements?

6.6 In Figures 6.11A and B, fill in the risk fields for maintainability in a fashion analogous to the usability styles.

6.7 Try to specify a purpose for the following maintainability requirements in Figure 6.11A and B: R1, R3, R5, R7, and R9.

6.8 Which maintenance activities are covered by each of the maintainability requirements R1 to R11?

Exercises

6.9 Case project
For one of the case studies (16.1 to 16.5) do the following:

a) Set up a quality grid to identify the most important quality factors in the project.

b) Define some usability requirements. Justify the requirements.

c) Assess security risks for the project, and define some security requirements. (This question is trivial for Journal Circulation; you might use the Ticket Machine project instead.)

d) Define some maintenance requirements. Justify the requirements.

e) Define quality requirements for any missing, but important, quality factors according to the quality grid.

6.10 Find examples of quality requirements
Find examples of quality requirements in

a) the Shipyard case (Chapter 11).

b) the Midland Hospital case (Chapter 12).

c) the Tax Payers' case (Chapter 15).

Comment on possible weaknesses in the quality requirements.

6.11 Error message problems
Users at West Zealand County complain about incomprehensible error messages from their COTS-based system. Analysts estimate that each of about 200 users waste about half an hour each day trying to recover from these messages. The county's own IT staff, who operate the system, suggest contracting with the COTS supplier to improve the situation. In principle, it is an easy matter to change error messages once you know what the new messages should say.

a) Suggest requirements for this improvement project.

b) It is likely that the COTS supplier will change some of the messages and then claim that the system is adequate, so your requirements should be very precise.

c) What is the maximum amount the customer should be willing to pay for the revised product?

6.12 Analyze security safeguards

Section 6.8.3 mentions safeguards against a long list of threats.

a) For each of these safeguards, specify whether it is a prevention, a detection, or a repair safeguard.

b) If you feel that any important safeguard is missing, suggest an additional safeguard.

Chapter 7 Exercises: Requirements in the product life cycle

Discussions

7.1 What are the roles of customer and supplier for each requirement activity in the product life cycle in an in-house project? In a tender project? In a COTS purchase?

7.2 The Midland Hospital requirements (Chapter 12) ask the supplier to specify how he can meet each requirement. Look at the details at the first page of the specification (section 4.1, proposal format). Are the supplier's specification a priority? An option? Something with open metrics or open targets? Or something else?

7.3 For each requirement example in section 7.6 (design and programming), describe how you could verify it during acceptance testing and how this differs from verification during design and programming.

7.4 Which of the requirement examples in section 7.6 (design and programming) would be easy to handle with embedded trace information? Which would be hard, and why?

Exercises

7.5 Compare proposals

In the Tax Payers' Association (Chapter 15), several kinds of suppliers are considered.

a) Which factors would you use to compare their "proposals"?

b) Which kind of supplier would you recommend to the customer?

Chapter 8 Exercises: Elicitation

Discussions

8.1 Which techniques could be used to overcome each of the elicitation barriers ("users cannot express what they need", …)?

8.2 Which techniques could be used to elicit user tasks? To elicit a data model? To elicit feature requirements? To elicit quality requirements?

8.3 If you know the Soft Systems Methodology (Avison & Fitzgerald 1988; Checkland 1981), you will know about Rich Pictures and CATWOE. What are their roles from an elicitation point of view? Which types of intermediate work products do they describe?

Exercises

8.4 Case project

For one of the case studies (16.1 to 16.5) do the following:

a) Make a preliminary stakeholder analysis (your own best guess).

b) Suggest elicitation techniques for the project.

c) List whom you would involve in the techniques and when to use the technique.

d) Outline the business goals for the project.

e) Outline a cost/benefit analysis for the project (don't go into details with the numbers, but identify important hard and soft factors).

f) Outline a goal-domain trace matrix for the project.

g) List the largest risks in the project. Suggest approaches to reduce the risks.

8.5 Run a focus group

Run a focus group for one of the case studies (16.1 to 16.5). Even on a course, you should include some real stakeholders in the focus group. On professional courses, case project 16.4 (project management) is a good choice, since many of the participants are potential stakeholders. On university courses, case project 16.5 (education management) is a good choice for similar reasons. The remaining three case studies might be used for focus groups, since most courses have some participants that could be stakeholders. However, these projects are more narrow in scope, and fewer surprising ideas will turn up.

a) Follow the procedure for a focus group. Define stakeholder groups and have representatives for each of them (some role-playing might be appropriate on a course, but not in a real project).

b) End up with top priority issues for each stakeholder group.

c) If you have done the earlier requirements exercises for this project, try to compare your findings at the focus group with the requirements you came up with earlier. Discuss the differences.

8.6 Shipyard business goals and cost/benefit
Figure 8.6 shows a cost/benefit analysis for the shipyard. It covers some of the business goals, but not all.

a) Extend the cost/benefit analysis to include all the business goals. See section 8.5 and Chapter 11 (section 4.1 of the specification).

b) Find a way to clearly show how the business goals map into the cost/benefits.

8.7 Clear up the QFD attempt for the shipyard
Figure 8.7B shows an unsuccessful attempt at making a QFD (Quality Function Deployment) matrix for the shipyard case.

a) Study section 8.7.1 carefully to identify some of the defects in the example.

b) Set up a "correct" QFD matrix.

8.8 Cost/benefit calculation for West Zealand Hospital
The West Zealand Hospital could clearly define the business goals of their roster planning system, as shown in section 8.5.

a) Outline a cost/benefit analysis that corresponds to the business goals (don't go into details with the numbers, but identify important hard and soft factors).

8.9 Set up a task-feature matrix for the hotel system
Section 8.8 mentions that you can set up a task-feature matrix, which shows how each task relates to the product features. However, no example is given.

a) Set up a task-feature matrix for the hotel system.

b) Discuss to what extent it duplicates functional requirements styles from Chapter 3 and 4.

8.10 Plan an interview with a supplier of membership administration software
Assume that you worked as a consultant for the Tax Payers' Association, trying to help them purchase a membership administration system as specified in Chapter 15. In this exercise we ask you to plan a meeting with a potential supplier of such systems.

a) What would you ask at the meeting?

b) Which other activities would you suggest to find out whether the supplier is a good candidate?

c) Find a way to show that your questions and activities cover everything.

8.11 Shipyard conflict

In the shipyard case (Chapter 11), there was a hidden conflict between the sales department and the production people (the foremen, workers, etc.). The production people were annoyed that they often had to work overtime to finish ships because of unrealistic deadlines promised by the sales department. They wanted to have their say in the delivery time promised to customers, and they saw IT with on-line production plans as a tool to help them. Sales, however, knew that is was necessary to give optimistic deadlines and argue about this with production staff later. Otherwise the shipyard might not get the order and it might not survive. (In addition, sales people were given bonuses according to order size, which further encouraged them to promise unrealistic deadlines.)

a) Would it be a good idea to run a focus group? (Section 10.2 may give you some ideas.)

b) If so, how would you proceed?

c) If not, how would you elicit needs and wishes?

d) How would you try to settle the conflict?

8.12 Goal-requirements for an e-learning product

Company TeleX contacts a Web-application software house asking them to develop an e-learning system. The e-learning system should train the employees at TeleX to support customers better, for instance when customers phone to report problems with the services they receive from TeleX. The software house has developed other e-learning systems on a time-and-material basis. TeleX doesn't want a time-and-material-based contract, because they are not sure they will get value for money.

a) Suggest suitable requirements for the situation (hint: look at the goal-design scale).

b) Suggest a suitable project model and contract model (see section 1.7).

Chapter 9 Exercises: Checking and Validation

Discussions

9.1 Compare the Task & Support approach with the IEEE criteria (correct, complete . . .). Which criteria does it support, which must be met in other ways?

9.2 The Midland Hospital case (Chapter 12) has priorities for each requirement. The customer had great difficulty coming up with anything but "top priority" for all the requirements. How could you elicit these priorities?

9.3 Can the analyst make some of the checks alone or are users/customers necessary?

9.4 The checking techniques are intended for checking the almost finished specification. Could some of them be used earlier? If so, which ones?

9.5 The Tasks-with-Data style might be used as a checking technique. What kind of checking would it be? Could it replace other checking techniques?

Exercises

9.6 Check an existing requirements specification
Analyze the Midland Hospital spec in Chapter 12 (the specs in Chapters 11, 14, or 15 might be used instead):

a) Complete the checklist forms in section 9.4 for the specification. (Read the additional instructions in the text.)

b) If you had one work day available to improve the spec, what would you improve?

9.7 The power of the checking techniques
How do the various check questions contribute to the IEEE factors (quality of a specification)?

Chapter 10 Exercises: Techniques at work

Discussions

In the "unbelievable demands" example (focus groups, section 10.2), the top priority was "do as you promise".

10.1 How would you turn that into requirements?

10.2 What would you suggest that the software vendor should do to meet the demand?

Exercises

10.3 Classify issues
Look at the "ideal e-mail" case (focus groups, section 10.2).

a) How many issues would you have to deal with to satisfy the top four issues for all stakeholder groups?

b) How many issues would you have to deal with to give each stakeholder group at least one of their top four issues?

c) Trace each final issue to issues from earlier steps. Critically review each final issue to find out whether it correctly reflects earlier issues and whether a "why" should be added.

d) Which issues would you call solution ideas? Which are problems to be solved? Which are requirements?

e) Find a final issue that is very close to being a good requirement, and a final issue that is very far from being a requirement. Turn the latter into requirements.

References

This chapter contains two lists of the same literature: (1) arranged according to subject, (2) annotated and arranged according to author. Some of the references are mentioned under more than one subject, for instance under "requirements books" and "systems development".

In general we don't include references to the origins of classical topics or compare what different experts have said. Instead we give a few references that will allow a practitioner to read more when needed. Many of the topics are covered by several comprehensive requirements books, and we don't refer to each of these, but we list the books under "requirements books".

Some topics are recent or controversial. In these case we have references to different views of them.

References according to subject area

Requirements books

Avison, D.E. & Fitzgerald, G. (1988) *Information systems development – methodologies, techniques and tools*. Blackwell Scientific Publications, Oxford.

Checkland, P.B. (1981) *Systems Thinking, Systems Practice*. John Wiley & Sons, Chichester.

Davis, A.M. (1994) *Software requirements*. Prentice Hall, New Jersey.

DeMarco, T. (1979) *Structured Analysis and Systems Specification*. Prentice Hall, New Jersey.

Dorfman, M. & Thayer, R.H. (eds) (1990) *Standards, Guidelines, and Examples on System and Software Requirement Engineering*. IEEE Computer Society Press, London.

IEEE Guide to Software Requirements specifications. ANSI/IEEE Std. 830-1993 or 1998.

Kotonya, G. & Sommerville, I. (1998) *Requirements Engineering, Processes and Techniques.* John Wiley & Sons.

Kovitz, B.L. (1999) *Practical Software Requirements. A Manual of Content & Style.* Manning Publications, Greenwich, CT.

Macaulay, L. (1996) *Requirements Engineering.* Springer, Berlin.

Robertson, S. & Robertson, J. (1999) *Mastering the Requirements Process.* Addison-Wesley.

Sommerville, I. & Sawyer, P. (1997) *Requirements Engineering: A Good Practice Guide.* John Wiley & Sons.

Wiegers, K.E. (1999) *Software Requirements.* Microsoft Press, Redmond, Washington.

Yourdon, E. (1989) *Modern Structured Analysis.* Prentice Hall, New Jersey.

COTS

Brownsword, L., Oberndorf, T. & Sledge, C.A. (2000) Developing new processes for COTS-based systems. *IEEE Software,* July/Aug, 48–55.

Carney, D. & Long, F. (2000) What do you mean by COTS? *IEEE Software,* March/April, 83–86.

Maiden, N.A. & Ncube, C. (1998) Acquiring COTS software selection requirements. *IEEE Software,* March/April, 46–56.

Natt och Dag, J., Regnell, B., Carlshamre, P., Andersson, M. & Karlsson, J. (2001) Evaluating Automated Support for Requirements Similarity Analysis in Market-Driven Development. *Proceedings of the seventh International Workshop on Requirements Engineering – REFSQ '2001,* Interlaken, Switzerland, June 2001.

Regnell, B., Host, M., Natt och Dag, J., Beremark, P. & Hjelm, T. (2000) Visualization of agreement and satisfaction in distributed prioritization of market requirements. *Proceedings of the sixth International Workshop on Requirements Engineering – REFSQ '00,* Essener Informatik Beiträge, 125–136.

Use cases, scenarios and object-oriented systems

Booch, G., Rumbaugh, J. & Jacobson, I. (1999) *The Unified Modeling Language, User Guide.* Addison-Wesley, Reading, Massachusetts.

Campbell, R.L. (1992) Will the Real Scenario Please Stand up? *SIGCHI Bulletin,* April, pp 6–8.

Cockburn, A. (1997) Structuring use cases with goals. *Journal of Object-Oriented Programming,* Sep-Oct, 35–40 & Nov-Dec, 56–62. See also: http://members.-aol.com/acockburn/papers/usecases.htm

Cockburn, A. (2001) *Writing Effective Use Cases*. Addison-Wesley, Reading, Massachusetts.

Constantine, L. & Lockwood, L.A.D. (2001) Structure and style in use cases for user interface design. In *Object Modeling and User Interface Design* (ed. M.V. Harmelen), Addison-Wesley, Reading, Massachusetts.

Jacobson, I., Christerson, M., Jonsson, P. & Overgaard, G. (1994) *Object-oriented Software Engineering – A Use Case-driven Approach*. Addison-Wesley, Reading, Massachusetts.

Lauesen, S. (1998) Real-life object-oriented systems. *IEEE Software*, March/April, 76–83.

Lauesen, S. & Mathiassen, M. (1999) Use cases in a COTS tender. *In Proceedings of the Fifth International Workshop on Requirements Engineering* (eds A.L. Opdahl, K. Pohl and E. Dubois), REFSQ '99, Presses Universitaires de Namur, 115–129.

Maring, B. (1996) Object-oriented development of large applications. *IEEE Software*, May, 33–40.

Rumbaugh, J., Jacobson, I. & Booch, G. (1999) *The Unified Modeling Language Reference Manual*, Addison-Wesley, Reading, Massachusetts.

Stevens, P. & Pooley, R. (2000) *Using UML, Software Engineering with Objects and Components*. Pearson Education, London.

Weidenhaupt, K., Pohl, K., Jarke, M. & Haumer, P. (1998) Scenarios in system development: Current practice. *IEEE Software*, March/April, 34–45.

Quality requirements

Gilb, T. (2001) Requirements-Driven Management Using Planguage. Free for download from http://www.result-planning.com.

ISO/IEC TR 9126 (1991) *Information technology, software product evaluation, quality characteristics and guidelines for their use.* International Organization for Standardization, Geneva.

McCall, J.A. & Matsumoto, M. (1980) Software Quality Metrics Enhancements, Vol. I–II, Rome Air Development Center.

Spool, J.M. (1997) Market maturity. *Eye for Design*, Jan./Feb.

Response times and queuing theory

Kleinrock, L. (1976) *Queuing Systems. Volume 1, Theory. Volume 2: Computer applications*. John Wiley & Sons, New York.

Schioler, H. (2001) Queue distributions for the M/D/1 model. To appear in *IEEE Transactions on Computers*. See also Henrik Schioler on http://www.control.auc.dk/~henrik or e-mail: henrik@ control. auc.dk

Tanenbaum, A.S. (1988) *Computer Networks*. Prentice Hall, New Jersey.

Usability

Bailey, R.W., Allan, R.W. & Raiello, P. (1992) Usability testing vs. heuristic evaluation: a head-to-head comparison. *Proceedings of the Human Factors Society 35th Annual Meeting*, 409–413.

Card, S.K., Moran, T.P. & Newell, A. (1980) The keystroke-level model for user performance time with interactive systems. *Communications of the ACM* **23**(7), 396–410.

Carlshamre, P. & Karlsson, J. (1996) A Usability-Oriented Approach to Requirements Engineering. *Proceedings of ICRE '96*, IEEE Computer Society Press, 145–152.

Cuomo, D.L. & Bowen, C.D. (1994) Understanding usability issues addressed by three user-system interface evaluation techniques. *Interacting with Computers* 6(1), 86–108.

Desurvire, H.W., Kondziela, J.M. & Atwood, M.E. (1992) What is gained and lost when using evaluation methods other than empirical testing? *Proceedings of HCI 92*, Cambridge University Press, 89–102.

Dumas, J.S. & Redish, J.C. (1993) A practical guide to us-ability testing. Ablex Publishing Corporation, Norwood, New Jersey.

Jorgensen, A.H. (1990) Thinking aloud in user interface design: a method promoting cognitive ergonomics. *Ergonomics* **33**(4), 501–507.

Shneiderman, B. (1998) *Designing the User Interface*. Addison-Wesley, Reading, Massachusetts.

User interface design

Beyer, H. & Holtzblatt, K. (1998) *Contextual Design. Defining Customer Centered Systems*. Morgan Kauffmann, San Francisco.

Carlshamre, P. & Karlsson, J. (1996) A Usability-Oriented Ap-proach to Requirements Engineering. *Proceedings of ICRE '96*, IEEE Computer Society Press, 145–152.

Catledge, L.D. & Potts, C. (1996) Collaboration during conceptual design. *Proceedings of ICRE '96*. IEEE Computer Society Press, 182–189.

Constantine, L. & Lockwood, L.A.D. (1999) *Software for Use: A practical guide to the models and methods of usage-centered design*. Addison-Wesley, Reading, Massachusetts.

Lauesen, S. & Harning, M.B. (2001) *Virtual Windows. IEEE Software*, July/August, 67–75.

Shneiderman, B. (1998) *Designing the user interface*. Addison-Wesley, Reading, Massachusetts.

Security

British Standard BS 7799. Part 1: Code of Practice for Information Security Management. Part 2: Specification for Information Security Management.

Pfleeger, C.P. (1997) *Security in Computing*. Prentice Hall PTR, New Jersey.

Systems development and notations

Avison, D.E. & Fitzgerald, G. (1988) *Information Systems Development – methodologies, techniques and tools*. Blackwell Scientific Publications, Oxford.

Beizer, B. (1990) *Software Testing Techniques*, 2nd edition, Van Nostrand Reinhold, New York.

Checkland, P.B. (1981) *Systems Thinking, Systems Practice*. John Wiley & Sons.

DeMarco, T. (1979) *Structured Analysis and Systems Specification*. Prentice Hall, New Jersey.

Ellsberger, J., Hogrefe, D. & Sarma, A. (1997) *SDL, Formal object-oriented language for communication systems*. Prentice Hall.

Pressman, R.S. (2000) *Software Engineering: a practitioner's approach*. McGraw-Hill, Maidenhead, Berkshire, England.

Weidenhaupt, K., Pohl, K., Jarke, M. & Haumer, P. (1998) Scenarios in system development: Current practice. *IEEE Software*, March/April, 34–45.

Yourdon, E. (1989) *Modern Structured Analysis*. Prentice Hall, New Jersey.

Project management and process improvement

Emam, K.E. & Madhavji, N.H. (1995) Measuring the success of requirements engineering processes. *IEEE*, 0-8186-7017-7/95, 204-211.

Lauesen, S. & Vium, J-P. (1996) Lessons learned from assessing a success. Fifth European Conference on Software Quality, Dublin, September 1996, 335–344.

Lauesen, S. & Vinter, O. (2001) Preventing requirement defects. An experiment in process improvement. *Requirements Engineering Journal* **6**, 37–50, Springer-Verlag, London.

Martin, E.W. Martin, E.W., Brown, C.V., DeHayes, D.W., Hoffer, J.A. & Perkins, W.C. (1999) *Managing Information Technology. What managers need to know*. Prentice Hall, New Jersey.

Pressman, R.S. (2000) *Software Engineering: a practitioner's approach*. McGraw-Hill, Maidenhead, Berkshire, England.

Sikkel, K., Wieringa, R. & Engmann, R. (2000) A case base for requirements engineering: Problem categories and solution techniques. *Proceedings of the sixth International Workshop on Requirements Engineering – REFSQ '00*, Essener Informatik Beiträge, 80–85.

Thayer, R.H. (ed.) (1997) *Software Engineering Project Management*. IEEE Computer Society Press, Los Alamitos, CA.

Function points

Furey, S. & Kitchenham, B. (1997) Why we should use function points/The problems with function points. Point - Counterpoint. *IEEE Software*, March/April, 28–31.

Thayer, R.H. (ed.) (1997) *Software Engineering Project Management*. IEEE Computer Society Press, Los Alamitos, CA.

Risk

Boehm, B. (1989) *Software Risk Management*. IEEE Computer Society Press, Los Alamitos, CA.

Jones, C. (1994) *Assessment and Control of Software Risks*. Prentice Hall, Englewood Cliffs, NJ.

Elicitation

Beyer, H. & Holtzblatt, K. (1998) *Contextual Design. Defining customer centered systems*. Morgan Kauffmann, San Francisco.

Carlshamre, P. & Karlsson, J. (1996) A Usability-Oriented Approach to Requirements Engineering. *Proceedings of ICRE '96*, IEEE Computer Society Press, 145–152.

Constantine, L. & Lockwood, L.A.D. (1999) *Software for Use: A practical guide to the models and methods of usage-centered design*. Addison-Wesley, Reading, Massachusetts.

Davis, B.G. (1982) Strategies for information requirements determination. *IBM Syst. Journal* **21**(1), 4–30.

Goals, cost/benefit and QFD

Brown, P.G. (1991) Echoing the voice of the customer. *AT&T Technical Journal* March/April, 18–32.

Cooper, A. (1996) Goal-directed software design. *Dr. Dobb's Journal* Sept., 16–22.

Evans, J.R. & Lindsay, W.M. (1996) *The Management and Control of Quality*. West Publishing Company, St. Paul, MN.

Parker, M.M. & Benson, R.J. (1988) *Information Economics*. Prentice Hall, New Jersey.

Rao, A., Carr, L.P., Dambolena, I., Kopp, R.J., Martin, J., Rafii, F. & Schlesinger, P.F. (1996) *Total Quality Management: A cross-functional perspective*. John Wiley & Sons, Chichester.

Other

Davis, A.M. (1992) Why industry often says 'no thanks' to research. *IEEE Software*, November, 97–99.

Fisher, R. & Ury, W. (1991) *Getting to Yes*. New York, Penguin.

Solingen, R., Berghout, E. & Latum, F. (1998) Interrupts: Just a minute never is. *IEEE Software*, Sept./Oct., 97–103.

Spool, J.M. (1997) Market maturity. *Eye for Design*, Jan./Feb.

Annotated references (in alphabetical order)

Avison, D.E. & Fitzgerald, G. (1988) *Information systems development – methodologies, techniques and tools.* Blackwell Scientific Publications, Oxford. Explains and discusses several methods for dealing with the early phases of systems development. Although these topics are central to requirements, the word "requirement" is hardly mentioned. One of the methods explained is Soft Systems Methodology, by Checkland.

Bailey, R.W., Allan, R.W. & Raiello, P. (1992) Usability testing vs. heuristic evaluation: a head-to-head comparison. *Proceedings of the Human Factors Society 35th Annual Meeting*, 409–413. Bailey et al. studied a very small system where 50 experts had found 31 usability problems by means of heuristic evaluation. They found that only two of the problems were worth correcting, in the sense that there was no measurable effect of correcting the remaining 29 problems. Author's comment: They would probably have found an effect of correcting a few more of the 31 usability problems if they had used more varied test tasks, but the trend seems clear: Heuristic evaluation finds many false positives.

Beizer, B. (1990) *Software Testing Techniques*, 2nd edition, Van Nostrand Reinhold, New York. A classic in software testing.

Beyer, H. & Holtzblatt, K. (1998) *Contextual Design. Defining customer centered systems.* Morgan Kaufmann, San Francisco. A solid approach to work analysis and redesign of work. Uses affinity diagrams to find the common structures and variants in user tasks. Also shows how to study documents and other artifacts to get ideas for new systems.

Boehm, B. (1989) *Software Risk Management.* IEEE Computer Society Press, Los Alamitos, CA.

Booch, G., Rumbaugh, J. & Jacobson, I. (1999) *The Unified Modeling Language. User Guide.* Addison-Wesley, Reading, Massachusetts. A definition and explanation of UML. See later developments at www.rational.com. The Object Management Group (OMG)'s definition of UML is available at http://cgi.omg.org/cgi-bin/doc?ad/99-06-08.

British Standard BS 7799. Part 1: Code of Practice for Information Security Management. Part 2: Specification for Information Security Management. A comprehensive survey of safeguards to be considered, primarily on the management level. Often, however, the reader has to guess at the corresponding threats.

Brown, P.G.: QFD (1991) Echoing the voice of the customer. *AT&T Technical Journal* March/April, 18–32. A short, thorough description of QFD with a good example.

Brownsword, L., Oberndorf, T. & Sledge, C.A. (2000) Developing new processes for

COTS-based systems. *IEEE Software*, July/Aug, 48–55. How the development process should be modified to cater for COTS.

Campbell, R.L. (1992) Will the real scenario please stand up? *SIGCHI Bulletin*, April, 6–8.

Card, S.K., Moran, T.P. & Newell, A. (1980) The keystroke-level model for user performance time with interactive systems. *Communications of the ACM* **23**(7), 396–410. Breaks down the user part of the task into basic elements and measures the time used for each type of element.

Carlshamre, P. & Karlsson, J. (1996) A Usability-Oriented Ap-proach to Requirements En-gi-neering. *Proceedings of ICRE '96*, IEEE Computer Society Press, 145–152. A simple, effective approach to task analysis and usability testing.

Carney, D. & Long, F. (2000) What do you mean by COTS? *IEEE Software*, March/April, 83–86. Discusses the various dimensions of COTS, e.g. modifiability and supplier type.

Catledge, L.D. & Potts, C. (1996) Collaboration during conceptual design. *Proceedings of ICRE '96*. IEEE,182–189. A study of actual initial design in industry.

Checkland, P.B. (1981) *SystemsThinking, Systems Practice*. John Wiley & Sons. A classic about joint development of the human and the computer part of the new system, known as Soft Systems Methodology (SSM).

Cockburn, A. (1997) Structuring use cases with goals. *Journal of Object-Oriented Programming*, Sep-Oct, 35–40 & Nov-Dec, 56–62. Also in: http://members.-aol.com/acockburn/papers/usecases.htm. The now classical paper on various meanings of use cases and good examples of Cockburn's goal-oriented use cases.

Cockburn, A. (2001) *Writing Effective Use Cases*. Addison-Wesley, Reading, Massachusetts. The full approach of goal-oriented use cases on various levels. Lots of good advice on what to do and what not. Many real-life use cases. Has a good way of integrating stakeholder viewpoints into the use cases. Excellent discussion of UML versus text-based use cases. Insists on use cases describing the split between user and product – in that way limiting creative solutions and leading to problems of whether we describe the new or the old system.

Constantine, L. & Lockwood, L.A.D. (2001) Structure and style in use cases for user interface design. In *Object Modeling and User Interface Design* (ed. M.V. Harmelen), Addison-Wesley, Reading, Massachusetts. A solid discussion of various use case styles and why most of them fail to describe true technology-independent tasks.

Constantine, L. & Lockwood, L.A.D. (1999) *Software for Use: A practical guide to the models and methods of usage-centered design*. Addison-Wesley, Reading, Massachusetts. Describes a systematic design method for user interfaces, starting with elicitation of essential use cases, and ending up with prototypes and usability testing. Also has a good section on helping users to get from novices to experts. As in other usability and design books, the weakest part is how the screen design "pops out of the air".

Cooper, A. (1996) Goal-directed software design. *Dr. Dobb's Journal*, Sept., 16–22. Discusses the many aspects of goals, for instance the conflicts between personal goals, official goals, and official requirements.

Cuomo, D.L. & Bowen, C.D. (1994) Understanding usability issues addressed by three user-system interface evaluation techniques. *Interacting with Computers* 6(1), 86–108. Compares problems detected by a usability test with those predicted by three evaluation techniques: heuristic evaluation, cognitive walk-through, and guidelines. Heuristic evaluation detects about 60% of the problems detected in usability testing, and reports 50% false positives. Also compares the kinds of problems reported by the three evaluation techniques.

Davis, A.M. (1994) *Software Requirements*. Prentice Hall, New Jersey. A classic in the area. Discusses the goal levels: a requirement on one level, is the solution on the level above. Good sections on state diagrams and many other techniques.

Davis, A.M. (1992) Why industry often says 'no thanks' to research. *IEEE Software*, Nov. 97–99. Explains that researchers usually know too little about industry to help.

Davis, B.G. (1982) Strategies for information requirements determination. *IBM Syst. Journal* 21(1), 4–30. How to elicit requirements through questionnaires, studies of existing systems, critical success factors, decision studies, and prototypes. Also discusses mental weaknesses that make elicitation difficult.

DeMarco, T. (1979) *Structured Analysis and Systems Specification*. Prentice Hall, New Jersey. A classic on dataflow, essential versus physical models, etc.

Desurvire, H.W., Kondziela, J.M. & Atwood, M.E. (1992) What is gained and lost when using evaluation methods other than empirical testing. *Proceedings of HCI 92*, Cambridge University Press, 89–102. Compares heuristic evaluation against usability testing. Reports 44% hit-rate of heuristic evaluation, and 50% false positives, which they call "potential problems".

Dorfman, M. & Thayer, R.H. (eds) (1990) *Standards, guidelines, and examples on system and software requirement engineering*. IEEE Computer Society Press, Los Alamitos, CA. Includes several standards, for instance British Standard BS6719 with an excellent checklist of things to include in the requirements. Also has examples of full requirements specifications, for instance a complete spec of ATM requirements based on dataflow diagrams, decision tables, pseudo-code, etc. Also has an example of a spec based on object classes.

Dumas, J.S. & Redish, J.C. (1993) *A Practical Guide to Usability Testing*. Ablex Publishing Corporation, Norwood, New Jersey. A comprehensive guide to most aspects of usability testing and usability in general.

Ellsberger, J., Hogrefe, D. & Sarma, A. (1997) *SDL, Formal object-oriented language for communication systems*. Prentice Hall. A thorough description of SDL, which is used as a standard in telecommunications and is useful for specifying other technical interfaces.

Emam, K.E. & Madhavji, N.H. (1995) Measuring the success of requirements engineering processes. *IEEE*, 0-8186-7017-7/95, 204-211. Gathered and ranked expert opinions of the most important factors in requirements work. Point to many factors that are not normally considered, for instance the most important one: that the customer is able to see the consequences of the new system.

Evans, J.R. & Lindsay, W.M. (1996) *The Management and Control of Quality*. West Publishing Company, St. Paul, MN. Includes a good description of QFD at work.

Fisher, R. & Ury, W. (1991) *Getting to Yes*. Penguin, New York. The classic book on successful negotiation on all levels, from your own private affairs to international affairs.

Furey, S. & Kitchenham, B. (1997) Why we should use function points – The problems with function points. Point – Counterpoint. *IEEE Software*, March/April, 28–31. A good, short discussion of the importance of Function Points versus the weaknesses of the approach.

Gilb, T. (2001) Requirements-Driven Management Using Planguage. Free to download from http://www.result-planning.com.

IEEE Guide to software requirements specifications. ANSI/IEEE Std. 830-1993 or 1998. A classic with suggestions for what to write and what not to write in a requirements specification. The only addition in the 1998 version is a five page comparison with IEEE/EIA 12207.1-1997.

ISO/IEC TR 9126 (1991). Information technology, software product evaluation, quality characteristics and guidelines for their use. International Organization for Standardization, Geneva. An international standard for quality factors.

Jacobson, I. , Christerson, M., Jonsson, P. & Overgaard, G. (1994) *Object-oriented Software Engineering – a use case driven approach*. Addison-Wesley, Reading, Massachusetts. Introduced the use case concept and showed the relation to object-oriented modeling.

Jones, C. (1994) *Assessment and Control of Software Risks*. Prentice Hall, Englewood Cliffs, NJ.

Jorgensen, A.H. (1990) Thinking aloud in user interface design: a method promoting cognitive ergonomics. *Ergonomics* **33**(4), 501–507. A short, thorough description of practical experiences with the thinking-aloud version of usability testing. The designers made the test, and it worked fine. They were surprised at the number of problems detected. This caused them to change attitude, improve the user interface, and actually remove many of the problems.

Kleinrock, L. (1975, 1976) *Queuing Systems. Volume 1: Theory, 1975. Volume 2: Computer applications, 1976*. John Wiley & Sons. Queuing theory is the basis for computing the response times. In spite of its age, this is still the "Bible" of queueing theory.

Kotonya, G. & Sommerville, I. (1998) *Requirements Engineering, Processes and Techniques*. John Wiley & Sons. Discusses elicitation, validation, management, modeling, and "viewpoints" (almost the same as stakeholders' viewpoints). There are few examples of actual requirements, although there is a tentative case study that uses a viewpoint approach.

Kovitz, B.L. (1999) *Practical Software Requirements. A Manual of Content & Style*. Man-ning Publications, Greenwich, CT. A different way of looking at requirements. Discusses the domain concept, the product concept, and the interface concept – with slightly different terms. Classifies projects into a few types of "problem frames". Shows a complete requirements specification for a "bug log" program for in-house use. Refuses to accept usability requirements or other domain-oriented issues as valid requirements - the interface has to be designed before it becomes requirements.

Lauesen, S. & Vium, J-P. (1996) Lessons learned from assessing a success. Fifth European Conference on Software Quality, Dublin, September 1996, 335–344. A longer description of the shipyard case, what actually happened and what the customer believed had happened.

Lauesen, S. (1998) Real-life object-oriented systems. *IEEE Software*, March/April, 76–83. A study of industrial object-oriented projects and the basic architectures used. Also discusses to what extent the promises of OO came true.

Lauesen, S. & Mathiassen, M. (1999) Use cases in a COTS tender. *In Proceedings of the Fifth International Workshop on Requirements Engineering* (eds A.L. Opdahl, K. Pohl and E. Dubois), REFSQ'99, Presses Universitaires de Namur, 1999, 115–129. The first published version of the Task & Support concept, how it was developed, and how it worked in the first experiments.

Lauesen, S. & Harning, M.B. (2001) Virtual Windows. *IEEE Software*, July/August, 67–75. Shows how Virtual Windows are developed, why they produce better user interfaces than traditional approaches, and outlines how they are turned into final screens. Uses a slightly simplified version of the hotel system as an example.

Lauesen, S. & Vinter, O. (2001) Preventing requirement defects. An experiment in process improvement. *Requirements Engineering Journal* **6**, 37–50. Springer-Verlag, London. Reports on the process improvement experiment at Bruel & Kjaer, how the existing requirements problems were analyzed to arrive at a new requirements approach, and what the results were when using the approach in the next project.

Macaulay, L. (1996) *Requirements Engineering*. Springer, Berlin. Covers notations and techniques from Rich Pictures to QFD and Future Workshops (focus groups). Discusses the customer-supplier relationship and various process models, including tenders. Few examples of actual requirements, however.

Maiden, N.A. & Ncube, C. (1998) Acquiring COTS software selection requirements. *IEEE Software*, March/April, 46–56. An interesting report on experiences when buying commercial software and how to deal with requirements.

Maring, B. (1996) Object-oriented development of large applications. *IEEE Software*, May, 33–40. A discussion of the experiences at Schlumberger when using object-oriented development. One experience was that understanding the business logic in a truly object-oriented approach was like "reading a road map through a soda straw". They didn't succeed until they separated the business logic from the data objects.

Martin, E.W., Brown, C.V., DeHayes, D.W., Hoffer, J.A. & Perkins, W.C. (1999) *Managing Information Technology. What managers need to know*. Prentice Hall, New Jersey. Many wonderful case studies of system acquisition, some include part of the actual requirements.

McCall, J.A. & Matsumoto, M. (1980). Software Quality Metrics Enhancements, Vol. I–II, Rome Air Development Center. An early, solid approach to defining software quality factors. It is still my favorite basis for quality requirements.

Natt och Dag, J., Regnell, B., Carlshamre, P., Andersson, M. & Karlsson, J. (2001) Evaluating Automated Support for Requirements Similarity Analysis in Market-Driven Development. *Proceedings of the seventh International Workshop on Requirements Engineering – REFSQ '2001* – Interlaken, Switzerland, June 2001. A case study of keeping track of thousands of product requirements and using techniques to avoid duplicates.

Parker, M.M. & Benson, R.J. (1988) *Information Economics*. Prentice Hall, New Jersey. The classic in analyzing costs and benefits, hard as well as soft. An appendix contains lists of typical benefit factors in various business sectors.

Pfleeger, C.P. (1997) *Security in Computing*. Prentice Hall PTR, New Jersey. A comprehensive coverage of most security areas, including threats, technologies, legal and ethical issues. Somewhat weak on managerial issues.

Pressman, R.S. (2000) *Software Engineering: a practitioner's approach*. McGraw-Hill Publishing Company, Berkshire, England. A recent, comprehensive introduction to most software engineering techniques and notations.

Rao, A., Carr, L.P., Dambolena, I., Kopp, R.J., Martin, J., Rafii., F. & Schlesinger, P.F. (1996) *Total Quality Management: A cross-functional perspective*. John Wiley & Sons, Chichester. Includes a good introduction to QFD.

Regnell, B. Host, M., Natt och Dag, J., Beremark, P. & Hjelm, T. (2000) Visualization of agreement and satisfaction in distributed prioritization of market requirements. *Proceedings of the sixth International Workshop on Requirements Engineering – REFSQ '00*, Essener Informatik Beiträge, 125–136. A case study of how a product developer, operating in the global market, collected and prioritized requirements, and how visualization techniques could improve the process.

Robertson, S. & Robertson, J. (1999) *Mastering the Requirements Process*. Addison-Wesley. Uses a specific, real-life project to explain the author's Volere approach, which includes a systematic elicitation and analysis process, and a comprehensive template for what to write. Focuses on requirements in feature style. Also deals with quality factors, although a bit simplistic. Covers primarily in-house or contract development. A good "how to" book.

Rumbaugh, J., Jacobson, I. & Booch, G. (1999) *The Unified Modeling Language Reference Manual*. Addison-Wesley, Reading, Massachusetts. A companion to Booch, Rumbaugh & Jacobson, *UML User Guide* (see above).

Schioler, H. (2001) Queue distributions for the M/D/1 model. To appear in *IEEE Transactions on Computers*. See also Henrik Schioler at http://www.control.auc.dk/~henrik or e-mail: henrik@conrol.auc.dk. Shows how to compute response times when the service time is constant. Sounds easy but it is much more difficult than when the service time is exponentially distributed.

Shneiderman, B. (1998) *Designing the User Interface*. Addison-Wesley, Reading, Massachusetts. Defines the usability factors *Time to learn*, *Speed of performance*, etc. The factors were defined already in the 1986 version. Covers usability from many points of view and gives examples of various kinds of interfaces.

Sikkel, K., Wieringa, R. & Engmann, R. (2000) A case base for requirements engineering: Problem categories and solution techniques. *Proceedings of the sixth international workshop on requirements engineering – REFSQ '00*, Essener Informatik Beiträge, 80–85. Introduces a taxonomy of problems to be handled by IT. Examples are COTS-extension problems, Architecture problems, and Unidentified problems. Shows generic questions that can be asked to clarify the problems.

Solingen, R., Berghout, E. & Latum, F. (1998) Interrupts: Just a minute never is. *IEEE Software*, Sept/Oct, 97–103. This article studied what happens when someone comes into your office and says "could you spare me a minute?" In most cases the result was an interruption of about 15 minutes. In addition to this, the interrupted person spent a significant time mentally returning to working full speed on what he had been doing. The amount of time thus wasted was difficult to measure and depended on the kind of work being done, but the authors suggest that it is another 15 minutes for intellectual work. Also suggests way to reduce this kind of waste.

Sommerville, I. & Sawyer, P. (1997) *Requirements Engineering: a good practice guide*. John Wiley & Sons. Explains small, tangible procedures such as how to enumerate requirements, how to use shall/will, how to use data models, how to resolve conflicts. Gives no real-life examples, but reports on costs and experiences with the different procedures.

Spool, J.M. (1997) Market maturity. *Eye for Design*, Jan/Feb. Shows that the key requirements change as a market develops. Functional requirements are important early, quality requirements later.

Stevens, P. & Pooley, R. (2000) *Using UML, Software engineering with objects and components*. Pearson Education, London. Another, more discussing, introduction to the Unified Modeling Language.

Tanenbaum, A.S. (1988) *Computer Networks*. Prentice Hall, New Jersey. Has a good, easy-to-read introduction to queuing theory.

Thayer, R.H. (ed.) (1997) *Software engineering project management*. IEEE Computer Society. Includes sections on Function Points and other cost estimation techniques.

Weidenhaupt, K., Pohl, K., Jarke, M. & Haumer, P. (1998) Scenarios in system development: Current practice. *IEEE Software*, March/April, 34–45. A study of several development projects that used scenarios – or use cases/tasks – as a basis for development. They report significant benefits in general, although the benefits were hard to measure financially.

Wiegers, K.E. (1999). *Software Requirements*. Microsoft Press, Redmond, Washington. Covers many aspects of requirements. Particularly strong areas are: rights and obligations for customer and developer, business goals and requirements priorities, requirements management, tracing and verification, requirements tools.

Yourdon, E. (1989) *Modern Structured Analysis*. Prentice Hall, New Jersey. A classic on dataflow, data modeling, state diagrams, etc.

Index